PHILANTHROPIC DISCOURSE IN ANGLO-AMERICAN LITERATURE, 1850–1920

PHILANTHROPIC AND NONPROFIT STUDIES
Dwight F. Burlingame and David C. Hammack, *editors*

Philanthropic Discourse in Anglo-American Literature, 1850–1920

Edited by
FRANK Q. CHRISTIANSON
and LESLEE THORNE-MURPHY

INDIANA UNIVERSITY PRESS

This book is a publication of

Indiana University Press
Office of Scholarly Publishing
Herman B Wells Library 350
1320 East 10th Street
Bloomington, Indiana 47405 USA

iupress.indiana.edu

© 2017 by Indiana University Press

All rights reserved

No part of this book may be reproduced or utilized in any form or by any means, electronic or mechanical, including photocopying and recording, or by any information storage and retrieval system, without permission in writing from the publisher. The Association of American University Presses' Resolution on Permissions constitutes the only exception to this prohibition.

The paper used in this publication meets the minimum requirements of the American National Standard for Information Sciences—Permanence of Paper for Printed Library Materials, ANSI Z39.48-1992.

Manufactured in the United States of America

Library of Congress Cataloging-in-Publication Data

Names: Christianson, Frank, editor. | Thorne-Murphy, Leslee, editor.
Title: Philanthropic discourse in Anglo-American literature, 1850–1920 / edited by Frank Q. Christianson and Leslee Thorne-Murphy.
Description: Bloomington : Indiana University Press, 2017. | Series: Philanthropic and nonprofit studies | Includes index.
Identifiers: LCCN 2017026849| ISBN 9780253029553 (cl : alk. paper) | ISBN 9780253029843 (pr : alk. paper)
Subjects: LCSH: Social problems in literature. | Humanitarianism in literature. | Charity in literature. | Literature and society—Great Britain—History—19th century. | Literature and society—Great Britain—History—20th century. | Literature and society—United States—History—19th century. | Literature and society—United States—History—20th century. | Social movements in literature.
Classification: LCC PR778.S62 P48 2017 | DDC 820.9/355—dc23 LC record available at https://lccn.loc.gov/2017026849

1 2 3 4 5   22 21 20 19 18 17

Contents

Preface: Telescopic Philanthropy Redeemed   *vii*
Acknowledgments   *xiii*

Introduction: Writing Philanthropy in the United States and Britain | Frank Q. Christianson and Leslee Thorne-Murphy   *1*

1. The Poverty of Sympathy | Lori Merish   13

2. Self-Undermining Philanthropic Impulses: Philanthropy in the Mirror of Narrative | Daniel Bivona   30

3. Education as Violation and Benefit: Doctrinal Debate and the Contest for India's Girls | Suzanne Daly   59

4. Urban Reform and the Plight of the Poor in Women's Journalistic Writing | Monika Elbert   85

5. Lady Bountiful for the Empire: Upper-Class Women, Philanthropy, and Civil Society | Dorice Williams Elliott   114

6. Patrons, Philanthropists, and Professionals: Henry James's *Roderick Hudson* | Francesca Sawaya   139

7. "Witnessing Them Day after Day": Ethical Spectatorship and Liberal Reform in Walter Besant's *Children of Gibeon* | Tanushree Ghosh   162

8. "The Orthodox Creed of the Business World"? Philanthropy and Liberal Individualism in Edith Wharton's *The Fruit of the Tree* | Emily Coit   190

9 Sustaining Gendered Philanthropy through Transatlantic
Friendship: Jane Addams, Henrietta Barnett, and Writing
for Reciprocal Mentoring | Sarah Ruffing Robbins   *211*

Conclusion | Frank Q. Christianson and Leslee Thorne-Murphy   *236*

Afterword: Follow the Money | Kathleen D. McCarthy   *240*

Index   *247*

Preface
Telescopic Philanthropy Redeemed

When Peggy Bartels was awoken by the phone at 4 a.m., she assumed it was a relative calling from Ghana. She was right. It was her cousin calling to announce that her uncle had passed away and that she had been selected to take his place as King of Otuam, a coastal African Fante village of approximately seven thousand people. Groggy and disbelieving, she mulled over the unsettling news as she prepared for her day's work as a secretary at the Ghanaian embassy in Washington, DC. How could she, a naturalized US citizen employed in DC, possibly function as king of a village in Ghana?

In *King Peggy: An American Secretary, Her Royal Destiny, and the Inspiring Story of How She Changed an African Village*, Bartels and her coauthor, Eleanor Herman, recount her eventful first few years as King of Otuam.[1] Holding down her job at the embassy, Bartels kept in daily contact with her advisers in Otuam, learning her duties and attempting to circumvent those who hoped to benefit from her absence. When she took a prolonged vacation leave for her "enstoolment" (coronation) and resided in Otuam for several weeks, she realized that the competing members of her council were banking on her residence in the United States and her submission to male authority in order for them to continue embezzling village funds and wielding local power unconscionably. She would have none of that. The ensuing narrative is a study in maneuvering the politics of local governance, as she battled with her cunning council members, worked within a mix of ancestral and postcolonial government systems, and eventually took the first steps toward bringing clean water, education, and modern health care to her village.

Bartels's book is part autobiography, part spiritual memoir, and part history of the Fante people and customs. At times, it is delightfully humorous. And, perhaps more importantly, it is a fundraising tool. Overt mention of this aspect of the book is tucked away in the last few pages of her narrative, where Bartels recounts the efforts of Pastor Be Louis Colleton and the congregation of the Shiloh Baptist Church in Maryland, who raised funds to provide a well for the village and laid plans to provide a school. She outlines the immense impact these efforts had already had on the well-being of her people. In the epilogue, she describes the congregation's future plans and directs readers to its website to make their own donations.

Though this fundraising information comes late in the narrative and is quite understated, the logic of philanthropy informs the entire narrative. Bartels and her coauthor set out to demonstrate that she is an efficient, reliable, and trustworthy ruler who not only respects her ancestral culture but also appreciates the contributions colonial rulers brought with them. She is at ease in both the political climate of Washington, DC, embassy life and the political climate of her Ghanaian village. She is a woman who can outmaneuver male prejudice, she is an African who is attuned to Western technology and philanthropy, and she is an American who can both praise and critique American culture and people. She is morally upright, refusing to use her position to benefit herself, instead depleting her own bank account and time reserves in order to serve her people. In short, she is the ideal person to whom one could donate funds, knowing that the money would not be squandered on excessive administrative costs or corrupt officials.

Philanthropy relies on cultivating just such a relationship of trust in the face of recurring fears of mismanagement, political intrigue, and condescension. To create an attractive object of philanthropic effort, Bartels must deal with her readers' assumptions about the legacy of British Gold Coast colonialism and the transatlantic slave trade, must inculcate sympathy for a people half a world away, and must convince her (presumably) American readers that a donation on their part will have a purely beneficial influence, in no way doing any harm or demonstrating inappropriate condescension. This is no easy task.

One might say that Bartels's narrative rewrites what Charles Dickens famously called "telescopic philanthropy."[2] In Dickens's 1852 novel, *Bleak House*, the renowned philanthropist Mrs. Jellyby works frantically on behalf of the Africans of the fictional "Borrioboola Gha." Yet her efforts result in dismal failure; her heavy-handed practice of philanthropy is misinformed and condescending, and her efforts even take a deadly turn when the settlers she sends to Africa are slain by the native population. In essence, Bartels's successes reverse Mrs. Jellyby's failures. Both women consider it their duty to serve an African population. Whereas Bartels's narrative demonstrates her competence and trustworthiness, Mrs. Jellyby's narrative establishes her complete ineffectiveness. Bartels manages the difficult politics of her village council, while Mrs. Jellyby cannot even govern the politics of her own household, let alone the politics of the African settlement she establishes. Bartels's narrative establishes sympathy for herself and her people, while Mrs. Jellyby's philanthropy is fixed on a distant object with which she bears no immediate relation and has no sympathetic bond. In her twenty-first-century rendering of telescopic philanthropy, Bartels corrects Mrs. Jellyby's failures, as she points us toward the small village of Otuam and allows us to see the possibilities of philanthropic success.

The rhetorical strategies that Bartels employs have their roots in the philanthropic logic of Dickens's time. In the wake of the industrial revolution, increasing urbanization, and the political implementation of principles of political economy, concerned citizens on both sides of the Atlantic took alleviating rampant poverty and want into their own hands. Philanthropic organizations proliferated, successfully establishing volunteerism and giving as vital aspects of civil society.

As Brian Harrison reports, "Of 640 London charities alive in 1860, no less than 279 were founded between 1800 and 1850, and 144 between 1850 and 1860; by the 1860s they were raising annually about as much as the total annual expenditure of the Poor Law system in the whole of England and Wales—not to mention the voluntary labour involved and the numerous private and unrecorded acts of charity."[3] Similarly, Frank Prochaska notes, "When *The Times* announced in 1885 that London's charitable receipts exceeded the budgets of several European states, it was a source of national and imperial pride."[4] These numbers account for charities only in London, but other major cities in the United Kingdom, in the United States, and even in Britain's colonies were similarly arrayed.

Likewise, Kathleen McCarthy argues that the sum total of philanthropic organizations in antebellum America grew exponentially.[5] They emerged in part to mitigate the social impact of modern industry, which propelled the growth of an urban working poor population tied to a wage-labor system that was largely unregulated and unstable. It marshaled a wide cross-section of American society in collective reform efforts addressing abolition, labor, and education policies and practices, as well as moral reform initiatives such as temperance and other evangelizing movements growing out of the Second Great Awakening.

We could find a parallel to the transatlantic burgeoning of philanthropic activity during the nineteenth century in our current global nongovernmental organization (NGO) initiatives, what the Johns Hopkins report "The State of Global Civil Society and Volunteering" describes as "a 'global associational revolution,' a major upsurge of organized, private, voluntary and nonprofit activity, [that] has been under way around the world for the past thirty years or more."[6] Today's NGO climate echoes the energy and innovation that defined nineteenth-century philanthropy. Indeed, the definition of a nonprofit institution adopted by the United Nations in 2003 could double as an apt definition of a nineteenth-century philanthropic association: "We define the non-profit sector as consisting of (a) organizations; that (b) are not-for-profit and, by law or custom, do not distribute any surplus they may generate to those who own or control them; (c) are institutionally separate from government; (d) are self-governing; and (e) are non-compulsory."⁷ *Philanthropy* in the nineteenth century was a broad term that signified more than large-scale giving. It encompassed or overlapped with our concepts of volunteerism and corporate giving, and with the types of organizations we know as NGOs, nonprofit institutions, and registered charities. Studying the texts generated by nineteenth-century philanthropy allows us to better understand the discursive underpinnings of our own burgeoning third sector.

This book approaches the field of philanthropic studies from the perspective of literary studies. Our contributors examine fiction, promotional material, correspondence, tracts, and other texts to piece together the rhetorical maneuvers of philanthropic effort. While other scholars have documented the social history of philanthropic work, this collection focuses on the underlying discourse that unifies the disparate elements of the transatlantic philanthropic endeavor, from traditional notions of patronage to scientific theories of poverty, and from Scottish enlightenment ideals of sympathy to Darwinian notions of social organization. As a whole, the collection gives us an opportunity to focus our own eyepiece on the philanthropic literature of a century and a half ago to gain a refined perspective on our philanthropic inheritance.

Notes

1. Bartels and Herman, *King Peggy*.
2. Dickens, *Bleak House*, 49.
3. Harrison, *Peaceable Kingdom*, 217.
4. Prochaska, *Christianity and Social Service*, 24.
5. McCarthy, *American Creed*.
6. Salamon et al., "The State of Global Society and Volunteering."
7. United Nations, *Handbook on Non-profit Institutions in the System of National Accounts*, para. 2.14.

Bibliography

Bartels, Peggielene, and Eleanor Herman. *King Peggy: An American Secretary, Her Royal Destiny, and the Inspiring Story of How She Changed an African Village*. New York: Anchor Books, 2012.

Dickens, Charles. *Bleak House*. London: Penguin, 2003.

Harrison, Brian. *Peaceable Kingdom: Stability and Change in Modern Britain*. Oxford: Clarendon, 1982.

McCarthy, Kathleen. *American Creed: Philanthropy and the Rise of Civil Society*. Chicago: University of Chicago Press, 2003.

Prochaska, Frank. *Christianity and Social Service in Modern Britain: The Disinherited Spirit*. Oxford: Oxford University Press, 2006.

Salamon, Lester M., S. Wojciech Sokolowski, Megan A. Haddock, and Helen S. Tice. "The State of Global Society and Volunteering: Latest Findings from the Implementation of the UN *Nonprofit Handbook*." Johns Hopkins University Comparative Nonprofit Sector Working Paper no. 49, March 2013. http://ccss.jhu.edu/wp-content/uploads/downloads/2013/04/JHU_Global-Civil-Society-Volunteering_FINAL_3.2013.pdf.

United Nations. *Handbook on Non-profit Institutions in the System of National Accounts*. New York: United Nations, 2003. http://unstats.un.org/unsd/publication/seriesf/seriesf_91e.pdf.

Acknowledgments

EACH OF THE scholars who wrote chapters for this book was unfailingly patient and committed to making a meaningful contribution to the study of nineteenth-century literature and philanthropy. Our association with these colleagues has enriched our own understanding of this subject immeasurably.

We are grateful for the community of competent professionals who make books like this one possible. We thank our colleagues in the Brigham Young University (BYU) English Department and College of Humanities for their support over the course of this project. The staff at Indiana University Press, including director Gary Dunham and acquisitions editor Janice Frisch and her assistants, Peggy Solic and Kate Schramm, provided excellent and sure-handed guidance as the manuscript came together. The manuscript as a whole benefited from the attention of the series editors and anonymous reviewers, who offered careful, unstinting feedback. In the last stage, Mel Thorne, Jennifer McDaniel, and their team at the BYU Faculty Editing Service helped with final edits and indexing.

Finally, we must acknowledge the support of our family members, who, through their constancy and faith, embody the charitable ideal to which this book is dedicated.

Philanthropic Discourse
in Anglo-American Literature, 1850–1920

Introduction
Writing Philanthropy in the United States and Britain

Frank Q. Christianson and Leslee Thorne-Murphy

As part of the Chicago World's Fair in 1893, thousands of philanthropists from the United States and Europe convened for a weeklong International Congress of Charities, Correction, and Philanthropy. They discussed remedies for pauperism, lauded the new science of sociology that informed the Charity Organization movement, compared the merits of philanthropic systems from Europe and the United States, and debated the advantages of coordinating state and voluntary poor relief. Florence Nightingale sent a paper discussing nursing reform; Robert Treat Paine (president of Boston's Charity Organization Society) addressed the problem of urban poverty; and her Royal Highness the Princess Christian (Queen Victoria's daughter) prepared a paper on charitable medical care. Every conceivable aspect of social reform and philanthropy seemed to have a dedicated session led by the most prominent workers in the field.[1]

These sessions attracted notably sizable crowds, since the fair itself boasted entertainment enough to lure away even the most devoted attendees. The fair, officially named the World's Columbian Exposition to commemorate the four hundredth anniversary of Columbus's arrival, was simultaneously a display of high nationalism and incipient globalism. Over the course of six months, the gate tallied some twenty-seven million visits to a world's fair that dwarfed its predecessors in scale and variety of exhibits. Approximately two hundred new buildings covered six hundred acres that displayed the culture and achievement of forty-six participating countries. However, the fair centered on the United States in a moment of industrial and cultural coming-of-age.

The Columbian Exhibition provided the perfect opportunity for the United States to demonstrate its ability to play on a world stage, and the Congress on

Charities was an ideal scene to stage, since it drew on an informal transatlantic exchange of ideas and practices that had been in place for decades. Given their shared language, the philanthropists from England and the United States in particular had long traded and debated social reform philosophies and methods, from the abolitionist movement to the settlement movement and from poor-law reform to temperance efforts. This transatlantic philanthropic exchange was evident at the fair even beyond the bounds of the Congress on Charities. The printed report of the Congress noted that most of the participating nations sent "charitable and correctional exhibits" as part of their national displays.[2] Certainly England did. Its exhibit space in the Woman's Building included a large selection of materials regarding philanthropic work. In fact, the philanthropy portion contained more items than any other part of Great Britain's exhibits in the Woman's Building, aside from the collection "Portraits of Eminent British Women" (many of whom were philanthropists). Britain's philanthropy exhibits contained "Specimens of Handicraft Work" made by those trained and educated in philanthropic establishments, maps detailing the locations and extent of charitable institutions, and photographs and sketches of schools, infirmaries, and charitable work. Most importantly, the country's philanthropy exhibits contained five bound volumes of extensive typewritten reports on the philanthropic work of women in hundreds of organizations throughout the British Isles.[3]

This documentary record had been gathered by a committee of women appointed by Princess Christian of Schleswig-Holstein, daughter of Queen Victoria, head of the committee coordinating the Woman's Building exhibits and, of course, a prominent patron of philanthropic efforts. To head the committee, she appointed Angela Burdett-Coutts, whose career dispensing funds from the banking fortune she inherited had made her an international celebrity. Burdett-Coutts and her colleagues sent letters to every identifiable philanthropic organization in the British Isles, requesting a report on the work that women had contributed.[4] These reports functioned not only as exhibits for the fair but also as raw material for several papers presented at the conference and as the subject matter for a book written and edited by Burdett-Coutts and her committee members to be sold at the fair.

In the preface to this book, titled *Woman's Mission: A Series of Congress Papers on the Philanthropic Work of Women*, Burdett-Coutts described the transatlantic culture of philanthropy that the exhibit sought to capture:

> In an unusual degree the blood of many races runs in our veins; but we are bound together in the one historic record of the English-speaking peoples. One language unites us; one Bible, one literature. The poetry and prose of past centuries, and the first achievements of Englishmen in the dim twilight of scientific discovery, are a common heritage of both nations. In the past fifty years the genius of both, sometimes divided, sometimes intermingled, has kept the light burning. To the sacred lamp of literature American authors have added

a peculiar radiance of their own, and the field of discovery and invention has been illuminated by the splendid achievements of American research. And as in these two great branches of progress we are at once co-inheritors and fellow-workers, so the philanthropic work of Englishwomen, commingled by practice and example with the work of American women, must, I feel, have an absorbing interest for those who, like ourselves, have drawn their national being from the Anglo-Saxon race.[5]

Burdett-Coutts's comments register several ideas integral to the chapters in this book. First, they reflect the degree to which women had taken leadership in social welfare efforts—philanthropy had become *the* arena of public life most amenable to women's professional development, and Burdett-Coutts sought to both embody and document the place of women in civil society. Second, they capture the transatlantic nature of philanthropic influence. Burdett-Coutts's history drew on an established mythology racially rooted in English scientific and cultural achievements over the course of the eighteenth and nineteenth centuries. The germinal account of Anglo-Saxon development had been widely adopted in the late-Victorian period as a way of framing the relationship between the United States and Britain. That history was explicitly racialized to assert northern European heritage as a foundation for an Anglophone empire. Although troublingly exclusive to modern ears, this model continued to inform social and political perspectives well into the twentieth century. Fifty years before Winston Churchill would formally launch the Cold War by invoking "the fraternal association of the English-speaking peoples,"[6] Burdett-Coutts expressed her version of the Special Relationship on a platform of charitable giving. Modern philanthropy, according to Burdett-Coutts, was the result of this historic narrative, a culminating point in the shared history of progress.

Finally, the Congress demonstrated that philanthropy was more than a set of economic and social practices or a discrete group of institutions. Burdett-Coutts's narrative reimagines the collective practices of modern civil society into a discourse with the power to motivate forms of affiliation across geographic, national, and social boundaries. For Burdett-Coutts, this discourse, or set of written traditions and conversations, became the founding concept behind transatlantic philanthropic endeavor.[7] She refers to a shared "language" and "literature," complete with "the poetry and prose of past centuries," alongside ongoing "scientific discovery" as the "commingled" source of an Anglo-Saxon nationalism, a common "national being."

A Discourse of Philanthropy

This collection of essays by literary scholars traces developments in the discourse of philanthropy that emerged during this period to become, as dramatized in the Columbian Exhibition, a hallmark of Anglophone-Atlantic civilization. As it adapted eighteenth-century systems of social order, philanthropy assumed a variety of cultural forms that, in turn, registered a new state of relations within and among classes. Beginning in the first half of the nineteenth century, a literature of philanthropy proliferated on both sides of the Atlantic, as increasing urbanization and industrialization created new demands on traditional social structures. Print matter represented philanthropy—through works of fiction and social science as well as political and economic treatises—as a primary means of managing class relations, civic engagement, and political reform. Philanthropy, as a discursive tradition, was a key factor in the development of the nineteenth-century transatlantic social imagination.

The chapters in this collection demonstrate that philanthropy revolved around several key concepts. First, it concerned the definition and nature of poverty, particularly the urban poverty that was a hallmark of the increasingly industrialized cities on both sides of the Atlantic. In the process of confronting the problem of burgeoning urban poverty, what had traditionally been considered publicly minded altruism, benevolence, and charity developed into a much more rationalized system that sought to alter the course of civil society through giving and voluntarism. Primary among the efforts of philanthropists were repeated attempts to differentiate between the "deserving" and "undeserving" poor and to negotiate the often-conflicting roles of public aid and private relief. Both these concerns were addressed directly in writing generated by the Charity Organization Societies (COS), first established in London in 1869 and soon spreading to other urban centers in the United States and Britain. The COS organizations offered to coordinate relief among the many private organizations that offered similar services, referring those in need to the organizations best suited to provide for them, and investigating the claims made by applicants to reduce the risk of impersonation and fraud. Workers in these organizations took part in the nascent methods of social science, developing the concept of casework and bringing what they considered a scientific, academic methodology to philanthropic work. Eventually, the new philanthropy movement brought academic study to the poorest of urban environments in the settlement-house movement and brought philanthropic work to an academic setting with the advent of degree programs in philanthropy at the University of Chicago and elsewhere. These efforts generated a literature that adopted new perspectives and methods while incorporating the Enlightenment concept of sympathy as well as established notions of class, ethnic divides, patronage, and benevolence. In addition, these efforts provided a field of endeavor notable for attracting women to its cause, both women of means like Burdett-Coutts, who could fund philanthropic endeavor, and women who devoted their time and, increasingly, expertise. Defining the nature and roles of women, then, became integral to the representation of philanthropy.

During a period when civil society was the primary front (or occupied its most historically prominent place) in addressing the adverse effects of industrialism, these widespread discussions of poverty, urbanization, women's work, and sympathy provided a means of understanding and debating social reform. While the twentieth century would see the advent of modern social welfare policy, the culture of philanthropy in the preceding period exhibited a uniquely entrepreneurial and diverse field of endeavor. The period from 1850 to 1920 constitutes a discrete epoch in the history of philanthropy, a period when giving gained an unprecedented measure of cultural authority as it changed in kind and degree, and the system of narratives that developed around modern philanthropy sought to explain changing social conditions in ways that transcended national boundaries. In hindsight, these changes appear as a central modernizing agent in the development of Anglophone culture on both sides of the Atlantic.

Literary Scholarship and Philanthropy

Within literary studies over the past decade, philanthropy and related concepts of charity, humanitarianism, and social reform have been employed to register broader changes in the sociology of class, gender, and race. A wide range of studies has shown how philanthropy influenced literary development and how writing about philanthropy shaped public perceptions of the new forms of civil action. Dorice Williams Elliott's *The Angel out of the House* (2002) and Andrea Geddes Poole's *Philanthropy and the Construction of Victorian Women's Citizenship* (2014) exemplify this tradition in detailing how writing by and about women's roles invoked philanthropy as both an expansion of and escape from the Victorian domestic arena.[8] Jill Bergman and Debra Bernadi's collection *Our Sisters' Keepers* (2005) explores a similar dynamic in what they term "benevolence literature" by American women in the nineteenth century.[9] Benevolence, as a ritualized behavior, is also central to Daniel Siegel's *Charity and Condescension* (2012), which considers the ways charity helped sustain ostensibly outmoded forms of paternalism.[10] Literary scholarship dealing with philanthropy and class identity tends to emphasize literature's response to the profound demographic shifts propelled by the industrial revolution. The rise of an urban working poor and an expanding middle class inspired a large body of work attempting to document the new urban experience and offer systems to classify social position and thereby manage it in an increasingly unstable environment. Studies such as Seth Koven's *Slumming: Sexual and Social Politics in Victorian London* (2004), Daniel Bivona and Roger Henkle's *The Imagination of Class* (2006), and Gavin Jones's *American Hungers* (2007) show how poverty was understood as a cultural condition by novelists, journalists, and sociological investigators.[11] A related strand of scholarship examines philanthropy in conjunction with other traditions, such as political economy. Claudia Klaver's *A/Moral Economics* (2003), Lauren Goodlad's *Victorian Literature and the Victorian State* (2003), and Ilana Blumberg's *Victorian Sacrifice: Ethics and Economics in Mid-century Novels* (2013) consider the ways philanthropic discourse represents the consequences of industrialism offering a sometimes complementary, and other times contradictory, account from that of classical economic thought.[12]

Recently, literary scholars such as Amanda Claybaugh and Frank Christianson have begun to explore how philanthropy operated as a transatlantic phenomenon.[13] In her book *The Novel of Purpose* (2007), Claybaugh traces the lines of affiliation among various reform movements that crisscrossed the Atlantic as part of a network of private and institutional connections informing literature's response to social problems.[14] Claybaugh's analysis proceeds from the premise that nineteenth-century Anglophone literature was much more transnational than was the literature of the twentieth century. A "literature-in-English" model superseded investments in national distinctiveness, making it possible to imagine a coherent literary culture with many avenues of mutual influence. Christianson's *Philanthropy in British and American Literature* (2007) modifies Claybaugh's model of continuity by showing how American cultural nationalism sought a literary tradition free of the burdens of British cultural inheritance.[15] American perspectives on philanthropy, as both private charity and institutional giving, played a central role in how the nation distinguished itself in economic, social, and moral terms. British and American philanthropies informed the role of the state and the place of the individual in collective efforts to maintain civil society.

Seen together, these studies foreground philanthropy's integral role in the literature of a period known for a new fictional mode: social realism. Writers used the language of philanthropy to discuss matters integral to the experience of rapid industrialization. This collection aims to make explicit and to further our understanding of philanthropy's place in nineteenth-century print culture.

Philanthropic Writing in the Anglo-American Tradition

The chapters in this book build on the scholarly tradition while also attempting to advance the conversation in new directions. Drawing on a wide sampling of the documentary record, from manifestos to fundraising tracts and from correspondence to novels, the book engages key contexts for transatlantic associational culture in the late industrial period. The essays specifically address this corpus from a literary studies perspective, identifying the philosophical, ideological, and aesthetic values that motivated and shaped that record rather than tracing the histories of specific philanthropic institutions or practices. Contributors examine novels, letters, pamphlets, and more in order to piece together the intellectual world in which philanthropists reasoned through their efforts, experimented imaginatively with reform methods, and, along the way, examined their own motives.

Both the content and the context of Burdett-Coutts's manifesto suggest the international scope of that discourse. This collection takes a transnational perspective in order to better understand the issues that informed philanthropists on both sides of the North Atlantic. In particular, the collection juxtaposes chapters dealing with the United States, Britain, and Britain's most influential colony, India. It offers explicitly transnational topics alongside national themes to reveal the patterns, philosophies, and unsettled questions that were all part of the rich and vibrant transatlantic philanthropic community.

Among the least settled questions for writers of the period were the effects of increasing urbanization. As Tanushree Ghosh demonstrates in chapter 7, "'Witnessing Them Day after Day': Ethical Spectatorship and Liberal Reform in Walter Besant's *Children of Gibeon*," often philanthropists set out to investigate the sites of urban poverty in order to educate themselves and to offer their own solution to the conditions they encountered. These efforts required both donors and recipients to negotiate the underpinnings of philanthropy in an urban setting. Besant's work represents late Victorian literature's effort to address the ethics of class conflict, economic philosophy, gender norms, and aesthetic values through the prism of philanthropy. These issues were not limited to the London needlewomen who are Besant's subject. Sarah Robbins's "Sustaining Gendered Philanthropy through Transatlantic Friendship: Jane Addams, Henrietta Barnett, and Writing for Reciprocal Mentoring" (chapter 9) explores the rhetorical relations between two women at the forefront of the urban-settlement movement, one in London and the other in Chicago. By tracing the influence these women had on one another, Robbins reveals the interchange of ideas that defined an informal philanthropic network spanning the Atlantic. Much as Addams and Barnett developed their professional identities by encountering the urban poor, Margaret Fuller and Louisa May Alcott developed new forms of representation in response to the poverty they encountered on the streets of New York City. Monika Elbert's "Urban Reform and the Plight of the Poor in Women's Journalistic Writing" (chapter 4) traces the transformation in each of these women's writing as they narrate their urban experiences in both private and public forms of reportage. She suggests that urban poverty demanded a different aesthetic vision that unsettled the literary conventions associated with romantic and transcendental traditions.

Robbins's and Elbert's chapters are among five that foreground to varying degrees another defining feature of modern philanthropy: its role as a professionalizing vehicle for women. Both essays suggest how women's writing helped advance reform agendas while also articulating forms of leadership unique to women in the civic space. The kinds of professional-public navigation apparent in these studies take on an extra layer of complication when removed to the colonial context of nineteenth-century India, where would-be women philanthropists confronted the challenges of working within and among the patriarchies of the colonial regime and the indigenous cultures. Suzanne Daly (chapter 3) and Dorice Williams Elliott (chapter 5) examine debates over initiatives led by women to ameliorate suffering among Britain's colonial subjects in India. Collectively, these chapters demonstrate how philanthropic activity was gendered and how women, as benefactors and beneficiaries, navigated a coded system that could both enable and circumscribe certain forms of activism.

While the consequences of urban industrialization remained a foundational concern, philanthropy's conceptual underpinnings drew on the legacy of Enlightenment economic thought, which framed relations between classes. Adam Smith's notion of sympathy, at the heart of his theory of moral sentiments, was particularly important to the nineteenth-century representation of philanthropy. Lori Merish, in "The Poverty of Sympathy" (chapter 1), traces this concept in depictions of poor, unmarried mothers in factory literature, showing how this specific literary and social type exposes the limits of sympathetic identification in philanthropic literature. Daniel Bivona adds to this discussion in "Self-Undermining Philanthropic Impulses: Philanthropy in the Mirror of Narrative" (chapter 2). Bivona engages with the competing concepts of sympathy elaborated by Adam Smith and Edmund Burke, demonstrating that the intellectual inheritance of both philosophers contributed to philanthropic representations in the novels of Charles Dickens and George Gissing. In doing so, he pieces together a progressive dialogue of sympathetic identification and ultimate rationalization that haunts the fictional worlds created by both novelists. Emily Coit continues to develop our understanding of economic discourse in the realm of philanthropy, introducing a discussion of Andrew Carnegie and Alfred Marshall into her analysis of Edith Wharton's *The Fruit of the Tree*. In "'The Orthodox Creed of the Business World'? Philanthropy and Liberal Individualism in Edith Wharton's *The Fruit of the Tree*" (chapter 8), Coit demonstrates that Wharton used her novel to engage and question liberal economic thought, in spite of her own professed allegiance to liberal causes.

As philanthropists negotiated the variables of economic philosophy, they inevitably encountered the realities of economic disparity, whether based on traditional notions of class, on wealth, or on perceived ethnic or racial difference. Several chapters consider how literature of the period represented and questioned the culture of patronage that persisted in domestic and colonial contexts into the early twentieth century. Francesca Sawaya confronts these issues directly in her exploration of traditional patronage applied to artistic production. In "Patrons, Philanthropists, and Professionals: Henry James's *Roderick Hudson*" (chapter 6), Sawaya traces the potential for wealthy, elite patrons of the arts to enable or curtail artistic sensibility. Elliott continues this discussion in the realm of upper-class women's philanthropy, exploring how the class variables changed and developed as British and native women used philanthropic work to engage in civil society, both in England and in colonial India. In "Lady Bountiful for the Empire: Upper-Class Women, Philanthropy, and Civil Society" (chapter 5), she traces these processes in the work of three women novelists: Florence Willford, Alice Perrin, and Swarnakumari Debi. Suzanne Daly explores this topic from a different perspective, investigating how philanthropists from differing social and religious backgrounds functioned in colonial India. In "Education as Violation and Benefit: Doctrinal Debate and the Contest for India's Girls" (chapter 3), Daly outlines the contested field of education and religion, a field that she shows has continued resonance for twenty-first-century philanthropic work.

Collectively, the chapters explore some of the most significant philanthropic developments in the Anglo-American narrative tradition. The afterword, by Kathleen McCarthy, reviews recent trends in the scholarship of philanthropy and suggests productive avenues for continuing this work. As she notes, the study of philanthropy necessarily engages with issues of economic philosophy, of civil society, of gender and class disparity, and of wealth and influence. Philanthropy offers an ideal means of examining the wide sweep of civic engagement across the nineteenth and twentieth centuries.

From the mid-nineteenth century until the rise of the modern welfare state in the early twentieth century, philanthropy played a singular role in the making of civil society. The chapters in this book explore the rhetorical ways and means of this discrete sphere of voluntary action and the culture it produced. Although industrialization proceeded unevenly across the Atlantic world, the literary archive speaks to certain cultural effects that constitute philanthropic discourse. They show how that culture provided a platform for new narratives of class and gender relations. They examine how philanthropy drew on and shaped other modernizing discourses, including religion, economics, and social science. Ultimately, they demonstrate how the public sector was redefined by a dynamic and highly contested system of social ethics informed by both local realities and globalizing trends.

FRANK Q. CHRISTIANSON is Associate Professor of English at Brigham Young University. He is author of *Philanthropy in British and American Fiction: Dickens, Hawthorne, Eliot and Howells*.

LESLEE THORNE-MURPHY is Associate Professor of English at Brigham Young University.

Notes

1. See "For Fair Congresses: Dates Arranged for the Various Sessions to Be Held," *Chicago Daily Tribune*, April 17, 1893; "Public Treatment of Pauperism: Program Prepared for Its Discussion during the Congress of Charities," *Chicago Daily Tribune*, May 10, 1893; "For Social Reform: Program for the Congress to Begin Work This Week," *Chicago Daily Tribune*, June 4, 1893; "Way to Aid the Poor: Sermon to the Charities and Correction Conference," *Chicago Daily Tribune*, June 12, 1893; "To Revive the Unfit: Charity of Later Years Is Broad in Aims and Methods," *Chicago Daily Tribune*, June 13, 1893; "In Charity's Cause: World's Congress Discusses the Care of the Helpless," *Chicago Daily Tribune*, June 14, 1893; Alive to Good Deeds: Congress of King's Daughters Begins at the Art Institute," *Chicago Daily Tribune*, June 15, 1893; "Paupers and Darwin: Laws of Natural Selections Do Not Produce Mendicancy," *Chicago Daily Tribune*, June 16, 1893; and "Society as a Study: Dr. E. B. Andrews of Brown University Presents His Views," *Chicago Daily Tribune*, June 17, 1893. See also *General Exercises*; Billings and Hurd, *Hospitals, Dispensaries, and Nursing*; and Gilman, *The Organization of Charities*.
2. *General Exercises*, 26.
3. Department of Publicity and Promotion, *World's Columbian Exhibition, 1893*.
4. Burdett-Coutts, *Woman's Mission*, x–xi.
5. Ibid., xxi.
6. Churchill, "The Sinews of Peace."
7. Our use of the term *discourse* draws on literary and cultural studies that designate a discrete set of discursive or textual traditions as a means of exploring cultural assumptions, power relationships, and acknowledged or unacknowledged reactions against prevailing authority. As a number of studies have shown, philanthropic writing in the nineteenth century represented an increasingly coherent set of institutions and practices (see, for example, Friedman and McGarvie, *Charity, Philanthropy, and Civility*; McCarthy, *American Creed*; Prochaska, *Christianity and Social Service*; Himmelfarb, *Idea of Poverty*; and Mandler, *Uses of Charity*). Within this framework, philanthropy becomes a rhetoric or topos that appears across a broad spectrum of published materials. This corpus is the object of our collective discourse analysis.
8. Elliott, *Angel out of the House*; Poole, *Philanthropy*.
9. Bergman and Bernadi, *Our Sisters' Keepers*.
10. Siegel, *Charity and Condescension*.
11. Koven, *Slumming*; Bivona and Henkle, *The Imagination of Class*; Jones, *American Hungers*.
12. Klaver, *A/Moral Economics*; Goodlad, *Victorian Literature and the Victorian State*; Blumberg, *Victorian Sacrifice*.
13. Notable in the history of transatlantic philanthropy is the work of Thomas Adam. See Adam, *Buying Respectability*; and Adam, *Philanthropy, Patronage, and Civil Society*.
14. Claybaugh, *Novel of Purpose*.
15. Christianson, *Philanthropy in British and American Fiction*.

Bibliography

Adam, Thomas, ed. *Buying Respectability: Philanthropy and Urban Society in Transnational Perspective, 1840s to 1930s.* Bloomington: Indiana University Press, 2009.
———. *Philanthropy, Patronage, and Civil Society: Experiences from Germany, Great Britain, and North America.* Bloomington: Indiana University Press, 2004.
Bergman, Jill, and Debra Bernadi. *Our Sisters' Keepers: Nineteenth-Century Benevolence Literature by American Women.* Tuscaloosa: University of Alabama Press, 2005.
Billings, John S., and Henry M. Hurd, eds. *Hospitals, Dispensaries, and Nursing: Papers and Discussions in the International Congress of Charities, Correction and Philanthropy, Section III, Chicago, June 12th to 17th, 1893.* Baltimore: Johns Hopkins Press, 1894.
Bivona, Daniel, and Roger Henkle. *The Imagination of Class: Masculinity and the Victorian Urban Poor.* Columbus: Ohio State University Press, 2006.
Blumberg, Ilana. *Victorian Sacrifice: Ethics and Economics in Mid-century Novels.* Columbus: Ohio State University Press, 2013.
Burdett-Coutts, Angela, ed. *Woman's Mission, A Series of Congress Papers on the Philanthropic Work of Women by Eminent Writers.* New York: Charles Scribner's Sons, 1893.
"Chicago Daily Tribune (1849–1993)." *ProQuest Historical Newspapers.* http://www.proquest.com/products-services/pq-hist-news.html.
Christianson, Frank. *Philanthropy in British and American Fiction: Dickens, Hawthorne, Eliot, and Howells.* Edinburgh, UK: Edinburgh University Press, 2007.
Churchill, Winston S. "The Sinews of Peace." Speech given at Westminster College, Fulton, MO, March 5, 1946. http://www.nato.int/docu/speech/1946/s460305a_e.htm.
Claybaugh, Amanda. *The Novel of Purpose: Literature and Social Reform in the Anglo-American World.* Ithaca, NY: Cornell University Press, 2007.
Department of Publicity and Promotion, ed. *World's Columbian Exhibition, 1893: Official Catalog, Part XIV: Woman's Building.* Chicago: W. B. Conkey, 1893.
Elliott, Dorice Williams. *The Angel Out of the House: Philanthropy and Gender in Nineteenth-Century England.* Charlottesville: University Press of Virginia, 2002.
Friedman, Lawrence J., and Mark D. McGarvie, eds. *Charity, Philanthropy, and Civility in American History.* New York: Cambridge University Press, 2002.
General Exercises of the International Congress of Charities, Correction and Philanthropy, Chicago, June 1893. Baltimore, MD: Johns Hopkins Press, 1894.
Gilman, Daniel C., ed. *The Organization of Charities, Being a Report of the Sixth Section of the International Congress of Charities, Correction, and Philanthropy, June, 1893.* Baltimore, MD: Johns Hopkins Press, 1894.
Goodlad, Lauren. *Victorian Literature and the Victorian State: Character and Governance in a Liberal Society.* Baltimore, MD: Johns Hopkins University Press, 2003.
Himmelfarb, Gertrude. *The Idea of Poverty: England in the Early Industrial Age.* New York: Knopf, 1984.
Jones, Gavin. *American Hungers: The Problem of Poverty in U.S. Literature, 1840–1945.* Princeton, NJ: Princeton University Press, 2007.
Klaver, Claudia. *A/Moral Economics: Classical Political Economy and Cultural Authority in Nineteenth-Century England.* Columbus: Ohio State University Press, 2003.
Koven, Seth. *Slumming: Sexual and Social Politics in Victorian London.* Princeton, NJ: Princeton University Press, 2004.

Mandler, Peter. *The Uses of Charity*. Philadelphia: University of Pennsylvania Press, 1990.
McCarthy, Kathleen. *American Creed: Philanthropy and the Rise of Civil Society*. Chicago: University of Chicago Press, 2003.
Poole, Andrea Geddes. *Philanthropy and the Construction of Victorian Women's Citizenship: Lady Frederick Cavendish and Miss Emma Cons*. Toronto: University of Toronto Press, 2014.
Prochaska, Frank. *Christianity and Social Service in Modern Britain: The Disinherited Spirit*. Oxford: Oxford University Press, 2006.
Siegel, Daniel. *Charity and Condescension: Victorian Literature and the Dilemmas of Philanthropy*. Athens: Ohio University Press, 2012.

1

THE POVERTY OF SYMPATHY

Lori Merish

IN THE *THEORY of Moral Sentiments*, Adam Smith describes how the condition of impoverishment is a barrier to sympathy as well as to the social visibility or intelligibility on which it apparently depends. Assessing the "disposition to admire, and almost to worship, the rich and the powerful, and to despise, or at least, to neglect, persons of poor and mean condition," Smith describes how the "poor man goes out and comes in unheeded, and when in this midst of the crowd is in the same obscurity as if shut up in his own hovel."[1] This chapter locates the impoverishment of sympathy that Smith describes in the displacement of traditional forms of social benevolence and what Bruce Robbins calls the "privatization of love" associated with the rise of a liberal political economy.[2] This absence of sympathy for the poor is conspicuously evident in antebellum discourses of poverty; shaped by the English Poor Law debates and the rise of economic liberalism, as well as by the increased visibility of the urban poor in the early decades of the century, this discourse initiated a new skepticism about poverty and a hardening in attitudes toward the poor.[3]

A central figure in this discourse was the poor, unmarried mother, whose entitlement to both sympathy and relief was increasingly questioned, and who was seen to pass what reformer William Ellery Channing termed the "fatal inheritance" of poverty on to her offspring.[4] The cultural prominence of this figure reflects the influential theories of Thomas Malthus, who assailed the traditional system of poor relief for encouraging excessive reproduction among the poor, with potentially catastrophic consequences—a process checked only by the disciplinary force of female chastity. For Malthus, it is to the "fatal effects" of an unrestrained "increase in population" that we may attribute the "very natural . . . superior disgrace which attends a breach of chastity in the woman, [more] than in the man," so that "a woman should be at present almost driven from society" for committing this "offence," a "custom" best dictated less by "state necessity" than by "female delicacy" and morality.⁵ This chapter examines how the diminishment of sympathy for poor, unmarried mothers was both registered and contested in two texts from 1850: George Foster's collection of sketches, *New York by Gaslight*, and the popular pamphlet novel *Mary Bean: The Factory Girl*. Both texts at once gesture toward and unsettle the widespread sensational, phobic construction of poor women's sexual stories; both incorporate surprisingly moving oral narratives or testimonials of female economic suffering, which become textual sites for mobilizing and remembering residual forms of sympathy and care for poor women. The chapter ends with a discussion of the writings of former factory girl and working-class activist Jennie Collins, whose 1871 book *Nature's Aristocracy: A Plea for the Oppressed* comprises just such testimonials; Collins determines to write so that the "shades of the hungry, toil-killed, and heart-shattered ... women shall tell their tales to the world in death, as they told them to me in life." Collins at once critiques the capitalist organization of charity—a system in which a "man gives back to his victims ... a part of the sum of which he deliberately robbed them" and is then "lauded to the skies as an example of mortal perfection"—and locates true benevolence and sympathy in the hearts and communal practices of working-class women.⁶

In her essay "Sympathy and Its Vicissitudes," Gillian Silverman emphasizes the importance of narrative for catalyzing sympathy's affective exchange; for Silverman, "sympathy ... is contingent upon discourse; we enter into vicarious suffering only by entering into language and storytelling." Silverman notes that, for Adam Smith, "the 'first question which we ask is, What has befallen you?' and '[t]ill this be answered ... our fellow-feeling is not very considerable.'"⁷ Although this class matrix and history have generally been obscured in the cultural and literary history of US sentimentality, the public performance of "tales of woe" was central to traditional scenes of poor relief. In Britain and in the colonies, poor relief in the eighteenth century was governed by the English poor laws and was structured as parish relief. Individuals would perform their tales of woe before bodies sometimes known, sentimentally enough, as the Guardians of the Poor; the Guardians would be elite men in the community, often intimately acquainted with the teller and with her or his history of suffering. As scripted by this scenario, the poor would reveal to their superiors their impoverished condition, while the rich publicly, and quite palpably, revealed their beneficent nature.

In the early nineteenth century, urbanization, as well as the increased influence of liberal economic ideology that underwrote an expanded market society, facilitated a recasting of these scenes of sympathetic exchange and their forms of ritualized public sentiment; in particular, liberal economic theory initiated a new skepticism about and distrust of the poor. Beggars were envisioned as duplicitous actors, and their tales of suffering were reimagined as counterfeit rather than sincere testimonials; one English poor law reformer spoke of the "false tale of distress" regularly recounted by the "idle laborer" bent on deceiving and swindling the public. Such views were widely circulated in the American press; George Fitzhugh's *Cannibals All!* quotes a long passage from the *Edinburgh Review* describing various categories of "beggar imposters" who victimize kindhearted urban inhabitants with "long, pitiful got-up tale[s] of pretended distress."[8] While the United States never experienced the intense anxiety about overpopulation (and poor women's reproductivity) that Malthus's theories generated in England, the increased visibility of the urban poor and the rapidly expanding welfare rolls in cities in the years after 1815, and especially after the Panic of 1819, effected what historians of social welfare describe as a similar hardening in attitudes toward the poor and changes in welfare policies. As in Britain, a number of scientific reports—aiming to temper what one reformer termed the "blind sympathy" of earlier relief practices—were issued inquiring into the causes of poverty and the identity, number, and condition of the poor, and Societies for the Prevention of Pauperism were established in every sizable northern city. Most of these bodies recommended substantial changes in the distribution of poor relief, in particular a shift from "outdoor relief" (cash pensions) to indoor relief (the almshouse and workhouse, with the stigma of shame that would serve as a spur to work) and were marked by a "deepening distrust" and growing "contempt" toward the "increasing throng" of the "dependent poor."[9]

Indeed, according to one historian, "The influence of the classical economists . . . and the idea that public relief tended to pauperize and demoralize recipients" met "even more rigid acceptance in the United States than in England." Precisely the idea(l) that, in America, poverty need not exist encouraged a "harsh and suspicious view of the poor."[10] Poverty was increasingly read as moral failure: in this context, the recipient of the tale of woe was encouraged not to sympathize with the sufferings of the bearer of the tale but to search for the moral failings and vices to which this suffering might be attributed—to find their hidden but underlying moral causes. By the 1820s, as Bruce Dorsey observes, "public sentiments alleged that improvidence caused poverty and indiscriminate charity encouraged pauperism."[11] Reflecting these views, Ezra Stiles Ely, in his 1822 article "Prevention of Pauperism," observes that the majority of paupers landed in almshouses because of their own "drunkenness, idleness, extravagance, improvidence, laziness, lust and the righteous curse of unchastity." While acknowledging that "the laboring population . . . appear not to obtain a proportionate share of the growing prosperity around them," reformers such as Ely promoted the view that since the causes of poverty and destitution are "chiefly moral," they "admit only moral remedies."[12]

This reformulation of sympathy was scripted into and by the writings of poverty reformers. As Silverman notes, in Smith's *Theory of Moral Sentiments*, "the achievement of fellow feeling relies on cognition and understanding rather than on any automatic or blind responsiveness." Silverman illustrates the point with the following quotation from Smith: "The compassion of the spectator must arise altogether from consideration of what he himself would feel if he was reduced to the same situation, and, what perhaps is impossible, was at the same time able to regard it with his present reason and judgment."[13] Mobilizing this reason and judgment, antebellum writers about poverty (in dialogue with British poor law reformers) aimed to delimit indiscriminate almsgiving as the product of unregulated emotion. As Boston reformer R. C. Waterston notes in his "Address on Pauperism" (published in 1844 by the Society for the Prevention of Pauperism), "The idea of generosity is agreeable to our nature, and the delicate sympathies of the heart are gratified in the act of benevolence," so that "when applications are made, the first impulse is to give at once, and to give without investigation."[14]

However, for this and other poor law reformers, such impulses must be controlled, and such investigation is crucial; reformers would engage in home visits and interviews to determine the moral character of the poor to combat what Waterston terms the "great evil" of "indiscriminate almsgiving"—itself the cause (following the Malthusian logic) of "increasing pauperism."[15] Whereas innocent children are worthy of what Charles Burroughs in his "Discourse on Pauperism" (1835) terms the "tenderest sympathies and most generous relief," the adult poor—especially the able-bodied poor—are the object of increased skepticism.[16] Is their poverty the consequence of legitimate ill fortune, or—more likely—the consequence of vice? Or worse, is it the sham performance of what Burroughs calls the "professional beggar"? Especially when there are "applications from strangers," one should exercise the necessary "caution" until a proper "investigation . . . has been made"; "true benevolence will seek to manifest itself in the wisest way," and this requires "serious reflection" about the probable consequences of one's almsgiving.[17]

The textualization of sympathy in sentimental texts can be seen to facilitate and affirm the distanced, reflective stance toward the poor, which is recommended by Smith and by these poverty reformers; it also can be seen to affirm what Dorsey describes as the spiritualization of poverty, the focus on the spiritual and moral versus bodily needs of the poor—specifically, the view that, in Waterston's description, "a kind word spoken will be of more benefit . . . than the charity bestowed." Recommending a new emphasis on "spiritual" versus "temporal" wants, Waterston writes, "We must strive not merely to alleviate wretchedness, but to reform character" and "thus elevate the moral condition of the poor."[18]

On the one hand, the reformulated sympathy recommended by poverty writers aimed to displace what Burroughs called the "charity of compulsion" of traditional relief practices.[19] Writers traced the problem to the 1601 Act of 43 Elizabeth, chapter 2, known as the Old Poor Law, since American poor laws were "derived . . . from the code of that country from which we descended."[20] That belief that the act "produces such sympathies between [the poor] and the rich, and binds together in such a golden union these two remote classes, by such expressions of kindness on the one side, and by such a deep sense of gratitude on the other," Burroughs argues, is a sentimental myth. In truth, the poor tax is paid "without any consciousness of a charitable disposition." And the pauper receives legislative aid "not as a charity, but as a right." Instead of producing binding sympathies, Burroughs contends, the Old Poor Law in fact produces a "gulf of separation between the rich and the poor," for the parties "regard each other as natural enemies," as "hardhearted oppressors" and "poachers," respectively.[21] While assailing traditional forms of benevolence as emotionally impoverished, reformers such as Burroughs recast relief, as suggested earlier, in spiritual rather than material terms.

The displacement of material relief—the new tendency during home visits to distribute tracts, not alms—is evident in the strikingly material metaphors through which sympathy is depicted, especially the figuration of sympathy as food. In a June 1837 letter from Jane Sedgwick to her sister Catharine (author of the 1837 novel *The Poor Rich Man and the Rich Poor Man*, which is an important text for the refiguration of sympathy and poverty I describe here), this metaphorization is plainly evident. Jane writes to Catharine, "Of all the abundant good gifts you have received with such liberality from God, there is not one for which you ought to be so grateful as the power of your sympathy. What would your genius do without it for those poor exiles, what for that host of children who are fed with your smiles, for all that crowd of poor in spirit who are the chief paupers in our community!"[22]

A central target of poverty discourse—as with the discourse surrounding the Poor Law Amendment Act in Britain—was the poor unmarried mother. Under the notorious and highly controversial "Bastardy Clause" of the British New Poor Law (1834), single mothers were prohibited from naming fathers and from expecting the parish to extract money from the father or receive any cash payment; if she could not support her child, she would have to enter a workhouse.[23] As Lisa Cody notes, Liberal and Whig critics of the Old Poor Law who engineered the New Poor Law characterized single mothers as "pests of society," burdens, villains, strumpets, and cunning manipulators of men and charity. These discourses transformed poor women into deceitful calculators who became pregnant either to force their partner into marriage or to live idly on the relief that the parish would provide in lieu of the father's support; the poor, unmarried mother became a self-interested speculator whose womb was a kind of factory for the production of excess profit.[24]

American poverty writers took up these themes as well. Extending relief to unmarried mothers as a regular stipend from the public purse "whenever the female cannot find a profitable father for her offspring" affords "countenance and encouragement" to vice—and is thus (following the Malthusian logic) a "breeding ground" for pauperism. Several writers objected to women's "unblushing effrontery," and their "exacting as a *right* what ought never to have been granted, even as a charity," in appealing for relief. Since respectable poverty "shrinks from public view," the appeal for relief is itself a morally suspect performance, approximating itself to the "abominable arts, which make beggary and parish relief a better trade than labor."[25] The very notion that respectable poverty "shrinks from public view" itself affirmed the moralization of poverty, its construction as "secret shame" (a view evident in the pamphlet novel *Mary Bean*, discussed below). Several cities, including Boston and Philadelphia, crafted poor laws that mirrored British developments; by the 1820s, poor women were increasingly seen to bear the burden of the responsibility, morally and economically, for premarital sexuality.

The impoverishment of sympathy toward poor women was at once registered and contested in *Mary Bean: The Factory Girl*, an 1850 pamphlet novel written by "Miss J. A. B. of Manchester." *Mary Bean* features the perils of courtship in the industrial capitalist era, when the economic and social risks of premarital sex intensify for women, and, in the narrator's words, "the obtaining of a good husband is like drawing a prize in a lottery, where all the tickets but one are blanks."[26] Like the revolutionary-era seduction narratives analyzed by Cathy Davidson, the story provides a kind of gender pedagogy, adapted to the conditions of antebellum industrial life.[27] Mary is a country girl brought by her would-be seducer, George Hamilton, to the factory town (in this instance, Manchester, New Hampshire); here the passage to the factory town is not the prelude to but the vehicle of seduction, plotted as part of "the course which her *lover* had so ingeniously marked out" to facilitate her sexual "fall" and her subsequent career as his mistress.[28] The story exploits the seduced factory maid as literary type: the title page describes her tale as "illustrating the trials and temptations of factory life"—though in fact, the heroine's native village is the setting in which George melodramatically "mould[s] [Mary] to [his] wishes," and the factory tour (where Mary is introduced to "the various machines used in the manufacture of the goods," as well as the "pretty factory girls") is a male plot device.[29] Even Mary's factory work is scripted under the sign of male desire: claiming that, because of failed investments, he "lacks the means" to provide her with "a maintenance becoming of [her] situation, and one worthy [of] the love" Mary bears him, George convinces her to seek a position in the factory, where she can "earn something for the two of them." Male economic bankruptcy here signifies as female erotic ruin, and it is unprotected poor women who are most vulnerable to the vicissitudes of the market.[30] Mary's lover is a murderer as well as a seducer, his utter disregard for life is underscored by the narrative pairing of these two acts, and Mary ultimately dies at the hands of an abortionist to whom she is sent by George in an effort to free himself from unwanted dependents. The antebellum discourse about poverty, with its curtailment of sympathy, provides the social matrix that makes the ubiquitous *seduced* and *abandoned* stories intelligible. The new contempt for poor women, underwritten by liberal political economy, legitimates their sexual objectification and abandonment and their treatment as social outcasts; male sadism toward economic dependents (the unborn child, the pregnant lover) are given emphatic, and horrific, narrative expression.

In *Mary Bean*, seduction is scripted as the negation of sentimental intelligibility. Lowell mill woman Harriet Robinson, describing the practice among married workingwomen of changing their names as a way to protect their wages from the grasp of estranged (or abusive) husbands, depicts anonymity as freeing and empowering for workingwomen; in *Mary Bean*, urban anonymity fuels female victimization.[31] The romantic narrative is contextualized within traditional forms of social welfare and care; resistance to seduction is aligned with the interest and gaze of the social. The spell George casts on Mary, signifying the destructiveness of mesmeric possession rather than preservative care, depends on secrecy: they initially pass surreptitious notes at a dinner party, they meet for the first time in the woods, and Mary's initial objections center on what the "world would think" to find her in company with George. "How can I escape the scorn and derision of my . . . acquaintances," she asks him, and risk the "suspicions of [my] friends?"[32] Such passages, and the moral voice of the narrator, articulate a socialized understanding and value of love, and they script romantic love in the language of social benevolence. This traditional understanding of love and pity are associated with the village peddler, Prosperity Jones, who describes buying some gingerbread and cheese in a grocery store and, when approached in the street by an old woman who is hungry, shares his dinner with her; Mary later remarks that his story "manifested a benevolent heart."[33]

Bereft of such forms of benevolence and care, Mary, even when pregnant, finds she has limited claims on her lover. A "ruined girl—forsaken of friends," she recognizes that "Hamilton was the only one she felt she had a claim upon, and he, as the cause of her ruin, was bound, in pity and in honor, to protect her from suffering and want." Abandoned by Hamilton, she locates him in Boston and successfully pleads her case, "throwing herself upon his pity and protection" and "mov[ing] his heart."[34] But his sympathy is short-lived. Soon thereafter he takes her to the notorious abortionist, Dr. Savin, at whose hand she dies, and the heartless Hamilton "felt himself relieved of a burden"—in particular because "none lived to tell the fearful story" of her seduction and murder. Not only is this incident meant to reveal the inhumanity of a system that would destroy rather than care for the offspring of unwed pauper mothers; it also literalizes the violence of a textual system that—ever suspicious rather than sympathetic to poor mothers—would pry open their deceitful forms to expose the shameful secrets hidden within. In the era of Victorian sexual mores, a woman's *fall* is utterly shameful, and men like Hamilton rely on women's internalization of sexual shame to consign them to silence. In *Mary Bean*, Mary's deep grief and melancholy reflect the material and social losses—losses in benevolence and social care—that fuel and attend this constriction of voice, the poor woman's diminished control over her sexual story. Believing that "to make her conduct known would be sure ruin to her reputation," Mary succumbs, in the end, to the poverty of sympathy.[35]

The curtailment of sympathy toward poor unmarried mothers is portrayed in a range of antebellum texts; taken together, these texts underscore the key role of poor women to the literary history of benevolence, even while they unsettle the reflective distance promoted by Smith and poverty reformers (a distance affirmed through sentimental textualization) by memorializing the embodied, oral performances of the poor. For example, the vexed rhetorical terrain Harriet Jacobs must navigate in *Incidents in the Life of a Slave Girl*, in recounting "Linda Brent's" life as an unmarried mother of two children while evoking readerly sympathy and support, is shaped at once by the purported degradation of the slave and the stigmatization of the impoverished unwed mother.[36] As I examine elsewhere, a concern with the "condition" of poor and working-class women was a primary focus of social reformers (especially labor and urban reformers) in the antebellum United States; such a concern shaped factory debates in England and in America as well as sociological studies of urban life.[37]

In courtrooms and charitable institutions, as well as in cross-class encounters on urban streets, laboring and poor women were asked to bear witness to the burdens of poverty and provide moving testimonies to economic suffering. Such narratives shaped literary discourse in complex ways. For example, a range of midcentury fictional and nonfictional literary texts (including Lydia Child's *Letters from New York* and George Foster's *New York by Gaslight*) include scenes in which a wealthy man or woman encounters a female stranger who orally recounts a poverty narrative, her firsthand experiences of economic suffering and deprivation. Explicitly challenging reformer Charles Loring Brace's claim that the "poor *feel*, but they can seldom speak,"[38] numerous authors depict scenes in which poor women come to voice and articulate moving if attenuated life narratives. Such a repertoire made poor women's narratives a conventional part of antebellum oral and written culture but radically simplified their stories and created exceptionally narrow frameworks for representing poor women's and workingwomen's experiences.

For example, attunement to poor women's narratives of economic distress interrupts the predominantly visual emphasis—the construction of poor women as spectacle—evident in *New York By Gaslight*. Like most sensational exposés (and as his title signals), Foster's narrative principally invokes the visual metaphor—"Go on with us, and see," he initially invites us, instructing the reader to "use our eyes" together. However, in his fifth chapter, he incites us to listen, recording "brief but instructive autobiographies" of poor women turned prostitutes.[39] Foster asserts that these "personal narratives were taken down from the lips and in nearly the very words of those who enacted them"; he claims that these narratives were "collected from various sources, during a professional life of many years in the metropolis, as a daily reporter and journalist."[40] Like many sensational authors, Foster grounds his text in allegedly nonfictional reports or testimonials of criminality and illicit sexuality, delivered in what Shane White calls vernacular performance sites (street, courtroom, etc.) of urban lower-class life—arguably an important way in which oral narratives of the poor, or what scholars term *orature*, have entered the literary text.[41]

In *New York by Gaslight*, these narratives diverge from the romantic, picturesque representation of the poor commonly found in middle-class texts—a mode Herman Melville, in *Pierre*, ironically terms the "povertiresque"[42]—and their economical realism is often startlingly moving. The first narrator, from a rural background, describes her first sexual encounter, as a fifteen-year-old girl, with her beloved cousin Tom: "He was a handsome young man, and . . . so deferential and soft in his manner that he completely won my child's-heart." Afterward, her cousin is struck with remorse, "accusing himself of being [her] destroyer," while the narrator's "childish simplicity" is affirmed by her belief that she "didn't dream of any thing wrong." "I'm as good as ever I was," she assures Tom before the two swear "eternal fidelity." A few months later, she discovers she is pregnant; Tom is in the city "attend[ing] the lectures," and the narrator sees "no other chance than to break the hearts of my poor parents by telling them of my disgrace." A secret sexual encounter does not obliterate "good[ness]"; unwed motherhood, with the child as what reformers called the "badge of shame," is a familial "disgrace." Beside herself with worry, she goes to the minister to "ma[k]e a clean breast of it" and seek advice; the minister agrees to help her but extorts the "same favors I had done to cousin Tom" in repayment. The poor woman's "choice" of an abortion to solve her problem is clarified by a consideration of her alternatives; fearing her family's reaction and without the father's support, her options are limited.[43]

Although there was an extensive system of privately funded orphanages in the antebellum period (notably, institutions that were racially segregated), these group homes did not accept foundlings or abandoned children. According to Julie Miller, "As illegitimates, the children of unmarried mothers bore a moral taint, with the result that, in the words of one administrator of a post–Civil War foundling asylum, 'some may say that, because they were the offspring of guilty parents, it were better that their existence in this world should be extinguished at its dawn.'"[44] In *New York by Gaslight*, the girl's lover abandons her—as the narrator sarcastically states, "Of course, it wouldn't do for a man's *honor* that he marry a poor girl after he had ruined her!"—and her parents ultimately discover her secret. It destroys them: her mother "took it to heart dreadfully," and her health deteriorates, while her father starts drinking, loses his farm, and ends up in the county poorhouse. Meeting not sympathy but exploitation and reiterated misogynist treatment, as a poor woman and as an instrument for men's sexual use, the narrator moves to New York to work in the sex trade, filled with hatred and rage. "Is it strange that I have grown hard-hearted and reckless and learned to look at life as a game of cards, at which he who wins most is . . . best?"[45]

The narrator of Foster's second "brief but instructive autobiograph[y]" describes a bleak childhood of urban poverty: "I haven't any fine romance and innocent babyhood, and all that sort of thing, to amuse you with," she tells her interlocutor, noting, "the first thing I can remember is being cold and hungry, and half naked and ragged, and sent out in the rainy mornings into the streets barefooted, to sweep the crossings and beg for pennies." The narrator depicts her damp, dark, broken-down tenement in detail: "We lived in a little back cellar down in an alley in Orange street, where I don't remember . . . ever to have seen the sun enter. The floor was only loose boards, and the black mud and slime used to ooze up through the cracks all about. . . . The damp used to come out on the walls, and stand there year after year, in big, gummy drops. . . . I remember all of these details very vividly, because they constituted the home of my childhood, and I knew no other place of shelter in the world where I could set my foot."[46] She continues, "In this one cellar my father and mother, my two brothers and sisters and myself . . . ate, slept, cooked, washed and ironed, did everything in this one dank and noisome hole . . . [the] squalid, loathsome, suffocating home of my childhood." She notes, "My relatives . . . were mostly kind to me and to each other. They never beat me when I had been unlucky in my day's work; but oftener, when I came home crying bitterly, with my little frozen fingers almost empty . . . my mother's face has beamed with an expression of genuine sympathy and affection."[47]

Her parents drink, and while initially she "loathed the smell and distaste of it," she quickly discovers alcohol's appeal: "After I had drank it I felt like another being; it seemed as if I was handsome and delicate, and wore fine clothes and had on pretty shoes and stockings, showing my white bare legs, like the fine little ladies I saw walking in Broadway with their mamas." "At other times, I pined and longed for I knew not what; and a vague but fierce feeling of despair and revenge filled my little heart almost to bursting." Prostitution, like alcohol, becomes a vehicle of escape from physical deprivation and absolute wretchedness: "I was ambitious; and finding that I was going to be handsome, I determined to make my own way through the world. I had already reflected a good deal, and had come to the conclusion that I couldn't be worse off, any how." Her plan is facilitated by acquaintance with "a dashing, splendidly dressed lady" who occasionally stopped "to give me a sixpence and talk to me." At ten the narrator has made "considerable progress in my grand but very indefinite schemes": "I had gradually and cautiously secreted money enough to buy some second-hand clothes, which struck me as being overwhelmingly grand." Here and elsewhere in her autobiographical tale, the narrator affirms the powerful if often trivialized importance of clothes for poor women, which were both signs of desire and, as Carolyn Steedman asserts, means of entry into nineteenth-century society.[48]

The narrator is ultimately recruited by the "dashing, splendidly dressed lady" as a prostitute, playing the "grand part of interesting and tender child—in which [she] was sold over and over again, during several years, to rich old lechers, blind with debauchery and palsied with age." Prostitution was clearly a means of escape from the abject poverty, endless labor, and "squalid, loathsome, suffocating home" of her childhood: "When I contrast my condition then with what it is now, I feel as if I ought to be pretty well satisfied with the way I have managed to get on in the world. I live freely and generously, dress like a princess, drink, eat and sleep like a king's mistress, and care for nobody on earth." She admits that she feels at times "a kind of heart sickness," but a glass of whisky blots it out. Notably, Foster does not editorialize in this section but allows these voices and these stories to resonate; in the end, he "commend[s]" his narrative to "the hospitality of [his readers'] affections."[49]

My final text, working-class writer Jennie Collins's *Nature's Aristocracy: A Plea for the Oppressed* (1871), directly addresses both the impoverishment of sympathy for poor women that accompanied the rise of economic liberalism and the conventional uses to which poor women's narratives were put—in part by recontextualizing those narratives in her own collection of poor women's oral materials. In one of Collins's sketches, she suggests how the new skepticism toward poor women could engender highly scripted, conventionalized performances of poverty—what historian Peter Mandler calls "the theatrical assumption of 'deserving' traits"[50]—that were at once verbal and bodily: as one poor mother notes, "The world was a great stage, upon which each character must appear in a proper dress. I was a beggar! and while my dress was whole, my face washed, and my hair combed, no one would give me a farthing. So I tore this dress, disarranged my hair, and rent my shoes that men might believe my story."[51] But Collins is especially intent on recording "the simple tales of real life which have occurred within the limit of my personal acquaintance," and in doing so, she places working-class women, as subjects of sympathy, firmly within the narrative frame. Asking rhetorically, "What audience would gather to listen to a reformed woman?" in listening attentively to the story of her former friend Martha Varley, "who rose like a meteor and like a meteor fell," Collins assembles that audience through her text and grounds it in the "generous friendship" of the poor—a generosity usually invisible to the middle-class reader.[52]

Collins's text provides multiple, emphatic examples of the everyday acts of kindness and generosity of poor and working-class people, for "it often happens that the most charitable are never heard of by the world."[53] "Outcast mendicants," including "thieves and beggars," tend to a poor, sick, homeless widow whose former wealthy associates ignore her plight; the loyal, enduring friendships born among workers in factories is given its own chapter. Overall, Collins's text affirms the findings of twenty-first-century studies that poor and working-class people give a greater percentage of their earnings to charity than the wealthy do, although it is the wealthy donors of huge sums who are known for their philanthropy and whose benevolent acts are (in Collins's phrase) "noised abroad" and "emblazoned on the banners of worldly praise."[54] Like Harriet Wilson in *Our Nig*, Collins insists on the moral authority of the "kitchen-girl,"[55] for it was commonplace for people in need of food to come to the kitchen door of large houses; thus it was female servants who were best positioned to hear the stories of the poor. Collins recounts several such kitchen encounters with "poor beggar-wom[e]n" and men and relates to her readers the "simple stor[ies]" they tell, enlightening her readers with the narrative wisdom the "kitchen-girl" holds: "Ah, ye drawing room beauties and afternoon belles, ye cannot see the phases of life which the kitchen-girl sees. . . . If you would but go to the kitchen door in the cold winter mornings when that hesitating, gentle rap comes upon the panel, or that timid pull at the bell, and would look into the little pleading faces as they tremblingly ask for food, you would find a field of useful work." The kitchen is thus an incubator of sympathy, a school of "generosity and kindness"; the "infection" with which domestic servants were frequently associated is here envisioned as at once affective and morally beneficial.[56]

While the kitchen-girl meets the pleas of needy visitors with unheralded acts of benevolence and generosity, Collins describes how wealthy men routinely "turn a deaf ear" to supplicants' "heartfelt appeal[s]" and "touching stor[ies]." Complaining that women are often faulted in men's texts for being unkind and malicious toward other women, Collins reveals workingwomen to be "exceedingly charitable toward those of their own sex." Indeed, Collins argues that, precisely because men have the opportunity for advancement and can achieve material benefit by alignment with the capitalists—thus becoming "a fit tool for tyranny, and hence an 'excellent overseer'"—they are less reliable instruments of class benevolence and are less instrumental in preserving the kitchen-girl's moral economy of feeling.[57] Preserving that feminine ethic is critical, for "this is an age of bargains and contracts. Those good old days of generous hospitality, of friendly assistance, and of mutual good-will have passed into history as a thing that existed once, but can never come again." Collins imagines the workingwomen's text as a kind of archive, one that textually memorializes and preserves a social ethos of "hospitality" in the kitchens, in the "friendly treatment" of the poor toward one another, in the "sister[hood]" of shop girls, in the abiding "attachments" and loyal friendships forged in the "community" of the factories and workshops, and in the solidarity of the unions.[58]

Reflecting her interest in spiritualism, Collins depicts writing as a form of mediumship, a gesture of communion with the dead:

> These are sad tales indeed I have to tell. Too full of sorrow and suffering, defeats and discouragements, oppression and cruelty to be sought by the gay, and too true to attract the novelist. Yet I must write them. The world shall hear them, though the recollection brings tears and the repletion a shudder. Sad faces! How they crowd upon me now that I open the gate of memory! Lonely wives, oppressed daughters, tearful toilers at the needle and loom, broken-hearted victims, and lifeless suicides.
>
> Must I live it over again? Must I look once more into those tearful eyes and see those outstretched hands? . . . Yea, I will tread fearlessly back along the thorny path of my short life; and the shades of the hungry, toil-killed and heart-shattered men and women shall tell their tales to the world in death, as they told them to me in life.[59]

Writing during the Depression, proletarian author Meridel Le Sueur describes her work as "epitaphs marking the lives of women who . . . leave no statistics, no record, obituary or remembrance."[60] Like Le Sueur, Collins imagines her writing as a bearer of class memory, a means of honoring, preserving, and transmitting the voices of the dead as well as a female moral economy of class feeling.

As Collins's writing suggests, workingwomen's rearticulation of sympathy was crucial to their feminist working-class politics. Workingwomen's texts contribute forcefully to our understanding of the politics of sympathy in the antebellum era; indeed, they forcefully remind us that sympathy in fact *had* a (class) politics. Importantly, "sympathy" was a key word in socialist debates, in the work of Owenites and especially Fourierists and Saint-Simonians; hegemonically defining the meaning of *sympathy* was thus essential to the operations of class power. Describing this process in Britain, Mary Poovey argues that sentimentalism, with its doctrine of innate and spontaneous humanitarian benevolence, anchored the moral authority of the bourgeoisie; as economic strategy, its paradigm of innate benevolence "sanctioned . . . and helped underwrite" the laissez-faire individualism that gradually transformed England from a paternalistic hierarchy to a modern class society while allowing the bourgeoisie to usurp from the aristocracy the role of England's moral conscience.[61]

In bourgeois society, this benevolence was largely circumscribed within the nuclear family—thus domesticating and privatizing traditional forms of social benevolence associated with a paternalist social order. As I argue elsewhere, antebellum factory women responded forcefully to the class parameters of bourgeois sentimentality, especially as it was increasingly localized within the domestic sphere. Factory women's critique of sentimentality objects to the ways in which antebellum sentimental literary texts domesticate sympathy and gender it feminine while using it to underwrite novel but supposedly natural versions of female subjectivity. In particular, they challenged the view that poor women might be imagined as objects of sympathy only if they did not behave as subjects of desire.[62] Workingwomen's texts such as Collins's, I suggest, contribute a critical if thus far unremarked chapter in the history of sentimentality. In particular, in contesting the normalization of domestic sentimentality, their writings made legible other versions of sympathy as a class affect that was at once marking and memorializing, mobilizing and preserving structures of feeling marginalized in the liberal-capitalist social order.

LORI MERISH is Associate Professor of English at Georgetown University. She is author of *Sentimental Materialism: Gender, Commodity Culture, and Nineteenth-Century American Literature* and *Archives of Labor: Working-Class Women and Literary Culture in the Antebellum United States.*

Notes

1. Smith, *The Theory of Moral Sentiments*, 61, 51.
2. Robbins, *Servant's Hand*, 180.
3. There is little published scholarship on antebellum discourses of poverty. For a valuable overview of social and political discourses of poverty and the poor, see Glickstein, *American Exceptionalism, American Anxiety*. In antebellum literary studies, Jones, *American Hungers*, has initiated a conversation that has barely begun. See also Ryan, *Grammar of Good Intentions*.
4. Channing, *Discourse on the Life*, 14.
5. Malthus, *Principle of Population*, 70–71.
6. Collins, *Nature's Aristocracy*, 11, 143.
7. Silverman, "Sympathy and Its Vicissitudes," 11.
8. Fitzhugh, *Cannibals All!*, 143.
9. Dorsey, *Reforming Men and Women*, 58, 74, 59.
10. Trattner, *Poor Law*, 55.
11. Dorsey, *Reforming Men and Women*, 81.
12. Ely, "Prevention of Pauperism," 232.
13. Silverman, "Sympathy and Its Vicissitudes," 12.
14. Waterston, "Address on Pauperism," 20.
15. Ibid., 21.
16. Burroughs, "Discourse on Pauperism," 41.
17. Waterston, "Address on Pauperism," 38.
18. Dorsey, *Reforming Men and Women*, 82; Waterston, "Address on Pauperism," 38, 46.
19. Burroughs, "Discourse on Pauperism," 56.
20. Ibid., 44–45.
21. Ibid., 56–57.

22. Dewey, *Life and Letters*, 269.
23. See Trattner, *Poor Law*. According to Theodore Parker, mothers "bequeath" their economic powerlessness and poverty to their children. Parker, *Perishing Classes*, 4.
24. Cody, "Politics of Illegitimacy," 132.
25. Rothman, *Almshouse Experience*, 29, 96, 6.
26. B., *Mary Bean*, 8.
27. Davidson, *Revolution and the Word*.
28. B., *Mary Bean*, 17.
29. Ibid., 10, 21.
30. Ibid., 24.
31. Robinson, *Loom and Spindle*, 67.
32. B., *Mary Bean*, 17, 18.
33. Ibid., 22.
34. Ibid., 35, 34.
35. Ibid., 39, 26.
36. Jacobs, *Incidents in the Life of a Slave Girl*.
37. Merish, *Archives of Labor*.
38. Brace, *Dangerous Classes*, 119 (emphasis added).
39. Foster, *New York by Gaslight*, 69, 77, 99.
40. Ibid., 97.
41. White, *Stories of Freedom*.
42. Melville, *Pierre*, 88.
43. Foster, *New York by Gaslight*, 97, 98.
44. Miller, *Abandoned*, 48.
45. Foster, *New York by Gaslight*, 99.
46. Ibid., 99, 100.
47. Ibid., 100–103, 101.
48. Ibid., 101, 102; Steedman, *Landscape for a Good Woman*, 89.
49. Foster, *New York by Gaslight*, 102–103, 197.
50. Mandler, *Uses of Charity*, 23.
51. Collins, *Nature's Aristocracy*, 20.
52. Ibid., 15, 45, 39, 44.
53. Ibid., 160.
54. Ibid., 44, 144, 142.
55. Wilson, *Our Nig*. See also Merish, *Archives of Labor*.
56. Collins, *Nature's Aristocracy*, 20, 21, 85.
57. Ibid., 28, 65, 123.
58. Ibid., 87, 89, 65, 105.
59. Ibid., 11.
60. Le Sueur, "Women on the Breadlines," 166.
61. Poovey, "Ideology and *The Mysteries of Udolpho*," 317, 308, 314.
62. Merish, *Archives of Labor*.

Bibliography

B., Miss J. A. *Mary Bean: The Factory Girl*. Boston: Hotchkiss, 1850.

Brace, Charles Loring. *The Dangerous Classes of New York and Twenty Years' Work among Them.* New York: Wyncoop and Hallenbeck, 1872.
Burroughs, Charles. "Discourse on Pauperism." In *The Jacksonians on the Poor: Collected Pamphlets*, edited by David J. Rothman. New York: Arno Press, 1971.
Channing, William Ellery. *Discourse on the Life and Character of the Rev. Joseph Tuckerman.* Boston: William Crosby, 1841.
Child, Lydia Marie. *Letters from New York.* Edited by Bruce Mills. Athens: Georgia University Press, 1999.
Cody, Lisa. "The Politics of Illegitimacy in an Age of Reform: Women, Reproduction, and Political Economy in England's New Poor Law of 1834." *Journal of Women's History* 11, no. 4 (2000): 131–156
Collins, Jennie. *Nature's Aristocracy: A Plea for the Oppressed.* Edited by Judith Ranta. Lincoln: University of Nebraska Press, 2010.
Davidson, Cathy N. *Revolution and the Word.* New York: Oxford University Press, 1986.
Dewey, Mary E., ed. *Life and Letters of Catharine M. Sedgwick.* New York: Harpers, 1872.
Dorsey, Bruce. *Reforming Men and Women: Gender in the Antebellum City.* Ithaca, NY: Cornell University Press, 2006.
Ely, Ezra Stiles. "Prevention of Pauperism." *Presbyterian Magazine* 2 (March 1822): 230–232.
Fitzhugh, George. *Cannibals All! or, Slaves without Masters.* Edited by C. Vann Woodward. Cambridge, MA: Harvard University Press, 1960.
Foster, George G. *New York by Gaslight and Other Urban Sketches.* Edited by Stuart M. Blumin. Berkeley: University of California Press, 1990.
Glickstein, Jonathan A. *American Exceptionalism, American Anxiety: Wages, Competition, and Degraded Labor in the Antebellum United States.* Charlottesville: University of Virginia Press, 2002.
Jacobs, Harriet A. *Incidents in the Life of a Slave Girl.* Edited by Jean Fagan Yellin. Cambridge, MA: Harvard University Press, 1987.
Jones, Gavin. *American Hungers: The Problem of Poverty in U.S. Literature, 1840–1945.* Princeton, NJ: Princeton University Press, 2009.
Le Sueur, Meridel. "Women on the Breadlines." In *Harvest Song: Collected Essays and Stories*, 166–171. Albuquerque, NM: West End Press, 1990.
Malthus, Thomas. *An Essay on the Principle of Population.* New York: Penguin, 1983.
Mandler, Peter. *The Uses of Charity.* Philadelphia: University of Pennsylvania Press, 1990.
Melville, Herman. *Pierre; or, The Ambiguities.* New York: Penguin, 1996.
Merish, Lori. *Archives of Labor: Working-Class Women and Literary Culture in the Antebellum United States.* Durham, NC: Duke University Press, 2017.
Miller, Julie. *Abandoned: Foundlings in Nineteenth-Century New York City.* New York: New York University Press, 2008.
Parker, Theodore. *A Sermon of the Perishing Classes.* Boston: Benjamin H. Greene, 1847.
Poovey, Mary. "Ideology and *The Mysteries of Udolpho*." *Criticism* 21, no. 4 (1979): 307–330.
Robbins, Bruce. *The Servant's Hand: English Fiction from Below.* New York: Columbia University Press, 1986.
Robinson, Harriet. *Loom and Spindle.* Boston: Applewood Books, 2011.
Rothman, David J., ed. *The Almshouse Experience: Collected Pamphlets.* New York: Arno Press, 1971.
Ryan, Susan M. *The Grammar of Good Intentions: Race and the Antebellum Culture of Benevolence.* Ithaca, NY: Cornell University Press, 2006.

Silverman, Gillian. "Sympathy and Its Vicissitudes." *American Studies* 43, no. 3 (2002): 5–28.
Smith, Adam. *The Theory of Moral Sentiments*. Edited by D. D. Raphael and A. L. Macphie. Indianapolis, IN: Liberty Fund, 1984.
Steedman, Carolyn Kay. *Landscape for a Good Woman: A Story of Two Lives*. New Brunswick, NJ: Rutgers University Press, 1987.
Trattner, Walter I. *From Poor Law to Welfare State*. New York: Free Press, 1998.
Waterston, R. C. "Address on Pauperism." In *The Jacksonians on the Poor: Collected Pamphlets*, edited by David J. Rothman. New York: Arno Press, 1971.
White, Shane. *Stories of Freedom in Black New York*. Cambridge, MA: Harvard University Press, 2002.
Wilson, Harriet E. *Our Nig: Sketches in the Life of a "Free" Black*. Edited by P. Gabrielle Foreman and Reginald Pitts. New York: Penguin, 2009.

2

SELF-UNDERMINING PHILANTHROPIC IMPULSES

Philanthropy in the Mirror of Narrative

Daniel Bivona

THE EIGHTEENTH-CENTURY ENLIGHTENMENT supplied a useful philosophical justification for extending aid to those who suffer, one that was based less on the notion that we are all children of God than on the premise that we are all human and periodically suffer. As Frank Christianson argues, "Unlike charity, which had strong associations with an ethos that was simultaneously Christian and individualist, philanthropy was informed by a collective Enlightenment project of rationalised social advance."[1] In other words, it is the recognition that the social order is improving and must continue to improve that authorizes a secular obligation for philanthropic assistance. In assisting others, we acknowledge our kinship with those who suffer, and in theorizing that kinship, Enlightenment intellectuals found a new glue to bind together a social order consisting of self-interested individuals.

This secular ethical principle would be adopted and promoted widely in the most influential literary form of the nineteenth century, the novel. Yet in that novelistic tradition, one sees developing, by the mid to late nineteenth century, a move away from Enlightenment optimism and toward a profound skepticism about the nature of our common humanity and whether or not those bonds entail a moral obligation on those of us who are not suffering. The novelistic works of Charles Dickens and George Gissing are exemplary in this sense and are the main focus of this chapter.

I concentrate my attention here on Dickens's *Bleak House* (1852–1853), which was directly influenced by the *Morning Chronicle* reports of Henry Mayhew, and George Gissing's two novels of the late 1880s, *Thyrza* (1887) and *The Nether World* (1889), which engage more directly than any of Gissing's other novels with the issues that beset philanthropy in the late nineteenth century. While Dickens was not at all uncritical of the misapplication of sympathy, he is closely identified with a mid-Victorian commitment to the moral obligation of sympathetic engagement with those who suffer. My contention is that one can trace through the novels of both of these writers the outlines of a process whereby philanthropy, by the 1880s, is beginning to lose moral authority in the culture as the disinterestedness central to its exercise becomes harder to achieve, and as disinterested behavior itself is increasingly interpreted as a convenient cover for very "interested" motives. In moving from Charles Dickens to George Gissing, one moves from a complex, if satirically tinged and critical, engagement with Exeter Hall philanthropy (in the work of Dickens) to a more thoroughgoing rejection of philanthropy as inevitably self-undermining, and thus literally *de-moralizing* (in the work of Gissing).

Institutional Sympathy

With little hope of state intervention to improve the lot of the poor and the working classes in nineteenth-century Britain, private philanthropic enterprises shouldered most of the burden of addressing poverty and its social effects for most of the century. Among the better-known private organizations were such entities as the Charity Organizations Society (COS), which provided housing for the working class; workingmen's colleges; Temperance Societies; the Salvation Army; cultural interventions such as the settlement movement at Toynbee Hall (an institution based on the idea that the lot of the poor could be improved simply by having young Oxford and Cambridge men live among them); and the People's Palace.[2] Completed in 1887 and modeled on a scheme first advanced by a character in Walter Besant's 1882 novel *All Sorts and Conditions of Men*, the People's Palace was designed to bring the experience of culturally enriching pleasures to East Londoners lacking any experience of them.[3]

Many of these private institutions—and the COS is perhaps the prime example—were governed by a strict set of rules created in the belief that they were needed to protect people from the debilitating consequences of receiving relief.[4] The fear was that, like a vaccination gone awry, the very interventions undertaken to alleviate poverty might themselves spread the infection, in particular, the debilitating infection of dependency. As a result, the COS, for example, was preoccupied with drawing fine distinctions between the "deserving" poor (who could be given relief because it would help launch them toward independence) and the "undeserving" poor (who would, it was felt, inevitably become dependent on charitable relief if given it and thus spiral downward into a worse condition).

The focus on the "deserving" poor means that often the somewhat better-off members of the working class, rather than the residuum, benefited most from the award of relief. Thus, the director of the COS, Octavia Hill, attributes her success in improving COS-managed housing to her practice of evicting those who fall behind in their rent, noting that none of the tenants in the housing taken over by the COS were allowed to remain if they fell more than two weeks in arrears. Indeed, she attributes her success precisely to this willingness to draw a bold line between "deserving" and "undeserving" tenants and does not hesitate to link what she calls "improvement" both to her readiness to evict and to a variety of other "cleansing" measures she would take in the aftermath of an eviction:

> As soon as I entered into possession, each family had an opportunity of doing better: those who would not pay, or who led clearly immoral lives, were ejected. The rooms they vacated were cleansed; the tenants who showed signs of improvement moved into them, and thus, in turn, an opportunity was obtained for having each room distempered and painted. The drains were put in order, a large slate cistern was fixed, the wash-house was cleared of its lumber, and thrown open on stated days to each tenant in turn.[5]

While the linkage between poverty, disease, irresponsibility, and filth here is a common enough Victorian topos, the more interesting observation Hill makes is to be found in her remark that she looks for "signs of improvement" in the tenants who are asked to stay. In identifying the deserving, the philanthropist recognizes a bit of her own hardworking self—the subject of a narrative of self-improvement—in the behavior of the other. When she fails to see it (as here), she consigns the poor person to oblivion. Ultimately, the careful surveillance practiced by philanthropists such as Hill is based on this implicit specular linkage between philanthropist and needy person. The deserving are recognized both for what they reflect back to us in the present and what that reflection seems to guarantee of their future trajectory—and ours. The image in the mirror hints at narrative depths.

The roots of this mimetic model of social relationships can be found in the Enlightenment discussion of sympathy and sympathetic relationships. What emerges from this discourse is a persistent characterization of the scene of sympathy as a theatrical one, and the central figure in this tradition is Adam Smith. In the words of his influential *Theory of Moral Sentiments* (1759), "The compassion of the spectator must arise altogether from the consideration of what he himself would feel if he was reduced to the same unhappy situation, and, what perhaps is impossible, was at the same time able to regard it with his present reason and judgment."[6] David Marshall reminds us that the theatricality inherent in the Smithian scene of sympathy necessarily implies some distance between the feelings of the one in distress and the feelings of the spectator:

> For Smith, acts of sympathy are structured by theatrical dynamics that (because of the impossibility of really knowing or entering into someone else's sentiments) depend on people's ability to represent themselves as tableaux, spectacles, and texts before others.[7]

The implications of Marshall's claim are that the theatricality that invests the scene of sympathy has the potential to undermine the philanthropist's desire to extend aid to the earnestly deserving. What if I cannot read the scene correctly? What if what appears to be his suffering is only playacting? These questions haunt the history of sentimental philanthropy.

Smith addresses these questions directly in 1759 but by highlighting rather than eliminating the contradictions in play. In Marshall's words:

> Adam Smith bases his *Theory of Moral Sentiments* on the presumption of a universal need for sympathy, he describes a society in which sympathy seems unlikely and even impossible—not so much because people are disinclined to enter into sentiments or situations that are painful or distressing, but rather because (in Smith's view) people know the characters and sentiments of others only through representations they form in their imaginations of what they think others feel.[8]

In other words, since inner states of mind and feeling can be plumbed only by those who read and interpret the behavior of the sufferer, decoding the scene of sympathy accurately becomes the central problem in the sympathetic tradition. Hence the disciplinary function of reiterated scenes of sympathy that appear especially in nineteenth-century fiction, a literary form that takes on the work of rendering inner states of mind and feeling accessible, albeit in the form of fictional narrative. In Christianson's words, "Not a feeling, then, but a way of communicating feelings . . . explains the emergence of sympathy as a literary idea and its subsequent appeal for nineteenth century fiction writers."[9] The complex philosophical and linguistic problem involved in decoding other people's enactments of pain and suffering is not easily solved, even if novelistic representations of it eventually help to reinforce its social importance, as Christianson argues. In Rae Greiner's view, Victorian fiction writers "fashioned realism to equip the mind to comprehend a reality that was itself sympathetic, a reality whose realism found sanction in the imaginative fellowship we have with others."[10]

Earlier in the eighteenth century, David Hume worried that to extend sympathy to another, one had to take into account nothing less than differences in "manners, character, country, education, custom, or language": all complicating psychological and social differences that make true sympathy unlikely to be achieved in many cases.[11] Smith himself acknowledges that even the most dispassionate of spectators of suffering can never truly know for certain if he has replicated in himself the suffering of the person in pain:

> After all this, however, the emotions of the spectator will still be very apt to fall short of the violence of what is felt by the sufferer. Mankind, though naturally sympathetic, never conceive, for what has befallen another, that degree of passion which naturally animates the person principally concerned. That

imaginary change of situation, upon which their sympathy is founded, is but momentary. The thought of their own safety, the thought that they themselves are not really the sufferers, continually intrudes itself upon them; and though it does not hinder them from conceiving a passion somewhat analogous to what is felt by the sufferer, hinders them from conceiving any thing that approaches to the same degree of violence.[12]

Not only are the feelings of the spectator likely to be "less violent," but also, no matter how much spectators claim to be able to feel the other's pain, spectators soon enough find refuge in quite other feelings, perhaps drawing comfort from the conviction that the other's anguish is finally not their own.

Yet another important Enlightenment figure, Edmund Burke, brings the inadmissible to light in his theorization of the scene of sympathy, and he does so two years before the publication of Smith's *Theory of Moral Sentiments*—in 1757, in his influential treatise on aesthetics, the *Philosophical Enquiry into Our Ideas of the Sublime and the Beautiful*. Like Smith, Burke also sees sympathy as grounded in a theatrical relationship between sufferer and spectator, and in his work that relationship is quite explicit. He poses the questions Aristotle asks in his *Poetics*: Why do we spectators enjoy the spectacle of suffering onstage? How does one account for the disjunction between the painful feelings portrayed onstage and the pleasurable feelings they stimulate in the spectators? Unlike the other Enlightenment theorists of sympathy, Burke is less interested in understanding how we can feel the other's pain than he is in arguing that the other's pain stimulates an opposite feeling in the spectator—pleasure in observing the agonies of the sufferer. For Smith and Hume, the crucial question is how self-interested individuals become willing to bind themselves to their neighbors in an implicitly disinterested social exercise of sympathy. Smith's solution—the theorization of an imagined metaphorical resemblance between the sufferer's pain and the spectator's imagination of his pain—does not, for Burke, fully address the central issue. For the latter, the central question is how to reconcile the portrayal of suffering with the spectator's evident experience of pleasure in the other's suffering: the spectator's "delight," as he calls it, which is presumably the opposite feeling to that endured by the sufferer. Moreover, the motivating power of this pain/pleasure disjunction is crucial to an understanding of what allows an other-regarding social order to be formed from an otherwise savage band of individuals focused too intently on their own self-interest:

> As our Creator has designed that we should be united by the bond of sympathy, he has strengthened that bond by a proportionable delight, and there most where our sympathy is most wanted,—in the distresses of others. If this passion was simply painful, we would shun with the greatest care all persons and places that could excite such a passion; as some, who are so far gone in indolence as not to endure any strong impression, actually do. . . . The delight

we have in such things hinders us from shunning scenes of misery; and the pain we feel prompts us to relieve ourselves in relieving those who suffer; and all this antecedent to any reasoning, by an instinct that works us to its own purposes without our concurrence.[13]

The persuasiveness of this social justification of Schadenfreude rests on the premise that pleasure, rather than pain, is the main impetus behind sympathetic behavior by the spectator. Burke's claims also suggest a trenchant recognition on his part of what Freud would later call the "ambivalence of the emotions," and Burke's acknowledgment that the process is "instinctual" suggests he sees it as a fundamentally unconscious, rather than consciously calculated, activity. Sharing the other's pain, as the other theorists of sympathy would have it, has the potential to paralyze the spectator by curbing his willingness to act benevolently. Thus, Burke concludes that the delight we take in the spectacle of the other's suffering must be, however paradoxically, what enables us to extend aid to those in pain.

If theatrical metaphors dominate the discussion of sympathetic relationships in the late eighteenth century, the nineteenth century sees the emergence of the novel as the cultural form dedicated to dramatizing the complexities involved in our philanthropic duties to others. The novel takes on the major social role of representing the psychological and social effects on the individual of both poverty and philanthropy, dramatizing how sympathy can corrupt as well as aid in the process of self-transformation. Constructed around plots composed of individual narratives, the novel also helps to teach its readers to conceptualize the devastating effects of suffering in narrative, rather than simply in static, terms.[14] As Audrey Jaffe argues, novelistic representations generally taught Victorian readers to project themselves imaginatively into the lives of others by establishing dynamic, but specular, sympathetic relationships across the class divide (a divide that parallels the divide between reader and novel, spectator and sufferer):

> The "objects" of Victorian sympathy are inseparable from Victorian middle-class self-representation precisely because they embody, to a middle-class spectator, his or her own potential narrative of social decline: they capture the fragility of respectable identities psychically positioned between high and low, defined within the parameters of a narrative of rising and falling.[15]

Moreover, Jaffe's analysis allows for the possibility of admitting *Schadenfreudliche* delight in the other's suffering as a chief motivating factor. Thus, some novels construct a democracy of suffering that ties together characters and readers, the latter of whom cannot readily insulate themselves emotionally from the compelling spectacle of impoverished suffering with which the novel brings them into contact. Indeed, they do not want to do so. That these "scenes" of suffering ultimately generate pleasure effects central to the popularity of fiction (as well as drama) would seem to be beyond doubt, even had the late eighteenth century not conveniently furnished the well-known example of Goethe's Werther, whose fictional suicide induced paroxysms of readerly sympathetic anguish across Europe after *The Sorrows of Young Werther* was published in 1774.

Dickens and Gissing at least begin with a set of assumptions that rule the sentimental tradition dating back to Smith and Burke in the late eighteenth century and that can be considered a Victorian development of that tradition: the implicit claim that the foundation of human sympathy lies in constituting the other as human through a mirror-style recognition that, in Jaffe's terms, breaks from the static confines of the mirror metaphor to offer a recognition of a dynamic, narrative process to which the other is bound. In other words, we not only accord "humanity" to the other by identifying with her in a static moment of reflection, but we recognize the dynamic plot that she is living out as a possible one of our own. What motivates philanthropy initially, in many cases, is the psychological recognition that the other is in pain and that that pain is something we all might feel, even if only metaphorically, or (in the case of Burke) that our delight in the spectacle of suffering ultimately enables us to assist those in pain. What undermines the philanthropic impulse, however, is the fear that assistance to the poor may make them, ironically, not more like the middle-class spectator but less—the center of a delightful spectacle of suffering we wish to prolong rather than a fellow human whose sufferings we wish to see ended. What is at stake, finally, in the argument over sympathy is the very status and possibility of disinterested behavior.

Dickens and Philanthropy

In his most direct novelistic attack on misplaced philanthropy, the novel *Bleak House*, Dickens fires at both easy targets and hard ones. Among the easier targets is what he calls the "telescopic philanthropy" of Mrs. Jellyby, the embodiment of Exeter Hall philanthropy.[16] Mrs. Jellyby is so intensely focused on improving the lot of West Africans that she does not even notice that one of her children has his head stuck between two iron railings outside her London home.[17] She is inattentive to moral and medical crises originating in her own domestic sphere because she has displaced her concern to remote areas of the globe, substituting for proper maternal care for her own children a passionate concern for the welfare of people she has never seen. As Bruce Robbins argues, she plays a central part in the novel's deeply ambivalent representation of professionalized philanthropy as less concerned with taking care of orphans than with tending to itself.[18] In that sense, she is little but a satirical butt to Dickens: an embodiment of maternal neglectfulness, an image of mid-nineteenth-century charity as an institution absorbed mainly in serving its own professional goals. Her self-absorption and indifference to the need to aid those close to her echoes the professional self-absorption of the most important institutional villain in the novel—the Court of Chancery.

She also becomes symbolically important insofar as her behavior foreshadows the more complicated and ambivalent behavior of the most important "mother" in the novel, Lady Dedlock, who distances herself from her daughter, Esther Summerson, out of intolerably mixed motives. Lady Dedlock needs to hide her sexual past from her husband and the lawyer Tulkinghorn, who is blackmailing her (and thus Lady Dedlock cannot acknowledge Esther as her own child for most of the novel), but she has difficulty renouncing the pleasure of a different narrative she can experience only at a vicarious distance. In this ghostlike narrative, she feels a mixed *Schadenfreudliche* delight in raising her own daughter to maturity, and she lives this narrative only vicariously by spying on Esther, or so the novel suggests (Esther is, of course, both her "ruin" and the innocent daughter she guiltily abandoned). The ambiguous expression of these conflicting motives, the mixture of self-torment and vicarious maternal pleasure that cannot relieve itself in the form of direct help to her daughter, can be seen in Lady Dedlock's furtive surveillance of the daughter she resembles, an attentiveness that, until later in the novel, often feels less like the recognition of a loving mother caught in a tragic dilemma than the sinister surveillance of an officious poor-law inspector.[19] One might call it a disturbing, if metaphorically displaced, form of "telescopic philanthropy" that involves a studiously careful reluctance to provide any self-implicating assistance to her daughter until late in the novel.

Speaking of "condescension" and recognition in Dickens's novel, Daniel Siegel highlights the inescapable role of mirroring as a means of representing the consolidation of metaphorically linked oppositional identities: "Condescension is a kind of mirror, an encounter through which both subordinate and superior see themselves as constituted by the recognition of the other."[20] In *Bleak House*, identity itself is often tied up with one's ability to identify with the other in the mirror; it is not, however, invariably based on a master-slave distinction, an inescapable inequality of power, as Siegel argues here.[21] As Esther says in the "Telescopic Philanthropy" chapter:

> At first I was painfully awake and vainly tried to lose myself, with my eyes closed, among the scenes of the day. At length, by slow degrees, they became indistinct and mingled. I began to lose the identity of the sleeper resting on me. Now it was Ada, now one of my old Reading friends from whom I could not believe I had so recently parted. Now it was the little maid woman worn out with curtsying and smiling, now some one in authority at Bleak House. Lastly, it was no one, and I was no one.[22]

Not only is Esther running through—however unknowingly—the various "identities" (identifications, really) she performs throughout the narrative, identifications that imply a growing sense of her own power, from sister of Ada to little maid woman to "some one in authority at Bleak House," but she also looks forward—in a gesture whose meaning cannot be fully disclosed to the reader until Nemo is introduced later in the novel—to becoming a "no one" who is, ironically, "some one." She is, of course, the daughter of the man whose place is felt as an absent presence haunting the novel, a man who is never recognized except by the child Jo, who cannot confer paternal recognition on Esther, and whose apposite name literally means "no one"—Nemo. In locating this episode in the "Telescopic Philanthropy" chapter, Dickens is no doubt suggesting that philanthropy is both crucial, because it is imbricated with the process of conferring identity (stimulated by identification, it is also a mechanism for bestowing recognition), and too often misplaced—especially by those whose professional service amounts mainly to self-serving busyness.

The Jellyby and Pardiggle episodes finally raise an important unanswered, but large, question about the novel: Does Dickens see all philanthropy as telescopic? Is philanthropy by definition an all-too-convenient means of disburdening oneself of one's social responsibilities in the guise of serving others in need? Does the Burkean "delight" we experience in observing the spectacle of suffering lead us, ironically, to entertain a guilty wish to prolong it rather than alleviate it? Are the motives that drive disinterested benevolence untrustworthy, ultimately, because they are detached from any direct connection to authentic need and self-interested desire—from feeling, in short? Are the motives of the philanthropic, then, inevitably objects of legitimate suspicion?

The "Telescopic Philanthropy" chapter of *Bleak House*, thus, also stages a discussion between Ada Carstone and Esther Summerson about the motives of the most important philanthropist in the novel, John Jarndyce, the owner of Bleak House, who has made his home a refuge for Esther as well as for Ada and her cousin Richard Carstone, the latter two wards of Chancery, as they await a long-delayed judgment on their fate from that eminently plodding institution. In exploring Jarndyce's ambiguous motives, the novel raises questions about the motives that guide philanthropy more generally—in particular, the morality of disinterestedness. As the novel shows, Jarndyce's generosity to Richard ultimately fails to achieve its aim, for Richard eventually falls victim to Chancery-induced hallucinations of the gentility to which he comes to believe himself entitled. Likewise, Jarndyce's repeated forgiveness of his friend Harold Skimpole for his "childish" behavior does not correct that behavior but instead prolongs it, raising disturbing questions about why Jarndyce indulges Skimpole's irresponsibility.[23] If, as Esther's narrative suggests early on, Jarndyce appears to be free of selfish motives, his oft-stressed reluctance to be acknowledged and thanked for his goodness seems to compel us to interpret it as one more sign of his benevolent selflessness. The complex problem of selfless detachment is precisely what the author has in his sights. The notion that Jarndyce's charitable behavior is prompted by purely selfless motives does not quite wash, though, despite what the text says, because the novel suggests plenty of possible selfish or self-interested motives for his behavior. At one point early in the novel, Esther even wonders if he might actually be her father, thus suggesting his charitable treatment of her might be seen as a Lady Dedlock–like, and deeply self-interested, secret reparation for earlier paternal neglect.[24] Unfortunately, when given an opportunity to ask him precisely that question, Esther stifles herself, preferring instead to say only that her trust in him requires her not to ask anything: "If my whole reliance and confidence were not placed in you, I must have a hard heart indeed. I have nothing to ask you, nothing in the world."[25] Literally a lie (we know Esther manifestly does have an important question to ask him at this point about her own parentage), this response by Esther to Jarndyce's invitation outlines the dilemma: speak the question on one's mind (and thus express distrust in the other) or stifle one's curiosity (and thus surrender the attempt to know the narrative of one's own past). The disinterested, it turns out, are ultimately untrustworthy because they often misrepresent their own feelings. The implication of this observation is troubling, and not only because the unanswered question about Esther's parentage leaves open, for a while anyway, the possibility that Jarndyce, in proposing marriage later, is violating the incest taboo. It might also suggest that the good acts performed by knowledgeable people are morally contaminated because they only pretend to be motivated by disinterest. This, strangely, seems to leave ignorance—indeed, lack of self-knowledge—as the only morally trustworthy path to goodness. If the portrayal of disinterestedness cannot be trusted (because its direct connection with human feeling is not directly observable), how are we to know it enacts an intention of furthering the good?

The complexity of motive that underlies philanthropic behavior in this novel is thus bound up with the problematic everyday notion of authentic desire itself. If human behavior were a reliable index of individual feelings and thoughts, simple sincerity—speaking one's mind—would allow one to negotiate the thicket of otherwise obscure motives reliably. However, speaking in Dickens is seldom a simple matter of representing one's feelings and thoughts in a direct way, despite his continual valorization of earnestness in his fiction.[26] Dickens was well aware of the social reality that human desires are complexly mediated affairs and, thus, that we often fail to speak what is "on our mind" not simply to mislead the other (although that is one prominent motive) but rather—to take just one example—in order to affirm trust in the other even if we do not feel trustful, or to inspirit the other with a hopefulness that we may not even share. Dickens underlines that purpose in the episode in which Ada and Esther critique Mrs. Jellyby's neglectfulness:

> Ada laughed and put her arm about my neck as I stood looking at the fire, and told me I was a quiet, dear, good creature and had won her heart. "You are so thoughtful, Esther, she said, and yet so cheerful! And you do so much so unpretendingly! You would make a home out of even this house."
>
> My simple darling! She was quite unconscious that she only praised herself and that it was in the goodness of her own heart that she made so much of me![27]

Here we have something of a hall of mirrors in which the distinction between original image and reflected image, between original "goodness" and reflected "goodness," has been rendered hopelessly problematic, despite Ada's confidently authoritative assertion that Esther is not playacting. Esther's praise of Ada's goodness can be read as a further expression of Esther's own goodness (which, of course, must pass the ethical test of unselfishness by being expressed indirectly through the claim that Esther recognizes it in the other—Ada). Here, mirroring undermines the authority of origins, forcing us to see each girl's recognition of the other's goodness as an expression of their own collective goodness, thus rendering pointless the pursuit of an original impulse to goodness residing in a single source. Indeed, the novel renders problematic the attempt to capture knowledge of the other-in-herself at all, valorizing instead performance over knowledge. This seems to be one of the implications of Esther's well-known claim that "the poor" are ultimately unknowable: "What the poor are to the poor is little known, excepting to themselves and God."[28] The statement lays down an epistemological boundary that the middle-class reader presumably cannot cross. Ultimately, however, it is a claim with broad psychological and epistemological significance, positing the futility of all attempts to know individuals in themselves despite what cues their behavior gives us, whether they are poor or well off. In that sense, the claim that the poor are ultimately unknowable "excepting to themselves and God" issues a challenge to Smith's confident claim that we can at least know the other's mind and feelings from a metaphorical distance. Moreover, it seems to render problematic even a Burkean attempt to assure us that where there is *Schadenfreudliche* delight in another's suffering, there are the grounds for earnest philanthropy. Dickens certainly seems to be even more dubious than the Enlightenment theorists about our ability to see into the mind and heart of the other.

The independence that Victorian philanthropy seeks to foster is paradoxically a result of this Dickensian surrender in a moment of intimate bonding with an other. And this rule applies not only among the characters but to the relationship between the reader and those characters. In other words, when I confront the suffering other, the not-me is not me—at least not yet. But it is potentially me; hence my interest in it. I live vicariously the perilous narrative of the other, but I am tenuously preserved from the other's fate by virtue of observing that fate rather than living it (Smith would say, "in imagination"). Dickens's word for describing this process (in *Bleak House*) is "transference," a word that implies that the condition for experiencing sympathy is theatrical separation of the spectator from the spectacle (and a surrender of the utopian desire to know the other-in-herself in favor of a claim to know her only by analogy with oneself). The separation of subject from object is the condition that ironically ties humans to one another (and to estranged parts of themselves) through relationships of analogy or metaphor rather than identity (a point asserted by Smith in his *Theory of Moral Sentiments*, as we have just discussed). Above all, what this suggests is that Dickens distrusts "disinterested" philanthropy because he rejects the notion that most ties between people are purely rational—that is, self-interested in the political economic sense. Like Burke, who argues that the pleasure we take in the suffering of others makes it possible for us to extend aid to them, Dickens seeks to build a community of individuals linked together through specular ties of feeling not among equals but rather among unequals, unequal because one of the pair is often suffering: the one who extends aid regards the suffering one from the privileged perspective of one who secretly enjoys the spectacle of suffering. Burke insists that our "delight" in the spectacle of suffering ultimately (and paradoxically) serves the goal of drawing both pitier and pitied into communal, if unequal, relationship. Moreover, only the spectator's delight in the spectacle of suffering before him enables the latter to suspend his reaction of disgust or fright long enough to extend aid to the sufferer. The pleasure we take in others, even if it is a guilty pleasure in the spectacle of someone else suffering, is what finally motivates philanthropy.

To put this in terms that Dickens's novel might prefer, Burke's "instinct" may seem sadistic, selfish, and antisocial in operation, insofar as it relies on our experiencing pleasure in the spectacle of the other's suffering to motivate our sympathy, but ironically it actually works to encourage what most would recognize as a benevolent end, insofar as it enables one to extend aid to the other—to practice something that looks like philanthropy, we might say. Moreover, the dissymmetry of power between spectator and sufferer, which is central to Burke's analysis of the dynamics of pitying, is generally resolved as Dickens has his main characters occupy both roles at different times—most obviously, Esther herself, who accords sympathy to a figure like Jo and later becomes an object of sympathy herself when her face is marred by the smallpox she contracts from him.

I am not by any means the first to make the argument that Victorian "disinterestedness" has nothing to do with the weak version usually on display in the twentieth century because the Victorian valorization of "detachment" usually demands an often painful surrender of one's self-interest—a conscious renunciation—rather than a weakly mechanical obedience to purely rational promptings to realize the good. As Amanda Anderson argues in *The Powers of Distance*,

> The cultivation of detachment involves an attempt to transcend partiality, interests, and context: it is an aspiration toward universality and objectivity. The norms through which that aspiration finds expression may be situated, the aspiration may always be articulated through historically available forms, but as an aspiration it cannot be reduced to a simple form of illusion, or a mere psychological mechanism.[29]

The key word here is "aspiration": it is an aspiration toward a goal seldom achieved, but one that is important nonetheless because it embodies a significant cultural ideal.

Ultimately, Dickens makes use of "transference" to establish metaphorical links among the different subplots of the novel to suggest that while knowledge of others is produced in this novel, it is knowledge *known* in advance of knowledge—foreknowledge of a sort gained from the recognition of the other's narrative. And what knowledge of this sort demonstrates is the intimate interconnection of all humans, the inescapability of playing, at various times, both roles in the matched pair that is the sufferer and the philanthropist. Thus, for instance, Esther *knows* her mother's life is tied up with her own life in advance of actually learning it with certainty, because Lady Dedlock's surveillance of her is surely a form of recognition even if Esther cannot identify it as positive or negative until late in the novel. A more obvious example of the linkage between foreknowledge and specular relationships occurs early in the novel, when Guppy, touring Chesney Wold, dilates on a portrait of Lady Dedlock, whose resemblance to Esther suggests simultaneously metaphorical likeness and difference between the two: "I do assure you that the more I think of that picture the better I know it, without knowing how I know it!"[30] What is happening here is not a confrontation with the returned repressed in the Freudian sense but rather its opposite: a staging of foreknowledge derived from the observation of resemblance that then leads characters and readers to draw inferences about Lady Dedlock's narrative trajectory—the gradual unfolding of a tragic fallen-woman plot glimpsed by others, however dimly, through foreknowledge of narrative ends. What Guppy "knows" from scrutinizing Lady Dedlock's portrait is her resemblance to Esther, but that realization interpellates Lady Dedlock as the subject of a narrative, opening the door to the inference that Lady Dedlock is a fallen woman desperately attempting to disguise her fall and that Esther is the innocent victim in that narrative. In other words, what is recognized in looking at Lady Dedlock's face is Lady Dedlock's narrative trajectory (and, by extension, the disgrace to be inherited by her innocent daughter).

Ultimately, the marring of Esther's face by the smallpox she contracts from Jo moves her from being the privileged observer, the subject par excellence and narrator of the first part of the novel, to the consummate object of pity, the philanthropist who is victimized by the very *disease*—poverty—she attempted to alleviate in the case of one small boy. The transference of smallpox is symbolically a transference of the markings of abject poverty. Its vector extends to those higher up in the social scale: from the dying Jo (who "caught" it from Esther's father Nemo) to Charley (who eventually recovers) and to Esther Summerson herself.

The end of the novel, however, attempts to right John Jarndyce's motives by having him renounce the plan to take Esther as his wife in favor of Allan Woodcourt. In other words, Dickens moves Jarndyce from the position of self-interested lover to more disinterested father. After releasing her from her pledge to marry, he then behaves more like a father than a lover, awarding the newly married couple with a miniature version of Bleak House in which to live. Ultimately, though, this gesture does not resolve the ambiguity of his motives. It is an ambiguous gesture that appears to announce both his disinterested philanthropic interest in them and his unwillingness to see them rise to his level through the possession of a full-sized Bleak House. The novel ties up its complicated plots with Richard unable to free himself from the psychological chains of Chancery despite Jarndyce's efforts on his behalf, with Esther learning that she is the illegitimate daughter of Lady Dedlock, and with Jarndyce offering a helping hand to the newly married couple in the form of a somewhat bizarre gift of a shrunken Bleak House.

The puzzle of Jarndyce's motives is never completely solved at the end, although his behavior seems to be approved by the author ultimately because (we infer) his motives are disinterested in Anderson's sense: that is, he presumably suffers in surrendering Esther to the man she really loves, Allan Woodcourt. Nonetheless, the novel suggests no happy Smithian access to metaphorical knowledge of his motives. Instead we are left with more of a Burkean disjunction between a desire to do good by Esther and a conflicting desire to suppress actual motives that ought not to see the light of day. Is Jarndyce's wedding gift to them of a shrunken Bleak House, then, a poor substitute for the real thing—an expression of insuppressible, but perhaps unconscious, spite—or, as Esther chooses to see it, a metaphorical gift of a loving, "fatherly," philanthropic man? Even if it is the latter, what is the guarantee that a *fatherly* father invariably operates solely on wholly singular, and morally pure, motives as he gives his daughter-lover in marriage to a man who was, until recently, a rival in love? The novel seems to strain to get its readers to accept Esther's all-forgiving view of Jarndyce's motives, and perhaps this points to the central problem of philanthropy itself in Dickens: a gesture ostensibly of disinterested benevolence, its disinterestedness a guarantee of the moral probity of the philanthropist's motives, philanthropy is implicitly at odds with Dickens's interest in the spirit of passionate, and earnest, loving that comes from the heart but is, by virtue of that fact, notably interested and sometimes deeply ambivalent. As Burke clearly warns us, what comes from the heart is, at best, an ambivalent desire: a *delight* in the other's pain that prompts one to reparative action without conjuring away the emotional ambivalence that underwrites the scene of sympathy. It installs the observer in a position of superiority to the sufferer as a condition of making his or her efforts to help efficacious. Moreover, the *observer* here refers both to the philanthropic individual represented in the text and the sympathetic reader of the text. The novel represents within its own pages the sympathetic relationships it presumably generates in its own readers who are emotionally engaged with the novel's compelling characters.

Gissing and Philanthropy

The novelist George Gissing, who was heavily indebted to Dickens, takes on the problem of extending sympathy across class lines in a number of his works but particularly in the two novels he published at the end of the 1880s: *Thyrza* and *The Nether World*, the former focused mainly on the respectable working class and the latter delving more deeply into the lives of the residuum. The former appeared, not accidentally, in the same year that Queen Victoria dedicated the newly built People's Palace on Mile End Road in the East End, one of the most important symbolic moments in the history of culturalist philanthropy in the late Victorian age. Walter Besant's novelistic sketch of a working-class warren transformed by the introduction of its people to an Arnoldian, or aestheticist, project of elevating pleasure is treated with withering skepticism in the novel *Thyrza*.

In the novel, a pretty member of the respectable working class develops a crush on an upper-class male philanthropist named Egremont, whose name and passionate social idealism evoke the hero of Benjamin Disraeli's classic 1845 "condition of England" novel *Sybil; or, The Two Nations*. Egremont, in Gissing's novel the heir of a successful businessman rather than a second son of the aristocracy, is immersed in various projects of culturalist philanthropy from the beginning. He is described by Gissing as "an idealist," determined to "cleanse" the "foulness" of the East End by "spiritual education of the upper artizan and mechanic class," committed to a philanthropic project directed toward the grand goal of social improvement through, implicitly, drawing a line between *deserving* and *undeserving* and extending opportunities to the former.[31] Trying but failing to interest working-class men in a series of lectures on literature that, to his disappointment, are increasingly poorly attended, Egremont turns to the idea of converting an empty church building into a free library, filling it with books he has purchased, and hiring a self-taught working-class reader named Gilbert Grail to run it as chief librarian. Grail, the most attentive listener to Egremont's literary lectures, spends his days working in a soap and candle factory and his nights improving himself with heavy reading. Grail's fiancée, Thyrza, meanwhile, takes to visiting the library during the day as Egremont is busy stacking books on the shelves in preparation for its opening. The result of these visits is a growing passionate attachment between Egremont and Thyrza that soon becomes awkward for both involved.

Although scrupulously careful not to offer overt encouragement to Thyrza's growing attachment to him, Egremont nonetheless continues to meet with her and ultimately falls for her despite his friend Mrs. Ormonde's hypocritical warning to him not to "fill her head" with unrealizable dreams of self-transformation.[32] Indeed, Egremont's attractions to Thyrza are soon enough depicted as inseparable from the erotic attractions that underwrite slumming in this period; it is his fascination with imagining a different life he might have lived, one closer to the instincts in the more *natural* social sphere of Thyrza, that drives his interest in her:

> It seemed to him that he had thrown off a great deal of what was artificial in behaviour and in habits of speech, that he had reverted to that self that came to him from his parents, and he felt better for the change. The air of simplicity in the room and its occupants was healthful; of natural refinement there was abundance, only affectation was missing. Would it have been a hardship if his father had failed to amass money, and he had grown up in such a home as this?[33]

While what is described in this musing seems more like a return to the imagined innocence of a middle-class childhood than the erotic experience of frisson in Bohemia that inspires the slumming of, say, Baudelaire or the Goncourt brothers, this is, nonetheless, a concession to the fact that Lambeth mobilizes Egremont's desires while only ostensibly inspiring his conflicted social conscience.[34] Moreover, the musing reveals Egremont's tendency to idealize a loss of status while being supposedly engaged in a project that helps working-class people attain precisely what he is musing about losing. The story of philanthropy in this novel has become as much the story of the philanthropist's physical attraction to the working-class figure—and its consequences—as the story of the working-class girl's attraction to the goals of philanthropy. In other words, Gissing engages the question of whether philanthropy's motives must be guided by disinterestedness. Philanthropy in this Gissing novel is depicted as a weak expression of love serving as a useful cover for a more powerful sexual desire, the kind of sexual desire that is mobilized in trifling.[35] Like Dickens, Gissing is suspicious of benevolent behavior that is not grounded in authentic desire, and more so than Dickens, he is reluctant to imagine that disinterested benevolence, the disavowal of self-interested motives, can do anyone any good.

Mrs. Ormonde is a prominent philanthropist who devotes herself to the project of taking ill working-class children from the warrens of East and South London to her house in Eastbourne for rehabilitation. At one point early in the novel, she takes in an ill Thyrza to improve her health and her outlook on life, while inadvertently filling her head with exactly the self-transformative desires she later warns Egremont to steer her clear of. Thyrza's first view of the sea at Eastbourne guarantees both the success of the Arnoldian-aestheticist mission—she has learned to desire better things for herself—and its tragic failure, as even Thyrza herself later admits that the visit to the seacoast invested her with aspirations and desires that would inevitably make her dissatisfied with her life in Lambeth. Despite Mrs. Ormonde's warning, Egremont's own interest in Thyrza at this point has long since assumed the shape of erotic fantasy merely lightly clothed in the garb of disinterested philanthropy, and Egremont's own virginal status makes this experience of first love rather painfully stimulating for him:

> He sprang up, ghastly. He had not closed his eyes through the night, but had lain, and walked about the room, in torment. Desire, jealousy, frenzy of first passion, the first passion of his life; no pang was spared him. Oh, how had it grown so suddenly![36]

The emotional opposite of the spectator's Schadenfreude in the scene of sympathy is the lover's ambivalent experience of love as a form of suffering: sexual arousal experienced as unpleasure that causes Egremont here not to embrace Thyrza but to distance himself from her. Eros fails to bind previously sundered wholes (in the Aristophanic sense) here, because Gissing portrays arousal as unpleasurable and ultimately a threat to what ought to be the disinterested motives of philanthropy. The author seems to have innocence itself in his critical sights: the pull of first love propels the virginal, and idealistic, Egremont to distance himself from the woman who inspires that love, from what has become seemingly without his conscious knowledge an erotic entanglement. Egremont's own lack of self-knowledge or self-consciousness, his psychologically virginal status, is underlined here by the shock with which he recognizes, belatedly, that *it* had "grown so suddenly!" Sexual panic, in this case, occasions the shocking discovery that he is incapable of disinterested behavior toward Thyrza.

The conclusion of Gissing's novel sees Thyrza, avoided by Egremont, who increasingly fears the social awkwardness of his infatuation with her, seeking refuge in Lambeth, only to be rejected by the much-abused Gilbert Grail as—what else?—no longer "fit" for a life in South London. Meanwhile, Egremont turns to Annabel Newthorpe, who accepts his proposal of a loveless marriage that reinforces conventional class boundaries under threat of dissolution by philanthropic projects throughout the novel. Gissing's novel ends with an implicit concession to Disraeli's "two nations" thesis but without Disraeli's novelistic resolution, which dramatizes an optimistic—and tendentious—faith that working-class Britons could learn to be satisfied with social inequality, provided the wealthy and well-born do their social duty by them. *Thyrza*, by contrast, has philanthropists involved in reinforcing the boundary between the "two nations, the rich and the poor," while thoroughly rejecting Disraeli's idealistic Tory faith that being consigned to one side of the line need not be a bar to happiness.[37] Moreover, the novel ends with a hypocritical rejection of the efficacy of philanthropy by characters such as Mrs. Ormonde, whose own self-undermining philanthropic work is revealed to produce individuals dissatisfied with their lot in life by infecting them with the worm of vain hope for class transcendence—a transcendence that, in contradictory fashion, she sees as her mission to prevent. Gissing depicts the failure of philanthropy as a failure, finally, of the erotic project of the philanthropist: the failure to love the poor enough to desire to help them surmount the barriers of class. Egremont is one of a series of emotionally constricted Gissing males, whose self-imposed frigidity belies their powerful responsiveness to the erotic threat posed by their own desires and the frightening spectacle of the responses they awaken in the other (Thryza). Ironically, the unwelcome discovery that Egremont cannot be disinterested converts his relationship with Thyrza into a conventional trifling melodrama, with Thyrza as his victim.

Refusal of sexual entanglement in this novel, however, is not to be understood solely as an expression of personal squeamishness on Egremont's part or even just as moralistic recoil from the disillusioning discovery by a sexual innocent of the erotic nature of his own desires—a discovery, in other words, that his relationship with Thyrza cannot be disinterested. The undertone to the novel is also subtly neo-Malthusian, as Gissing's Egremont pulls himself back desperately from the erotic attraction that his trifling with Thyrza has awakened in both, the fear of sexual entanglement with her underwriting implicitly the threat that the working-class girl's sexuality poses for the upper-class male's attempt to distance himself from the coupling that he desires but that would draw him into class miscegenation. The class barrier that is being rather desperately shored up at the end of this text is fundamentally both sexual and political, although Gissing is much more reticent on this topic in *Thyrza* than he will be two years later when he writes *The Nether World*. Philanthropy is presented, in *Thyrza*, in powerfully contradictory ways, as both a social duty the upper class owes to the lower classes and as an implicit threat to social stability when it blossoms, as it does here, into full-fledged romantic love: as Malthus reminds us, unrestrained sexual behavior is the root cause of poverty, so Egremont's refusal to marry Thyrza enacts a moralistic lesson about sexual renunciation as the means to consolidate and retain one's upper-middle-class status.[38] The novel finally implicitly repudiates the very disinterestedness that is at the heart of Smith and Burke's notion of our social duty to the sufferer by drawing a line, an uncrossable line of class, between the one who suffers and the one who seeks to alleviate suffering. Moreover, rather than generating sympathetic feelings for Thyrza's plight, Egremont's reaction converts his own sexual attraction to her into a frightening recoil from the threat of eugenic contamination—the potential for which, he discovers, has infected even his own emotions.

If *Thyrza* is a novel that finally rejects the notion of class permeability and upward mobility for at least the more genteel members of the working class, *The Nether World*, published two years later, offers an even darker, and hesitatingly tragic, view of the prospects for philanthropy. Philanthropy in *The Nether World* is not only driven by unknowable mixed motives residing in the philanthropist but also revealed to be a sinister attempt to control other people—and seldom for their ultimate individual good. In Burke's vision of sympathy, suffering offers a spectacle that produces delight in the spectator, which is then converted, through the magic of unconscious motive, into an attempt to assist the sufferer. He who brings aid to the suffering is driven by his fascination in observing the spectacle of suffering. Through the common Victorian novelistic technique of will-shaking, *The Nether World* portrays philanthropy as a coldly inhumane exercise of power over others. Moreover, the novel takes a very broadly metaphorical view of philanthropy, associating it not only with institutional charity but with the extension of any kind of interpersonal aid to others that springs out of motives of sympathy. More often than not in this novel, this help neither benefits its recipients nor makes the Nether World a better place.

The main philanthropist in the conventional sense in the novel is Michael Snowdon, who inherits a fortune in Australia from his oldest son and then returns to East London, where he rescues his granddaughter Jane from the sinister Peckovers, who have been using her as a household drudge. However, the most compelling philanthropist in the broader metaphorical sense here is Sidney Kirkwood, a member of the respectable working class who involves himself deeply in the lives of both the Hewett family and the Snowdons, and who functions throughout the text as both the chief spectator outside of the drama (the main register of the inhumanity of working-class life in Clerkenwell for readers) and chief actor on stage. He is the principal philanthropist within the novel, a Jarndyce without the means, whose marital choice at the end rewards the selfish and undeserving Clara Hewett while punishing the long-suffering innocent Jane Snowdon out of what appears to be an exaggerated concern for his own moral reputation. It is Kirkwood who knits the two main plots together—the Snowdon plot and the Hewett plot—by developing love interests in both Clara Hewett and Jane Snowdon and then ultimately deserting the long-suffering and meritorious Jane for the facially scarred, and pitiable but self-absorbed, Clara. The choice Sidney is presented with at the end of the novel—whether to marry Jane or Clara—is a Hobson's choice, admittedly, because it will inevitably embitter whomever he refuses. The choice is Gissing's way of dramatizing philanthropy as a competitive Darwinian contest with a clear winner and loser. In both of the main philanthropists of the text, one can see motives of humane pity gradually congealing into inhumanely principled behavior, as Gissing offers his most searching critique of not only institutionalized philanthropy but also an individualized ethical code that traces its roots to the eighteenth-century moral imperative of sympathy.

Like Dickens's *Bleak House*, *The Nether World* makes much of faces, and each heroine's face functions as a mirror, as the narrator's facial reading provides narrative clues to each heroine's ultimate destiny. The most beautiful (and ultimately scarred) face in the novel belongs to Clara Hewett, who at seventeen, before her facial scarring, seems to possess the features of "a very uncommon type, at once sensually attractive and bearing the stamp of intellectual vigour."[39] Perhaps most telling at that time, however, is the description of her face as the face of "one who intensified in her personality an inheritance of revolt."[40] Her face foretells her story: she combines an inheritance of rebelliousness with a personality that intensifies that quality. Marked here for these inherited and acquired traits, Clara seems headed down a road of tragedy, a narrative trajectory guaranteed by Gissing's numerous cheerful reminders that the mechanism of degeneration—Lamarckian inheritance of acquired traits—means that we are all ruined by the circumstances of our own life experiences, the traces of which can be found written into our bodies. Of course, Gissing marks out the downward narrative trajectory by associating virtually every character in Clerkenwell with it, his narrator noting that, not just people but even the very streets of Clerkenwell testify to the inevitability of degeneration. Sydney, we are told, lives on Tysoe Street, Clerkenwell, "a short street, which, like so many in London, begins reputably and degenerates in its latter half."[41] No Ada Carstone or Esther Summerson, whose faces tell the tale of their goodness, Clara has facial beauty that bespeaks a promised destiny of disappointment and ruination even before it is literally scarred with acid by a rival actress. As Dickens might say, we know it even before we know we know it: she is the daughter of a man scarred by hereditary drunkenness and the sister of a man who will pass criminality to the next generation. Precisely because Clara seems a cut above most of her neighbors, she is inevitably headed for a fall. However, Gissing generalizes her case to include all children of the poor whose birth embitters their parents, in short, all the inhabitants of Clerkenwell, reduced through Gissing's metaphors to "hapless spawn" whose birth is an "abortion":

> On all the doorsteps sat little girls, themselves only just out of infancy, nursing or neglecting bald, red-eyed, doughy-limbed abortions in every stage of babyhood, hapless spawn of diseased humanity, born to embitter and brutalise yet further the lot of those who unwillingly gave them life.[42]

In language here that is coldly sociological and intimately ghastly at the same time, Gissing converts the unconscious motives that drive Burke's philanthropist to do good on a personal level into unconscious biological compulsions that lead to the overproduction of babies who, as a result of their numbers and their birth to lower-class parents, compel disgust rather than sympathy.

Gissing's overwrought tone when addressing the subject of overpopulation, however, actually looks coolly measured and objective compared to that of some of his contemporaries. The Reverend Andrew Mearns's investigation of the social depredations of abject poverty, titled *The Bitter Cry of Outcast London*, which appeared in the *Pall Mall Gazette* in 1883, is perhaps the best-known from this period, although, when it comes to hysteria about overpopulation, few outdo Gissing's contemporary, Arnold White. A liberal enthusiast for eugenics, brimming with Malthusian fears, rather than a melodramatic Christian missionary like Mearns, White advocated in his *The Problems of a Great City* (1886) a brutally efficient eugenic solution to the problem of long-term poverty: the forced sterilization of the poor. His description of incipient criminality in the youngest of East End children makes Gissing's discussion of the overproduction of "abortions" seem relatively humane by comparison:

> Criminal and pauperized classes with low cerebral development renew their race more rapidly than those of higher nervous natures. Statesmen idly stand by, watching in such moments as they can spare from the strife of party the victory of battalions destined to misery and crime over the struggling army of the prudent and the self-controlled. Birth into certain quarters of London is birth into an environment from which there is no escape. At three years old baby lips lisp oaths so bestial as to be coarse in the betel-stained mouths of the crew of a Coromandel dhoney. At six, little girls are initiated by their mothers into practices so loathsome the gorge rises at the thought. At ten, girls and boys alike are unclean spirits limited in their power for evil only by their abilities. Dynasties of criminals and paupers hand down from generation to generation hereditary unfitness for the arts of progress and all that brings greatness to a nation, and engage themselves in warring against all forms of physical and moral order. Where a man is criminal himself, the cause of crime in others, and the begetter of criminal posterity, it seems to be an act of mere self-protection on the part of this generation to segregate him.[43]

What is described here goes beyond, in its horror, Gissing's description of passive "abortions" idling on the tenement stoops dandled by their hopeless child-mothers whose lives they will live to embitter. Instead, White describes menacing predatory animals actively at war with civilized order almost from birth, the products of regrettable sexual congress between the thoughtless poor, readying themselves for lives of criminality. What unites White with his fear of growing criminality among the poor and Gissing with the latter's warnings about overpopulation is the implicit agreement between the two that the poor no longer resemble the members of the respectable classes and are committed to foul narrative ends that will only be exacerbated by conventional philanthropy.

Self-Undermining Philanthropic Impulses | 51

Jane Snowdon, by contrast, presents an even more troubling case: a tragic and ineffectual Little Dorrit figure, bound to a life of unceasing disappointment, who loses the man she loves at the end. She is a consistent victim of the Nether World invested with sympathetic agency. She endures abuse from the Peckovers before her grandfather arrives to save her, and she takes on the unwelcome duty of enacting his inhumane project despite her own misgivings. When Sidney discovers that she has finally become capable of laughter after an early life of consistent suffering at the hands of the Peckovers, he initially feels a "profound sympathy was transforming him."[44] It restores his faith in "nature," and he concludes, through a mistaken reading of her narrative that he will shape, that nature seems to have intended her for "one of the most joyous among children."[45] Yet her capacity for joy is not enough to save her, any more than the surface geniality of her father, J. J. Snowdon, protects him from disaster. No sooner does Sidney meet her father, in fact, than he begins to see in the depths of his face something that tells against him and thus ultimately his daughter: "But his face was against him; the worn, sallow features, the eyes which so obviously made a struggle to look with frankness, the vicious lower lip, awoke suspicion and told tales of base experience such as leaves its stamp upon a man for ever."[46]

Gissing's Lamarckian reading of the father's face, which reveals the troubling signs of base experience in life, then begins to infect his reading of the face of Jane when he examines that face again and, this time, recoils in disgust from the woman with whom he had, shortly before, convinced himself he had been falling in love:

> All the more repugnant was this face to Sidney because it presented, in certain aspects, an undeniable resemblance to Jane's; impossible to say which feature put forth this claim of kindred, but the impression was there, and it made Sidney turn away his eyes in disgust as often as he perceived it.[47]

The ties of sympathy toward Jane are virtually sundered in this moment, as Sidney's moment of homosexual panic, brought on by Jane's growing facial resemblance to her degenerate father, occasions a larger conviction that Jane's whole *line* is contaminated and that Sidney's desire to marry into a degenerate line bespeaks a dangerous attraction to the degenerate sufferer that must be stifled. More than merely an aesthetic recoil, Sidney's reaction of disgust is a repudiation of the ethical imperative of sympathy, even if Gissing softens the moral implications of Sidney's cruel decision to flee Jane by having him return to the disfigured Clara, whom he also proves powerless to help.

Michael Snowdon functions as a novelistic demonstration that a philanthropic mission makes one inhumane, a philanthropic monster who borrows, and exaggerates, some of the contradictory features of Mrs. Ormonde in *Thyrza*. After involving Jane in charitable activities in the middle of the novel, Snowdon reveals the secret of his wealth to her, demanding that, in return for his making her his heir, she undertake to spend it only on charity and social work (and to accept a life of celibacy). Snowdon's demand that Jane take vows of celibacy marks him as a monstrous idealist, making demands of his granddaughter that he never considered adopting himself, and testifies to the growing centrality in the novel of the neo-Malthusian theme. However, we have already seen at this point in the novel that although Gissing may use the celibacy requirement as a marker of Snowdon's growing inhumanity, Gissing himself nonetheless sees the refusal of sexual congress as the only solution to the problem of poverty and inherited criminality. With a father like J. J., Jane's most charitable gesture toward the rest of humanity would be to give up breeding altogether: indeed, the vow of celibacy extracted by her grandfather is both a mark of his inhumanity and the only viable solution to the problem of poverty. Although Jane reluctantly accepts her grandfather's mission for her, Snowdon's project is doomed to failure, ultimately, when Jane, heartbroken by Sidney Kirkwood's desertion of her for the once-beautiful Clara Hewett, falls out of her grandfather's favor just before he dies and his will is lost, thus insuring that the remains of his estate after his death will go to the undeserving J. J. Snowdon.

Sidney Kirkwood, who initially plans to propose to Jane once she knows the details of her grandfather's plans and can make an informed choice, had been justly irritated by Michael Snowdon's escalating demands on his own granddaughter and, in particular, by his insistence that she not be educated, even though she is to be an heiress. In fact, after Snowdon dictates a new demand not only that Jane give away her inherited fortune by following his strict instructions to the letter but also that she remain celibate for the rest of her life, Gissing's narrator remarks, "Michael had taken the last step in that process of dehumanisation which threatens idealists of his type."[48] Moreover, Jane's very simplicity, the innocence that makes her akin to a Dickensian moral heroine, makes her averse to Michael's grand project, for its coldly sociological ambitiousness frightens her: "Consecration to a great idea, endowment with the means of wide beneficence—this not only left her cold, but weighed upon her, afflicted her beyond her strength."[49] Although Jane in her purity seems intended for an Esther Summerson role of quiet, unassuming, individualized heroism, she achieves no such apotheosis and experiences no such rewards. She is purely a victim here, a good woman who will never recover from the loss of the one man who seems to believe in her. Indeed, Gissing here is repudiating philanthropy itself in depicting Jane's recoil from its grand promises and associating the authors of idealistic philanthropic schemes with degeneracy. The sneering language that Gissing uses in the text in discussing "sensuality" suggests that it is not merely Snowdon's corrupt idealism that the text is troubled by: it is, as in *Thyrza*, the binding power of sexuality itself; the cure for poverty, in Gissing's view, can never be Eros because Eros is the chief cause of poverty and demoralization. The ironically optimistic Burkean vision of a social order made whole by the philanthropic work of spectators delighted by the very suffering that spurs them to alleviate it is implicitly rejected here, as the novelist embraces the very campaign against sex that his main character criticizes when it is articulated by the grandfather, Michael Snowdon. Gissing endorses Sidney's registering of the "inhumanity" of Snowdon's scheme but then, ironically, has Sidney perform that inhumanity himself by leaving Jane to a life of celibate despair.

Although initially destined, seemingly, to play the mediating figure who registers the inhumanity of Snowdon through his conscious awareness of it, Kirkwood is unable to transcend his own limitations and fails in his philanthropic mission to redeem Jane from a life of misery. As a philanthropic act, the bestowal of Sidney's love on an unworthy object—Clara Hewett—leaves much to be desired precisely because it cannot be redemptive, because it cannot interpellate the limited Clara, finally, into a redemptive narrative. Moreover, Kirkwood's recoil from Jane, whom he once attempted to love, is only ostensibly triggered by his fear that his motives have been misunderstood as venal ones. Fundamentally, Kirkwood recoils from Jane's degenerate physicality, from the narrative written across her face, a face that resembles her father Joseph's and thus conveys her story in advance of her having lived it. Sidney reads her the way Octavia Hill reads tenants who fall into arrears: she is bound to a narrative of decline regardless of what she wishes, her own history in the East End ensuring, through the mechanism of Lamarckian inheritance of acquired traits, that her narrative will take a degenerate turn. Moreover, Gissing subtly plays with the mirror image here, transmuting Michael Snowdon's idealist fanaticism into Joseph Snowdon's degenerate physicality, which, in turn, manifests itself in the suffering face of the disappointed Jane from whom Sidney turns away in fear, unable to find her even remotely as "scientifically interesting" as Joseph Conrad's more detached Marlow jokingly finds Europeans who go to the Congo in the 1890s.

Conclusion

The facial marks of smallpox notably serve a dual role in Dickens, physically identifying Esther Summerson with the poverty she hoped to alleviate but also with the stigmata that mark her as destined for secular sainthood. In Gissing, however, the corrupted idealism of the philanthropist father has become the son's inheritance in the form of a degeneracy that, the novelist assures us, will surely drag his daughter Jane down one day. Sidney cannot help reading Jane's face as a promise that she is bound to a degenerate end, and in rejecting her physically, he consigns her to a life of disappointed hope.

The reading of narrative ends in the other, associated in Dickens with conventionalized melodramatic plots of rising or falling, becomes naturalized in

Gissing's novel as the Snowdon family is unable to escape its destined end in degeneracy. Gissing rejects the optimism of Burke's or Smith's Enlightenment vision for sympathy as the consummate social-ordering principle built on a foundation of sensation with a much more hopeless vision of entire families—the Hewetts in particular—condemned to eugenic hell.

Like Dickens's work, *The Nether World* seems to accept the notion, central to the sympathetic tradition, that human bonds of sympathy, forged in a moment of self-recognition in the other, are the necessary foundation of any social order consisting of individuals. To feel a metaphorical version of the other's pain (or even to delight in it) is to take the first step to aid those who suffer. In Dickens's novel, this complicates immensely the motives of especially his unsaintly characters, who, like John Jarndyce, are driven to help by obscure motives that are, nonetheless, evidently anchored in strong feeling, no matter how inadmissible those actual feelings may be. Jarndyce is an example of a Dickensian character who works for the betterment of individuals even if his philanthropy seems to be driven by something less than the pure motives Dickens insists that Ada and Esther possess: a reparative motive, perhaps, that should be applauded even if the wrong being repaired is never fully exposed to the light of day in the novel.

However, Gissing draws the implication that philanthropic motives cannot fail to be self-serving, finally. Both *Thyrza* and *Nether World* feature male protagonists who are significantly emotionally and sexually constricted. Neither Egremont nor Kirkwood allows himself to display even the predatory vitality of a dangerously repressed Dickensian figure such as Bradley Headstone. While Kirkwood's erotic investments in Clara and Jane, no matter how they are overlaid with philanthropic pretenses, at least allow him to avoid the icy distancing stance of Egremont toward Thyrza, Kirkwood experiences a bodily recoil from the poor when he notes the symptoms of degeneracy. His mirror reflects a monster, as the Jane of his observation moves from potentially Dickensian heroine to join the lower species to which she was born. Described in Dickensian terms as "faithful to the past, and unchanging" in the end,[50] both object of philanthropy and would-be philanthropist, Jane's stasis is by no means the redemptive sort of an Esther Summerson or Little Dorrit, spreading good wherever she goes, unable and unwilling to surrender her connection to the past, and applauded by Dickens for insistently retaining her allegiance to that past, which is ultimately a token of the coherence of her narrative life. Jane is instead a living mark of the futility of philanthropy that, even were it successful, would not produce a redeemed future and social progress. Faithful to the past here essentially means she is a prey to atavistic instinct.

Finally, it is clear that the Burkean celebration of sympathy for the suffering at least suggests Burke has faith that human social order may be renewed by philanthropic effort, even if the underlying motives driving philanthropy ought not to see the light of day. No matter how large a role guilty pleasure plays in propelling us to extend aid to the suffering, at least it plays that role in the Burkean schema. By contrast, the social world of Gissing's characters is one in which we do not see our best selves reflected back to us in the faces of the suffering. Instead, we behold the faces of the abject poor with whom we cannot identify and whose promised narratives cannot be improved by our intervention into their plots. Bodily disgust is all that springs from our recognition that the narrative trajectories of those we behold—and once loved—obviate the desirability of assisting them. In having Sidney Kirkwood register the inhumanity of Snowdon's demand for his granddaughter to remain celibate, the novel repudiates the very idea of philanthropy as a cure for poverty while, contradictorily, also placing the novel on the side of a Dickensian form of sympathy that it is powerless to endorse: the only humane way to deal with widespread poverty is to seek the extermination of the poor.

DANIEL BIVONA is Associate Professor of English at Arizona State University. His publications include *The Imagination of Class: Masculinity and the Victorian Urban Poor* (with Roger B. Henkle); *British Imperial Literature, 1870–1940: Writing and the Administration of Empire*; and *Desire and Contradiction: Imperial Visions and Domestic Debates in Victorian Literature*.

Notes

1. Christianson, *Philanthropy*, 9.
2. The now-classic study of female settlement houses is Martha Vicinus's *Independent Women*.
3. Joyce, "Castles in the Air," 514–525.
4. Jacques Donzelot argues that philanthropy in this era needs to be understood as a deliberate strategy of "depoliticization": "Philanthropy in this case is not to be understood as a naively apolitical term signifying a private intervention in the sphere of so-called social problems, but must be considered as a deliberately de-politicizing strategy for establishing public services and facilities at a sensitive point midway between private initiative and the state." Donzelot, *Policing of Families*, 55.
5. Hill, *Homes*, 38–39.
6. Smith, *Moral Sentiments*, I.I.11.
7. Marshall, *Surprising Effects*, 5.
8. Ibid., 180.
9. Christianson, *Philanthropy*, 33.
10. Greiner, *Sympathetic Realism*, 4.
11. Marshall, *Surprising Effects*, 180.
12. Smith, *Moral Sentiments*, I.I.36.
13. Burke, *Sublime and the Beautiful*, 31.

14. For a more positive view of the role of fiction in helping readers conceptualize "the common good" in the twentieth century, see Bruce Robbins's *Upward Mobility and the Common Good*.

15. Jaffe, *Scenes of Sympathy*, 9.

16. Moore, *Dickens and Empire*, 69.

17. Dickens, *Bleak House*, 52.

18. Bruce Robbins, "Telescopic Philanthropy."

19. "Supplying relief to those whose poverty did not conceal any ruse was not enough. This relief must also serve some purpose; it must also contribute to a rehabilitation of the family. This was why, in every request for aid, one had to locate and bring to light the moral fault that more or less directly determined it: that portion of neglectfulness, laziness, and dissolution that every instance of misery contained. In this new policy, *morality was systematically linked to the economic factor*, involving a continuous surveillance of the family, a full penetration into the details of family life." Donzelot, *Policing of Families*, 69 (emphasis in original).

20. Siegel, *Charity and Condescension*, 347.

21. I have remarked before that specular relationships are important to this text. The words *face* (noun and verb) and *faces* (noun and verb) appear 351 and 27 times in the novel, respectively. Bivona, "Poverty, Pity, and Community," 81.

22. Dickens, *Bleak House*, 60–61.

23. Christianson makes the convincing argument that Dickens has Harold Skimpole portray himself as simultaneously beneficiary and benefactor. Christianson, *Philanthropy*, 93.

24. Dickens, *Bleak House*, 96.

25. Ibid., 114.

26. Purton argues that, through his depiction of Skimpole, Dickens "systematically dismantles the previous generation's depiction of the 'Romantic child.'" Purton, *Dickens and the Sentimental Tradition*, 59.

27. Dickens, *Bleak House*, 62.

28. Ibid., 124.

29. Anderson, *Powers of Distance*, 33.

30. Dickens, *Bleak House*, 104.

31. Gissing, *Thyrza*, 9, 13.

32. Ibid., 212.

33. Ibid., 177.

34. In a recent essay, Diana Maltz notes that in the 1880s the term *slumming* generally referred both to visiting the poor out of philanthropic motives and for motives of "curiosity." Maltz, "Blatherwicks and Busybodies," 20.

35. The best recent work on the frisson generated by slumming is Seth Koven's *Slumming* (2004).

36. Gissing, *Thyrza*, 252.

37. Disraeli, *Sybil*, 87.

38. See Malthus, *Principle of Population*.

39. Gissing, *Nether World*, 26.

40. Ibid.

41. Ibid., 50.

42. Ibid., 130.

43. White, *Problems of a Great City*, 49.

44. Gissing, *Nether World*, 138.

45. Ibid., 139.

46. Ibid., 162.

47. Ibid.
48. Ibid., 177.
49. Ibid., 226.
50. Ibid., 390.

Bibliography

Anderson, Amanda. *The Powers of Distance: Cosmopolitanism and the Cultivation of Detachment.* Princeton, NJ: Princeton University Press, 2002.

Bivona, Daniel. "Poverty, Pity, and Community: Urban Poverty and the Threat to Social Bonds in the Victorian Age." *NCS: Nineteenth Century Studies* 21 (2007): 67–83.

Burke, Edmund. *A Philosophical Inquiry into Our Ideas of the Sublime and the Beautiful.* Vol. 1 of *The Works of the Right Honourable Edmund Burke.* London: John C. Nimmo, 1787.

Christianson, Frank. *Philanthropy in British and American Fiction: Dickens, Hawthorne, Eliot, and Howells.* Edinburgh, UK: Edinburgh University Press, 2007.

Dickens, Charles. *Bleak House.* London: New American Library, 1964.

Disraeli, Benjamin. *Sybil.* Vol. 14 of *The Works of Benjamin Disraeli, Earl of Beaconsfield.* New York: Walter Dunne, 1904.

Donzelot, Jacques. *The Policing of Families.* Translated by Robert Hurley. London: Random House, 1979.

Gissing, George. *The Nether World.* Edited by Stephen Gill. New York: Oxford University Press, 1992.

———. *Thyrza: A Tale.* Hassocks, UK: Harvester Press, 1974.

Greiner, Rae. *Sympathetic Realism in Nineteenth-Century Fiction.* Baltimore, MD: Johns Hopkins University Press, 2012.

Hill, Octavia. *Homes of the London Poor.* London: Macmillan, 1875.

Jaffe, Audrey. *Scenes of Sympathy: Identity and Representation in Victorian Fiction.* Ithaca, NY: Cornell University Press, 2000.

Joyce, Simon. "Castles in the Air: The People's Palace, Cultural Reformism, and the East End Working Class." *Victorian Studies* 39, no. 4 (1996): 513–538.

Koven, Seth. *Slumming: Sexual and Social Politics in Victorian London.* Princeton, NJ: Princeton University Press, 2004.

Malthus, Thomas. *An Essay on the Principle of Population.* London: J. Johnson, 1798.

Maltz, Diana. "Blatherwicks and Busybodies: Gissing on the Culture of Philanthropic Slumming." In *George Gissing: Voices of the Unclassed,* edited by Martin Ryle and Jenny Bourne Taylor, 15–28. Aldershot, UK: Ashgate, 2005.

Marshall, David. *The Surprising Effects of Sympathy.* Chicago: University of Chicago Press, 1988.

Mearns, Andrew. *The Bitter Cry of Outcast London.* London: Humanities Press, 1970.

Moore, Grace. *Dickens and Empire: Discourses of Class, Race, and Colonialism in the Works of Charles Dickens.* Chippenham, UK: Antony Rowe, 2004.

Purton, Valerie. *Dickens and the Sentimental Tradition: Fielding, Richardson, Sterne, Goldsmith, Sheridan, Lamb.* London: Anthem Press, 2012.

Robbins, Bruce. "Telescopic Philanthropy: Professionalism and Responsibility in *Bleak House.*" In *Nation and Narration,* edited by Homi Bhabha, 213–230. London: Routledge, 1990.

———. *Upward Mobility and the Common Good: Toward a Literary History of the Welfare State.* Princeton, NJ: Princeton University Press, 2007.

Siegel, Daniel. *Charity and Condescension: Victorian Literature and the Dilemmas of Philanthropy.* Athens: Ohio University Press, 2012.

Smith, Adam. *Theory of Moral Sentiments.* 1759. Reprint, London: A. Millar, 1790. http://www.econlib.org/library/Smith/smMS.html.

Vicinus, Martha. *Independent Women: Work and Community for Single Women, 1850–1920.* Chicago: University of Chicago Press, 1985.

White, Arnold. *The Problems of a Great City.* London: Remington, 1886.

3

EDUCATION AS VIOLATION AND BENEFIT
Doctrinal Debate and the Contest for India's Girls

Suzanne Daly

> Laura was raised in a missionary's home and just felt the burden for mission work.
> —John Sander, Laura Silsby's father¹

> All benevolence is "colonial."
> —Gayatri Chakravorty Spivak²

Preface: The Business of Educational Philanthropy

On January 29, 2010, seventeen days after a catastrophic earthquake struck Haiti, ten US missionaries from the Idaho-based Baptist ministry New Life Children's Refuge were arrested at the Haitian border as they attempted to enter the Dominican Republic with thirty-three Haitian children, none of whom carried identity papers. Officials discovered that the children, whom the missionaries' leader Laura Silsby had claimed were orphans, all had living parents or guardians who had surrendered them after being assured that they would have better lives, and better educations, in the adoptive homes that New Life could secure for them.³ One parent was quoted in the *Wall Street Journal* as saying, to his neighbors' nodded agreement, "The chance to educate a child is a chance for an entire family to prosper."⁴ The terms of this exchange, although implicit, could not be clearer: the missionaries had offered to cultivate the children's minds in return for the opportunity to cultivate their souls.⁵ The case attracted international attention, with analyses frequently pitting supporters of what Silsby termed a rescue mission against "secular child advocates"⁶ who decried the operation as at best misguided and culturally insensitive and at worst an unambiguous case of abduction and child trafficking.

Either way, the New Life missionaries' actions were largely portrayed as not only extreme but vaguely anachronistic, belonging to a repudiated if undefined past.

A deeper consideration of the story's historical and cultural antecedents suggests that the Silsby case cannot be neatly framed as a clash between outworn missionary practices and the rational procedures of secular modernity; the substantial and long-standing coexistence in Haiti of missionary-run and secular schools and orphanages, a situation mirrored in most of Europe's former colonies, blurs this narrative's temporal boundaries. Beyond that fact, however, the story's prehistory, particularly the piece located within the matrix of coercion, indoctrination, and enablement that has long defined colonial and neocolonial educational schemes, further complicates the picture. How did Silsby's plan come to be seen as acceptable to her supporters, and how did it come to be thwarted? One answer is that the events in Haiti, as well as the analyses that followed, were inflected by the many colonial and postcolonial settings in which conversion as a multivalent trope has structured the theory and practice of educating children, particularly those labeled "underprivileged." The subtle weave of ongoing negotiation that education in conditions of underdevelopment entails among missionaries, lay workers, nongovernmental organizations (NGOs), parents, students, and (not least) national, local, and foreign governments, in other words, has a long history shot through with unlikely lines of connection—between Methodist schools in South Africa and Singapore, for example, or, in this case, between British-controlled India in the nineteenth century and Catholic-majority Haiti, a former French colony. Debates on education in India, the site of missionary efforts that would come to exert a global influence on imperial educational philanthropy, offer one version of the past imagined to have irrupted in the Silsby case.

Although Haiti's colonial history differs vastly from that of India, several Protestant denominations influential in twentieth-century Haiti began their missionary endeavors in British-controlled India, which served as a laboratory and proving ground for their educational work.[7] India's extraordinarily rich mission archives provide a detailed record of how missionary practices evolved over the course of a century to become increasingly intertwined with the business of educating poor children. This essay therefore proposes that debates over the nature and aims of colonial educational philanthropy in nineteenth-century British India remain instructive for two reasons. First, they demonstrate why the lines of demarcation separating education, philanthropy, and imperialism in cases such as Silsby's are frequently less bright than they may first appear. The larger story of educational progress in the United States and Great Britain has often been mapped in terms of a transition from religious to secular, and it is from this perspective that Silsby's misadventures in Haiti were understood as a startling recrudescence of discredited (and criminalized) practices. By historicizing the staying power of faith-based colonial education, the India debates illuminate the tensions within this overly straightforward narrative of educational evolution.

Second, although the Victorian debates on the relative merits of secular and religious educational philanthropy are roughly analogous to questions raised in the Silsby case, their historical and geographic distance usefully estranges them. Analyzed from this remove, the tactical value of the doctrinal-versus-secular binary becomes clear: it virtually guarantees that no real debate will ever take place, because if both sides begin (as they almost inevitably do) by arguing that their opponents are unqualified to render judgment and therefore unworthy of engagement, the conversation will never move past that initial point of contention. The resulting cycle of mutual derogation serves to obscure or suppress the real terms of the debate, which concern the exercise of power by the educators and the nature and aims of the empowerment they wish to confer on their students. Yet these questions of power and rights may be discerned even within texts structured by rigidly oppositional views on secular versus faith-based education, and such moments obliquely suggest a means of navigating the divide. They do so by prefiguring or pointing toward what Gayatri Chakravorty Spivak has called the enabling violation, an act whose undeniably beneficial effects nevertheless do not, and cannot, justify its having been performed.[8]

In this chapter, my two central texts are educational reformer Mary Carpenter's *Six Months in India* (1868), in which she outlines a secular educational program for Indian girls, and a sharply critical review of Carpenter's book by Rosamond Webb, the longtime secretary of the Society for Promoting Female Education in the East (FES) and editor of its magazine, the *Female Missionary Intelligencer*. The FES, which trained female teachers and placed them in missionary-run girls' schools in Africa, Asia, and the Levant, was an interdenominational Protestant organization committed to Christian education, and Webb appears to have been passionately devoted to its cause. Webb's review of *Six Months in India* appeared over ten monthly issues of the *Female Missionary Intelligencer* in 1869; running an unprecedented 30,000 words in length, it is not so much a review as a polemic, a manifesto on colonial education in its own right. While both authors mount predictable (and predictably vexed) defenses of their respective schools of thought, each perceives in the other side's educational system a potential to cause unacceptable levels of individual and social harm to the population it is intended to serve.[9] In articulating these objections, Carpenter and Webb each begin to mount a critique of their antagonists' pedagogical practices—if not their own—as an imbalance of ethical imperatives. In so doing, they demonstrate an intellectual engagement with the commingling of damage and benefit that define the enabling violation.

The concept of the enabling violation emerges from Spivak's early theorizations of the structural violence of British colonialism and connects them to her ongoing considerations of what might constitute ethically responsible transformational practices under globalization. In the NGO-ized world of twenty-first-century global philanthropic capitalism, she cautions, "the necessary collective efforts... to change laws, relations of production, *systems of education*, and health care" will certainly fail if conducted under the old colonialist assumptions and without thorough attention to questions of complicity and responsibility on all sides.[10] To illustrate the enabling violation's potential to traverse the gap between the most abhorrent of acts and the most urgent of ethical imperatives, Spivak frequently invokes the child of rape, whose full humanity may neither be denied nor "advanced as a justification for the rape."[11] *Enabling violation* in Spivak's usage is therefore emphatically not a term of backhanded, partial, or retroactive absolution; nor is it a mandate to discern in any transgression a redeeming aspect. Not all violations are enabling. And I want to be absolutely clear: the attempt to spirit the Haitian children across a national border in the chaos following the earthquake was an unqualified violation, legally and ethically; enablement played no part in it. Amid scenes of unthinkable devastation, baiting besieged parents with vague promises of safety, education, and a future—any future—for their children constitutes entrapment, not aid. My point is that exclusive attention to cut-and-dried violations forecloses the possibility of comprehending the spectrum of philanthropic-pedagogical power relations of which such cases mark one end. Spivak consistently indicates that when speaking of the enabling violation, tension must be applied to both sides of the paradox that it names: the enablement or benefit must never be used to justify the violation, but neither may the benefit, once conferred, be rejected, denied, or prohibited from benefiting others. Only from a persistent and multifaceted critique of the enabling violation might a more ethical program emerge. As Spivak observes, "One cannot write off the righting of wrongs. The enablement must be used even as the violation is re-negotiated."[12]

Elsewhere, Spivak cautions that enabling violations are not equally or evenly enabling; while some Indians, she reminds us, benefited from colonialism in fairly straightforward if problematic ways, "the relationship of women, for example, or Dalits, to benevolent colonialism is very different: very oblique and very ambivalent. On the other hand, because there is violation, one can also think about the ways in which one could undo the violation, or rather how to sustain the enablement with a minimum of violation."[13] Issues of gender and education appear frequently in Spivak's examples and analyses of the enabling violation, in part because gender (as a category or concept-metaphor) and education (as a practice necessary to rulers and ruled) played a central role in both the construction and the dismantling of the British colonial project in India.[14] In the nineteenth century, British education in India exemplified the uneven development of cultural capital: prior to the adoption of the program outlined in Wood's Despatch of 1854, much of the population was either left out altogether or served by miscellaneous entities that operated with varying levels of governmental sanction, funding, and oversight. Wood's Despatch called for the establishment of education departments in each province that would found and oversee a system of government-run schools through the university level and forge affiliations with secular private schools, to which they would offer grants-in-aid. In the 1860s, the mandates of Wood's Despatch had not been fully implemented, and the question of how best to educate the different strata of society was far from settled either in England or in India.[15] In the latter, however, girls' education was scanted by the colonial government, both because it feared provoking a cultural backlash and because girls were seen as a bad investment: educated Indian women, it was thought, had no value as future workers in the service of the empire. At this historical juncture, private, gender-specific educational philanthropy emerged as a powerful means through which British women could gain legitimacy and assert authority in the colonial context by claiming the work of teaching as their mandate and their mission.

Like missionaries, British women had long been considered defective to the colonial enterprise. For women who wanted to work in (or on behalf of) British India, educational philanthropy therefore proved fertile ground, not least because it could be claimed as an extension of their natural duties.[16] The act of teaching has frequently been understood to involve the giving of something—oneself, one's knowledge, one's good example—for the betterment of others. Teaching, even volunteer teaching, is not inherently or necessarily philanthropic. Yet once teaching was defined as giving, it could be claimed as both philanthropy and women's work, particularly when the teachers were paid very little, as in the case of the FES. Conversely, imperial-philanthropic work that involved neither teachers nor students in the traditional sense often contained pedagogical elements, as when missionaries labored to inculcate "habits of industry" in the poor. The term *imperial educational philanthropy*, therefore, while descriptive of many Victorian schemes to educate British colonial subjects, may be said to denote areas of overlap and contestation rather than a single point of convergence.

For much of the nineteenth century, the majority of privately run British educational-philanthropic enterprises in India were overseen by missionaries who struggled to balance the competing demands of pedagogy and ground-level philanthropy—providing for the most desperately needy—while navigating the task that was at once central to their mission and most likely to undermine it: religious instruction designed to effect pupils' eventual conversion to Christianity. For missionaries, laboring to convert nonbelievers constituted perhaps the ultimate act of philanthropy because it enacted what they considered to be the highest expression of concern for human welfare—the desire to save souls. This placed them in an oddly doubled position: in terms of educating India's poor, these British missionaries had the field largely to themselves, yet neither their government nor their charges particularly wanted them to succeed in their ultimate aim. As much recent scholarship has demonstrated, detractors in the late eighteenth and early nineteenth centuries had argued forcefully, if ultimately unsuccessfully, that Christian proselytizing in India would serve no philanthropic purpose but would undermine both the East India Company's economic mission and the British Empire's civilizing imperative. Two central issues on which this scholarship focuses are the 1813 renewal of the East India Company's charter, into which Evangelical member of parliament William Wilberforce successfully inserted a clause requiring the Company to allow missionary activity in its territories, and the debates over the curriculum and language of instruction in government-run Indian schools, which pitted the so-called Orientalists against proponents of an Anglicized curriculum. Thomas Babington Macaulay's contribution to the latter debate was his 1835 "Minute" on Indian education, which derided "false religion" but stated, "Assuredly it is the duty of the British Government in India to be not only tolerant, but neutral on all religious questions."[17] This double move implicitly justified missionaries' conversion efforts while apparently foreclosing the possibility of official assistance. Although missionaries would eventually forge working relationships with colonial authorities in many cases, tensions remained. The FES's female teachers certainly faced official prejudice, but they also possessed key advantages in India: because women were less readily associated with religious authority, they were less threatening to governments and Indian parents alike. As women, moreover, they were the only European teachers who could be granted access to Indian women and girls over the age of eight or nine.

These, then, were some of the factors Mary Carpenter confronted when, in 1866, she decided to travel to India in order to stake a claim for the secular education of Indian girls. Although my analysis focuses largely on Webb's critique of Carpenter, I have no wish to recuperate one side at the other's expense. Rather, I pass over many of Webb's more chauvinistic beliefs simply because the ideological underpinnings of Victorian imperialism, and the excesses of missionary enterprises built on those foundations, have been thoroughly critiqued elsewhere.[18] Both Webb and Carpenter, moreover, premise their arguments on racialized (and largely unexamined) cultural and doctrinal hierarchies, the outlines of which will be familiar to any student of the period. Their arguments' value lies in making unusually visible the web of contradictory power dynamics that structure imperial educational philanthropy and in their suggestion that these contradictions cannot be avoided or overcome either by embracing or rejecting religious instruction in colonial classrooms. To teach may be to give of oneself, but the inverse formulation is that to impart knowledge, values, and modes of behavior is an unavoidable exercise of power. In a setting where partisans tended to see their favored system of education as inevitably enabling to the student, a perspective that blunted any ability to perceive concomitant violations, *Six Months in India* and Webb's response reveal an acute, if ultimately curtailed, sense of the enablement/violation dynamic that Spivak locates in colonial practices. Carpenter's argument that secularizing colonial education for girls would render it devoid of coercion shares with Webb's critique of Carpenter's blind trust in the (masculine) authority of the colonial government an ability to anatomize convincingly the bind of harm and benefit in the other's pedagogical program while remaining blind to the potential for damage within her own; hence the curtailment. Neither writer, moreover, questions the premise that imposing a foreign language and educational system on Indian children with the express purpose of inculcating beliefs, habits, and values unshared by the children's parents or their larger community is an unmixed good. Together, Webb and Carpenter make visible a cluster of suppositions that would be promoted and contested throughout the twentieth century. Their echoes may be heard in the New Life Children's Refuge statement of purpose, which outlines a mission to provide Haitian children with "a solid education and vocational skills" and to help "each child find healing, hope, joy and new life in Christ,"[19] as well as in the outraged response of Haitian officials to New Life's actions.[20]

In the interest of situating Carpenter's and Webb's conflicting views on the theory and practice of colonial pedagogy, the following section gives brief sketches of their intellectual and social coordinates. Despite their divergent class, educational, and religious backgrounds, each carved out a career involving publication, social action, and interaction with networks of female activists. Each, moreover, believed passionately in the cause of educating Indian girls, but in ways that reflect her specific formation, beliefs, and professional affiliations.

Webb and Carpenter: Biographical Background

Mary Carpenter (1807–1877) was far better known in her lifetime than was her contemporary Rosamond Webb, and her writing and activism have secured her a place in the histories of British feminism and of educational and prison reform. Her pioneering work is detailed in her best-known books, *Reformatory Schools for the Children of the Perishing and Dangerous Classes* (1851), *Juvenile Delinquents: Their Condition and Treatment* (1853), and *Our Convicts* (1864); they brought Carpenter wide recognition and established her reputation as an authority on the rehabilitation of criminal youth, a category she helped to bring into being.[21] Beyond this, Carpenter's writings on India and her associations with prominent feminists, activists, and cultural critics, including Frances Power Cobbe, Harriet Martineau, and Josephine Butler, have been studied by scholars of Victorian feminism, imperialism, and social-reform movements.[22] The oldest child of Unitarian minister Lant Carpenter, whom Frank Prochaska describes as belonging to "the intellectual aristocracy of English puritanism," Carpenter received an excellent education and ran a successful girls' school with her mother, Anna Penn, beginning in 1829.[23] She never married, but devoted her life to philanthropic work that included founding a visiting society in 1835 to promote the education of impoverished girls, founding a "ragged school" in 1846, founding the Red Lodge reformatory in 1854, advocating for the abolition of US slavery, and founding the Indian National Association in 1870.[24] Through her father, she was introduced to Raja Ram Mohan Roy, a founder of the Brahmo Samaj, shortly before his death in Bristol in 1833. Blending religious and social reform, Roy opposed the caste system and the oppression of women and advocated a modernized, monotheistic Hinduism based on ethical tenets; in this he was influenced by Unitarianism as well as his deep knowledge of Hindu scriptures. Roy's opposition to the forceful imposition of Christianity in India and his commitment to women's education clearly resonated with Carpenter, who after her father's death became, as Clare Midgley notes, "a key repository of memories of Roy's time in England" for members of the Brahmo Samaj who made pilgrimages to Roy's grave in the 1860s.[25] Meetings with these men led Carpenter to write *The Last Days in England of the Rajah Rammohun Roy* (1866); it was around this time that she began to imagine a role for herself in the movement for Indian social reform begun by the Brahmo Samaj. She dedicated *Six Months in India* to the memory of Roy, whom she calls "the great reformer of India, who first excited in the author's mind a desire to benefit his country."[26]

While Carpenter's personal independence and commitment to feminist and progressive causes would appear to differentiate her rather sharply from the low-church evangelical conservatism of Rosamond Webb, Carpenter cannot be seamlessly integrated into a secular (or secularizing) feminist narrative; rather, the circles in which she traveled reflect a high degree of educational and social privilege that allowed her to move among reformers and intellectuals of widely divergent beliefs. Carpenter never professed any dissent from her father's strain of religious thought, and accounts of her life and work routinely mention the depth of her commitment to Unitarianism; Barbara Ramusack calls Carpenter a "devout Christian," while Helen Rappaport observes that "all her life she would remain devoutly religious and dedicated to good works."[27] Carpenter's contemporaries could find her stringent religiosity off-putting; as Sally Mitchell details, Carpenter's friendship with Frances Power Cobbe foundered after Cobbe went to assist her at Red Lodge but found the work overwhelming, the living conditions unbearably severe, and Carpenter's "'stiff and prickly orthodoxy' and her constant references to Christ" uncongenial to her own beliefs.[28] Carpenter's copious use of scriptural references in her writing is notable even when compared to that of her Victorian peers, for whom such language was commonplace; Timothy Larsen has exhaustively documented the extent to which her prose relies rhetorically on biblically inflected, "sermonic" language and biblical quotation to advance forceful arguments in favor of Bible teaching for poor children and reformatory inmates. He further notes that Carpenter's summative late work, *Red Lodge Girls' Reformatory School, Bristol: Its History, Principles and Working*

(1875), remains consistent with her early books in these respects, suggesting that her habits of thought, rhetorical style, and pedagogical program underwent no significant shifts over the course of her career.[29] *Six Months in India*'s argument for secular education thus marks a departure from the practices Carpenter instituted at her British schools, whose students she presumed to be at least nominally Christian. It reflects a gradualist view of Christian influence that she attributes to Roy's teachings, such as his argument in *The Precepts of Jesus: The Guide to Peace and Happiness* (1820) that it would be wiser to expose the Indian people only to the New Testament's most widely applicable moral precepts rather than press them to abandon their faith all at once for "abstruse and difficult doctrines."[30]

On Rosamond Anne (sometimes Rosamund Anna) Webb (1821–1899), the historical record is much thinner; unlike Carpenter's, Webb's family was not prominent, and she spent her entire working life as the paid secretary of the FES. Her career is notable mostly for the ways that she appears to have made her job conform to her vocation, expanding the purview of her paid work until she came to function as the organization's indispensable center. As Rosemary Seton has observed, although the FES's public face was largely male when Webb was hired in 1841, Webb gradually took on a wide range of responsibilities: she corresponded extensively with the FES's agents and toured England to recruit teachers, organize working parties of committee members, and raise funds. Webb's name and home address appear in all of the FES's advertisements, announcements, and listings, and her extensive correspondence with missionary organizations throughout the world reveals the depth of the FES's commitment to interdenominational cooperation among Protestants. When the *Female Missionary Intelligencer* was launched in 1854, Webb became its editor in all but name, and she contributed content as well.[31] It is telling that almost immediately after her death in 1899, the FES ceased to exist as an independent organization and was folded into the Church Missionary Society (CMS).[32] Her obituary, which appeared in the *Female Missionary Intelligencer*'s final issue, notes that "it would be extremely difficult, if not impossible, to find anyone else who could in one person unite the various offices of General, Association, Financial, and Editorial Secretary."[33] It makes no mention, however, of Webb's family, personal history, or life outside the FES.

The FES did not rank among the largest or best-known Victorian missionary organizations, but it was one of the earliest to devote itself exclusively to female education, and it compels attention on other grounds as well: although its London founding is generally attributed to the Reverend David Abeel of the American Reformed Dutch Church, its teachers and students were all women; it was interdenominational and multinational; and its unique organizational structure came to be imitated by other entities later in the century.[34] The FES had little overseas infrastructure but instead recruited and trained unmarried female teachers in Great Britain and placed them with extant Protestant missionary enterprises of several denominations, matching recruits with organizations of their own faith. FES teachers thus represented a new kind of British imperial female presence, resident for professional rather than familial reasons. The FES also sponsored and promoted zenana education, or instruction in the women's quarters of private homes, and provided financial support to Protestant girls' schools in Africa and Asia, several of which were run entirely by women. The *Intelligencer*'s mission statement rehearsed its achievements explicitly in terms of the girls and women it employed and served, as in this example, printed on the last page of the January 1866 issue:

> The Society was established in the year 1834; its sphere of labour includes China, Burmah, India, Ceylon, Mauritius, Africa, and the Levant. The Committee have sent forth 117 qualified European teachers, and have trained 211 native schoolmistresses, now in employment. The work carried on by them comprises Zenana teaching for the ladies of the upper classes; Bible and sewing classes for the poor women; Orphanages, Boarding, Day, Infant, and Ragged schools. There are 269 schools in connection with the Society, containing more than 10,000 scholars.[35]

Not only does this description foreground gender; it also places a dual emphasis on the FES's geographic and social reach. The *Intelligencer* under Webb's direction took care to document its teachers' ongoing efforts to expand their means of outreach across religious and socioeconomic lines.

As the secretary to a missionary organization, Webb followed her father in occupation: born to a farming family in Stalham, Norfolk, Robert Webb moved to London in 1821 and by 1844 was listed as the corresponding secretary for the Moravian Missions London Association. In 1850, his daughter Rosamond is first listed as the assistant secretary of the FES.[36] Little else is known of her; census records reveal that she lived at her parents' home for her entire life, often with several of her six sisters, and that after her father's death she was listed as head of household. Even for the period, the family's fortunes were bound up with the Church of England and missionary endeavors to a notable degree; Rosamond's youngest brother, the family's first university graduate, attended Cambridge and took holy orders; another brother became a vicar. Her sister Ellen's marriage to the Reverend Edward Whately, the son of Richard Whately, Anglican Bishop of Dublin, connected the Webbs to an old and socially prominent family with whom Rosamond had a professional affiliation: Edward's sister Mary Louisa headed a girls' school in Cairo, and her correspondence frequently appeared in the *Intelligencer*.[37]

Rosamond Webb's sole independent publication appeared in 1869, the year her review was published: she edited a volume titled *Historical Notices of Events Occurring Chiefly in the Reign of Charles I*, by Nehemiah Wallington (1598–1658), a London Puritan who had throughout his lifetime kept voluminous personal diaries as well as notebooks in which he documented Royalist malfeasance. Webb's edition, published by Richard Bentley, was derived from her transcription of "a quarto volume of 281 folios"[38] held in the British Library. Its scholarly apparatus includes a lengthy introduction, copious footnotes (many of which identify works of the period from which Wallington quoted without attribution), and original research into Wallington's family records. The amount of time and labor Webb expended on *Historical Notices* must have been enormous. Yet the fact of this book's existence would itself barely qualify as a footnote except that it tends to confirm an impression conveyed by Webb's work for the FES: that she saw herself not merely as a paid employee but as a professional writer, scholar, and critic whose editorial duties both reflected and promoted her beliefs regarding the Christian faith and women's education.

Six Months in India

Carpenter's *Six Months in India* is a hybrid five-hundred-page work that chronicles her tour of Indian schools and concludes with briefs on educational and penal reform. These latter sections stand as the most complete statement of her vision for implementing secular education for Indian women and girls. After the 1866 trip on which *Six Months* was based, Carpenter would travel to India three more times and give many talks outlining her program, but she never substantially revised the plan provided in the book. When read alongside Webb's response, it reveals a number of cultural currents moving beneath the surface of the doctrinal-secular education divide: the education of Indian girls proves bound up with questions of social class, language politics, and gendered forms of indigenous and imperial authority. While Carpenter's overarching point is that replacing missionary schools with secular institutions will enhance the benefit to Indian girls by eliminating the harm of unwelcome religious indoctrination, numerous anecdotes and observations in *Six Months* suggest that imperial educational philanthropy is organized around so many nodes of enablement and violation that eliminating any one is unlikely to transform the system.

For most of volume 1, *Six Months* takes the form of a travelogue, as Carpenter narrates her journeys between Madras, Bombay, and Calcutta. Aided by colonial officials, she gains entrée to schools and prisons, stays at the homes of prominent colonial officials, meets with members of the Brahmo Samaj and their female relatives, and describes the flora, fauna, architecture, and local color that she encounters. Carpenter's previous writings on British prisons demonstrate her skill for sharp observation and shrewd analysis, yet *Six Months* is shaped less by the critical stance of the social reformer than by the well-established conventions of travel literature. All that she sees conforms to the genre's received truths: she finds Indian gardens inferior to those in England,[39] reads in Ahmedabad's buildings the traces of "a very superior race,"[40] now regrettably departed, and generally deplores India's pervasive ignorance, poverty, and idolatry. Carpenter perceives the salutary effects of British influence wherever she goes—not only in normal schools, government institutions, and the judiciary system but even, somewhat surprisingly, in Christian missions. Volume 2 summarizes her "general observations" on Indian culture and offers proposals for reforming its prisons and schools. Chapter 5, "Female Education," outlines her central recommendation, the "establishment of a Female Normal Training School" to supply female teachers. She writes,

> Feeling assured that the Government has hitherto held back from taking this course, not through any apathy respecting female education, but from a desire to be assured that the want is actually felt by enlightened natives, before taking any initiatory steps in the matter, I have, in the Madras and Bombay Presidencies, ascertained that enlightened native gentlemen are most anxious for the establishment of such schools, as they have testified to me in writing.[41]

Carpenter's anxiety to secure the consent of Indian men and her insistence on British governmental oversight correspond to her desire that education be uncoupled from religious instruction, a point to which I return in discussing Webb's review. Having aligned herself repeatedly with the British government's "principle of non-interference with the religion and the social customs of the natives," Carpenter here tacitly acknowledges the potential for violation in any imperial educational scheme.[42] Yet she clearly believes that her system will produce enablement without violation. This emphasis on consent and noninterference as ethical imperatives ironically provides Webb with the means to pick apart Carpenter's entire program. Through a remarkably detailed analysis of three prominent motifs in Carpenter's book—positive descriptions of mission schools, discussions of "idolatry," and elaborations on the question of interference—Webb gradually unravels Carpenter's assumptions that her conception of British education could easily be uncoupled from Christian doctrine and that a secularized system of education would necessarily be purged of coercion.

Although Webb and Carpenter situate themselves rhetorically on opposite sides of an ideological divide, the two antagonists shared many beliefs about the targets of their benevolence, Indian women and girls. While the secularizing aspect of *Six Months* was criticized by many evangelical commentators and lauded by British feminists, missionaries and feminists held strikingly similar (and often similarly misinformed) opinions on the extent, severity, and uniform nature of gendered oppression in India.[43] Anna Johnston observes, "the litany of woes understood to have beset Indian women in traditional society was rehearsed endlessly" in missionary literature, with "child marriage, infanticide (particularly female), *sati*, and widowhood" foremost among them.⁴⁴ Yet feminist magazines such as the *Englishwomen's Review* regularly decried these practices as well. The difference between the two camps lay not in the diagnosis of India's ills but in the cure prescribed for them—secular versus Christian education, with aggressive Anglicization and oversight by British women as common factors. Webb's outrage at Carpenter's critique of Christian education, while predicated on religious doctrine, reveals in addition a strong concern to protect and defend the status and moral authority of the FES. For each woman, the enablement not just of Indian girls but of her own British female cohort was at stake.

Webb's Response to Carpenter

Webb's review of *Six Months* provides both a detailed case study on the question of colonial education as enabling violation and a fascinating specimen of Victorian close reading. Although it is impossible to ascertain the degree to which Webb spoke for herself as well as her employer in any of the writing she produced for the FES, her review of *Six Months*, like all of her published work, appears to reflect a combination of organizational loyalty, authorial ambition, and deep personal commitment. Because no private writing of Webb's has survived, there is no means of determining whether any admixture of personal or corporate animus toward Carpenter or her Unitarianism underlies Webb's often-pointed rhetoric. What the review does convey is a sense of pleasure in its argumentative performance that complicates without undercutting the conviction with which that argument is presented. The attack, in other words, may be heartfelt, but it feels gleeful nonetheless. Webb's strategy is ingenious: rather than confront Carpenter directly, she quotes *Six Months* extensively in order to argue that not only is Carpenter woefully uninformed regarding India, but her writing on religious education is so riven with contradiction as to suggest that she does not know her own mind. Carpenter's *ipsissima verba*, Webb argues, prove that faith-based education for Indian girls is necessary, desirable, and virtually unavoidable.

Unsurprisingly, Webb's central disagreement with Carpenter is the latter's argument that religious instruction both impedes the larger cause of educational access and violates Indian girls' right to doctrinal noninterference. Yet Webb skirts this issue until the final installment, opting instead to undermine Carpenter's case on other grounds. Webb opens by praising *Six Months* for furnishing "much information, useful and practical, from which those, like ourselves, labouring in the same field, might profit largely" and acknowledging the sagacity of Carpenter's observation that "'accounts of India . . . are greatly coloured by the character and views of the narrator . . . [and] what may be true of one part of India is very incorrect of another.'"⁴⁵ The ironic purport of these courtesies soon surfaces, however, as Webb proceeds to attack the book on several related points:

first, Carpenter's cultural and linguistic incompetence, which prevents her from speaking directly to Indian women and forces her to rely heavily on information obtained from (male, educated, English-speaking) members of the Brahmo Samaj;[46] second, her inappropriately congenial relationship with colonial authorities, who appear unexpectedly throughout Carpenter's narrative with unsolicited offers of transportation and lodging, invitations, or letters of introduction, and from whom she blithely anticipates funding and support; third, Carpenter's determined erasure of mission schools, the primary Western educators of Indian girls, from both her sketch of current conditions and her blueprint for reform; fourth, Carpenter's out-of-hand refusal to consider mission-trained Indian women as a solution to what she identifies as India's greatest problem, the lack of female teachers; and finally, as the inevitable result of these combined missteps, Carpenter's regrettable focus on higher-caste women and concomitant failure to see or respond to the constituency to which Imperial Great Britain owes its greatest moral duty: the vast population of poor girls, whom the missionaries alone, in Webb's view, are struggling to educate.[47]

From a twenty-first-century perspective, it is difficult not to sympathize with many aspects of Webb's critique. Webb's motives must certainly have been mixed—Carpenter had been explicitly described as a competitor by the FES[48]—but Carpenter does come across as defensive about her lack of language skills,[49] overly enamored of her Indian interlocutors' mastery of British cultural norms,[50] and surprisingly naïve regarding what she sees as the unalloyed benevolence of the British government and its improving effects on India.[51] The prose in which Carpenter describes her endless round of visits to schools and prisons often feels detached from its context, and she rarely questions or complicates her passing observations, leaving them to stand as apparently unassailable truths. While the rhetorical style favored by women's missionary publications like the *Female Missionary Intelligencer* at times bears an uncomfortable resemblance to Wilkie Collins's memorable parodies of Evangelical prose, it is nevertheless true that when the FES teachers' published letters outstrip the boundaries of those conventions, they do so with an affective force nowhere to be found in Carpenter's narrative. Mrs. Buckley in Orissa, for example, describes an 1867 influx of famine refugees as "walking skeletons"; she continues, "Since the poor children have come to us in larger numbers, I and the elder school-girls have had an anxious and weary time of it. For two months I have not been able to spend a whole night in bed, so severe have been the sufferings of many of the famine children."[52] Affliction and stress inflect correspondence of a more quotidian nature as well: Mrs. Daüble's 1866 list of her sixty-nine charges at the Secundra orphanage notes that three have recently died, while eight are described as "weak," "suffering," or "ailing" from fever; four are blind, and four have lost an eye or the vision in one eye.[53] Carpenter asserts periodically that her role in India is "that of a learner," but she routinely renders imperious condemnations of the "lower orders," as when she expresses dismay at their "unregulated manners, loud discordant jabbering, and insufficient clothing."[54] The FES teachers were by no means immune to such opinions; their reports frequently sound jarring notes of anger, disgust, or frustration. But it is frustration on the ground, expressed by women who were attempting to do the work that Carpenter asserted was most necessary to uplift India's girls and, by extension, India as a whole: not just teaching girls but training them to be teachers.

Perhaps Webb's most devastating charge against Carpenter is that Carpenter disagrees with her own thesis regarding the impropriety of religious instruction. Webb quotes Carpenter at length to make the case that her apparent inability to suppress either her horror of "idolatry" or her belief in the superiority of Christianity severely undercut her claim that instructing Indian children in Christian doctrine violates their universal right to noninterference on religious matters. Carpenter's equivocal position is crystallized in a passage from the conclusion to *Six Months* with which Webb took particular issue:

> Though, as I publicly stated in every place I visited, I value Christianity above all things, as the guide of my life and the spring of my actions—though it is to me the pearl of unspeakable price, and I desire that all should share the privilege I hold so dear—though I believe that the sway of our Divine Master is destined to extend over all the nations of the earth, and that the acceptance of it would prove an inestimable boon to the people of Hindostan,—yet, respecting the individual freedom of every immortal being, as I value my own, I would not, if I could, obtrude my own religion upon them.[55]

Carpenter bases her hesitance regarding religious instruction on a lofty universal principle of "individual freedom," but she continues, "I believe, indeed, that injudicious or obtrusive efforts at the conversion of others, however praiseworthy the zeal which prompts them, hinder the very spirit they are intended to promote, and often arouse a spirit of antagonism, which is most unfavourable to it."[56] Principle here quickly gives way to, or at least aligns tidily with, tactical value; the question of whether any pedagogical program could ever be fully congruent with absolute respect for "individual freedom" never arises. Carpenter closes by attributing these thoughts to Roy and paraphrasing her ally Keshub Chunder Sen, leader of a breakaway Brahmo Samaj faction, to the effect that Christians in India should act as missionaries solely through their good example, "by living out the spirit of [their] religion before the native population."[57]

While Webb reads such equivocations as something akin to hypocrisy, this doubleness in Carpenter's prose may be comprehended less as conscious bad faith than as the inevitable result of an attempt to subordinate her own core beliefs to those of Roy and Sen, the authorities with whom she is most concerned to associate herself. The many moments of contradiction in *Six Months* (to which Webb is preternaturally alert) suggest that the two are ultimately irreconcilable, at least for Carpenter; Webb produces abundant evidence to support her assertion that Carpenter "would, we are persuaded, be among the first to acknowledge that it is to Christianity the nations of the west owe their superiority over those of the east—their civilization, the 'moral precepts' to which they profess allegiance, and, not least, the standing and position of the female sex."[58] Carpenter's private journals, extracts from which were published after her death, tend to support Webb's reading; in 1864, she writes of "going to India to promote the Christian work for the women," and 1866 entries describe her hope of working for "the elevation of women, and perhaps also for the planting of a pure Christianity" in India, and of "carry[ing] Christian sympathy and help" to Indian women.[59] That Carpenter (like Webb) holds Christianity and British culture above all others is evident in her writing, but what this means for India is that the program she proposes merely substitutes cultural conversion as another form of religious conversion. It is the colonization of consciousness by other means, as Webb suggests when she accuses Carpenter of wanting to "impart . . . results, ignoring the source from whence they spring."[60] Seen in this light, Carpenter's rapid acquiescence to the problematic idea that the female relatives of high-caste, British-educated men form the logical starting point for any pedagogical program for girls makes perfect sense, despite the fact that her entire career to this point had been focused on the British poor. Carpenter finds these women charmingly conversant with British culture and, therefore, the ideal subjects for her brand of educational reform.

As further evidence of Carpenter's willful self-delusion, Webb points out that she condemns missionary teaching in the abstract at every turn while delighting over each mission school she visits. This testimony, Webb dryly observes, "is all the more valuable, as being that of a witness who cannot be suspected of any undue bias in favour of missionary proceedings."[61] Yet Carpenter's praise does not address religion specifically—what delights her is that Christianity makes Indian people seem more English, whereas what she calls idolatry makes them appear threateningly foreign to her. She cannot untangle these threads; nor can she comprehend the source of the disgust she feels toward the crowds of impoverished Indians, wholly untouched by Anglicizing influences, that she encounters in public places. On the other side of the question, Webb claims that Christian duty to preach the Gospel is scripturally ordained and therefore cannot, despite Carpenter's assertions, be deemed "improper interference" by any true Christian.[62] Yet Webb insists, in the face of abundant evidence published in her own journal, that "there is nothing like pressure or compulsion to induce a profession of Christianity" in any mission school.[63] This flat denial of violation marks an impasse beyond which the debate cannot advance and exemplifies what Gil Gott has termed the arrested dialectic of imperial humanitarianism.[64]

Conclusion

This deadlock over the terms of enablement and violation articulated by Webb and Carpenter in the late 1860s came increasingly to characterize the larger arena of imperial educational philanthropy in the last quarter of the nineteenth century; perhaps inevitably, neither secular British feminists nor mission teachers gained the level of influence and control that they sought over Indian girls' education. Yet while missionaries' dreams of a Christian India failed to materialize, they played a pivotal role in the education of Indian girls, both directly and indirectly. As Parna Sengupta notes,

> Ultimately it was native Christian women, trained in mission schools, who came to dominate the [Indian] female teaching profession well into the twentieth century. Thus, the decision to expand upper-caste women's education paradoxically created greater educational opportunities for lower-caste, non-Hindu women.[65]

It is probably fair to say that British feminists, including Carpenter, had far less impact overall. Carpenter's biographers concur that her Indian efforts, which raised her profile substantially in England, met with far less success than her British reforms, although they offer different explanations for this failure. Certainly, British feminists arrived late to the scene; mission schools were securely established and Indian feminists and social reformers were beginning to do the very work they had envisioned performing themselves. In Carpenter's case, Webb probably comes as close to the truth as anyone: lacking knowledge and experience in the Indian context, Carpenter aligned herself with the Brahmo Samaj, an elite group so well-positioned to initiate reform within their own community that any aid she could offer was largely superfluous.

What neither Webb nor Carpenter could fully apprehend was that Indian women were themselves by this point advocating for greater educational opportunities both in concert with and independently of the Brahmo Samaj. Webb attenuates the impact of her critique and reveals her own lack of historical foresight by overrelying on her own group of male informants, including Alexander Duff, William Miller, and J. B. Tinling, all of whom she cites copiously in order to discredit not just Carpenter but the Brahmo Samaj, despite its work to promote women's education.[66] In Carpenter's case, the rise of Indian reform movements, including feminist organizations, in the last quarter of the nineteenth century rendered her concern for high-caste women largely unnecessary. Building from the foundations available to them, these women ultimately organized, and educated, themselves.[67]

To be fair, Carpenter tentatively endorses a distant future in which Indians would have greater autonomy, whereas no glimmer of this idea may be found in the *Female Missionary Intelligencer*. Yet in however compromised a fashion, the FES teachers were explicitly educating girls to take their places, preparing for a day when they would no longer be needed. The *Intelligencer* regularly published letters from these "native teachers," and while their carefully constrained prose cannot be said, in Gauri Viswanathan's resonant phrase, to "fragment and disperse the monumentality of the missionary archives,"[68] neither can these women be written out of history as neatly as Carpenter seems to want to do. Her discomfort with the idea of missionary-trained teachers is complicated, however: it stems from her distaste for missionary schools and may be partly class-bound as well, but it also signals her concern that the imposition of religion in the name of enablement constitutes a violation. Yet just as Webb and her fellow FES members could not acknowledge that violation, Carpenter could not perceive or build on the enablement bound up in it, enablement that the Indian teachers assert in their letters and that upper-caste women would readily claim when they sought these instructors for themselves. It is instructive to note that Carpenter deemed mission-trained, low-caste teachers to be tainted for her purposes—the fruit of a poisoned tree, so to speak—whereas the Indian women who wished to procure an education did not. This disjuncture between Carpenter's horror of mission-trained teachers and upper-caste Hindu women's embrace of them tends to confirm Spivak's assertion that every enabling violation exists in a condition of ongoing negotiation, as well as to support her claim that it is therefore necessary to engage in an ongoing consideration of how best to "sustain the enablement with a minimum of violation."[69]

My purpose, however, is not to restage a contest in which it is possible to discern winners and losers but to consider what these factions' insights into their antagonists' practices might suggest about the ways in which we comprehend the theory and practice of philanthropic and development projects in the present. In July of 2013, philanthropist Peter Buffett published an essay in the *New York Times* decrying "philanthropic colonialism," which he defined as the attempt to "solve a local problem . . . with little regard for culture, geography or societal norms"; the same week, *Times* columnist Nicholas Kristof felt compelled to defend "women's empowerment" through education as a noble and necessary global project.[70] We are still, it would seem, getting philanthropy wrong, and in the same ways. What, then, might the example of Carpenter and Webb offer to theorists and practitioners of educational philanthropy who wish to answer Kristof's call to arms without falling into Buffett's error?

For one, their example suggests that the terms of enablement and violation are most readily discernable at the point of ideological intractability. Yet to comprehend these terms often requires that we suspend—at least provisionally—our right to reject bad-faith critiques outright. It seems clear that Webb's review contains elements of turf protecting, professional jealousy, and doctrinal rigidity, but her sharply partisan reading of Carpenter is apposite nonetheless. In Carpenter's case, neither the banality of her brittle, touristic characterizations of India's unpleasant strangeness nor her Manichean rejection of missionaries renders invalid her fear of "improper interference," of ideological zeal misdirecting salutary impulses. Beyond that, their writing allows us to see that the enabling violation is not merely the coinage of a twentieth-century theorist but a concept that existed, long before it was named, as a problem with which educational philanthropists, as well as the objects of their benevolence, struggled. The enabling violation therefore provides a means of productively disrupting binary, either/or judgments without downplaying any real harm done.

A related point concerns the temporality of the enabling violation: the terms of the Webb-Carpenter dispute, which involved not only past harms but potential harms, and the fact that it took place at a time of burgeoning educational initiatives in British-controlled India, point us toward the realization that in the realm of pedagogy, at least, the enabling violation cannot be relegated to the past; it is not a relic of an outworn system that must be dealt with only until it dies out but a perpetual recurrence that appears in both new and familiar guises. Education, especially education that takes place outside the cultural and epistemological frames of reference of both student and teacher, necessarily involves something that is not nonviolent, regardless of whether we call this violation coercion, indoctrination, or epistemic, performative, or structural violence. By acknowledging the inevitability of such violence, and reading it through and against the archive of imperial educational philanthropy, it may be possible to recalibrate and mitigate present and emergent forms of violence, thereby producing from archival violation new forms of enablement.

SUZANNE DALY is Associate Professor of English at the University of Massachusetts Amherst. Her publications include *The Empire Inside: Indian Commodities in Victorian Domestic Novels* and "Food and Drink in the Nineteenth Century," a special issue of *Victorian Literature and Culture*, with coeditor Ross Forman.

Notes

1. Quoted in Millman and Ball, "Parents Defend Arrested Americans."
2. Quoted in Shaikh, "Gayatri Chakravorty Spivak," 176.
3. Quinn, "US Missionaries." For a fuller statement of the case, see King, "Owning Laura Silsby's Shame."

4. Millman and Ball, "Parents Defend Arrested Americans."

5. Charges against all defendants except Silsby were dismissed two months later, after a judge ruled that the children had indeed been voluntarily surrendered, and Silsby was convicted shortly thereafter on a reduced charge but sentenced to time served and released. See Joyce, *The Child Catchers*, chap. 1.

6. Moran, "Kidnapping or Caring?"

7. In Haiti under French rule, Catholicism was the sole legal religion until the 1791 Revolution. A few Protestant missions were established in the nineteenth century (Baptists arrived in 1834, for example, and Episcopalians in 1861), but their sphere of influence was fairly limited until the mid-twentieth century. For recent analyses of their rise to power, see Bellegarde-Smith, "Dynastic Dictatorship"; and Richman, "Voudou State."

8. For discussions of the enabling violation, see, for example, Spivak, *Post-colonial Critic*, 137; Spivak, "Thinking Cultural Questions," 347; Spivak, *Other Asias*, 15, 156.

9. Carpenter, *Six Months in India*; Webb, review of *Six Months in India*. Carpenter's criticism was directed at missionaries in general, not the FES specifically, and although I refer to a "dispute," to my knowledge Carpenter never responded specifically to Webb's review, if indeed she read it.

10. Spivak, "Cultural Talks," 340 (emphasis added).

11. Spivak, *Critique of Postcolonial Reason*, 371.

12. Spivak, *Other Asias*, 15.

13. Shaikh, "Gayatri Chakravorty Spivak," 176.

14. Spivak has also written extensively on her decades of work training teachers in rural West Bengal. For a brief overview of these endeavors, and her founding of the Pares Chandra and Sivani Chakravorty Memorial Rural Education Project, see Jasen, "Winner of Kyoto Prize."

15. Wood, "Despatch." For more on British education, see Müller, Ringer, and Simon, *Modern Education System*, chaps. 3–7. For more on Wood's "Despatch," see Singh and Nath, *Indian Education System*, chap. 6. For overviews of women's education in India in the 1860s, see Basu, "Century and a Half's Journey"; and Forbes, "Education for Women."

16. Frank Prochaska makes this case in his pioneering *Women and Philanthropy in Nineteenth-Century England*. See in particular his introduction, subtitled "Woman's 'Nature and Mission.'"

17. Macaulay, "Minute Recorded in the General Department," 170.

18. Also because—to state the obvious—the FES's religious mission was an abject failure: the mass conversion of Hindus that Webb believed imminent in the 1860s failed to materialize. I am more concerned with aspects of the educational-philanthropic debates that remain unresolved in the present day.

19. Eastside Baptist Church, "New Life Children's Refuge."

20. National Judicial Police Chief Frantz Thermilus, for example, was quoted as saying, "These people would never do something like this in their own country. We must make clear they cannot do such things in ours." Thompson, "Fear for Children."

21. An unsigned obituary in the *Spectator*, for example, calls her "one of the best-known of English philanthropists." Obituary of Mary Carpenter, 747.

22. Prominent studies include Burton, *Burdens of History*, chaps. 1, 4; Jayawardena, *White Woman's Other Burden*, chap. 4; Manton, *Children of the Streets*; Ramusack, "Cultural Missionaries"; and Schupf, "Single Women."

23. Prochaska further notes that "Piety, an exacting sense of obligation, and reforming principles marked the household" in which she grew up. Prochaska, "Carpenter, Mary

(1807– 1877)." Sally Mitchell describes Carpenter as "unusually well-educated." Mitchell, *Frances Power Cobbe*, 102. See also Gordon, "Carpenter, Lant (1780–1840)."

24. Johnson, "Biographical Sketch."
25. Midgley, "Brahmo Samaj of India," 368.
26. Carpenter, *Six Months*, 1:v.
27. Ramusack, "Cultural Missionaries," 121; Rappaport, "Mary Carpenter," 131.
28. Mitchell, *Frances Power Cobbe*, 105. The quotation is from Cobbe, "Personal Recollections."
29. Larsen, *People of One Book*, 157–167.
30. Carpenter, *Six Months*, 2:72. Roy's statement is in the introduction to *Precepts of Jesus*, xxvii–xxviii.
31. Seton, *Western Daughters*, 91.
32. The record of this transfer may be found in the archives of the CMS, which contain all of the FES's records; the archives are held by the University of Birmingham. See Keen, "Part 1."
33. Fox, "In Memoriam," 82.
34. Williamson, *Memoir of the Rev. David Abeel*, 145.
35. Mission statement, n.p.
36. Low, *Metropolitan Charities*, 179; Low, *Charities of London*, 415. Robert Webb's occupation is listed in the 1841 census as "Secretary to an institution" and in the 1871 census as "Secretary to a Religious Institution." His daughter Rosamond's is blank in both, but in the 1881 and 1891 censuses, she is listed as the head of the household and her occupation as "Secretary." I am deeply indebted to Dr. Patricia Bonner for her genealogical research on the Webb and Whately families; the conclusions drawn from that research, and any errors in this account of it, are my own.
37. See Brent, "Whately, Richard (1787–1863)." Brent describes the Whatelys as "a well-connected political and professional family of some distinction." See also Manley, "Whately, Mary Louisa (1824–1889)." Manley notes that Mary Whately founded the first Western school in Egypt for poor Muslim girls and was fluent in Arabic.
38. Webb, "Introduction," xxiii.
39. Carpenter, *Six Months*, 1:39–40, 167.
40. Ibid., 1:35.
41. Ibid., 2:143–144.
42. Ibid., 2:155.
43. An unsigned review of *Six Months* attributed to William Arthur that appeared in the Methodist *London Quarterly Review* in January of 1869, for example, offers a milder version of Webb's central criticisms. See Arthur, review of *Six Months in India*. Kumari Jayawardena and Antoinette Burton, among others, have documented the celebratory response in women's periodicals to the treatises on India's women produced by Carpenter and the feminist social reformers with whom she is typically grouped. For analyses of the feminist response to Carpenter, see Jayawardena, *The White Woman's Other Burden*, chap. 4; and Ramusack, "Cultural Missionaries." As Burton has noted, the tone and content of an 1868 article on "The Position of Women in India" by Mrs. Bayle Bernard in the *Englishwoman's Review*, which quotes extensively and approvingly from Carpenter's *Six Months in India*, are echoed in articles published in a range of women's magazines spanning the next two decades; Burton further observes that "readers of the *Englishwomen's Review* were encouraged to accept [Carpenter's] observations as scientific fact." Burton, *Burdens of History*, 106–108, 110. For more on the question of missionary writing on Indian women, see, for example, Suleri, *Rhetoric of English*

India; Viswanathan, *Masks of Conquest*; Viswanathan, *Outside the Fold*; Nayar, *English Writing and India*, chap. 4; and Johnston, *Missionary Writing and Empire*.

44. Johnston, *Missionary Writing and Empire*, 86.

45. Webb, review of *Six Months in India*, January 1869, pp. 10, 11. The Carpenter quotation is from *Six Months*, 1:16.

46. For a detailed analysis of Carpenter's relationship to the Brahmo Samaj, see Midgley, "Brahmo Samaj of India."

47. Webb, review of *Six Months in India*, September 1869, p. 177.

48. In May of 1868, the following passage appeared in the *Intelligencer*: "E. O. Heywood, Esq., the treasurer, read the report for the past year. It stated that the new educational movement projected in India, in consequence of Miss Carpenter's visit, would be an energetic one, but the committee feared not connected with religion. They therefore urged the giving of increased aid to the Society, whose schools and zenana teaching were based on thorough religious instruction, and where the aim of the teacher was not only to civilize, but also to Christianize." "Home Proceedings: Bath," 77.

49. Carpenter, *Six Months*, 1:23. The FES, on the other hand, took pride in its attention to teachers' language instruction and published essays asserting the importance of speaking vernacular languages.

50. Carpenter, *Six Months*, 1:22.

51. Ibid., 1:62.

52. "Letter from Mrs. Buckley," 51.

53. Daüble, "Our Orphans at Secundra." The former Miss Shaw, Mrs. Daüble was an American who went to Assam with a Baptist mission and became the second wife of Carl Gustav Daüble, a German missionary who served in the CMS. See Murray, "Daüble, Carl Gustav (1832–1893)," 170. She wrote an account of the 1867 cholera outbreak that was published in the CMS's *Church Missionary Gleaner* in 1868. Rev. Daüble is incorrectly listed in some accounts as having died in 1853; he died in 1893.

54. Carpenter, *Six Months*, 1:21, 27.

55. Ibid., 2:216–217.

56. Ibid., 2:217.

57. Ibid. For more on Carpenter's relationship with Chunder Sen, see Burton, *Heart of the Empire*, chap. 1.

58. Webb, review of *Six Months in India*, November 1869, p. 213.

59. Carpenter, *Life and Work*, 236, 245, 246.

60. Webb, review of *Six Months in India*, November 1869, p. 213.

61. Webb, review of *Six Months in India*, October 1869, p. 187.

62. Carpenter, *Six Months*, 1:149; Webb, review of *Six Months in India*, November 1869, p. 213.

63. Webb, review of *Six Months in India*, November 1869, p. 212.

64. Gott, "Imperial Humanitarianism."

65. Sengupta, *Pedagogy for Religion*, 104.

66. For example, Webb quotes the Reverend William Miller's characterization of the Brahmo Samaj as "shallow and superficial." Webb, review of *Six Months in India*, November 1869, 217n. The original quote appears in Miller, *Scottish Missions*, 36.

67. For more on Indian feminism of the period, see Anagol, *Emergence of Feminism*.

68. Viswanathan, *Outside the Fold*, 122.

69. Quoted in Shaikh, "Gayatri Chakravorty Spivak," 176.

70. Buffett, "Charitable-Industrial Complex"; Kristof, "Women as a Force."

Bibliography

Anagol, Padma. *The Emergence of Feminism in India, 1850–1920.* Aldershot, UK: Ashgate, 2005.
Arthur, William. Review of *Six Months in India*, by Mary Carpenter. *London Quarterly Review* 31, no. 62 (1869): 349–369.
Basu, Aparna. "A Century and a Half's Journey: Women's Education in India, 1850s to 2000." In *Women of India: Colonial and Postcolonial Periods*, edited by Bharati Ray, 183–207. New Delhi: Centre for Studies in Civilizations, 2005.
Bellegarde-Smith, Patrick. "Dynastic Dictatorship: The Duvalier Years, 1857–1986." In *Haitian History: New Perspectives*, edited by Alyssa Goldstein Sepinwall, 273–284. New York: Routledge, 2013.
Brent, Richard. "Whately, Richard (1787–1863)." In *Oxford Dictionary of National Biography*, edited by H. C. G. Matthew and Brian Harrison. Oxford: Oxford University Press, 2004. http://www.oxforddnb.com.
Buffett, Peter. "The Charitable-Industrial Complex." *New York Times*, July 26, 2013. http://www.nytimes.com/2013/07/27/opinion/the-charitable-industrial-complex.html.
Burton, Antoinette. *At the Heart of the Empire: Indians and the Colonial Encounter in Late-Victorian Britain.* Berkeley: University of California Press, 1998.
———. *Burdens of History: British Feminists, Indian Women, and Imperial Culture, 1865–1915.* Chapel Hill: University of North Carolina Press, 1994.
Carpenter, J. Estlin. *The Life and Work of Mary Carpenter.* 2nd ed. London: Macmillan, 1881.
Carpenter, Mary. *Juvenile Delinquents: Their Condition and Treatment.* London: W. and F. G. Cash, 1853.
———. *Our Convicts.* London: Longman, Green, Longman, Roberts, and Green, 1864.
———. *Reformatory Schools for the Children of the Perishing and Dangerous Classes.* London: C. Gilpin, 1851.
———. *Six Months in India.* 2 vols. London: Longmans, Green, 1868.
Census Returns of England and Wales, 1841. HO 107/738/11, pp. 41–42. Public Records Office, London.
Census Returns of England and Wales, 1871. RG 10/106, p. 37. Public Records Office, London.
Census Returns of England and Wales, 1881. RG 11/102, p. 4. Public Records Office, London.
Census Returns of England and Wales, 1891. RG 12/72, p. 22. Public Records Office, London.
Cobbe, Frances Power. "Personal Recollections of Mary Carpenter." *Modern Review* 19, no. 2 (1880): 279–300.
Dauble, M. S. "Our Orphans at Secundra." *Female Missionary Intelligencer*, February 1866, pp. 24–27, and March 1866, pp. 37–40.
Eastside Baptist Church. "New Life Children's Refuge: Haitian Orphan Rescue Mission." https://studylib.net/doc/18912891/new-life-children-s-refuge-haitian-orphan-rescue-mission.
Forbes, Geraldine. "Education for Women." In *Women and Social Reform in Modern India: A Reader*, edited by Sumit Sarkar and Tanika Sarkar, 58–77. Bloomington: Indiana University Press, 2008.
Fox, H. E. "In Memoriam: Rosamond Anne Webb." *Female Missionary Intelligencer*, July 1899, pp. 81–82.
Gordon, Alexander. "Carpenter, Lant (1780–1840)." In *Oxford Dictionary of National Biography*, edited by H. C. G. Matthew and Brian Harrison. Oxford: Oxford University Press, 2004. http://www.oxforddnb.com.

Gott, Gil. "Imperial Humanitarianism: History of an Arrested Dialectic." In *Moral Imperialism: A Critical Anthology*, edited by Berta Esperanza Hernández-Truyol, 19–38. New York: New York University Press, 2002.

"Home Proceedings: Bath." *Female Missionary Intelligencer*, May 1868, pp. 74–79.

Jasen, Georgette. "Winner of Kyoto Prize Donates Award Money to Rural Indian Schools." *Columbia News*, December 18, 2012. http://news.columbia.edu/content/winner-kyoto-prize-donates-award-money-rural-indian-schools.

Jayawardena, Kumari. *The White Woman's Other Burden: Western Women and South Asia during British Rule*. New York: Routledge, 1995.

Johnson, Irene Baros. "Mary Carpenter: Biographical Sketch." In *Standing Before Us: Unitarian Universalist Women and Social Reform, 1776–1936*, edited by Dorothy May Emerson, 229–231. Boston: Skinner House, 2000.

Johnston, Anna. *Missionary Writing and Empire, 1800–1860*. Cambridge: Cambridge University Press, 2003.

Joyce, Kathryn. *The Child Catchers: Rescue, Trafficking, and the New Gospel of Adoption*. New York: Public Affairs Press, 2013.

Keen, Rosemary, ed. "Part 1: Society for Promoting Female Education (FES) in China, India and the East, 1834–1899." In *Church Missionary Society Archive, Section II: Missions to Women*. Marlborough, UK: Adam Matthew, 1997.

King, Shani M. "Owning Laura Silsby's Shame: How the Haitian Child Trafficking Scheme Embodies the Western Disregard for the Integrity of Poor Families." *Harvard Human Rights Journal* 25, no. 1 (2012): 1–47.

Kristof, Nicholas. "Women as a Force for Change." *New York Times*, July 31, 2013. http://www.nytimes.com/2013/08/01/opinion/kristof-women-as-a-force-for-change.html.

Larsen, Timothy. *A People of One Book: The Bible and the Victorians*. Oxford: Oxford University Press, 2011.

"Letter from Mrs. Buckley." *Female Missionary Intelligencer*, April 1867, pp. 50–53.

Low, Sampson. *The Charities of London*. London: Sampson Low, 1850.

———. *Metropolitan Charities*. London: Sampson Low, 1844.

Macaulay, Thomas Babington. "Minute Recorded in the General Department, February 2, 1835." In *The Great Indian Education Debate: Documents Relating to the Orientalist-Anglicist Controversy, 1781–1843*, edited by Lynn Zastoupil and Martin Moir, 161–172. Richmond, UK: Curzon Press, 1999.

Manley, Deborah. "Whately, Mary Louisa (1824–1889)." In *Oxford Dictionary of National Biography*, edited by Lawrence Goldman. Oxford: Oxford University Press, 2004. http://www.oxforddnb.com.

Manton, Jo. *Mary Carpenter and the Children of the Streets*. London: Heinemann, 1976.

Midgley, Clare. "Mary Carpenter and the Brahmo Samaj of India: A Transnational Perspective on Social Reform in the Age of Empire." *Women's History Review* 22 (2013): 363–385.

Miller, William. *Scottish Missions in Madras: Two Lectures*. Edinburgh: Andrew Elliot, 1868.

Millman, Joel, and Jeffrey Ball. "Haitians, Parents Defend Arrested Americans." *Wall Street Journal*, February 5, 2010. http://online.wsj.com/news/articles/SB10001424052748704533204575047720443045194.

Mission statement. *Female Missionary Intelligencer*, January 1866.

Mitchell, Sally. *Frances Power Cobbe: Victorian Feminist, Journalist, Reformer*. Charlottesville: University of Virginia Press, 2004.

Moran, Terry. "Kidnapping or Caring? Missionaries in Haiti Tried to Take Children to U.S. after Earthquake." *ABC News*, February 3, 2010. http://abcnews.go.com/WN/haiti-earthquake-american-missionaries-arrested-kidnapping-children-proper/story?id=9736257.

Müller, Detlef, Fritz Ringer, and Brian Simon, eds. *The Rise of the Modern Education System: Structural Change and Social Reproduction, 1870–1920*. Cambridge: Cambridge University Press, 1987.

Murray, Jocelyn. "Daüble, Carl Gustav (1832–1893)." In *Biographical Dictionary of Christian Missions*, edited by Gerald H. Anderson, 170. Grand Rapids, MI: Eerdmans, 1999.

Nayar, Pramod. *English Writing and India, 1600–1920: Colonizing Aesthetics*. New York: Routledge, 2008.

Obituary of Mary Carpenter. *Spectator* 50, no. 2555 (1877): 747.

Prochaska, Frank. "Carpenter, Mary (1807–1877)." In *Oxford Dictionary of National Biography*, edited by Lawrence Goldman. Oxford: Oxford University Press, 2004. http://www.oxforddnb.com.

———. *Women and Philanthropy in Nineteenth-Century England*. Oxford: Oxford University Press, 1980.

Quinn, Ben. "US Missionaries Charged with Child Kidnapping in Haiti." *The Guardian*, February 4, 2010. http://www.theguardian.com/world/2010/feb/04/missionaries-charged-child-kidnapping-haiti.

Ramusack, Barbara. "Cultural Missionaries, Maternal Imperialists, Feminist Allies: British Women Activists in India, 1865–1945." In *Western Women and Imperialism: Complicity and Resistance*, edited by Nupur Chaudhuri and Margaret Strobel, 119–136. Bloomington: Indiana University Press, 1992.

Rappaport, Helen. "Mary Carpenter." In *The Encyclopedia of Women Social Reformers*, vol. 1, edited by Helen Rappaport, 131–133. Santa Barbara, CA: ABC-CLIO, 2001.

Richman, Karen. "The Voudou State and the Protestant Nation: Haiti in the Long Twentieth Century." In *Obeah and Other Powers: The Politics of Caribbean Religion and Healing*, edited by Diana Paton and Maarit Forde, 268–287. Durham, NC: Duke University Press, 2012.

Roy, Rammohun. *The Precepts of Jesus: The Guide to Peace and Happiness*. 2nd ed. London: Unitarian Society, 1824.

Schupf, Harriet Warm. "Single Women and Social Reform in Mid-Nineteenth Century England: The Case of Mary Carpenter." *Victorian Studies* 17, no. 3 (1974): 301–317.

Sengupta, Parna. *Pedagogy for Religion: Missionary Education and the Fashioning of Hindus and Muslims in Bengal*. Berkeley: University of California Press, 2011.

Seton, Rosemary. *Western Daughters in Eastern Lands: British Missionary Women in Asia*. Westport, CT: Praeger, 2013.

Shaikh, Nermeen. "Gayatri Chakravorty Spivak." In *The Present as History: Critical Perspectives on Contemporary Global Power*, 172–202. New York: Columbia University Press, 2007.

Singh, Y. K., and Ruchika Nath. *History of Indian Education System*. New Delhi: A. P. H., 2007.

Spivak, Gayatri Chakravorty. *A Critique of Postcolonial Reason: Toward a History of the Vanishing Present*. Cambridge, MA: Harvard University Press, 1999.

———. "Cultural Talks in the Hot Peace: Revisiting the 'Global Village.'" In *Cosmopolitics: Thinking and Feeling Beyond the Nation*, edited by Pheng Cheah and Bruce Robbins, 329–343. Minneapolis: University of Minnesota Press, 1998.

———. *Other Asias*. Malden, MA: Blackwell, 2008.

———. *The Post-colonial Critic*. New York: Routledge, 1990.

———. "Thinking Cultural Questions in 'Pure' Literary Terms." In *Without Guarantees: In Honour of Stuart Hall*, edited by Paul Gilroy, Lawrence Grossberg, and Angela McRobbie, 335–357. London: Verso, 2000.
Suleri, Sara. *The Rhetoric of English India*. Chicago: University of Chicago Press, 1992.
Thompson, Ginger. "Case Stokes Haiti's Fear for Children, and Itself." *New York Times*, February 2, 2010. http://www.nytimes.com/2010/02/02/world/americas/02orphans.html.
Viswanathan, Gauri. *Masks of Conquest: Literary Study and British Rule in India*. New York: Columbia University Press, 1989.
———. *Outside the Fold: Conversion, Modernity, and Belief*. Princeton, NJ: Princeton University Press, 1998.
Webb, Rosamond. "Introduction." In *Historical Notices of Events Occurring Chiefly in the Reign of Charles I*, edited by Rosamond Webb, ix–lvii. London: Richard Bentley, 1869.
———. Review of *Six Months in India*, by Mary Carpenter. *Female Missionary Intelligencer*, January 1869, pp. 9–16; February 1869, pp. 25–32; March 1869, pp. 40–46; April 1869, pp. 57–63; May 1869, pp. 79–88; July 1869, pp. 136–145; August 1869, pp. 155–164; September 1869, pp. 173–178; October 1869, pp. 187–201; November 1869, pp. 209–218.
Williamson, G. R. *Memoir of the Rev. David Abeel, D.D., Late Missionary to China*. New York: Robert Carter, 1848.
Wood, Sir Charles. "Despatch." In *Selections from Educational Records: 1840–1859*, edited by J. A. Richey, 364–393. 1922. Reprint, New Delhi: Government of India Press, 1965.

4

Urban Reform and the Plight of the Poor in Women's Journalistic Writing

Monika Elbert

> We should study pauperism and crime, as we do any other science, intimately connected with human beings, science, and its laws.
> —Abigail Alcott, "Reports while Visitor to the Poor of Boston" (1849)

R<small>ALPH</small> W<small>ALDO</small> E<small>MERSON</small>'s famous question, "Are they *my* poor?" in the context of his begrudging attitude toward charity in "Self Reliance," is answered with a resounding yes by several women writers who took up the crusade for the poor. Abigail "Abba" Alcott, the mother of Louisa May Alcott, would exemplify the need for charity even when confronting personal privations. In an 1846 journal entry, Abba records, "Our food is simple, our recreations not expensive, and yet I am constantly finding myself involved or perplexed for want of money."[1] Despite her own personal poverty, she became a social worker and missionary to the poor in Boston and considered the plight of the poor as she reported to the Ladies' Aid Society in 1850, "We do a good work when we clothe the poor. We do a better one when we make the way easy for them to clothe themselves. We shall do the best thing when we so arrange society as *to have no Poor*."[2] Adopting transcendentalism's emphasis on individual self-reliance, Abba nonetheless found problems with a political system that stifled the individual. She advised her charitable donors to "do the poor *justice*, and no alms giving would be required. . . . Let us infuse more love into our gift, and it will be doubly blest," and she reprimanded the privileged for not giving enough fair pay: "Employment is needed, but just compensation is more needed."[3] Although she did not become the type of scientific philanthropist who would appear later in the century, a reformer who would put organizations before individuals, she did enlist the support of a social system that would ameliorate the plight of the poor, as evinced in this chapter's epigraph. But she knew from her relation to her reformer husband, the famous transcendentalist Bronson Alcott, that dreaming was not enough. And she would enlighten her brother, Samuel Joseph May, a Unitarian minister who would become increasingly political as a reformer for women's rights and as an abolitionist. Her advice to him was pragmatic: "Oh, dear Sam, we want the Poem, but we must have the Protest."[4] In politicizing the cause, she took away the poetry, moving from aesthetics to action. As Abba's language became increasingly skeptical of sentimentality, she also implored her wealthy benefactors in Boston for immediate relief. Anticipating a time when political action would be stalled by red tape, she lamented to her brother Sam, "Our charitable societies are too complex, the poor are freezing and starving, while wrapped in our sables and picnicking on tea and toast we discuss resolutions."[5]

Abba Alcott was a kindred spirit to Margaret Fuller, who also moved from poetic visions to prose and protest with her eyewitness accounts and her journalistic writings for the *New-York Tribune*. Like Fuller, who would rethink the male transcendentalist clubhouse's focus on extreme individualism and idealism, Abba Alcott was forced to think in practical terms after her husband Bronson's tremendous failure at the transcendentalist utopia, Fruitlands. After witnessing urban poverty, Louisa May Alcott also followed the example of her mother in her reportage from the streets of New York and as her sentimental stories about charitable giving became more acrid. The urban landscape, often in the context of holiday observance, would move all three women reformers to shift from sentimentalism to an activistic, and at times sensational, realism to jar the sleepy eyewitnesses to take action. These key figures of the mid-nineteenth century, especially those with transcendentalist ideals or affiliations, shaped the public's view of the poor and disenfranchised by adopting a journalistic mode— but only after they had witnessed firsthand the suffering of the poor in the urban landscape.[6] Consequently, an emerging transcendentalist politics along with a transformative sentimental aesthetics coalesced for these radical women writers as they observed and responded to the grim realities of urban poverty. Fuller, working for the *New-York Tribune*, became the first female reporter of note in the nineteenth century, but Alcott also took on the role of journalist with her socially conscious correspondence, journals, and fiction.

The Urban Experience

If an increasingly urbanized Boston changed Abba's view of the poor, New York would provide consciousness-raising moments for both Fuller, who had enjoyed a comfortable and sheltered life in Boston teaching gentrified ladies the meaning of transcendentalism at her "Conversations" lectures, and Louisa May Alcott, who had imagined herself downtrodden but genteel as a result of her father's failure to provide for his family. The Alcott transcendental ethic, beatifying the concept of nonownership and economizing to the smallest denominator, simply did not translate to the urban environment. On a personal level, Fuller and Alcott, as observers and as journalists on the streets of New York, experienced a kind of catharsis as they moved from a sentimental concept of poverty to a jarring encounter with the reality of the poor. One could surmise that Fuller's and Alcott's experiences on their own had led them to their heightened state of sensitivity to others' needs. Fuller, in her letters to a would-be lover, James Nathan, exhibited a deep sense of isolation in the city when she wrote, in 1845, "In the city I feel alone among the multitude of men."[7] In her personal journals, Fuller described a deep sense of alienation: she felt like "a wandering Intelligence, driven from spot to spot . . . [and] from home to home."[8] Alcott, though she experienced the glitzy holidays with the wealthy during her short stay in New York, never forgot her humble origins, and her journals show the deep rift between the life of the poor she witnessed and the life of the rich she temporarily indulged in. In both cases, a personal sense of alienation led to introspection and a more proactive approach to the suffering poor.

When Fuller and Alcott depicted the poor and forgotten, sentiment sometimes got the better of them, but both authors quickly replaced a sentimental picture with a horrifying image to challenge the complacent contemporary nineteenth-century reader with a dramatic call for action. They were looking not for tears but for true acts of charity. Margaret Fuller looked forward to a time "when even a few shall dare to" campaign for the poor "with the whole heart."[9] When Fuller and Alcott give us a glimpse of the poor and disenfranchised, it is not in the stark manner of Jacob Riis, who would later barge into the tenement slums, without sympathy and respect, to expose how the other half lives in graphically surreal images of artistic photography. Nor is it maudlin or disempowering sentimentalism.

The views of Fuller and Alcott may initially sound like those of another contemporary female visitor to New York in the 1840s, Lydia Maria Child, but they actually break away from Child's sentimental (and debilitating) view of the poor. Child, for example, shows her bias in assigning a squalid life to a poor vagabond child she observed on the street because of her middle-class prejudices about the downtrodden in society.[10] In her *Letters from New York*, Child predicts a wretched destiny for the four-year-old street urchin selling newspapers, imagining his parents to be drunken sots who would force him to make money, no matter how, to appease their drinking habit. Child descends into a complacent middle-class rant about how a good mother might have saved him and provides the reader with an empty sentimental discourse: "The sweet voice of childhood was prematurely cracked into shrillness by screaming city cries, as he went shivering along. . . . At that moment, one tone like a mother's voice might have wholly changed his earthly destiny; one kind word of friendly counsel might have saved him."[11] Fuller and Alcott rejected such patronizing middle-class responses, although they did imagine a kind of communal mothering to be a palliative for social issues. Child, though a good friend of Fuller's and a staunch proponent of Indian and African American rights, ironically found Fuller's political transformation in New York a bit shocking, especially with Fuller's rewriting of "The Great Lawsuit" (1843) into *Woman in the Nineteenth Century* (1845). Horace Greeley, Fuller's editor at the *New-York Tribune*, encouraged Fuller to rewrite "The Great Lawsuit" after she had witnessed the plight of the urban poor in various settings. Child, who spent time with Fuller in New York, was taken aback by Fuller's book-length manifesto, especially her radical feminism, declaring that "I like it much. . . . It is a *bold* book, I assure you. I should not have dared to have written some things in it, though it would have been safer for me, being married."[12]

Fuller and Alcott's move from an abstract view of poverty toward a more immediate activism plays out as the tale of two spinsters turned reformers, Fuller on the streets of New York, as described above, and Alcott in various urban centers—Boston; Washington, DC (as a Civil War nurse); and New York. Certainly, life as a domestic in Boston provided Alcott with many Gothic images of the plight of the urban poor, and her stint as a Civil War nurse (as she confronted the horrors of the battlefield) was brief, because she contracted typhoid fever and suffered severely from the effects of mercury-containing calomel (and later opiates). During her visit to New York, Alcott witnessed a larger panorama of misery, of which she would be only a small part. While there, she took on the more balanced and objective perspective of an eyewitness reporter who removes herself from the immediate action.

Just as the male transcendentalist counterparts became more proactive, and political, when the horrors of slavery become too clear with the passing of the Fugitive Slave Act by the turncoat Daniel Webster in their beloved Massachusetts statehouse, so too did these sisters and daughters of transcendentalists become more engaged in their roles as reformers on the streets when confronted with the evils of inequality. Not surprisingly, some of the most poignant cityscapes are captured and recorded on holidays—Thanksgiving, Christmas, and the New Year, the times of the year when the middle and upper classes make friendly visits to the poor in the asylums and prisons to bestow gifts on them, perhaps to assuage their own guilty conscience. Emerson himself came to a similar conclusion in his meditation on the holidays, which describes the difficulty "at Christmas and New Year" of "bestowing gifts," since the idea of indebtedness is so disturbing: "It is always so pleasant to be generous, though very vexing to pay debts."[13]

Margaret Fuller's Documentary Charity

If Margaret Fuller's experiences in Transcendentalist New England made her introspective, her life in New York City in the mid-1840s (December 1844–July 1846) marked a growing activism and political consciousness. Here was a real change for the class-conscious editor and armchair reformer of the *Dial*, who led "Conversations" for fine middle-class ladies in Boston in the early 1840s. As editor of the transcendentalist *Dial*, Fuller had theorized about Christian charity in the most abstract utopian terms and published essays that were highly philosophical or geared toward middle-class views of reform. Thus, in the *Dial*, she included various essays about Brook Farm and Fourierism (one, in fact, by transcendentalist Elizabeth Palmer Peabody), about the role of art in society (such as Emerson's "Thoughts on Modern Literature"), as well as some of Bronson Alcott's teachings (including "Orphic Sayings"). Most tellingly, in the July 1843 issue of the *Dial*, Fuller included both her essay "The Great Lawsuit" (growing out of her Conversations) and Emerson's "Gifts," in which a narcissistic image of giving emerges. In the latter essay, Emerson asserts that gifts on a material level are meaningless: "Rings and other jewels are not gifts, but apologies for gifts." (Emerson professes, "The only gift is a portion of thyself. Thou must bleed for me.")[14] Though, as a lapsed Unitarian minister, he gestures to the Christian ideal of self-sacrifice; he does not envision descending into the trenches of an urban landscape to actually promote true giving.

As a journalist in New York City, Fuller witnessed firsthand the atrocities that accompanied a burgeoning industrialization and urbanization. Many of Fuller's writings dating from this period were written for the *New-York Tribune*, edited by the liberal and progressive Greeley. He himself found the socialist reform movements espoused by Fourier and later by Marx beneficial; his idea about poverty was exemplified in such statements as "Morality and religion are but words to those who crouch behind barrels in the street to cut the icy blasts, or fish in the gutters for the means to sustain life."[15] Fuller's articles for his newspaper concern themselves with poverty, charity, and prison and asylum reform, because she visited prisons, almshouses, and orphanages. Her thinking in the New York journalism shows how she evolved from the claustrophobic (and somewhat intellectually provincial), highly personalized, and individualistic view toward reform that is evident in her 1843 treatise "The Great Lawsuit: Man versus Men, Woman versus Women." She moves from an egocentric and highly individualized view that mirrors the perspective of fellow transcendentalists Emerson and Henry David Thoreau to a view that broadly redefines the values of Christian and communal sharing—in her journalistic writings but also in her expanded version of "The Great Lawsuit" in *Woman in the Nineteenth Century*. Indeed, Greeley recognized the power of the revised "Great Lawsuit" in the new and improved version, *Woman in the Nineteenth Century*, which drew its force from urban observations. Greeley gleefully told a fellow editor, "Margaret's book is going to sell. . . . I tell you it has the real stuff in it."[16] The "real stuff" was the misery Fuller witnessed as a reporter for Greeley in New York—in her visits to prisons on Blackwell's Island (now Roosevelt Island), to the prison Sing Sing on the Hudson, and to various prisons, almshouses, and halfway houses throughout the city.

And often the occasion of the holiday, province of the female experience, would lend itself to discussions of matters extending beyond the sanctity of the home—into the world of economic privilege and scarcity. Fuller's and Alcott's holiday writings appearing in various media inevitably culminate in discussions of charitable acts that, they argue, should be practiced all year round.

Though Emerson had solipsistically meditated on the meaning of holiday gift giving and charity in his essay "Gifts," Fuller saw a bigger picture. (As mentioned above, Fuller had actually published Emerson's very middle-class essay on "Gifts" in the July issue of the 1843 volume of the *Dial*.) As a journalist, in many of her *Tribune* essays dealing with holidays ("Thanksgiving," "Christmas," "Valentine's Day," "New Year's Day"), Fuller juxtaposed the happiness of the wealthy with her observations of the lot of the poor to emphasize the need for a more sincere and compassionate sharing. She laments, in the essay "Christmas," the fact that most Americans enjoyed holidays without ever giving a thought to the downtrodden:

> Our Festivals come rather too near together, since we have so few of them; Thanksgiving, Christmas, New Year's Day—and then none again till July. We know not but these four, with the addition of "a day set apart for fasting and prayer," might answer the purposes of rest and edification, as well as a calendar full of saints' days, if they were observed in a better spirit.—But Thanksgiving is devoted to good dinners; Christmas and New Year's Days to making presents and compliments; Fastday to playing at cricket and other games, and the Fourth of July to boasting of the past, rather than to plans how to deserve its benefits and secure its fruits.[17]

Fuller advocated moving beyond the self-indulgent and mundane practices associated with holidays—the sumptuous meals, the ornate gifts, the mindless games, the empty oratory. Surprisingly, she found that the Catholic Church fostered more of an awareness of those on the fringes of society on these holy days. Indeed, she preferred Catholic generosity to the needy and poor to Protestant idealization of self-reliance to the point of self-interest and greed. The Protestant observance of holidays seemed superficial and materialistic to her. In "Christmas," she continues, "The world has never seen arrangements which might more naturally offer good suggestions than those of the Church of Rome."[18] She laments the fact that Protestant Americans had lost the true meaning of Christmas, evoked by the giving spirit of the Magi, the Madonna, and Christ himself, often embodied in the beautiful art and music associated with Catholic religion and wrought by "sublime geniuses."[19]

Discouraged by vacuous American holiday practices that belied the true meaning of Christmas, Fuller asks, "When shall we read of banquets prepared for the halt, the lame and the blind, on the day that is said to have brought *their* friend into the world? When will the children be taught to ask all the cold and ragged little ones, whom they have seen during the day wistfully gazing at the displays in the shop windows, to share the joys of Christmas eve?"[20] She expounds on the positive aspects of Catholic giving—showing how much more generous Catholics are than Protestants—and in the remainder of this article points to true examples of selfless giving, even on the streets of New York. She evokes, for example, the picture of a young, impoverished girl of thirteen, a selfless girl who showed a "Madonna sweetness" in caring for the street children: a group "of poor children . . . she gathered daily to a morning school. She took them from the door-steps and the ditch; she washed their hands and faces; she taught them to read and to sew; and she told them little stories that had delighted her own infancy."[21] Fuller also, ironically, emphasizes the benevolence of the Catholic Church to show a way of ameliorating the ills of the underclass: she alludes to the beneficence of the Madonna, an image she had already used in a radical way in "The Great Lawsuit." In her *Tribune* article, she writes of the "prevalent idea that politeness is too great a luxury to be given to the poor," claiming that "in Catholic countries there is more courtesy, for charity is there a duty, and must be done for God's sake."[22] Though certainly anti-Catholic in her biases against priesthood and superstitious rituals, Fuller found the compassionate but independent quality of her secular version of the Virgin Mary appealing.[23] On the streets of New York, Mary was not simply an icon for middle-class womanhood, but she became the Madonna of the Slums, a beatified version of perfect womanhood that could appear on the faces of the most impoverished.

In her newspaper article "Thanksgiving," Fuller espouses the view that charity must extend beyond the home: "But, if charity begins at home, it must not end there; and while purifying the innermost circle, let us not forget that it depends upon the great circle, and that again on it; that no home can be healthful in which are not cherished seeds of good for the world at large. Thy child, thy brother are given to thee only as an example of what is due from thee to all men."[24] Though some of the "circular" language here seems to be drawn from Emerson's view of the oversoul in his essays "The Over-Soul" and "Circles," it is quite obvious that Emerson's reciprocal feeling toward man in need was defunct, as witnessed in his comment in "Self-Reliance" on the "wicked dollar" he sometimes gave to the begging man and the "miscellaneous charities" he refused to support. Emerson's contrary response to conventional charity in "Self-Reliance" is expressed quite strongly: "Do not tell me, as a good man did to-day, of my obligation to put all men in good situations. Are they *my* poor? I tell thee, thou foolish philanthropist, that I grudge the dollar, the dime, the cent I give to such men as do not belong to me and to whom I do not belong."[25] In Emerson's vehement support of transcendentalist self-reliance and individualism and the Protestant work ethic, he could not condescend to feeling for the poor. Thoreau, too, espoused some of Emerson's views of the poor, not by directly accusing them of creating their own poverty but by aestheticizing his own experience of self-enforced poverty in the "Economy" section of *Walden* (while he still had all the amenities in the settlement of Concord). He was unsympathetic toward—even contemptuous of—the Irish immigrant who worked long hours doing manual labor to provide for his large family. Thoreau, too, felt that it was important to encourage self-reliance, but he was a bit more benevolent in suggesting that true friends would find the meaning of intimacy in giving generously of themselves, in a primeval type of sharing that preceded a Christian sense of duty. In fact, he decries a Christian notion of philanthropy to get back to a simpler, more genuine notion of charity, which would begin at home and not end up in feigned gestures of artificial giving at the almshouse.[26] Moreover, Thoreau felt that a private sense of charity would be more conducive to reform than a mass reform movement: "All the abuses which are the object of reform with the philanthropist . . . are unconsciously amended in the intercourse of Friends."[27]

Fuller, on the other hand, moved from a rather private and personal view of change in "The Great Lawsuit" to an urban, cosmopolitan view of reform in her essays and editorials for Greeley's *New-York Tribune*. While her Boston experience was not necessarily provincial, her New York experience opened her eyes to the plight of all the oppressed (the poor, the handicapped, the immigrants, the prostitutes, the insane, the aged, the convicts). Her visits to various charities, prisons, and asylums in and around New York (and even on the streets of New York) did not lead her to become a Sister of Mercy, but her approach to the poor reflected Catholic sensibilities as she preached the need to ameliorate the plight of the oppressed classes. She became increasingly politically active, something she had not preached so adamantly in "The Great Lawsuit," in which she promoted the transcendentalist view that if one raised one's own consciousness, one would effect change in a roundabout way (by influencing others in personal, not legal or political, terms). In New York she was in the urban landscape, witnessing and testifying to the evils of complacent wealth. Granted, she was harsh on Irish immigrants in New York, who were held back by "their extreme ignorance, their blind devotion to a priesthood, [and] the pliancy in the hands of demagogues," but she lauded them for their hard work in America and forecasted a better day when the children were enlightened through education.[28] She reluctantly tried to remove the stigma of stereotyping, and her pronouncements about the Irish were somewhat less xenophobic than those of Thoreau in his limited environs of

Concord. Fuller's New York experience allowed her to transcend the smallness of thinking associated with New England provinciality and made her go beyond the confines of the personal that she so espoused in "The Great Lawsuit" and even, to some extent, in *Woman in the Nineteenth Century*. Indeed, in her New York views (and reviews) of charity, she was able to join political activism (the traditionally male, public sphere) with compassionate feeling (the traditionally female, private sphere). This raising of her consciousness (an interesting androgynous merging of the spheres she had recommended in *Woman*) in a political context paved the way for her political radicalism in Italy, when she became actively involved in the struggle for the rights of the disenfranchised.

Paula Blanchard, in writing about Fuller's stay in New York, asserts that Fuller had already become politicized before her arrival and critiques the biographers who attribute her more radical views to her time in New York:

> Some biographers have tended to attribute Margaret's apparently new interest in social reform to a sudden enlightenment brought about by Horace Greeley and the squalid realities of the New York streets. What a mercy it was (they imply) that Margaret Fuller escaped from the Never-Never-Land of Boston Transcendentalism into the real world. This is true only to the extent that the massive social problems of the larger city provided a focus for an already developing social consciousness.[29]

Granted, Fuller already had a well-defined philosophy of social change, especially for women, in "The Great Lawsuit," but it was somewhat too spiritualized and too transcendentally idealistic to have real political efficacy. In *Woman in the Nineteenth Century*, she still maintains that women look within themselves before they become political: woman would become more self-reliant by becoming "more a soul ... for nature is perfected through spirit."[30] Fuller did not believe that laws would change women's status but, rather, that "women are the best helpers of one another.... We only ask of men to remove arbitrary barriers.... But I believe it needs that Woman show herself in her native dignity."[31] Fuller calls for women to be social activists by first looking inward and then effecting change for the downtrodden: "Women must leave off asking them [men] and being influenced by them [men], but retire within themselves, and explore the ground-work of life till they find their peculiar secret."[32] Sounding very much like an amalgamation of Emerson and Thoreau, Fuller asserts that women, after a period of hibernation and introspection, would be able to return to society and know how to live peacefully (with their own distinctive voice) among the crowd: "When they come forth again, renovated and baptized, they will know how to turn dross to gold, and will be rich and free though they live in a hut, tranquil if in a crowd."[33]

This earlier attitude toward solitude and social interaction seems too romantically facile for Fuller's New York writing, where introspection gives way to a more active social consciousness, which would allow women to help other women in need. This change in perspective can be seen in Fuller's account of her visit to the women's prison at Sing Sing in *Woman in the Nineteenth Century*. In her typical style, Fuller contrasts the wealthy with the poor, to condemn the materialistic privileged woman: "A little while since I was at one of the most fashionable places of public resort."[34] Here she saw women who "went to their pillows with their heads full of folly, their hearts of jealousy, or gratified vanity.... These were American *ladies*."[35] Of her visit to the women's prison at Sing Sing, she writes, "Soon after, I met a circle of women stamped by society as among the degraded of their sex."[36] Fuller maintains that the wealthy "at the fashionable house" were to blame "for those women being in prison," for their love of opulence and their vanity has been transmitted to the women of the underclass, who envying their finery, have succumbed to theft and prostitution to enjoy the same kind of dress and excitement. Fuller's attitude at the time shows a partially condescending or presumptuous morality, but it also shows Fuller's belief in the redemptive power of maternal love; she advises her middle-class readership to "seek out those degraded women, give them tender sympathy, counsel, employment. *Take the place of mothers*, such as might have saved them originally."[37] The bias that underclass mothers were somehow to blame for their erring daughters replaced the original thought that the opulent fashionable women might be held accountable. In this passage, too, Fuller suggests that these degraded women were, after all, lost. One might make oneself feel good by showing charity, but their degradation could finally not be helped: "If you can do little for those already under the ban of the world,—and the best-considered efforts have often failed, from a want of strength in those unhappy ones to bear up against the sting of shame and the prejudices of the world, which makes them seek oblivion again in their old excitements, you will at least leave a sense of love and justice in their hearts"—and in so doing, these well-meaning middle-class women would "keep spotless" their "own hearts."[38] The suggestion here is that the impoverished are basically immoral; they are addicted to excitement and will seek escape in the pleasures of the world. But in her actual journalistic writing about Sing Sing, this type of smugness recedes: she recalls the image of the female prisoners singing a hymn "with as gentle and resigned an expression as if they were sure of going to sleep in the arms of the pure mother."[39] She then looked forward to acts of "wise and gentle care" that would ameliorate their lives and prepare them for reentry into society.

Fuller seemed haunted by beckoning and beseeching eyes in penitentiaries and in asylums, especially when she made her holiday visits, a practice observed by many benevolent visitors. Citing Emerson's poem "The World-Soul," Fuller moves from the symbolic to the literal in her article "Asylum for Discharged Female Convicts," where she notes, "These pleading eyes, these angels in a stranger's form we meet or seem to meet as we pass through the thoroughfares of this great city. We do not know their names or homes."[40] Fuller expressly points out the injustice of staring at the convicts, poor and insane, as objects or soulless humans in her newspaper article "Our City Charities: Visit to Bellevue Alms House, to the Farm House, the Asylum for the Insane and Penitentiary on Blackwell's Island." She condemns the gaze of the stranger when she visited the almshouse: "We are sorry to see mothers with their newborn infants exposed to the careless scrutiny of male visitors. In the hospital, those who had children scarce a day old were not secure from the gaze of the stranger."[41] She focuses on one young girl in the asylum, "a little Dutch girl, a dwarf," who "had been brought here to New York . . . by some showman and then deserted." She suggests that this girl might have inspired "a thousand poetical images and fictions to the mind of Victor Hugo or Sir Walter Scott," but then she deflates the romantic and idealized image by focusing on realistic details—her misshapen and woebegone appearance. As if to suggest that her scrutiny, like that of the stranger she had just condemned, was disempowered in this haven of horror, she shows that the young dwarf girl was really an entity unto herself, that she could not be deciphered: "No one could communicate with her or know her feelings."[42] Inscrutable, too, were the faces of the children at the Farm School and of the inmates at the Asylum for the Insane. She compares the condition of the inmates at the Asylum for the Insane to that of the inmates at the more progressive asylum at Bloomingdale, "where the insane showed in every way that they felt no violent separation betwixt them and the rest of the world." In the Asylum for the Insane, "the eye, though bewildered, seemed lively." The insane "crouched in corners: they had no eye for the stranger, no heart for hope, no habitual expectations of light."[43] With their eyes unaware of any onlookers, the insane seemed to have locked themselves in a world that remained untouched by the observer, and Fuller found herself looking away from the "poor sufferers" and observing a woman "of high poetical interest." At times, she did lapse into the artist's imagination—of distancing oneself from suffering and aestheticizing the experience: she saw a woman seated in her cell, with "her eyes large, open, fixed and bright with a still fire"; she recounts the story of how this woman had lapsed into insanity while studying to become a nun.[44] To Fuller, she seemed "a figure from which a painter might study for some of his consecrated subjects."[45] But this language of visual pain also strikes me as an early form of photojournalism.

Certainly Margaret Fuller did not share Jacob Riis's predilection, later in the nineteenth century, of intruding into the most desolate homes of the poor to take pictures for photojournalism, which would allow the middle-class and upper-class viewers a panoptic vision of the poor. Though she sometimes lapsed into her earlier condescending or romanticized view of the poor—as, for example, when she discussed the need for the depiction of the "Ideal Poor, which we need for our consolation so long as there must be real poverty" and associated her laundress with "an admirable sample of the . . . class, the Ideal Poor"—for the most part, her sensitivity toward the disempowered in society grew as a result of her New York experience.[46] In her newspaper article "Prevalent Idea That Politeness Is Too Great a Luxury to Be Given to the Poor," Fuller tells an anecdote about an upper-class woman who tried to upbraid a young impoverished boy for taking his charge, a little baby, out into the brisk air with insufficient clothing: "The child, whose only offence consisted in taking care of the little one in public, and answering when he was spoken to, began to shed tears at the accusations thus grossly preferred against him."[47] Quite rightly, Fuller condemns the effrontery and snobbery of the wealthy woman chiding the poor boy. She condemns the entire crowd, who did not come to the rescue of the boy being scolded. Fuller becomes the charitable voice of the crowd as she writes, "Woman! do you suppose, because you wear a handsome shawl, and that boy a patched jacket, that you have any right to speak to him at all, unless he wishes it, far less to prefer against him those rude accusations."[48] Fuller chastises the woman even further: "Your vulgarity is unendurable; leave the place, or alter your manners."[49]

Most of her *Tribune* writings about the poor challenge this misguided approach of instructing and improving the poor. She uses the example of a missionary to the poor who, having attained wisdom in his later years, saw the folly and insensitivity of his ways: "'When I recollect,' said he, 'the freedom with which I entered their houses, inquired into all their affairs, commented on their conduct and disputed their statements I wonder I was never horsewhipped and feel that I ought to have been.'"[50] Though in her *New-York Tribune* essays, Fuller does not show the meddlesome moralistic voice of her earlier accounts of the poor, she does, in fact, still manifest some of her earlier views about how change may emerge. She continues to distrust the bureaucracy of the government, maintaining that political parties are too fickle to effect any real change in charitable institutions: "It is a most crying and shameful evil, which does not belong to our institutions, but is a careless distortion of them, that the men and measures are changed in these institutions with changes from Whig to Democrat, from Democrat to Whig. Churches, Schools, Colleges, the care of the Insane and suffering Poor, should be preserved from the uneasy tossings of this delirium."[51]

Fuller also persisted in her transcendentalist leanings toward self-reliance and the dignity of the individual. She drew on this context in demanding respect for the convict: "The prisoner, too, may become a man. Neither his open nor our secret faults, must utterly dismay us. We will treat him as if he had a soul. We will not dare to hunt him into a beast of prey, or trample him into a serpent."[52] She believed in the power of the heart over the power of politics: "When even a few shall dare" to offer "solicitations on behalf" of the poor, "for only a pure heart can 'avail much' in such prayers—then all shall soon be well."[53] Like Thoreau in "Civil

Disobedience," Fuller believed in the power of one individual to effect change: "If the nation tends to wrong, there are yet present the ten just men," and she persisted in believing in "the light of Conscience."[54] She felt it imperative that society try to redeem even one suffering man: "Is not the hope to save, here and there *one*, worthy of great and persistent exertion and sacrifice?"[55] As a woman with a strong feminist voice, too, Fuller borrowed from her earlier writings to appeal to women on a sentimental level: "See those little girls huddled in a corner, their neglected dress and hair contrasting with some ribbon of cherished finery held fast in a childish hand. Think what 'sweet seventeen' was to you, and what it is to them, and see if you do not wish to aid in any enterprise that gives them a chance of better days."[56] In evoking the memory of the teenage memento, Fuller not only calls on a maternal response to fallen women but also contrasts their own happy adolescence, thus effecting change through an appeal to the sentiments and emotions of women.

Finally, one might wonder what personal kinship Fuller had with New York, especially as it appears in many of her journalistic writings as a quagmire of social ills and disease. In her article "The Rich Man—an Ideal Sketch," Fuller imagines walking through the city with "the sight of spacious and expensive dwelling houses now in process of building" and entertaining the reverie of an enlightened merchant, the new American aristocracy, who cares for the poor and disenfranchised, but her reverie ends with the all-too-real shriek of a "ragged, half-starved little street sweep," begging, "Please ye give me a penny." With that, Fuller's utopian dream is abruptly interrupted: "The fancied cradle of the American Utopia receded or rather proceeded fifty years at least into the Future."[57] But she also felt that New York was most suited to the experiment of American democracy, ironically enough, because of the magnitude of need felt by the impoverished: "We hope to see the two thousand poor people, and the poor children, better situated in their new abode, when we visit them again.... There is no reason why New-York should not become a model for other states in these things. There is wealth enough, intelligence, and good desire enough, and *surely, need enough*."[58] Interestingly, it was not the current predicament of New York that interested her but rather the possibilities it offered because of its desperate state: "If she be not the best cared for city in the world, she threatens to surpass in corruption London and Paris. Such bane as is constantly poured into her veins demands powerful antidotes."[59] In this realistic appraisal of the state of New York, I hear a vague transcendentalist murmur that brings me back to Thoreau's idyllic life at Walden Pond and his apocalyptic message at the end of *Walden* about forthcoming change and transformation for the better: "If we have had the seven-years' itch, we have not seen the seventeen-year locust in Concord."[60] The shrill screams of begging and vagrant children held as much promise for Fuller as did the locusts of Concord for Thoreau. Out of the urban horror, a better life might emerge.

Louisa May Alcott's Public Charity and Personal Poverty

Although Fuller's professional transformation went from hosting idealistic transcendentalist conversations to writing benevolent but scathing journalistic commentary, Alcott never toed the party line as a result of her early unhappy encounter with the New England movement. As the daughter of famed but impractical transcendentalist Bronson Alcott, Louisa May Alcott knew from her firsthand experience the meaning of genteel poverty. Her father, an economic failure as a transcendentalist reformer and creator of the utopian Fruitlands, nonetheless inculcated values of empathy and charity in his four daughters. Moreover, Louisa's mother Abba served as a type of early social worker for the poor in Boston—and she indoctrinated her daughters with the need for giving on a practical level to both family and society. Louisa herself had to hire herself out as teacher and domestic and finally was forced to write to compensate for her father's mismanagement of money. But even early on, Louisa was quite aware of the distinction between public charity and personal poverty—always placing herself in her imagination as the benevolent donor. For example, at the age of eleven, while at Fruitlands, Alcott wrote about a "lesson" taught her by the girls' tutor Charles Lane in his reading of a story, "The Judicious Father." The young Alcott described the story and its effect on her as follows:

> How a rich girl told a poor girl not to look over the fence at the flowers, and was cross to her because she was unhappy. The father heard her do it, and made the girls change clothes. The poor one was glad to do it, and he told her to keep them. But the rich one was very sad, for she had to wear the old ones a week and after that she was good to shabby girls.[61]

Alcott's response to the story is most stunning, as she placed herself not in the role of the poor child, though she and her family were starving at Fruitlands, but in the role of the charitable donor. Moralizing about the story, she declared, "I liked it very much, and I shall be kind to poor people." The next day, the antislavery reformer Parker Pillsbury arrived, and Alcott put herself again in the role of the sympathetic onlooker: "We talked about the poor slaves."[62] Several days later, she voiced her unhappiness about the family's poverty, declaring, after he read a story about "Contentment," "I wish I was rich, I was good, and we were all a happy family this day."[63] In expressing her discontentment about the family plight to her mother, Louisa learned a lesson: "Mother often says if we are not contented with what we have got, it will be taken away from us."[64]

Alcott, living with her family in genteel poverty, was in the awkward and contradictory position of feeling entitled but living a less than privileged life. She was obsessed with the lack of money from an early age and lamented having to be a seamstress, companion, governess, teacher, and domestic in various notebook entries and letters. In 1852, her mother, as a social worker, opened an "intelligence office" (or employment office) for wayward girls seeking domestic employment in Boston: the idea "grew out of her city missionary work and a desire to find places for good girls. It was not fit work for her, but it paid, and she always did what came to her in the way of duty or charity, and let pride, taste, and comfort suffer for love's sake."[65] Alcott, when she wrote this entry, was aware of the dire financial straits in which her family lived and appreciated her father's meager attempts at moneymaking ("father wrote and talked when he could get classes or conversations") and her mother's steadfastness in keeping the family together. During their Boston residence in the early 1850s, Louisa was also acutely aware of the sisters' part in staving off pauperism: "Anna and I taught. Lizzie was our little housekeeper,—our angel in a cellar kitchen, May went to school." Nonetheless, Alcott perceived the family as happy, even with, or perhaps because of, the frequent visits from the impoverished and desperate: "Our poor little home had much love and happiness in it, and was a shelter for lost girls, abused wives, friendless children, and weak or wicked men." The family deemed itself respectable because it was following its Christian path of helping others, even though they themselves had nothing: "Father and Mother had no money to give, but gave them sympathy, help, and if blessings would make them rich, they would be millionaires. This is practical Christianity."[66] In this same journal entry, Louisa wrote of the thrill of being paid for the publication of her first story, "The Rival Painters." Indeed, all of her meticulous end-of-the-year accounts in her journals would hereafter point proudly to the money she made during any given year. Still, she was tormented by the lowly positions, as housekeeper or seamstress, she had to accept, and was keenly aware of her father's failure as breadwinner: "Father idle, mother at work in the office. Nan and I governessing. Lizzie in the kitchen."[67]

Though she voiced her displeasure about being poor, and even worried about poverty once she was financially secure as an author, she often put herself in the role of benefactress. When she began to earn money as a writer, the listings she recorded of her earnings show the precarious financial situation in which she found herself and her family. Thus, she recorded gleefully in an early 1868 entry that she had earned $1,000 in 1867, having published thirty-seven stories and that she had "paid [her] own way, sent home some, paid up debts, and helped May."[68] Later that month, she lamented the fact that she had not written enough and made a curious statement that instead of writing, she had given up her time to charity, for a New England Suffrage Association: "Acting for charity upsets my work. The change is good for me, and so I do it, and because I have no money to give."[69] By late February 1868, Alcott was more at peace with herself, having written eighteen stories and accomplishing much editorial work, but she also applauded herself in a journal entry of February 28, 1868, for performing twelve times as an actress for charity. Although Alcott enjoyed bestowing gifts on her parents and family members, she also lamented, "I never seem to have many presents, as some do, though I give a good many."[70] Alcott finally moved from a solipsistic version of "poor me" to an appreciation of how the other half lives, although the idea of the domestic merging with the political is strong in her journal writing of the 1860s, as it is in her most famous novel, *Little Women* (1868–1869).

Alcott is at her best when she is moved to write after being politically engaged. For example, though she served as a Civil War nurse in Washington, DC (from December 1862 through January 1863, when she fell ill and returned to Concord), her writing of *Hospital Sketches* served her political cause more so than her unsuccessful stint at nursing. Though she published some of the sketches for the abolitionist magazine *Boston Commonwealth* in 1863, she later reissued the collection as a book, more to make money than in response to anything in post–Civil War 1868. She speaks of appeasing the potential book buyers: "By taking out all Biblical allusions, and softening all allusions to rebs, the book may be made 'quite perfect,' I am told. Anything to suit customers."[71] Alcott has an extraordinary way of combining the vernacular-domestic with the national-political realms: in a journal entry for January 22, 1868, she laments the fact that her bonnet has been damaged but proceeds to "make another in the P.M." and attends in the evening the "Antislavery Festival," where she meets politically minded colleagues, "all the old faces and many new." She celebrates her political persona after attending the annual meeting of the Massachusetts Antislavery Society; in her daily journal writing, she asserts, "Glad I have lived in the time of this great movement, and known the heroes so well. War time suits me, as I am a fighting *May*."[72] Just so, the gentrified Fuller moved from the parochial circle of women acolytes in her Boston Conversations to witness the stunning poverty of fallen and struggling women in New York, women who would not have had the luxury of savoring her lectures or been able to heed the advice given to middle-class women who could practice a modicum of self-reliance after reading her *Woman in the Nineteenth Century*. Both Fuller and Alcott moved from an inordinate sense of self to compassion for others in their transformation as witnesses to urban poverty.[73] Part of this transformation occurred as they incorporated a maternal sense of charity into their encounters with those women they saw almost as their own fallen daughters.

Elizabeth Palmer Peabody, a leading (female) intellectual of the transcendentalist circle, asserted in a letter to Alcott, expressing condolences at her mother's death: "Gifted by God with your mother's heart and your father's ideality you united them in yourself, and saw them both in God's idea of them."[74] Alcott captured these two competing impulses: if her mother represented the reform impulse at a communal level, and the heart of Christian charity, Bronson Alcott represented a larger, more collective, and more abstract vision of improvement for humankind through his transcendentalist philosophy. Peabody admitted she preferred the realistic mode Louisa inherited from her mother: "I do not think I ever enjoyed anybody's fictions as I have enjoyed *yours*. I have enjoyed it in imaginative sympathy with both your father and your mother,—but especially with the *latter* because she did not forecast the 'all is well'! as your imaginative father could do."[75] Peabody recognized the split between Alcott the romantic and Alcott the realist. In fact, Peabody, ever the social reformer and realist, became the surrogate for the now-defunct phantom mother, the representative ideal reader, who praised a like-minded daughter of her own imagination for her realistic appraisal of life; Peabody's commendation of a mother who did not "forecast the 'all is well'" points to a central value in Alcott's fiction, where her endings never espouse a (totally) happy but untrue conclusion.

Publishing *Little Women* in 1868 was a real coup for Alcott in terms of prestige and financial success, as it brought her family out of poverty. Ironically, this book, inspired by her own life as a gentrified poor inhabitant of Concord, was her "romance about charity," as Julia Ward Howe might have described it (in terms of her husband's charity toward the blind and disabled)—the kind that would "easily interest the public."[76] And just as easy charity occurs on holidays, the opening of Alcott's *Little Women* focuses on the occasion of a holiday: the March girls discuss the desire to get the perfect Christmas gift for their mother, while Marmee teaches them the real lesson of charitable giving, in terms of helping those in most need. Nevertheless, the book reveals Alcott's ambivalence toward the poor—a sympathy mixed with condescension. In *Little Women*, the Hummels, the poor German immigrant family, are the source of illness for the charitable March family (because the March family are being a bit too charitable) and epitomize a certain social pestilence. They are inadvertently the cause of Beth's scarlet fever and subsequent death; it is Beth who witnesses the death of the baby in the squalid Hummel home and who most definitely is scarred emotionally and physically for the remainder of her life. Marmee is concerned since Beth, now an invalid, sings sad songs and obsesses about dead babies. Because Beth has been directly touched by the condition of the Hummels' poverty, she cannot be released from the web of poverty. In the meantime, Amy, the spoiled daughter, can make light of the Hummels' poverty as she laments a failed dinner when her friends did not appear. Left with a surfeit of food after two days of eating salad and ice cream, Amy is sick of the food and wants to bring it to the Germans, for, as she condescendingly declares, they like "that kind of mess." Amy gives the injunction, "Bundle everything into a basket and send it to the Hummels; Germans like messes. I'm sick of the sight of this, and there's no reason you should all die of a surfeit because I've been a fool."[77] Thus, the poor immigrants become the waste receptacle for superficial Amy, who still, at this juncture, needs to learn the true meaning of charity.

It may be that Alcott was trying to distance herself from her own childhood of poverty when she cast off her fictional poor in favor of the well-behaved middle-class protagonist or reader, or that it was cathartic to think of herself as a redemptive figure, even though she was only a step above those poor people she would help; the latter attitude is certainly evident in her visit to the poor orphans at Randall's Island in New York. As Peter Stoneley notes, "Alcott explores the drama of poverty from a middle-class point of view. She uses her fiction to re-delineate the social boundaries that her real family was in danger of blurring."[78]

However, there is some ambivalence in Alcott's treatment of the poor in her private (candid) writings, her (sentimental) fiction, and her journalistic nonfiction, and these attitudes toward charity, as I show, reflect her conventional (and contradictory) views toward the poor. In the summer of 1875, she recorded in her notebooks, with some disdain, "Kept house at home, with two Irish incapables to trot after."[79] Shortly after, Alcott travelled to a Woman's Congress in Syracuse, where Julia Ward Howe was in attendance and sang the "Battle Hymn of the Republic," and where questions of social inequality were discussed.[80] Howe had become a social activist in 1868 and had campaigned for the women's suffrage movement (first, in the New England Suffrage Association).[81] Alcott, too, became increasingly aware of the power of organized charity. Theory became practice when she went to New York in the fall, making a "friendly visit" to the orphanage and asylum on Randall's Island on Christmas day, 1875, a common practice for well-meaning citizens during the holidays.[82] Alcott wrote a letter to her family in Concord and, with great aplomb, declared, "I've had a good variety of Christmases in my day, but never one like this before."[83] The spectacle appeal of observing those beneath one is all too apparent in her observations, but, in her letters to her family, she also assumed her journalistic voice. At the hospital, her "heart-ache began," but her sympathy was tinged with a popular judgmental view. She moralized that the handicapped babies were "born of want and sin, suffering every sort of deformity, disease, and pain." Alcott felt privileged that the children took her for the "mayoress," who had been expected, and then reveled in her charitable acts of giving candy and dolls to the orphaned and sick children. In visiting "the idiot house," she seemed enthralled that one addled French girl singing the "Marseillaise" "was so overcome by her new doll that she had an epileptic fit on the spot." After giving away two hundred dolls "and a soap-box of candy," Alcott was delighted that the children's "sticky faces beamed" at her and her Quaker guide and waved after them as if they were "angels who had showered goodies on the poor souls." Indeed, Alcott looked forward to visiting the Tombs, a New York City prison, with her guide on New Year's, for, she explained, "I like this [type of friendly visit] better than parties, etc."

Though not purposely dehumanizing, her private discourse, nonetheless, made the visit to the poor a dramatic spectacle, where she played the part of the beneficent lady. Yet the reality of visiting the Tombs resulted in a jarring account of prison life in an expository essay in the children's magazine, the *Youth's Companion*. In "A Visit to the Tombs," a narrative hardly appropriate for a children's periodical, Alcott describes the horrors of the prison. When Alcott received her visiting pass and went further into the depths of the prison, she witnessed the presence of a sick inmate, whose cries for help prompted his removal to the hospital, and Alcott was assured, in a macabre way, "that for him captivity was nearly over."[84] The most horrifying vignette is the final one, in which a heartbroken woman finds out that her beloved husband has been sentenced to prison, and Alcott describes the impending death of the husband as not half as terrifying as the reaction of the wife, who, knowing the impending doom, breaks "into passionate weeping."[85]

Between ornate parties and visits with the well-to-do in New York, Alcott witnessed hard times—in the intense moments that brought her face to face with the poor immigrants, disenfranchised workers, and fallen women who were not part of Concord's privileged landscape of gentrified poor and not part of the New York elite. Though Alcott's juvenile fiction about charity is fairly conservative, especially her Christmas stories, her nonfiction essays on holiday visiting are more strident in their attack on the empowered wealthy who were responsible for the plight of the poor.[86] Indeed, her "A New Way to Spend Christmas" (published in the *Youth's Companion* in March 1876), based on her visit to Randall's Island in New York, angrily decries a system that oppressed so many, especially its children. It is clearly a revision of the more careless tone of her private writing (described above): "Blackwell's Island is full of hospitals, alms and workhouses; Wards has a hospital for immigrants, a mental asylum, and the Potter's Field, but Randall's is devoted to children."[87] Her exposé is as scathing an attack as that of Fuller's description of Sing Sing and Fanny Fern's account of Blackwell's Island.[88] Of the forty girls she observed, thirty-one were suffering from the "blight of poverty" quite visibly—with defective eyes, deformities, and handicaps. Alcott occasionally resorted to sentimentalizing in describing her desire to help: "I longed to take these young creatures into some safe corner to grow up in the sunshine and pure air they needed."[89] Perhaps this sentiment is related to her transcendentalist upbringing in and appreciation of nature and to her revered mother's sense of nurturing.

Alcott's tone throughout the published sketch is naturalistic and biting, more sentimental than in her self-aggrandizing epistolary jottings. For example, she wanted to give a doll to one of the ailing bandaged children, but "there was no hand to grasp it." The girl moaned continuously and seemed to be "cursed with inherited afflictions too dreadful to describe." She could not even eat "bonbons," "for in that mouth even sweets were bitter."[90] The suffering of the poor is not glossed over in this account, even though the audience was the same as that of her other, tamer, children's fiction. She does highlight the good, charitable people who made visits to the poor, and especially Mrs. Gibbons: "For thirty years has the lady who led our party . . . visited the poor children in these various refuges, taking upon herself the duty of seeing that this holiday is not forgotten but kept as it should be, with goodies, gifts, kind words, and a motherly face to make sunshine in a shady place." She almost makes this woman a saint: "There seemed to be a sort of halo 'round the little black bonnet' of this woman who led the party to the orphanage."[91]

Alcott's observation of the very maternal Mrs. Gibbons, the reformer on Randall's Island, inspired her book *Rose in Bloom*, on the question of charity and reform. The passage below is one of the more positive commentaries about reform from the novel, which I contend could not have been written without Alcott's experience witnessing the pain on the streets of New York. The protagonist, the orphan Rose, ultimately finds her calling working for the disenfranchised, and she finds herself "moved and inspired" by her avuncular guardian Dr. Alec's good works for the poor and needy. Enlightened by his brush with death, she recalls "the sight of some good man's patient labor for the poorest of his kind," and she can finally appreciate her own gift of giving toward the conclusion of the narrative.

> If Rose had ever felt that the gift of living for others was a poor one, she saw now how beautiful and blessed it was, how rich the returns, how wide the influence, how much more precious the tender tie which knit so many hearts together than any breath of fame or brilliant talent that dazzled but did not win and warm. . . . Her heroes ceased to be the world's favorites and became such as Garrison fighting for his chosen people; Howe restoring lost senses to the deaf, the dumb, and blind; Sumner unbribable, when other men were bought and sold and many a large-hearted woman working as quietly as Abby Gibbons, who for thirty years had made Christmas merry for two hundred little paupers in a city almshouse, besides saving Magdalens and teaching convicts.[92]

Here Alcott includes a list of reformers and champions for the poor—William Lloyd Garrison, who had promoted emancipation for slaves and for women, and William Graham Sumner, who advocated a spirit of cooperation between the social classes. Focusing on Abby Gibbons in this context is most striking here: she becomes the personification of the Christmas spirit that Fuller had recognized as the proper source of Christian charity all year round and the individual that Alcott had most praised in her account of reform on the streets of New York. It is not surprising that Alcott brings up another exemplar of true charity in this passage, toward the end of *Rose in Bloom*: Samuel Howe, who established a school for the deaf and blind. As Howe's wife, the feminist spokesperson Julia Ward Howe, had recognized, charity required more toil than show: "The romance of charity easily interests the public. Its laborious details and duties repel and weary the many, and find fitting ministers only in a few spirits of rare and untiring benevolence."[93] Rose's guardian, Dr. Alec, is the personification of Christian charity in *Rose in Bloom*, although, as in *Little Women*, with the Hummel episode, there is a rampant fear in this book that foreign refugees will bring pestilence to the community. We hear that Alec has caught a "bad malignant fever" from some "poor emigrants whom he met wandering about quite forlorn in a strange city. He understood Portuguese and sent them to a proper place when they had told their story."[94] Although Dr. Alec lives and inspires his ward Rose to carry on with his good works, the idea that the outsider immigrant is the cause of social woes is a common thread in several of Alcott's novels. But if the novel depicts a happy ending and the "romance of charity," for the benevolent donor, Alcott's images of the urban poor on the streets of New York in her journalistic fiction convey a different story.

Sarah Elbert points out how "the vivid contrast between fashionable drawing rooms and Randall's Island became the focus for *Rose in Bloom*," the idea for which was brewing during Alcott's stay in New York.[95] In this 1876 sequel to *Eight Cousins*, Phebe, the erstwhile poor child, the servant in her aunts' household, becomes the famous singer, and Rose, the moneyed child, becomes less empowered, as she ventures into the business of charity. Although both are orphans, Rose has money because of an inheritance from her deceased parents. Thus, the tables are turned as the poor servant wins the upper hand, and the mistress she serves seems less fortunate. It may be that Alcott wanted to show that both are from similar backgrounds, as orphans, and that in romanticizing the poor beautiful orphan in the shape of Phebe, who even marries one of the Campbell clan, she is buying into the aestheticization of poverty—and its concomitant anestheticization of the reading audience (with its hunger for the "romance of charity").

Strangely, Rose becomes a professional philanthropist precisely because she has no creative talents (perhaps this is Alcott's ultimate critique of the philanthropist-reformer type), and even though her Uncle Alec teaches her about the value of servitude and duty—to "do good for its own sake"—one feels an emptiness in Rose as compared to Phebe, at least throughout the first two thirds of the narrative.[96] The sisterhood does not seem totally fair or equal, and when Rose finally devotes herself to various charitable causes, as in the betterment of the "Home for Decayed Gentlewomen," she realizes the drudgery involved in such work: "I didn't expect to make anything out of it, but I did think they would be grateful."[97] The ingratitude of the poor initially bothers Rose, but when she takes up individual projects, especially with orphan children whose destinies she can form, she feels more fulfilled. Thus, she adopts a child, whom she dubs Dulce, whose mother is deceased and whose father is a convict in prison, with the same fervor that she has trained the orphan Phebe earlier; as Mac tells her, "I'm sure

Phebe has turned out splendidly, and you began very early with her."[98] However, Rose feels as if it will be a harder chore bringing up Dulce to be a good woman, since she has the father's wicked past as her legacy. Indeed, it is almost as if she cannot live down her unfortunate past as the idea of nature overcomes nurture. Dulce is not the "pretty" poor child worshipped in sentimental children's stories. Instead, she is described as "a pale, pensive little creature, always creeping into corners and looking timidly out, as if asking leave to live." She lacks the resilience and energy of beautiful Phebe; we hear that this orphan "did not grow pretty and never was a gay, attractive child, for she seemed to have been born in sorrow and brought up in misery."[99]

Ultimately, Alcott shows that knowing the pain of poverty allows one to be more empathic toward those who are suffering—clear evidence of Alcott's own growing empathy toward the poor. And Rose, after being touched by her Uncle Alec's righteous life as a benevolent doctor and generous donor to the poor, reconstructs her life so that she considers charity as noble a vocation as art, which she has envied in the songstress Phebe. As her reward for her increased social awareness, she is awarded, at the end of the narrative, with a husband, who has a poetic vision of justice. Her cousin Mac appears to be an odd combination of Thoreau and Emerson, as he wants to initially just read books, but when he comes into his own, he becomes the "Poet" that Emerson had in mind as the harbinger of change. Mac is seen carrying around copies of *A Week on the Concord and Merrimack Rivers* as well as *Walden* and spewing out gems of truth to Rose. In fact, he encourages Rose to read both Thoreau and Emerson and especially to focus on four of Emerson's essays. Mac inspires Rose, who had felt too simple to read the transcendentalists, to read several of Emerson's essays. Not surprisingly, the sensitive Rose, with her maternal instincts, prefers Emerson's softer essays about giving, "Love" and "Friendship," rather than the more aggressively masculine ones Mac most admired, "Heroism" and "Self-Reliance."[100] Though Alcott is clearly not as revolutionary as Fuller in her notions about charity, she does show that the maternal aspect in women should be celebrated as the giving spirit that holds society and families together (and with that, Rose is blessed with a poetic husband).

Several years after their respective visits to New York, both Fuller and Alcott would take on maternal roles, Fuller as mother of her biological child and Alcott with the responsibility of caring for her deceased sister May's child. However, both women continued to act with agency as they were committed to remaining political and charitable, in the broader sense: Fuller fighting the good fight in the Italian Revolution, and Alcott campaigning for women's rights, such as suffrage. They were perhaps among the first feminists who could make the personal political. It was almost as if these two women were destined for greatness because of their charitable predispositions.

A phrenologist, studying Alcott's head during the November when Alcott resided in New York, reported that she was special, that she manifested "faith, hope, and charity, especially the latter."[101] If Alcott's early life taught her to be charitable and grateful, her later years—with the time spent in New York, and later still in Concord during the centennial preparations—would find her more politically vigilant, as she looked forward to the day when the "tax-paying women of Concord" and fellow Concordians would "utter another protest that shall be 'heard round the world.'"[102] Greeley also addressed Fuller's universal appeal in a tribute to Fuller after her tragic death. It speaks in Fuller's favor that many of the local charities had garnered support through Fuller's efforts: "For every effort to limit vice, ignorance, and misery, she had a ready eager ear, and a willing hand; so that her charities—large in proportion to her slender means—were signally enhanced by the fitness and fullness of her wise and generous counsel."[103] Greeley duly noted the power of her pen: "I doubt that our various benevolent and reformatory associations had . . . ever since, received such wise, discriminating commendation to the favour of the rich, as they did from her pen during her connection with the *Tribune*."[104] The secret of her power, as Greeley testified, was that she always saw herself in the "outcasts of [her] sex." She had defended the women at a Prison Association meeting in true charitable Christian fashion, by insisting on their commonality: "As women like myself, save that they are victims of wrong and misfortune."[105]

MONIKA ELBERT is Professor of English and University Distinguished Scholar at Montclair State University. She is coeditor of two recent collections of essays: *Romantic Education in Nineteenth-Century American Literature: National and Transatlantic Contexts* and *Transnational Gothic: Literary and Social Exchanges in the Long Nineteenth Century*.

Notes

1. Alcott, *My Heart is Boundless*, 149.
2. Ibid., 177 (emphasis in original).
3. Ibid., 170, 178 (emphasis in original).
4. Ibid., 144. Meanwhile, many of the male reformers believed that the poem would still move men to action, as noted in Emerson's and Whitman's call for the Poet to inspire the masses to change course.
5. Ibid., 172.
6. Sari Edelstein has recently placed the nineteenth-century woman's tradition of writing "between the journalistic and the novelistic." Edelstein, *Between the Novel*, 10. Fuller seems strangely absent in her book, but Edelstein does devote a chapter to Alcott as a type of

eyewitness reporter of the Civil War in her *Hospital Sketches*. Edelstein, *Between the* Novel, 88–100. I also include women's private correspondence as a way in which the female experience encompassed the everyday events that plagued the nation: not only does the woman writer enter into a discourse with the world, but she also finds an audience, if only in the family, as letters by women were often read to family members.

7. Fuller, *The Letters of Margaret Fuller*, 113.

8. Quoted in Murray, *Wandering Pilgrim*, 238.

9. Fuller, "Thanksgiving," 13.

10. Child describes in great depth how she was hardened to the horrors of the city. Like Emerson, but within a different context, she withheld her generosity because she had "not the means to gratify it." She then focused on her own pain in witnessing those suffering around her and having to harden her heart: "This is the misery of a city like New-York, that a kindly spirit not only suffers continual pain, but is obliged to do itself perpetual wrong. At times, I almost fancy I can feel myself turning to stone by inches." Child, *Letters*, 194.

11. Ibid., 95.

12. Quoted in Capper, *Margaret Fuller*, 186. Capper maintains that the main difference in Fuller's rewriting of "The Great Lawsuit" to *Woman in the Nineteenth Century* was her attention to sexual politics. *American Romantic Life*. I put more emphasis on her growing awareness of the indigent and downtrodden, as when she describes her visit to Sing Sing.

13. Emerson, *Essays and Lectures*, 535.

14. Ibid., 536.

15. Quoted in Fenimore, "Horace Greeley."

16. Quoted in Capper, *Margaret Fuller*, 187 (emphasis in original). After Fuller's death, Greeley wrote an introduction to the 1855 reprint of her essay (published by John Jewett and Co.) and complimented her: "She wrote as one who had observed, and who had deeply felt what she deliberately uttered." Greeley, "Introduction," 12. Both she and Greeley were horrified about the Great Fire of 1845 in New York. Fuller was always deeply aware of the suffering of others and showed sincere compassion about catastrophic news in the urban landscape. For example, she wrote of several victims of New York's Great Fire: a young man who was distraught about losing his wife of four months; a girl "found in convulsions in the Fulton ferry-house. Having been burned out and lost everything, she wandered a while homeless and then took laudanum"; and a clerk who had been so dutiful that the authorities found him "disinterred grasping in one hand charred ledgers, in the other some gold." Letter from Margaret Fuller to James Nathan, July 22, 1845, in Fuller, *The Letters of Margaret Fuller*, 136.

17. Fuller, "Christmas," 254.

18. Ibid.

19. Ibid., 255.

20. Ibid., 254 (emphasis in original).

21. Ibid., 255.

22. Fuller, "Prevalent Idea," 129.

23. One could assert that even in her *Dial* editorship days, Fuller was already drawn to the image of the Virgin Mary, evidenced by her symbolic rendition of liberated women in "The Great Lawsuit," in which the self-reliant but maternal archetype of the Virgin Mary is held up as a model for women to emulate.

24. Fuller, "Thanksgiving," 9–10.

25. Emerson, *Essays and Lectures*, 262 (emphasis in original).

26. See, for example, his privileging of a non-Christian sense of philanthropy as he turns to a more primeval mythologized vision of sharing that would entail genuine gestures of giving

of oneself, not simply from a sense of Christian duty. In his section on friendship in *A Week on the Concord and Merrimack Rivers*, he rejects institutionalized charity: "When the Friend comes out of his heathenism and superstition, and breaks his idols, being converted by the precepts of a newer testament; when he forgets his mythology, and treats his Friend like a Christian, or as he can afford; then Friendship ceases to be Friendship, and becomes charity; that principle which established the almshouse is now beginning with its charity at home, and establishing an almshouse and pauper relations there." Thoreau, *Concord and Merrimack Rivers*, 225.

27. Ibid., 218.
28. Fuller, "The Irish Character," 147–148. Her article on the Irish was published in two parts. In both parts, she is negative about the Catholic Church's patriarchal claims to Irish souls and its hold over their minds. See ibid. and Fuller, "The Irish Character (Part 2)."
29. Blanchard, *Transcendentalism to Revolution*, 229.
30. Fuller, *Woman in the Nineteenth Century*, 103.
31. Ibid., 101.
32. Ibid., 72.
33. Ibid.
34. Ibid., 86.
35. Ibid. (emphasis in original).
36. Ibid.
37. Ibid., 87 (emphasis added).
38. Ibid.
39. Fuller, "Thanksgiving," 12.
40. Fuller, "Asylum for Discharged Female Convicts," 136.
41. Fuller, "Our City Charities," 99.
42. Ibid., 100.
43. Ibid., 101.
44. Ibid. This is an example from Fuller of Catholicism at its worst; even though she celebrated the warmth of sharing implicit in Catholic holidays, she shared with most American feminist thinkers of the nineteenth century a fear of the convent as a negative, prisonlike institution.
45. Fuller, "Our City Charities," 102.
46. Fuller, "The Poor Man—an Ideal Sketch," 381.
47. Fuller, "Prevalent Idea," 128.
48. Ibid., 129.
49. Ibid., 128.
50. Ibid., 129.
51. Fuller, "Our City Charities," 103.
52. Fuller, "Thanksgiving," 12.
53. Ibid., 13.
54. Fuller, "New Year's Day," 17.
55. Fuller, "Asylum for the Discharged Female Convicts," 137.
56. Ibid., 136.
57. Fuller, "The Rich Man—an Ideal Sketch," 366.
58. Fuller, "Our City Charities," 103 (emphasis in original).
59. Ibid.
60. Thoreau, *Walden*, 380.
61. Alcott, *Journals*, 45.

62. Ibid.
63. Ibid., 46.
64. Ibid., 48.
65. Ibid., 67.
66. Ibid.
67. Ibid., 68.
68. Ibid., 162.
69. Ibid., 164.
70. Ibid., 167.
71. Ibid., 164.
72. Ibid.
73. Nathaniel Hawthorne's Zenobia might be an incarnation of Margaret Fuller, as many have duly noted. Zenobia's lament to Hollingsworth toward the end of Hawthorne's *The Blithedale Romance* could be read as Fuller's response to transcendentalist reformers like Emerson: "It is all self . . . nothing but self, self, self." Hawthorne, *Centenary Edition*, 3:218.
74. Letter from Elizabeth Palmer Peabody to Louisa May Alcott, December 1877, in Peabody, *Letters*, 382.
75. Ibid.
76. Howe, *Memoir of Dr. Samuel Gridley*, 19.
77. Alcott, *Little Women*, 245.
78. Stoneley, "Alcott and Social Power," 24. Richard Brodhead notes that in the late 1860s, when Alcott wrote *Little Women*, she found herself caught "between old style-virtuous domesticity and a new-style lavishness," and that in the novel, "an ethic of poor but honest virtue" is pitted "against the temptations of affluence." Brodhead, *Culture of Letters*, 96. The boundaries between the middle and upper classes (represented by Laurie in *Little Women*) became more delineated: "In 1868 the middle-class audience no longer needs to differentiate itself from the household economic order it was once imperfectly separated from but now needs to deploy its tools of self-definition against another threatening adjacency—the emerging leisure class world of the postbellum years." Brodhead, *Culture of Letters*, 95. Peter Stoneley takes up a similar argument about class consciousness and material wealth in Alcott's work. See Stoneley, "Alcott and Social Power."
79. Alcott, *Journals*, 196.
80. Elbert, *Hunger for Home*, 260.
81. It is noteworthy that this same type of suffrage meeting that Howe and Alcott attended in Syracuse made Howe, in 1866, step outside herself to see a larger picture of charity at the suffrage conference in Boston, causing her "conversion to the cause" of suffrage. Howe, "My Friends," 315. Howe herself admitted that observing the organizational skills by women during the Civil War made her aware that women's suffrage movements and increased political activism could effect change. Howe, "My Friends," 315–316.
82. Such friendly visits to institutions like hospitals, orphanages, asylums, and prisons were often made by well-respected citizens and intellectuals, especially around Christmas. Stephen Nissenbaum believes these Christmas visits eradicated pangs of conscience on the part of the visitor, but even the avid readers of the visitors' accounts could be relieved: "The social order [was] still held together" despite the wear and tear of industrial capitalism. Nissenbaum, *Battle for Christmas*, 248.
83 Alcott, *Selected Letters of Louisa May Alcott*, 201.
84. Alcott, *Journals*, 167.
85. Alcott, "A Visit to the Tombs," 167.

86. See Monika Elbert, "Charitable (Mis)Givings." I use here, with permission from Routledge, some of the material from that essay, though my focus there is Alcott's fictional Christmas stories for the children's writing market. However, even in her fictional Christmas stories, Alcott shows a heightened sensitivity to the plight of the poor after her experience in New York.

87. Alcott, "A New Way to Spend Christmas," 265.

88. Fanny Fern, in her roles as New York observer and journalist, had also written about the impoverished inmates and the incarcerated prostitutes at Blackwell's Island, pointing the finger accurately at the wealthy, powerful men with political clout who destroyed them by seducing them. Fern, "Blackwell's Island." Her argument was as strident as Fuller's, and that is perhaps why Hawthorne admired Fern—because he thought she wrote as if "the devil was in her." Letter from Nathaniel Hawthorne to William Ticknor, February 2, 1855, in Hawthorne, *Centenary Edition*, 17:308. Moreover, both Fern and Hawthorne believed that though charity should begin at home, it should also become a communal enterprise if domestic charity fails to function.

89. Alcott, "A New Way to Spend Christmas," 266.
90. Ibid., 269.
91. Ibid., 266.
92. Alcott, *Rose in Bloom*, 313.
93. Howe, *Memoir of Dr. Samuel Gridley Howe*, 19.
94. Alcott, *Rose in Bloom*, 310.
95. Elbert, *A Hunger for Home*, 261.
96. Alcott, *Rose in Bloom*, 242.
97. Ibid., 241.
98. Ibid., 250.
99. Ibid., 252.
100. Ibid., 269.
101. Alcott, "Phrenological Exam of L. M. Alcott," 48.
102. Alcott, "Woman's Part in the Concord Celebration," 202.
103. Greeley, "Recollections," 214.
104. Ibid., 215.
105. Ibid., 214.

Bibliography

Alcott, Abigail. *My Heart Is Boundless: Writings of Abigail Alcott, Louisa's Mother*. Edited by Eva LaPlante. New York: Free Press, 2012.

Alcott, Louisa May. *The Journals of Louisa May Alcott*. Edited by Joel Myerson and Daniel Shealy. Boston: Little, Brown, 1989.

———. *Little Women*. Edited by Anne K. Philips and Gregory Eiselein. New York: Norton, 2004.

———. "A New Way to Spend Christmas." In *Louisa May Alcott's Christmas Treasury: The Complete Christmas Collection*, edited by Stephen H. Hines, 265–272. Tulsa, OK: River Oak, 2002.

———. "Phrenological Examination of L. M. Alcott." In *L. M. Alcott: Signature of Reform*, edited by Madeleine B. Stern, 48. Boston: Northeastern University Press: 2002.

———. *Rose in Bloom*. 1876. Reprint, New York: Puffin, 1995.

———. *The Selected Letters of Louisa May Alcott*. Edited by Joel Myerson and Daniel Shealy. Boston: Little, Brown, 1987.
———. "A Visit to the Tombs." *Youth's Companion*, May 25, 1876, p. 167.
———. "Woman's Part in the Concord Celebration." In *L. M. Alcott: Signature of Reform*, edited by Madeleine Stern, 198–202. Boston: Northeastern University Press, 2002.
Bergmann, Hans. *God in the Street: New York Writing and the Penny Press to Melville*. Philadelphia: Temple University Press, 1995.
Blanchard, Paula. *Margaret Fuller: From Transcendentalism to Revolution*. New York: Delacorte, 1978.
Brace, Charles Loring. *The Dangerous Classes of New York, and Twenty Years' Work among Them*. New York: Wynkoop and Hallenbeck, 1872.
Brodhead, Richard H. *Culture of Letters: Scenes of Reading and Writing in Nineteenth-Century America*. Chicago: University of Chicago Press, 1993.
Capper, Charles. *Margaret Fuller: An American Romantic Life*. Vol. 2, *The Public Years*. New York: Oxford University Press, 2007.
Child, Lydia Maria. *Letters from New York*. New York: C. S. Francis, 1845.
Edelstein, Sari. *Between the Novel and the News: The Emergence of American Women's Writing*. Charlottesville: University of Virginia Press, 2014.
Elbert, Monika. "Charitable (Mis)Givings and the Aesthetics of Poverty in Louisa May Alcott's Christmas Stories." In *Enterprising Youth: Social Values and Acculturation in Nineteenth-Century American Children's Literature*, edited by Monika Elbert, 19–38. New York: Routledge, 2008.
Elbert, Sarah. *A Hunger for Home: Louisa May Alcott's Place in American Culture*. New Brunswick, NJ: Rutgers University Press, 1987.
Emerson, Ralph Waldo. *Essays and Lectures*. New York: Library of America, 1983.
Fenimore, David H. "Horace Greeley (1811–1872), Editor of the *New York Tribune*." 1996. http://webpages.charter.net/fenimore/greeley.html.
Fern, Fanny. "Blackwell's Island." In *Ruth Hall and Other Writings by Fanny Fern*, edited by Joyce Warren, 304–309. New Brunswick, NJ: Rutgers University Press, 1986.
Fuller, Margaret. "Asylum for Discharged Female Convicts." In Fuller, *Margaret Fuller, Critic*, 134–137.
———. "Christmas." In *Essays on American Life and Letters*, by Margaret Fuller, edited by Joel Myerson, 254–260. Lanham, MD: Rowman and Littlefield, 1977.
———. "The Great Lawsuit: Man versus Men, Woman versus Women." *The Dial* 4 (July 1843). http://transcendentalism-legacy.tamu.edu/authors/fuller/debate.html.
———. "The Irish Character." In Fuller, *Margaret Fuller, Critic*, 146–148.
———. "The Irish Character (Part 2)." In Fuller, *Margaret Fuller, Critic*, 155–160.
———. *The Letters of Margaret Fuller*. Vol. 4, *1845–1847*. Edited by Robert N. Hudspeth. Ithaca, NY: Cornell University Press, 1987.
———. *Margaret Fuller, Critic: Writings from the New-York Tribune, 1844–1846*. Edited by Judith Mattson Bean and Joel Myerson. New York: Columbia University Press, 2000.
———. "New Year's Day." In Fuller, *Margaret Fuller, Critic*, 14–19.
———. "Our City Charities: Visit to Bellevue Alms House, to the Farm School, the Asylum for the Insane, and Penitentiary in Blackwell's Island." In Fuller, *Margaret Fuller, Critic*, 98–104.
———. "The Poor Man—an Ideal Sketch." In Fuller, *Margaret Fuller, Critic*, 375–383.
———. "Prevalent Idea That Politeness Is Too Great a Luxury to Be Given to the Poor." In Fuller, *Margaret Fuller, Critic*, 128–130.

———. "Thanksgiving." In Fuller, *Margaret Fuller, Critic*, 8–13.
———. "The Rich Man—an Ideal Sketch." In Fuller, *Margaret Fuller, Critic*, 359–366.
———. *Woman in the Nineteenth Century*. Edited by Larry Reynolds. 1845. Reprint, New York: Norton, 1998.
Greeley, Horace. "Greeley's Recollections of a Busy Life." In *Love-Letters of Margaret Fuller*, edited by Julia Ward Howe, 208–222. New York: D. Appleton, 1903.
———. "Introduction." In *Woman in the Nineteenth Century*, by Margaret Fuller, edited by Bernard Rosenthal. New York: Norton, 1971.
Hawthorne, Nathaniel. *The Centenary Edition of the Works of Nathaniel Hawthorne*. Edited by William Charvat and Roy Harvey Pearce. 23 vols. Columbus: Ohio State University Press, 1962–1987.
Howe, Julia Ward. *Memoir of Dr. Samuel Gridley Howe*. Boston: A. J. Wright, 1876.
———. "My Friends." *Harper's Bazaar* 44, no. 5 (1910): 315–316.
"Louisa May Alcott." *Phrenological Journal and Science of Health* 72, no. 4 (1881): 186.
Murray, Meg McGavran. *Margaret Fuller: Wandering Pilgrim*. Athens: University of Georgia Press, 2008.
Nissenbaum, Stephen. *The Battle for Christmas: A Cultural History of America's Most Cherished Holiday*. New York: Vintage, 1996.
Peabody, Elizabeth Palmer. *Letters of Elizabeth Palmer Peabody: American Renaissance Woman*. Edited by Bruce A. Ronda. Middletown, CT: Wesleyan University Press, 1984.
Riis, Jacob A. *How the Other Half Lives: Studies among the Tenements of New York*. 1890. Reprint, New York: Penguin, 1997.
Stoneley, Peter. "'The Fashionable World Displayed': Alcott and Social Power." *Studies in American Fiction* 27, no. 1 (1999): 21–36.
Thoreau, Henry David. *A Week on the Concord and Merrimack Rivers*. 1849. Reprint, New York: Library of America, 1985.
———. *Walden*. 1854. Reprint, New York: Library of America, 1985.

5

LADY BOUNTIFUL FOR THE EMPIRE
Upper-Class Women, Philanthropy, and Civil Society

Dorice Williams Elliott

WHEN GYNETH DESHON, the heroine of Florence Wilford's 1862 novel, *A Maiden of Our Own Day*, writes a letter to the editor of the local newspaper, her beloved grandmother is "shocked and grieved," and Gyneth herself is distraught to think that she has "acted like one of the 'strong-minded women' whom she had been taught to hold in horror."[1] The daughter of a high-ranking military officer and closely related to members of the titled aristocracy, Gyneth is expected to be accomplished and intelligent but also feminine and submissive. Gyneth, however, is troubled by "ambitious longings" that motivate her not only to write to the newspaper but, more importantly, to work as a District Visitor or to do some other kind of volunteer work with the poor.[2] Gyneth's aristocratic family, though, opposes these desires to participate in civil society through involvement in philanthropic work. Not only is the threat of becoming a "strong-minded," and thus unfeminine, woman held up to her, but she is also warned against becoming a "charitable guerilla."[3] While such a term is reminiscent of Charles Dickens's "cast-iron Lady Bountiful," Mrs. Pardiggle in *Bleak House*, who is a parodic version of the interfering woman District Visitor, it seems to mean something more in *A Maiden of Our Own Day*.[4] For in Wilford's novel, the women castigated as "charitable guerillas" are not necessarily interfering or obnoxious, but they are all clearly middle-class women, beneath Gyneth and her aristocratic family in social position. Thus, Gyneth's longings to be involved in the civil society of England during the period of high colonialism are thwarted, at least initially, because of her class as well as her gender.

As is evident in Wilford's novel, both class and gender played a significant role in the late nineteenth-century discourse of philanthropy, especially as it related to direct participation in civil society. Literary works such as novels are a good place to look at how such ideologies sometimes clashed in philanthropic discourse, because even novels that are little known now influenced the opinions, and even actions, of many readers, particularly middle- and upper-class women. Novels by women writers concerned with philanthropy also show the possibilities that such women could imagine for themselves and for other women within the confines of civil society. Wilford's novel, for instance, helped establish a standard for aristocratic women who wished to participate in imperial civil society by modeling the kind of civility that could enable them to have a much wider influence without challenging either their domesticity or their class position. However, the sphere of useful action outside their own homes was largely closed to genteel English and Indian women living in India, even thirty years after such a model had been established in England. By the end of the century, though, both Anglo-Indian and Indian women writers began to imagine a role for aristocratic women in Indian civil society that was like that of their English sisters such as Gyneth Deshon. Doing so, however, was not unproblematic, as two turn-of-the-century novels, Alice Perrin's *Idolatry* (1908) and Swarnakumari Debi's *The Uprooted Vine* (1892), reveal. Since so many women were involved in philanthropic work in the nineteenth and early twentieth centuries, and because so many of them read novels such as these, the novels themselves became an important part of philanthropic discourse.

The Philanthropic Heroine and Civil Society

Women who did take part in philanthropic work in England were involved in civil society in several senses of the term. The philanthropic organizations, local parishes, missionary societies, and social science congresses in which they participated were all voluntary institutions fulfilling different purposes than and situated between the public sphere of the state and the market and the private sphere of the home.[5] This metaphorical space between public and private spheres has been conceptualized and named in different ways, including *the social*, the *social sphere*, and the *social domain*, as well as *civil society*, a related, though not identical, term.[6] Historians of the eighteenth century commonly locate civil society in actual physical spaces, such as coffee houses, which were explicitly public yet closed to women, as were the organs of public discourse such as newspapers and journals (women could read these, of course, but were not expected to write for or produce them). Nineteenth-century civil society, however, as conceptualized by modern sociologists, political scientists, and historians, expanded from a more or less physically locatable space to include all voluntary associations and public forms of discourse. For philanthropic organizations, the literal spaces of their operations were the homes of the poor, as well as the institutions—such as workhouses, prisons, asylums, and schools—frequented by the poor. In England, the homes of the poor were often more accessible to women than to men, and the institutions serving the poor became increasingly open to women throughout the century, thus making women's presence in such organizations not only useful, but often vital.

Using a different metaphor, Nancy Bermeo and Philip Nord describe civil society as "the network of voluntary associations that mediates between the individual and the state."[7] A *network* suggests a web or fabric that ties organizations and their members together in formal or informal ways. English women, who had already begun to participate in philanthropic associations even in the eighteenth century, were a mainstay of such voluntary organizations in England by the middle of the nineteenth century. By the 1860s, there were several hundred thousand women participating in volunteer philanthropic work of various sorts, and women staffed most of the over 640 charitable institutions in operation in England.[8] As an important strand of this network of organizations and activity, women's participation was in fact woven into the very concept of civil society defined in this way. Of course, participation in such a network involves power negotiations, as Lauren Goodlad reminds us, citing Michel Foucault's concept of governmentality. Using the similar metaphor of the web, Goodlad remarks that "Foucault's notion of empowered actors provoking one another through a dense web of indirect relations provides a fitting model for what the Victorians saw as a dynamic civil society."[9] In this view of civil society, power relations are inherent in any network of associations, but power is negotiated and diffuse, not a monopoly of the state. Within such a "web of indirect relations," women could take different positions, both in relation to men and to other women. Aristocratic women, for example, might be differentiated from women of the middling classes while both might be subservient to male directors or governors; women from different social classes and regions of the world might join together in all-female organizations, which would involve yet another set of power dynamics. All of these would be likely to position themselves above working-class men and women and, in the case of the colonies, above indigenous peoples.

Another key component of the term *civil society* is the notion of the *civilized* or *civil* subject. Closely related to the concept of the *citizen*, the notion of civility dates at least as far back as Aristotle. Civility is a way of behaving and interacting that makes it possible for "empowered actors provoking one another" to exist and work together for the public good, which is the avowed goal of civil society.[10] Dennis L. Peck, drawing from Stephen L. Carter, provides a revealing list of qualities he considers part of civility: "sacrifice, generosity, trust, duty, morality, gratitude, communication, respect, self-restraint, fair and honest disagreement, obligation, and a firm resolve to right that which is defined by the community as wrong."[11] This list of values is similar to those that characterized the new gentleman, one who merited this title instead of merely inheriting it. However, a number of these values, it should be noted, were also especially associated with women: sacrifice, which heads the list, was an essential attribute of the domestic woman, as were generosity, trust, duty, morality, gratitude, respect, and self-restraint. The inclusion of so many attributes of the domestic woman in such modern definitions of civility suggests that nineteenth-century women who were allowed into civil society helped define its essence. Self-restraint, for instance, is especially linked to middle- and upper-class women, but it is also essential for anyone desiring to participate in civil society. As Peck conceives it, the "civilizing process requires acceptance of a cultural ethos that emphasizes self-control."[12] Those who were presumed to be unrestrained—the working classes with their political unrest and their unruly sexual desires that resulted in too-large families, sexualized women such as prostitutes, and heathen indigenous peoples—were banned from civil society and depended on those who were "civilized" to represent their interests and ameliorate their afflictions.

Because women seemed naturally to possess so many aspects of civility, they were assumed to be ideally qualified to teach civility to those defined as uncivilized. Thus, philanthropic women became an integral part of "the networks through which civility is produced and reproduced."[13] These women's "civilizing" mission not only aimed to impart civility to those they taught—in schools, hospitals, asylums, or Indian zenanas[14]—but also guaranteed their own civility and qualified them to act in a "civil society [that] consists of individuals acting in concert to pursue shared goals in the public arena."[15] Theoretically, the more civility a woman could claim—and civility was traditionally most identified with the aristocratic classes—the greater her claim to participate in civil society and thus fulfill her ambitious desires, even if that civility was, ironically perhaps, manifest in her extreme humility and willingness to sacrifice. Thus, while middle-class women participated widely in civil society, aristocratic women, who were supposed to exhibit the essence of civility, were thought to be uniquely qualified to lead because they could model and teach civility both to the "uncivilized" and to their fellow workers, middle-class women.

By the mid-nineteenth century, of course, England's civilizing mission was seen to stretch much beyond its own borders to include the various colonies and indigenous peoples belonging to the British Empire, such as India, supposedly Britain's crown jewel. Given their success in infiltrating civil society through philanthropic work at home, it is not surprising that English women also sought to spread normative feminine and Christian values, as well as to achieve their own ambitious desires, through volunteer charitable activities in an imperial context. Nineteenth-century Anglo India also had a highly developed civil society, but it was different from England's in some key ways, especially in that it excluded women, whether English or indigenous Indian. Although English women arguably entered civil society in England early in the nineteenth century partly through their efforts to civilize Indians by raising money to send Bibles and missionaries there and agitating for the English Parliament to abolish the Indian practice of *sati*, or widow burning, within India itself the opportunities for women to participate in the social sphere were very limited.[16] When inroads were made, it was primarily because the homes of the indigenous people—particularly the zenanas to which Indian women of the middle and upper classes were confined—were open only to women of the higher classes. There were a few English women who could be said to have participated in Anglo-Indian civil society by founding schools for Indian orphans, while famous English philanthropists like Mary Carpenter were invited to visit and make recommendations for improving Indian schools and prisons, as Suzanne Daly discusses in chapter 3. By and large, however, Englishwomen did not ordinarily perform volunteer charitable work even in the second half of the nineteenth century.[17]

The claim to superior civility that justifies a woman's participation in civil society is evident in the case of Gyneth Deshon, who learns to subdue all unruly desires and exemplify the qualities Peck lists as necessary for civility. When women familiar with this English model of participation in civil society are represented in a colony like India, however, the situation becomes more complicated. Anglo-Indian writer Perrin's *Idolatry*, for instance, features an upper-class English woman who does not perform philanthropic work in India because it is too dangerous for a beautiful aristocratic lady; instead, while in India she learns to discipline her desires into the ultrafeminine form that allows her to work in English civil society once she returns to the metropole. Thus, India serves as a training ground for English civility rather than offering it as an example for the aristocratic Englishwoman in India itself. The English model portrayed in *A Maiden of Our Own Day* is even more problematic for indigenous author Debi. For her, the image of the superfeminine woman participating in civil society was obviously appealing, since Debi herself managed to join civil society to some extent by helping form a supposedly philanthropic society. In her novel *The Uprooted Vine*, however, she offers the English model only as an imagined possibility that her heroine Snehalata cannot yet fulfill, despite exemplifying all the qualities of supercivility that Gyneth Deshon and Anne Crivener, the heroine of Perrin's novel *Idolatry*, do. The constraints of Indian society, and the role women were expected to play in it as the colony gradually moved toward independence from England, leave Debi unable to actually represent the aristocratic female philanthropist as an active participant in civil society in colonial India, though she can imagine it.

For upper-class women in England like Gyneth Deshon, there was already a template for performing charitable acts and leading philanthropic ventures: the figure of Lady Bountiful, the mistress of the manor who was traditionally responsible for the education and welfare of the tenants, laborers, and servants on the estate, as Jessica Gerard, among others, has discussed.[18] The Lady Bountiful, however, was primarily a rural figure, while women like the heroines of the novels I am discussing lived in urban settings without so many "dependents." For them, working with the urban poor could be viewed as transferring the Lady Bountiful role to the city, where aristocratic women could teach civility to the lower classes just as the lady of the manor did in the country. This "civilizing" of the urban poor by aristocratic women in England could be represented as especially necessary since the urban working classes were most often characterized as unruly rather than deferent and obedient like their rural counterparts. Likewise, many of the indigenous people of the colonies, in this case specifically India, were both urbanized and "uncivilized" by virtue of not being English. Thus, the civilizing mission of the aristocratic woman would seem logically to extend to colonies like India, despite the actual difficulties faced by such women when attempting to enter civil society there; however, imperial philanthropy, especially for upper-class women, proved more difficult to represent, as these novels demonstrate.

Besides the Lady Bountiful figure, another, more specific model for the aristocratic philanthropic heroine was Florence Nightingale, probably the most famous nineteenth-century British woman philanthropist. Nightingale, like Gyneth Deshon, expressed frustration with the round of visiting and other social duties that were supposed to constitute her contribution to civil society as the daughter in an aristocratic family, and she wished for a larger sphere of useful action, as she details in *Cassandra*.[19] It may be difficult now to think of Nightingale as superfeminine and submissive like Gyneth, since Nightingale is known for her skillful administrative work in setting up schools for nursing and her extensive writing on nursing and other medical issues. However, at the time that Wilford was writing *Maiden of Our Own Day*, just a few years following the Crimean War, Nightingale was being portrayed in the press as the "Lady with the Lamp," the symbol of compassion and femininity.[20] She was a model for many young women with ambitious desires, including upper-class girls like Gyneth, who longed to accomplish something beyond the domestic sphere, perhaps something that would take them out of England and into the empire, through philanthropy.

Like Wilford's *Maiden of Our Own Day*, Perrin's *Idolatry* and Debi's *Uprooted Vine* represent upper-class women with desires to actually participate in civil society, not just to donate money as aristocratic women in both England and India had done for centuries. However, even more than Wilford's Gyneth, these women are dogged by the figure of the *charitable guerilla*, the middle- or lower-class woman who is allowed to engage in charitable work but is perceived as less feminine than the standard upheld for aristocratic women. To be permitted to enter into and take an appropriate leading role in civil society, avoiding the opprobrium attached to the charitable guerilla, the aristocratic woman must acquire extraordinary self-restraint and demonstrate submission to authority. In doing so, all three of the heroines I discuss can be cast as examples to other aristocratic women and men of the desirability of aristocratic women becoming part of civil society, even if this can only be imaginatively projected into the future. Thus the figure of the new aristocratic woman, as it is conceived in these novels, moves beyond the traditional rural charity of the Lady Bountiful figure into not only the urban spaces of England but, increasingly, the empire. Even though this model does not translate easily into Anglo-Indian or indigenous Indian society, it is at least envisioned as a possibility in these novelistic instances of philanthropic discourse.

Wilford's *A Maiden of Our Own Day* and English Women's Philanthropy

Gyneth Deshon, the "maiden" of Wilford's title, is the daughter of a colonel in the army and a woman whose family includes titled nobility. When the novel opens, Gyneth, the second daughter in a large family who spent her first eight years with them in the West Indies, has since been living with and educated by her paternal grandmother in England while the rest of her family has been stationed in Corfu with her father's regiment. Gyneth's mother has obviously married an ambitious and respectable gentleman, but her concern about her daughters' marriages and her husband's worries about his sons' professions indicate that they are anxious about maintaining the social status of the family. There are continual hints that it is hard to keep such a large family in appropriate style on the colonel's income. The family is thus on the margins of the aristocracy; the possibility of sinking into the middle class is a real possibility. Hence, her mother hopes that Gyneth will marry her aristocratic cousin, the Honorable Anthony Waller, not the colonel's cousin, Lewis Grantham, a mere London barrister. Additionally, since the book is also consciously "high church," Gyneth is under the obligation both to live a Christian life and to help maintain her family's gentility. The way that Wilford imagines her maiden achieving both of these goals is by having her demonstrate an ultrafeminine domesticity, in addition to the array of female accomplishments expected of women of her class.

Gyneth, however, is also "of our own day." Like the more aggressive Nightingale, she has "ambitious longings" and desires to know "the busy outer world, that world of struggling, thinking human beings, about which she was wont to perplex herself so vainly."[21] All around her are women engaged in philanthropic work. The "Charitable Guerillas," as Gyneth's best friend Rose characterizes them, are mostly middle-class women who approach charity in an aggressive and unsupervised way: they "prefer fighting against ignorance and vice in their own independent fashion, instead of enrolling themselves in the regular army, with the Rector for their head."[22] This military metaphor is significant in this novel about the daughter of a colonel. Gyneth's job, like a soldier's, is to submit herself to proper authority—her father and the rector—and not pit her own desires against their superior knowledge. Although there are also a couple of exemplary charitable women closer to Gyneth's own social standing doing charitable work in ways that are more acceptable for an aristocratic woman, Gyneth's parents fear that taking a District Visiting route or visiting among the working-class wives of soldiers, as Gyneth desires, might endanger her or destroy her maidenly innocence and damage her marriage prospects. Colonel Deshon explains to his daughter that she could not visit the poor "without seeing and hearing what it is better [she] should be guarded from."[23] The only solution that Gyneth's friend and adviser, Rose, has to offer is to "do the little scraps of duties that fall in one's way, and be such a good, patient, proper, ordinary little darling, that at last the general of the regular army [the rector] will begin to say to himself, 'Ah, this little person has more in her than I thought; she hasn't joined the Guerillas, she knows how to be patient, and keep in her proper place, I will enlist her as a recruit forthwith.'"[24] Thus Gyneth must resign herself to subordination, male authority, and "her proper place," learning to embody a standard of femininity even beyond that of her middle-class counterparts.

Like other philanthropic heroines, before Gyneth can engage in philanthropic work outside her own home and her family's immediate circle of friends, she must discipline her "ambitious longings" as severely as her erotic or romantic ones, learning the extreme self-restraint supposedly required of aristocratic women who yearn to participate in civil society rather than simply taking their appropriate place as social ornaments and proper mothers to the nation's future leaders.[25] Paradoxically, even wishing to serve the poor is characterized as a potentially illicit desire for a properly feminine aristocratic woman. Therefore, far from rebelling against her parents or the expectations of her class, Gyneth does learn always to be submissive to her parents and brothers, never asserting herself or her opinions and certainly not writing any more letters to the editor. She is then finally allowed a happy ending: she marries her cousin Lewis Grantham, with whom she has been in love since the first page. Even more significantly, as his wife she is allowed to engage not only in legalized sex but also in (properly supervised) philanthropy, thus fulfilling both her erotic and ambitious desires.

Gyneth finally receives her reward of being able to participate in civil society through philanthropy because she has learned the self-restraint that she lacked on her first attempt to enter it by writing her opinions to the editor of a newspaper. There are several indications that Gyneth has now earned the right to engage in voluntary work for the public good. Not only has she become a model daughter to her parents, but she has become a competent teacher of civility—she has tamed her rebellious younger sister Fanny, brought out the manly nature of her timid little brother Edgar, and feminized the officious Augusta Weatherhead, daughter of the rector. Gyneth is now ready to be a leader, as someone with her social status should be. Because she avoids self-serving "fine-ladyism" in her work alongside shopkeepers' daughters—"'those sort of people' whom one longs to unite with oneself in any little schemes of doing good"[26]—she is able to guide them into teaching civility, rather than acting as the charitable guerillas who force themselves and their officious charity on the poor. The final proof that she has now acquired all the qualities that qualify her for doing public good is given at the end of the novel, when she asks her husband-to-be about the London philanthropies in which she hopes to be involved: "But will you trust me to do these things without you?" "Will I not?" he answers. "'Is it for nothing that I have chosen so discreet and modest a little lady, so submissive to all clerical and proper authority?"[27] Modesty, discretion, and submission to authority—these are the lessons a *lady* must learn in order to enter civil society, where she will lead by modeling civility to women of all the classes beneath her, a civility that, significantly, does not encourage even women of the highest class to compete with men.

Englishwomen and Philanthropy in India

Although it is not emphasized in the novel, the life of Gyneth Deshon in *A Maiden of Our Own Day* is linked to the empire in crucial ways. Her early years spent in the West Indies, her family's long sojourn in Corfu, and even her own sewing of clothing to be distributed by missionaries to Indian children all connect her to Britain's imperial mission and remind us that it is quite literally that mission that permits Gyneth to pursue her own ambitions, however altruistic. In the nineteenth century it was typical for women philanthropists in England to be involved with missionary societies devoted to civilizing the indigenous peoples of the various colonies, as Dickens satirizes in the figure of Mrs. Jellyby, with her "telescopic philanthropy."[28] Historian Clare Midgley dates female involvement in English politics to the late 1820s, when English women formed groups to petition Parliament to abolish *sati*, or widow burning, and claims that interventions of English women into Indian women's lives "became a way of promoting their own claim to a place in the national body politic."[29] These women's organizations in the earlier part of the nineteenth century grew out of the evangelical "foreign mission" movement of the 1790s, which continued throughout the century. As early as 1821, the Ladies Committee of the British and Foreign School Society had raised enough money to send a female missionary to India to develop schools for Indian girls.[30] However, most women involved in missionary work in India and other colonies throughout the century were the wives of missionaries—a position that Jane Eyre famously refuses to take in Charlotte Brontë's 1847 novel.

Although single female missionaries and missionary wives were obviously engaged in philanthropic work through precisely the kind of organization that modern theorists describe as central to civil society, in India there was a huge divide between the religious work of the missionaries and the forms of civil society associated more closely with the colonial government. Politically speaking, the policy of the East India Company and, to a lesser extent, the colonial government established in 1858, was not to interfere with native customs and religion, a practice that helped the English maintain their imperial power without fomenting indigenous rebellion, despite the small number of English people in India. The East India Company, in fact, had not allowed missionaries in India until Parliament passed the Charter Act of 1813, which forced the company to accommodate missionaries, however grudgingly.

By the second half of the nineteenth century, when many more English women had come to India as wives of civilian officials and military officers, there was not only a clash in attitudes regarding the civilizing of the indigenous peoples but a striking class divide between the definitively middle-class missionary women and the *memsahibs*, who formed the aristocracy of British India (whatever their origins in England). There was also a perceived division between officers' wives and civilian officials' wives, with at least one civilian wife overtly claiming superiority in civility:

> The military and civilians do not generally get on very well together. There is a great deal of very foolish envy and jealousy between them, and they are often downright ill-bred to each other, though in general the civilians behave much the best of the two. One day an officer who was dining here said to me, "Now I know very well, Mrs—, you despise us all from the bottom of your heart; you think no one worth speaking to in reality but the Civil Service. Whatever people may really be, you just class them all as civil and military—Civil and military; and you know no other distinction. Is it not so?" I could not resist saying, "No; I sometimes class them as civil and uncivil."[31]

Significantly, the civilian wives, those who like Maitland laid claim to a superior civility, were more likely to engage in philanthropic work in India. Lady Lena Campbell Login, for instance, felt she was "of real use to [her] husband in his political work" because of her visiting with upper-class indigenous women in the zenanas.[32] Lady Charlotte Canning, a governor-general's wife and friend of Florence Nightingale, visited many mission schools, reporting her observations in letters to Queen Victoria.[33] Many of the other wives, daughters, and sisters of civilian officials, as well as some of the officer's wives, visited, donated money, and participated in fancy fairs to raise money for charities, usually schools for Indian children.[34] The headmistresses and teachers of the schools, however, were almost always missionaries, missionary wives, or teachers sent out by missionary societies, and these missionary women usually had little contact or influence with the civil society of the cities, military camps, and government stations. Even when upper-class women were associated with philanthropy, like Lady Campbell Login, they did not participate in civil society on the same scale and with the same acceptance as their counterparts in England did. Rosemary Raza reports, for instance, that "although records indicate that women did play a part in philanthropic work," women like Honoria Lawrence "who had come fresh from Britain, considered that the efforts of those in India compared poorly with endeavours at home."[35] This was not entirely, as Lawrence seemed to believe, because of the inactivity or unwillingness of upper-class Anglo-Indian women, but because they faced more resistance from male members of civil society.

In his important book, *Civility and Empire: Literature and Culture in British India, 1822–1922*, Anindyo Roy addresses the complex ways in which civility was constructed and used to shore up the power of English masculinity in nineteenth-century India. His argument, not surprisingly, has corresponding implications for understanding the middle- and upper-class women trying to establish their own place in Anglo-Indian civil society. Before the opening up of the civil services to university-educated Indians after the 1870s, Roy explains, the professional class of English men who formed the upper class of Anglo-English society felt that they were best qualified not only to hold government offices, but also to dominate civil society in India. After 1870, however, there was a "deep discrepancy that lay within the order of 'civility' that had been the basis for defining citizenship."[36] The discrepancy that Roy identifies is the possibility that newly empowered, educated Indian men and the New Women who were agitating for political power in England might also lay claim to the civility that had so far guaranteed the masculine power of civic officials in India. The name given to the bureaucracy of the colonial government, in fact, was the *Civil* Service, designating both its male authority and its masculine civility (as well as distinguishing it from the military). However, the "ruling tenets of male civility" were "infected with a sense of uncertainty," claims Roy. One of the places in which he locates this "crisis of civility" is in the late-century Anglo-Indian romances, many of them authored by women and portraying "Englishwomen as independent and aggressive individuals," reminiscent of Wilford's charitable guerillas.[37] Despite such portrayals, in India, philanthropy had not given women the same access to civil society that it had in England, even though many Anglo-Indian women had attempted to duplicate their philanthropic roles in India.

What access upper-class English women in India did find to civil society mostly came through their involvement with the education of Indian women. In the zenana they found a space that English men, however powerful or highly positioned, could not penetrate. Missionary women had been educating Eurasian girls, as well as lower-class Indian girls and especially orphans, since early in the century. However, as Geraldine H. Forbes points out, Indian "prejudice against female education prevented the early schools from attracting large numbers."[38] Plus, as Raza notes, most of this kind of philanthropic work with Indians was "limited in scope, and dependent for success on the enthusiasm and commitment of the individual concerned."[39] Philanthropic work for women of both the missionary and the upper classes achieved far more support and encouragement when the potential subjects were the middle- and upper-class women confined in the Muslim and Hindu zenanas. The "private domain of the *zenana*, which Indian men had so jealously guarded," writes Janaki Nair, "comprised an absence in the constitution of colonial discourse," and many felt that India would never be really civilized until the zenana was known or even abolished.[40] By the second half of the century, even many Western-educated Indian men who wanted to be part of civil society began to desire education, though not conversion, for their wives, so that they could have the companionate marriages that characterized "civilized" domestic life. The English (male) rulers were equally desirous to know what went on in the zenanas, which they suspected were sites of political intrigue as well as unruly sexuality, and to civilize upper-class Indian women, who seemed totally beyond their reach and thus dangerous. The famous English philanthropist Mary Carpenter, who toured India at the invitation of the Indian government to propose a plan for the education of Indian women, in fact hoped that the tutelage of English women would bring upper-class Indian women into civil society: "Education must coax the middle and upper classes out of the walls in which they are immured" and exercise a "refining influence" on the classes beneath them, as upper-class Englishwomen were supposed to do through their participation in English civil society.[41] Paradoxically, however, as Jenny Sharpe and others have pointed out, Anglo-Indian women who sought a role for themselves in civil society through civilizing Indian women needed to define their colonialized sisters as *un*civilized in order to maintain their own position.[42] Yet it is in the field of women's education that most philanthropic work in nineteenth-century India was undertaken, whether by missionaries or upper-class women.

Learning to Serve in India: Alice Perrin's *Idolatry*

Few nineteenth-century Anglo-Indian novels portray women of any class doing philanthropic work in India, as the philanthropic heroine novels in England did from the 1860s on—another indication that women's entry into civil society in India was more problematic than in England. There are many existing travel narratives, memoirs, and diaries written by Anglo-Indian women, especially missionary women, that describe working with or visiting schools for Indian and Eurasian children or visiting in the zenanas.[43] In 1909, however, Alice Perrin, a popular Anglo-Indian romance writer like the ones Roy mentions, published

Idolatry, a book set mostly in India and portraying both a government station and a mission compound. The heroine, Anne Crivener, comes from an aristocratic background and has been a much sought-after heiress in London before the death of her grandmother and the loss of the fortune she and others thought she would inherit. With an income of only 125 pounds a year, she decides to go out to India to live with her mother and her stepfather, a missionary in Sika. Although she hides her motives from everyone, Anne's real reason for going to India is that she has discovered that her mother lives in the same city as a former suitor, Dion Devasse, who has recently inherited a large fortune, and, although she does not love him, she intends to rekindle his love for her and get him to renew his proposal of marriage.

Not surprisingly, Anne's cynical materialism is challenged once she is in India. She finds her mother, formerly a great beauty, sadly faded and worn out from the climate and the hardship of the missionary work she has undertaken as the partner of her second husband:

> Year after year of conscientious fulfillment of duty in a trying climate, of teaching native children, training native girls, expostulating with native women, economizing on a moderate income, battling with inferior servants had withered her body and planed her mind to the straight level of a narrow board.[44]

The repetition of the word *native* emphasizes her difference—and superiority—as an Englishwoman, what many would call her complicity with empire.[45] Yet far from feeling energized and powerful as an agent of civil society, Anne's mother, Mrs. Williams, has lost nearly all feeling along with her English beauty, while any romantic or ambitious desires she may once have had have all "withered." This is a result partly of her missionary work but also of her lowered class position, which has necessitated "economizing on a moderate income" and "battling with inferior servants." Although Mrs. Williams retains a remnant of her former social status and is "ladylike" enough to visit some of the zenanas, the gentility that forms a crucial part of civility for aristocratic women has been eroded. Anne recognizes this loss in her mother and feels compelled to use her own brighter spirits and authority to protect her, especially as Mrs. Williams approaches her early death—unfortunately, a common fate for missionary women.[46]

Although at first she finds her stepsister Sophia Williams, who is a paid missionary in her own right, uninteresting, unsophisticated, and not at all refined, Anne comes to admire her devotion and unselfishness as she teaches and visits in lower-class native schools, homes, and orphanages, as well as middle-class zenanas. Sophia, she learns, despite a life spent entirely in Indian missionary service, is not merely a caricature of a missionary; nor is she a charitable guerilla. She genuinely cares about the people she teaches and works with, and she is able to exert her independence while still submitting to male authority. Anne finds Sophia "refreshingly brisk and cheerful"; her stepsister uses mild slang, enjoys novels, and plays tennis (traditionally an aristocratic sport), giving her an individual personality, and she adores Anne.[47] The sisters, despite their differences in class and background, become friends, a significant step for the aristocratic Anne.

On the other hand, somewhat to her own surprise, Anne finds Mrs. Stapely, the wife of Devasse's commanding officer, Colonel Stapely, and thus the first lady of the local society, rather boring and provincial. Perrin uses Colonel Stapely himself to suggest the dismissive attitude of the colonial aristocracy toward the missionaries:

> He cared nothing, and knew little, about the Williams family except that the missionary and his wife, and the missionary's daughter by a former marriage, were an ardent trio who worked very hard at their native schools and orphanages, their meetings and services and efforts at conversion—with what result he had not troubled to investigate. Idolatry at Sika certainly would not appear to be lessening in spite of missionary exertion.[48]

Not only the class difference but also the differing aims of the missionary and military communities are apparent. While the missionaries hope to civilize India by converting Indians to Christianity, Colonel Stapely recognizes that the natives are far too numerous to convert and believes instead that they can only be efficiently governed and controlled by superior English gentlemen like himself. Women are clearly unnecessary to this aim and, indeed, Anne herself finds the local aristocratic women aimless and dull.

What really changes Anne, however, is the influence of the missionary Oliver Wray, a man from her own social class who has chosen to give up his wealth and social advantage to dedicate himself to the cause of spreading the gospel of Christ. A charismatic preacher and tortured soul, Wray also finds himself attracted to Anne, whose English femininity (and sexuality) disrupts his devotion to the notion of the Indian as an equal in the sight of God. His first sight of her is described as follows:

> She was alone in the bazaar, unwitting of the contemptuous relish in the eyes that gazed upon her; of the remarks that were being uttered by lips attuned from babyhood to all that was gross. In one burning moment all his concern and devotion for the spiritual welfare of these people, to whom he was dedicating his life, went from him, driven out by a savage instinct of antagonism and defence. The men around him were no longer his equals in the sight of God, to be pitied for their blindness to the truth, to be loved, and saved, and helped, and excused; but members of a vitiated race devoid of chivalry, without reverence for womanhood, to whom the female is naught but a necessary evil, or at best an instrument for pleasure.[49]

Although Wray sees Sophia and her stepmother, along with other missionary women, enter the bazaar and associate freely with Indian men and women every day, it is Anne, with her aristocratic femininity, who brings out the latent racial prejudice that underlies his Christian principles. Like Gyneth Deshon, Anne is more feminine than the middle-class philanthropists Sophia and Mrs. Williams; significantly, though, she is also more sexualized. While the plain, thirty-seven-year-old Sophia and the faded Mrs. Williams pose no temptation to either Indian or English men, Anne both attracts sexual attention and feels sexual attraction herself:

> It might be still more interesting to see [Wray] in love—he would make an ardent, masterful lover.—At this point Anne checked her thoughts aghast at her own vulgarity. Never before had she speculated as to the kind of lover a man would make! Was it possible that the climate and surroundings of this unspeakable country had already worked a deteriorating effect upon her mind?[50]

Here it is clear that Anne's erotic desires are stimulated by her Indian experience, just as her ambitious ones will soon be. It is worth noting that Perrin uses the word *vulgarity* to describe Anne's sexual imaginings, thus associating them directly with classed behavior. However, by blaming the thoughts on the "climate and surroundings," Perrin also acknowledges that in some way Anne has also become like the sexualized Indians. Presumably the memsahib Mrs. Stapely, who never visits the bazaar, would never have such thoughts.

Ultimately, however, Anne has to discipline her desires severely. She breaks off her engagement to Dion Devasse, despite the fact that it would bring her social position and financial security, because she comes to recognize that it is selfish to marry for such reasons without love. She comes to sympathize with and be able to comfort the annoyingly spoiled child of the Stapelys, further developing her real femininity. And, at the moment when Wray finally admits his passion for her, she refuses him so that he can devote himself to his higher calling among the Indians. Her self-restraint and humility finally proven, she returns to England and begins contentedly working for the generically named Charitable Association. Her old associates observe that "her expression held a sympathy and softness that before had been absent; there was a sweet depth in the eyes that had learnt to look with compassionate understanding upon suffering, want, and sorrow. A new strength, added by victory over self, lay in the curves of her mouth and chin."[51] Her aristocratic civility now perfected by developing ultrafemininity and severe self-restraint, she is allowed to participate—and lead—in England's civil society. In the end, she gradually falls in love with and marries Devasse, who supports and helps her with her charitable projects, and thus Anne acquires wealth to add to her aristocratic civility, potentially enabling her to found her own philanthropic organizations. Significantly, however, even though the book was published in 1909, Perrin still does not give her aristocratic heroine a role in civil society within India. Though it is her stay in India that leads Anne to recognize and discipline her own desires, and to develop the supercivility of the aristocratic female philanthropist, the heavily masculinized structure of Anglo-Indian civil society does not allow her to participate in it there. To participate in civil society, she must take her newly developed supercivility back to England.

Moving toward an Indian Civil Society: Swarnakumari Debi's *The Uprooted Vine*

If becoming involved in civil society was more difficult for English women in India than it was in England, it was even more daunting for middle- and upper-class Indian women, those confined, both literally and metaphorically, in the zenanas that were so crucial for would-be Anglo-English women philanthropists. Although there was an ancient tradition of high-caste women participating in philanthropy, it was almost entirely through "almsgiving to mendicants and students" or "wealthy women, especially queens and wives of wealthy merchants, giving wealth and houses to monastic orders, endowing temples, and building tanks and wells for public use."[52] Even very late in the century, it was unusual for high-caste Muslim and Hindu women to participate as volunteers in philanthropic or other organizations, because of their seclusion in the zenana.

Somewhat ironically, as Indira Ghose points out, it was actually the Western-educated men who were most likely to restrict their wives and daughters to the home: "Modelling themselves on English gentlemen and imbued with the ideology of domesticity, this class had a stake in the seclusion of their wives as a means of differentiation from lower classes."[53] Such seclusion, however, could also be seen not as an imitation of the English but as a rejection of England and its power. Even early in the nineteenth century, according to Kumkum Sangari and Sudesh Vaid, Indians constructed their own version of the private sphere "as an indigenist alternative to western materialism" that "comes into its own as a nationalist discourse" later in the period.[54] This nationalist trend glorified "women who fulfill their wife and mother roles with exceptional ardour [and] placed an enormous burden on the women who came within its defining scope. It was the women, their commitment, their purity, their sacrifice, who were to ensure the moral, even spiritual power of the nation and hold it together."[55] Indian women held this power, many nationalists believed, because they were less influenced by Western norms. As Tanika Sarkar expresses it, "The man, they said, had already been transformed by alien knowledge, whereas the woman, still largely governed by religious-ritual norms, embodied freedom, cultural authenticity, and, ultimately, the nation of the future."[56] The domestic woman, secluded within the women's space of the home, thus marked not only class but also nationalist aspirations, both of which militated against her entering civil society in her own right.

Nonetheless, by the late 1870s there were Indian women doing social work and figuring in reform circles. Some of these activities, as Antoinette Burton has shown, were documented by British feminists in the *Englishwomen's Review*, although, she also points out, British feminists generally had a stake in portraying Indian women as passive and in need of rescuing.[57] The most famous nineteenth-century Indian woman to make a name for herself through her involvement in civil society was Pandita Ramabai, who formed a women's organization in Pune in 1882 and started Sharada Sadan, a home and school for widows, in 1889.[58] Educated by her father and widowed at a young age, Ramabai was also a Christian convert, which helped make her a heroine for English and American, as well as some Indian, women.[59]

Like Ramabai, Swarnakumari Debi, a member of the "elite Tagore family" of Bengal, was also a social reformer.[60] Debi herself started an organization called Sakhi Samiti in 1886. Her Ladies Association was composed of "upper-class, educated women like herself with the avowed intention of promoting goodwill among them and helping widows and destitute women. The Samiti wished to educate these women so that they could earn their livelihood by teaching girls who were still confined within their homes."[61] Thus, these aristocratic women would literally teach civility to other women, who would, in turn, teach still more women. However, in their introduction, the translators of *The Uprooted Vine* explain that "Sakhi Samiti did not achieve much success in this project, though it served its purpose as a meeting ground for women of respectable families who could come together to exchange ideas and organize cultural activities."[62] They staged plays and held craft fairs in which the women could exhibit their talents and get recognition from others. It was thus a unique forum for Bengali women who had just started emerging from the seclusion of their homes to take part in larger, social activities. Debi later set up the Hiranmoyee Widow's Industrial Home.[63] She also attended the annual sessions of the Indian National Congress in 1880 and 1890.[64]

In addition to these reformist activities, Debi also had a prominent literary career; she wrote several novels, in addition to editing and writing for the journal *Bharati* for eighteen years. Thus, Debi not only played a key role in civil society herself but also used her novels, including *The Uprooted Vine*, to engage people in civic discourse who might not have read a political journal, attended congresses, or encouraged the setting up of women's associations. *The Uprooted Vine*, or *Snehalata ba Palita*, was published in serial form between 1889 and 1891 in *Bharati*, the journal that Debi edited. The book was published in volume form in 1892. Although some of Debi's novels were translated into English near the time of publication, including at least one translation by Debi herself, *The Uprooted Vine* has been translated only recently (2004). Given Debi's own participation in civil society, it may seem somewhat strange that her novel portrays a woman—a child widow who cannot, by Indian custom, remarry—who exemplifies the supercivility demonstrated by Gyneth Deshon and Anne Crivener yet cannot participate in civil society and instead faces only tragedy. Yet the novel does forcefully represent the need for such an outlet for women like Snehalata, its heroine.

The Uprooted Vine recounts the story of Snehalata's life as a child widow shuttled between homes after the death of her husband before the marriage is even consummated. Snehalata, "the Foster-Child" (which is the English translation of "ba Palita") is lovingly educated by her foster father, Jagat Babu, though her presence in the family sparks continual jealousy and spite from his wife and daughter. Unbeknownst to anyone, including herself, Snehalata loves the son Charu, a poet and one of a group of well-educated, professional, and reform-minded—though ultimately weak and flawed—young men featured in the novel. Snehalata is married off to a young man named Mohan before she is thirteen; Mohan is kind and sensible and the marriage seems to hold promise, but Mohan dies almost immediately, leaving Snehalata under the control of her in-laws, including the powerful and shrewish aunt Jethima and Mohan's dissipated and greedy older brother Kishori.

Snehalata is an ideal domestic woman—beautiful, intelligent, long-suffering, submissive, and kind. She serves unselfishly in each of the three households she inhabits during the novel, taking on most of the household duties and enduring abuse from other women in the zenana. These characters demonstrate that women who are secluded are by no means without power. Although they are not performing philanthropy, since this was not a possibility for women secluded in zenanas, these women could be likened to the charitable guerillas that haunt upper-class women desiring to participate in civil society. Focused more on their own need for power than on modeling civility through their exemplary femininity and discretion, such women do not symbolize what is best in their class and the nation, as the new nationalist men wanted them to, but instead dominate their homes and everyone in them. The men seem powerless to control or even contradict them, though they are blamed for whatever problems the women may cause. It is also important to note that, although Westerners expended so much sympathy on child wives, men often did not fare much better in their domestic lives, as Debi's narrator points out.[65] They had little more choice than their wives did in choosing a partner, since the bride and groom did not meet until midway through the wedding ceremony. Mohan's cousin Jiban, for instance, has had a glimpse of Snehalata and believes that she is the woman he is marrying; however, when the veil is drawn back during the ceremony, he discovers with despair that it is her foster sister Tagar that he has married, and their marriage is a very unhappy one. Tagar, following her mother's example, exerts unfeminine power over her husband and spends her time in idle, selfish pursuits. Yet it is Snehalata, the good domestic woman, who faces abuse and tragedy.

In one sense, Snehalata's tragedy stems from men's desire for her. After she is widowed and again living at Jagat Babu's home, Charu tries to convince her to marry him, violating the taboo against widow remarriage. Charu presents this to Snehalata as an instance of his commitment to reforming such unjust customs, but this hypocrisy only covers his lust. During their conversations about remarriage, Snehalata questions whether there might be another possibility for women besides marriage: "But is marriage the only goal of life? I believe there are many unmarried women in the West who devote their whole life to the service of others. We do not permit women to remain unmarried in our country, but widows . . ." Charu cuts off her speculations, which are essentially about women entering civil society, by reinforcing the "instinctive attraction between the sexes" that "divert[s] the course of their lives in another direction."[66] Charu's pretended commitment to reform through allowing widow remarriage is couched in even more constricting terms for women. Significantly, he brings up *sati*, which had long been outlawed, to claim that women have only one function—to love men. Since he knows that Snehalata loves him, this puts her in a very painful position. However, she remains true to her religious beliefs and flees the house, only to be further abused by her in-laws and eventually thrown out of their house when she refuses the advances of the equally lustful Kishori.

The only other explicit mention in *The Uprooted Vine* of the possibility for women to enter civil society is in a discussion between Jiban, who is the closest thing to a hero in the novel, and his father-in-law, Snehalata's guardian, Jagat Babu. Their discussion of the importance of women to Indian society goes on for five pages. Jiban, the chief spokesman for the reform of laws and customs that oppress women, makes clear the relation between the condition of women and the nation when he says, "The debate that has currently started in our society regarding women's education and independence and the abolition of child marriage signifies that we have begun to realize to some extent that the welfare and progress of the nation is contingent on the improvement in the condition of women." Jagat Babu, who now believes that it was too much education that caused all of Snehalata's problems, maintains that women's "glory lies in love and kindness. They should remain satisfied with that. Too much of reading is likely to pervert their nature."[67] Jiban's answer invokes the aristocratic feminine civility that we have seen in the other novels to argue for a place for high-caste Indian women in civil society:

> There is no doubt that the glory of women lies in the supremacy of their hearts, but doesn't the heart become expansive as a result of proper education and intellectual exercise? Doesn't the emergence of women like Miss Nightingale,

Miss Carpenter, and Miss Manning show the good consequence of the spread of higher education in the community?[68]

Jagat Babu, however, blames England for what he considers masculinized female behavior and is shocked that Indian women are "involving themselves in social action through organizations and conferences like men! How absurd it is!" At this, Jiban loses his temper and, in a bitterly ironic tirade, attacks the zenana system:

> How can the greatness of our countrymen find expression, unless they ridicule what is good? True enough. When women sit at home and quarrel and gossip about others, their tender feelings are suitably expressed but when they launch Sakhi Samitis and work for widows and orphans, they go against their feminine nature and hurt the sensibilities of nice people with their masculine hardness. I believe this kind of hardness is not proper for men either, is it?[69]

Significantly, Jiban here attacks the civility of men who resist the entrance of women into civil society. Jiban claims that the hearts of supremely feminine women like Snehalata will expand if they are allowed education and entrance into civil society. His language is reminiscent of reformers and feminists in England who argued not that women were equal to men but that the larger world needed the woman's voice and touch—thus expanding not only women's hearts but the domestic sphere itself, including it as a necessary component of civil society.[70]

Shortly after this conversation between Jiban and Jagat Babu, Snehalata is betrayed by Charu and commits suicide, Jagat Babu erroneously believing that she died out of shame and that her tragedy was caused by her education. Although Snehalata is not allowed to participate in civil society, as Jiban advocates, her story is a dramatic representation of the need for positive, active roles for women, especially young widows, outside the seclusion of their homes—like the ones available to Gyneth Deshon and Anne Crivener in England. The fact that the women's organization Jiban mentions as an example of what women like Snehalata should be able to join—Sakhi Samiti—is the name of the group in which Debi herself participated directly links her representation of Snehalata's tragic story with historical reality. If more such organizations were formed in order to give women access to civil society, such tragedies as the one portrayed in *The Uprooted Vine* need not happen. Thus, though such societies are not actually represented, the novel nonetheless makes a strong argument for them. At the same time, it uses the character of its heroine to outline the ultracivil characteristics that would qualify women for participating in them without threatening their femininity or caste.

Conclusion

The three novels that I discuss here are important because, at a time when many were worrying that women were becoming too aggressive and unfeminine, they showed how their female authors imagined a way for women of the upper classes to participate in imperial civil society, not despite but because of their gentility. All three novels thus portray upper-class women learning a kind of super-civility that, at least in imagination, equips them to model and teach civility to others, especially to women of the middle classes who are too independent or assertive—the ones that Wilford calls "charitable guerillas." By developing and displaying the qualities characteristic of civil society to an even higher level than that required of men, these authors suggest that upper-class women should be able to fulfill prominent roles in civil society appropriate to their class status, working alongside male directors and professionals as leaders of other women and even men of lower classes. Although the path to civil society is not easy in any of the novels, especially in Debi's, where it is only imagined, the claims that these heroines can make to a special kind of civility hold out the possibility of fulfilling their own ambitious desires—always represented as wholly altruistic—in ways considered appropriate and nonthreatening to male authority within that domain. As a key arena of civil society, philanthropy, which had historically provided aristocratic women with opportunities to influence society outside of the limited sphere of their homes, again proved useful in an imperial context—as long as the Lady Bountiful of the empire could demonstrate that she could be trusted to be civil wherever she was and whatever the temptation to be otherwise.

DORICE WILLIAMS ELLIOTT is Associate Professor of English at the University of Kansas. She is author of *The Angel Out of the House: Philanthropy and Gender in Nineteenth-Century England*.

Notes

1. Wilford, *Maiden*, 15, 17.
2. Wilford, *Maiden*, 281.
3. Wilford, *Maiden*, 119.
4. Dickens, *Bleak House*, 150–159. The term "cast-iron Lady Bountiful" was used in a review of *Bleak House*. Dyson, *Dicken's Bleak House*, 50–51. Gyneth herself refers to Mrs. Pardiggle as a negative example of a philanthropic woman in Wilford, *Maiden*, 126.
5. This definition of civil society has been debated. For instance, while Jean L. Cohen and Andrew Arato include the family as part of civil society, Craig Calhoun makes a clear distinction between the family and the voluntary relations of civil society. Nancy Bermeo and Philip Nord leave out the family altogether. Cohen and Arato, *Civil Society*, ix; Calhoun, "Civil Society/Public Sphere," 1897–1903; Bermeo and Nord, "New Research," 174–180.
6. Riley, *Am I That Name?*, 49; Elliott, *Angel Out of the House*, 112–127; Poovey, *Making a Social Body*, 5–8.
7. Bermeo and Nord, "New Research," 174.

8. Thomson, *The Victorian Heroine*, 28.
9. Goodlad, *Victorian Literature*, 16.
10. Peck, "Civility," 359.
11. Peck, "Civility," 361. Peck's list is a summary of Carter's *Civility*, 277-292.
12. Ibid.
13. Walzer, "Civil Society Argument," 90.
14. In upper-class Indian and other South Asian homes, the zenana was the part of the house reserved for women, much like the more commonly used term *harem*. The zenana was originally an Islamic custom but spread to much of the Hindu population in India following the Muslim conquest of India from the thirteenth to the sixteenth centuries.
15. Fine and Harrington, "Tiny Publics," 347.
16. On women entering civil society through the campaign against *sati*, see Midgley, "Female Emancipation."
17. Indira Ghose summarizes Carpenter's visit to India in *Memsahibs Abroad*, 114-124.
18. See Gerard, "Lady Bountiful."
19. See Nightingale, *Cassandra and Other Selections*.
20. See Poovey, *Uneven Developments*, 164-198.
21. Wilford, *Maiden*, 7.
22. Ibid., 119.
23. Ibid., 191.
24. Ibid., 119.
25. See Elliott, *Angel Out of the House*, 187-188.
26. Wilford, *Maiden*, 121.
27. Ibid., 397-398.
28. Dickens, *Bleak House*, 85. The term "telescopic philanthropy" is the title of chapter 4 of *Bleak House*.
29. Midgley, "Female Emancipation," 95-96.
30. Ibid., 101.
31. Julia Charlotte Maitland, quoted in Ghose, *Memsahibs Abroad*, 255.
32. Login, *Lady Login's Recollections*, 41.
33. Allen, *Glimpse of the Burning Plain*, 43.
34. A letter written by Isabella Fane to Caroline Chaplin describes a charity bazaar in Calcutta:

> Tuesday 12th This morning Christine and I were occupied from ten till one at the Town Hall in arranging things on a table for a fancy sale which was to take place for the benefit of some schools here. We were requested to take a table, which as a duty we consented to do. It was very fatiguing work, and we came home with aching feet and streaming faces.
>
> Wednesday 13th The sale began at ten. I dreaded it very much, for I thought I should make some confusion in the accounts, never having undertaken an affair of the sort before. However, it did very well. We made excellent shop girls and puffed off our goods in such fine style that our table produced more than any of the others. We got about 400 rupees, i.e., £40, and when one considers the rubbish we had to sell I think it was doing pretty well. Several natives attended. One very polite fellow, so beautifully drest, announced he wished particularly to make some purchases at our table, which he did accordingly. There were others also, but they were monsters and tried to bate down our articles.

Quoted in Pemble, *Miss Fane in India*, 90-91.

35. Raza, *In Their Own Words*, 129.

36. Roy, *Civility and Empire*, 3.
37. Ibid., 90–91.
38. Forbes, "Pure Heathen," WS-2.
39. Raza, *In Their Own Words*, 132.
40. Nair, "Uncovering the Zenana," 11.
41. Carpenter, *Six Months in India*, 1:85, 188.
42. Sharpe, *Allegories of Empire*, 10–11.
43. One of these is the Society for Promoting Female Education in China, India, and the East's *Female Agency among the Heathen*. It includes an account of the women in England who formed the society, describes the selection process for the women they sent out, and details the experiences of many of the women they sponsored.
44. Perrin, *Idolatry*, 53.
45. See, for instance, Forbes, "Pure Heathen," WS-8; and Paxton, "Feminism under the Raj," 334, 336.
46. There are many examples of female missionaries who met early deaths in India in the Society for Promoting Female Education, *Female Agency among the Heathen*.
47. Perrin, *Idolatry*, 64.
48. Ibid., 47.
49. Ibid., 116–117.
50. Ibid., 122.
51. Ibid., 383, 385.
52. Sundar, "Women and Philanthropy," 273.
53. Ghose, *Memsahibs Abroad*, 113.
54. Sangari and Vaid, introduction to *Recasting Women*, 10.
55. Tharu, "Tracing Savitri's Pedigree," 263.
56. Sarkar, "Enfranchised Selves," 351.
57. Burton, *Burdens of History*, 110–116.
58. Sundar, "Women and Philanthropy," 275.
59. Burton, *Burdens of History*, 118.
60. Sundar, "Women and Philanthropy," 276.
61. Sogani and Gupta, introduction to *The Uprooted Vine*, viii–ix.
62. Ibid., ix.
63. Sundar, "Women and Philanthropy," 276.
64. Sogani and Gupta, introduction to *The Uprooted Vine*, viii.
65. Debi, *Uprooted Vine*, 67.
66. Ibid., 150, 151.
67. Ibid., 233, 235.
68. Ibid., 235.
69. Ibid.
70. Elliott, *Angel Out of the House*, 10.

Bibliography

Allen, Charles. *A Glimpse of the Burning Plain: Leaves from the Indian Journals of Charlotte Canning*. London: Michael Joseph, 1986.

Bermeo, Nancy, and Philip Nord. "New Research Planning Group: Civil Society before Democracy: Lessons from 19th-Century Europe." *Historical Social Research* 20, no. 4 (1995): 174–180.

Burton, Antoinette. *Burdens of History: British Feminists, Indian Women, and Imperial Culture, 1865–1915*. Chapel Hill: University of North Carolina Press, 1994.

Calhoun, Craig. "Civil Society/Public Sphere: History of the Concept." In *International Encyclopedia of the Social and Behavioral Sciences*, edited by Neil J. Baltes and Paul B. Baltes, 1897–1903. Oxford, UK: Elsevier, 2001.

Carpenter, Mary. *Six Months in India*. 2 vols. London: Longmans, Green, 1868.

Carter, Stephen L. *Civility: Manners, Morals, and the Etiquette of Democracy*. New York: Basic Books, 1998.

Cohen, Jean L., and Andrew Arato. *Civil Society and Political Theory*. Cambridge, MA: MIT Press, 1992.

Debi, Swarnakumari. *The Uprooted Vine (Snehalata Ba Palita)*. Translated by Rajul Sogani and Indira Gupta. New Delhi: Oxford University Press, 2004.

Dickens, Charles. *Bleak House*. New York: Penguin, 1971.

Dyson, Anthony Edward, ed. *Dickens's Bleak House: A Casebook*. London: Macmillan, 1969.

Elliott, Dorice Williams. *The Angel Out of the House: Philanthropy and Gender in Nineteenth-Century England*. Charlottesville: University of Virginia Press, 2002.

Fine, Gary Alan, and Brooke Harrington. "Tiny Publics: Small Groups and Civil Society." *Sociological Theory* 22, no. 3 (2004): 341–356.

Forbes, Geraldine. "In Search of the 'Pure Heathen': Missionary Women in Nineteenth Century India." *Economic and Political Weekly* 21, no. 17 (1986): WS2–WS8.

Gerard, Jessica. "Lady Bountiful: Women of the Landed Classes and Rural Philanthropy." *Victorian Studies* 30, no. 2 (1987): 187–210.

Ghose, Indira, ed. *Memsahibs Abroad: Writings by Women Travellers in Nineteenth Century India*. Delhi: Oxford University Press, 1998.

Goodlad, Lauren M. E. *Victorian Literature and the Victorian State: Character and Governance in a Liberal Society*. Baltimore, MD: Johns Hopkins University Press, 2003.

Login, E. Dalhousie, ed. *Lady Login's Recollections*. 2nd ed. Punjab, India: Languages Department, 1970.

Midgley, Clare. "Female Emancipation in an Imperial Frame: English Women and the Campaign against Sati (Widow-Burning) in India, 1813–30." *Women's History Review* 9, no. 1 (2000): 95–121.

Nair, Janaki. "Uncovering the Zenana: Visions of Indian Womanhood in Englishwomen's Writings, 1813–1940." *Journal of Women's History* 2, no. 1 (1990): 8–34.

Nightingale, Florence. *Cassandra and Other Selections from Suggestions for Thought*. Edited by Mary Poovey. New York: New York University Press, 1992.

Paxton, Nancy L. "Feminism under the Raj: Complicity and Resistance in the Writings of Flora Annie Steel and Annie Besant." *Women's Studies International Forum* 13, no. 4 (1990): 333–346.

Peck, Dennis L. "Civility: A Contemporary Context for a Meaningful Historical Concept." *Sociological Inquiry* 72, no. 2 (2002):358–375.

Pemble, John, ed. *Miss Fane in India*. Gloucester, UK: Alan Sutton, 1985.

Perrin, Alice. *Idolatry*. London: Chatto and Windus, 1909.

Poovey, Mary. *Making a Social Body: British Cultural Formation, 1830–1864*. Chicago: University of Chicago Press, 1995.

———. *Uneven Developments: The Ideological Work of Gender in Mid-Victorian England*. Chicago: University of Chicago Press, 1988.

Raza, Rosemary. *In Their Own Words: British Women Writers and India, 1740–1857*. New Delhi: Oxford University Press, 2006.
Riley, Denise. *Am I That Name? Feminism and the Category of "Women" in History*. London: Macmillan, 1988.
Roy, Anindyo. *Civility and Empire: Literature and Culture in British India, 1822–1922*. London: Routledge, 2005.
Sangari, Kumkum, and Sudesh Vaid. "Recasting Women: An Introduction." In *Recasting Women: Essays in Indian Colonial History*, edited by Kumkum Sangari and Sudesh Vaid, 1–26. New Brunswick, NJ: Rutgers University Press, 1990.
Sarkar, Tanika. "Enfranchised Selves: Women, Culture and Rights in Nineteenth-Century Bengal." *Gender and History* 13, no. 3 (2001): 546–565.
Sharpe, Jenny. *Allegories of Empire: The Figure of Woman in the Colonial Text*. Minneapolis: University of Minnesota Press, 1993.
Society for Promoting Female Education in China, India, and the East. *Female Agency among the Heathen: Being the History of the Society for Promoting Female Education in the East, Founded in the Year 1834*. London: Suter and Alexander, [1847].
Sogani, Rajul, and Indira Gupta. Introduction to *The Uprooted Vine (Snehalata Ba Palita)*, by Swarnakumari Debi, translated by Rajul Sogani and Indira Gupta, vii–xiv. New Delhi: Oxford University Press, 2004.
Sundar, Pushpa. "Women and Philanthropy in India." In *Women, Philanthropy, and Civil Society*, edited by Kathleen D. McCarthy, 271–286. Bloomington: Indiana University Press, 2001.
Tharu, Susie. "Tracing Savitri's Pedigree: Victorian Racism and the Image of Women in Indo-Anglian Literature." In *Recasting Women: Essays in Indian Colonial History*, edited by Kumkum Sangari and Sudesh Vaid, 254–268. New Brunswick, NJ: Rutgers University Press, 1990.
Thomson, Patricia. *The Victorian Heroine: A Changing Ideal, 1837–1873*. London: Oxford University Press, 1956.
Walzer, Michael. "The Civil Society Argument." In *Dimensions of Radical Democracy: Pluralism, Citizenship, Community*, edited by Chantal Mouffe, 89–112. London: Verso, 1992.
Wilford, Florence. *A Maiden of Our Own Day*. 4th ed. London: Charles Taylor, 1899.

6

Patrons, Philanthropists, and Professionals
Henry James's Roderick Hudson

Francesca Sawaya

"Artists have always had patrons," writes Marjorie Garber in *Patronizing the Arts*. "From the time of Maecenas . . . to the Medicis and later the popes, and then to Isabella Stewart Gardner and the Guggenheim and MacArthur Foundations," she continues, "rich sponsors have often supported painters, sculptors, and poets."[1] This sponsorship, Garber argues, is "not a *problem* per se. . . . Rather, it is a condition of art-in-the-world."[2] Nonetheless, she identifies what she sees as the central challenges that emerge from a dynamic in which the "artist had the talent, and the patron the money": the "over-, and underestimation" of the arts. Art has been overestimated in the sense of being seen as transcendent and priceless and, therefore, as tainted by financial support; it has been underestimated in the sense of being seen as merely supplementary to the important work of economics, politics, and business. At the same time, the dynamic of talent versus money in patronage has also led to a complex psychological relation between the patron and the artist (*patron* is a word, Garber notes, etymologically linked to *pater*, or father). This "libidinal economy" mixes "deep gratitude and powerful resentment" and "often follows the psychic structure of a love affair." Garber's goal in her book is therefore twofold: to bring about renewed commitment to art sponsorship in an era of cutbacks and to equalize the relation of patron and artist, to create "a mode of patronage without patronization."[3]

Garber's contemporary polemic is useful for thinking about the question with which this chapter grapples: namely, how to define and analyze the significance of patronage and philanthropy for literature *within* modern capitalism. The "standard narrative" of economics in literature is that the emergence of modern capitalist markets freed the writer from the need for sponsorship.[4] In the eighteenth century, a constraining system of patronage gave way, literary historians argue, to a free market and professionalism, where the writer is carefully trained and able to support himself or herself through specialized, disciplined, and meritorious work.[5] In contrast, Garber asserts that "artists have always had patrons," that sponsorship was and remains a significant part of cultural production in the West across time and national boundaries, and therefore that the artist is wrongly often seen as an *"amateur,"* who works for love of art, rather than a trained *"professional."*[6] Capitalism, in Garber's argument, has not freed the artist economically or provided him or her with the status of a professional, as literary historians presume.[7]

Nonetheless, if Garber usefully challenges the "standard narrative" about the free market, her argument has a number of puzzling features, the most striking of which is her difficulty in defining what patronage is. Early on in the book, for example, Garber undermines her claim that artists and intellectuals have always had patrons by arguing that patronage is a relatively minor issue for modern literature (as opposed to modern art). She uses Samuel Johnson's famous 1755 letter breaking with his patron Lord Chesterfield to argue, as literary historians characteristically do, that the emergence of copyright and the expansion of the market in cultural goods in the eighteenth century enabled writers to bypass elite patronage and the dependency it created. But having created this opposition between patronage and the market in literature, Garber then abruptly returns to her original thesis. She discusses the continuing forms of individual patronage in modern literature and then closes down any contradiction by making patronage an infinitely capacious term. She suddenly asserts that "contracts, agents and editors, bookstores, magazines, and journals"—all factors usually associated with markets—are simply the "patronage units of the present day." Patrons, to Garber, are indistinguishably individuals, governments, corporations, universities, and markets.[8]

One way to support Garber's insight that sponsorship remains crucial for artists and writers *within* capitalism, while avoiding both contradiction and analytical imprecision, is to historicize her transhistorical account of patronage. Many historians and sociologists who study the changing practices of sponsorship would use the term *philanthropy*, rather than *patronage*, to describe modern and contemporary sponsorship of literature and the arts.[9] For these scholars, patronage is a premodern social practice that links individuals in self-interested and personalized ways across institutionalized hierarchies or divides, within contexts of inequality, such as feudal or aristocratic societies.[10] Philanthropy, in contrast, while having a premodern history in patronage and charity, is often seen as a modern social practice. Robert Gross, for example, focuses on the historical differences between charity and philanthropy, arguing that charity is premodern, linked to religious belief, and characterized by face-to-face interaction, whereas philanthropy is an "innovation of the market revolution's" joint-stock company of the seventeenth century and seeks "to apply reason to the solution of social ills and needs" through "abstract and institutional forms."[11] Philanthropy is thus etymologically and historically associated with disinterested and impersonal, rather than self-interested and personal, forms of sponsorship or aid.

Such distinctions between patronage and charity, on the one hand, and philanthropy, on the other, provide useful analytical leverage. At the same time, they do not completely solve the problem of imprecision. *Patronage*, for example, is a term we continue to use to describe systematic forms of sponsorship that highlight social inequality and mutual self-interest in business, politics, and culture. Similarly, many sociologists and historians read philanthropy as deeply self-interested, as an intraclass and transatlantic bourgeois practice that works both to create distinction among elites—within and across nations—and to stabilize the status quo, rather than disinterestedly distributing access.[12] Patronage blurs easily into philanthropy and vice versa. In short, we need better tools for analyzing the range of changing social practices that are part of capitalism and its markets.

In this chapter, I begin to ask some of the questions that might help us develop such tools for literature. Relying on the useful, albeit blurred, definitions of *patronage* and *philanthropy* outlined above, I examine Henry James's early novel *Roderick Hudson* (1874) and its representation particularly of the historical relation between patronage and modern philanthropy within capitalism. The novel is an important one in the James canon. James himself described it as his "first attempt at a novel, a long fiction with a 'complicated' subject" and revised and republished it twice (in 1878 and 1909).[13] While James criticism exhibits enormous theoretical sophistication in analyzing the relation between economics and aesthetics, critics have rarely focused on the significance of cultural patronage and philanthropy in his work. They have instead focused on what Michael Anesko calls James's "friction with the market," meaning James's critique of and uneasy adaptation to what is implicitly described as a free and competitive economic system.[14] While such a focus has been illuminating, we need to rethink the way James depicts capitalist markets—not as free or competitive but instead as shaped by the social practices of patronage and philanthropy. Adapting from Karl Polanyi's famous argument, we might say that James's depiction of capitalism focuses on the "intervention[ism]" that creates markets, not on what Polanyi calls the "utopian" fiction of free and competitive markets.[15] Rather than disputing the contemporary focus on James's critique of and engagement with markets, I am suggesting instead that we can ask new questions in relation to it by analyzing his depictions of patronage and of philanthropy's intervention in markets.

Roderick Hudson is usually read as a *künstlerroman* that rehearses debates about romanticism and realism, passion and self-discipline, homosociality and homosexuality in art, and the position of the American artist in the world.

Economic issues are subordinated to other concerns in contemporary analyses of the novel, perhaps because the market—as typically described in James criticism—appears to be relatively absent in the text. In addition, while the economics of the patron-artist relation cannot be avoided, that relation is usually read as being symbolic of purely psychological or aesthetic issues.[16] I argue instead that the novel's affective and aesthetic issues are indissolubly linked to economic ones—to the depiction of the market as constituted by forms of social "interventionism." James, in contrast to both the "standard narrative" of literary history and Garber's contradictory transhistorical one, provides a historical interpretation of the centrality of the patron, a centrality that James suggests is being transformed ideologically and practically into philanthropy within capitalism. Through his story of a sculptor and his patron, James describes a shift not only from individual to systematic forms of sponsorship but also from self-interested to putatively disinterested ones.

In telling this story, the novel's relation to the transatlantic is complex. James implicitly reads aesthetic patronage and philanthropy as a transatlantic elite phenomenon. Aristocratic European art sponsorship provides the backdrop for the story. But while James's story is largely set in Europe, he emphasizes that this is an American story and focuses on American artists and sponsors. The novel was written during the great institution-building period for American art, to which James directly alludes in the novel. In 1870, 1872, and 1877, respectively, the Boston Art Museum, the Metropolitan Museum of Art, and the Philadelphia Museum of Art were founded—each of which embodies the kind of activities we associate with patronage but even more with philanthropy. The "collecting mania" of the postbellum period—in which the US industrial elite bought up European art and placed it in the new urban museums—could be seen simply as an American version of old-fashioned European art patronage and philanthropy; however, James emphasizes that if his story is linked to the traditions of sponsorship in Europe, the story also must be read in terms of specific American cultural and historical developments.[17] Particularly, James depicts American patronage and philanthropy as having been shaped by the history of Puritanism. In addition, James's emphasis on professionalism and elite benevolence evokes the contemporary US cultural context. The large-scale institution building of the 1870s both embodied and created the need for more systematic forms of elite sponsorship and new kinds of professional expertise—in fundraising, museum management, art history, and art dealership. At the same time, these new institutional forms entailed a new ideology of elite benevolence that sought to describe civic health as best fostered when private and public sectors combine their forces. In short, James interprets his contemporary moment as one in which American patronage is changing and becoming philanthropy, without one social practice being reducible to the other. He furthermore suggests such change is taking place in dialogue with, but also in distinction from, aristocratic European forms of patronage and philanthropy.[18]

Even as James distinguishes patronage and philanthropy and suggests there are national variants of these social practices, he also links the practices together as part of a "libidinal economy," as Garber would say. James describes his wealthy patron as driven by an old-fashioned, and particularly American, Puritan ethos of morality and duty as well as by more modern, sentimental, and apparently benevolent motivations. Both the older and newer motivations are, in James's account, complexly constituted by what Friedrich Nietzsche identified as *ressentiment*. Nietzsche defined *ressentiment* as a revengeful envy, a will to power, disguising itself as morality or benevolence.[19] But as Fredric Jameson points out in his analysis of this central "ideologeme" of the nineteenth century, while Nietzsche associates such ressentiment with the "slave" morality of the powerless, the concept has an "unavoidably autoreferential structure," reflecting as much on bourgeois intellectuals like Nietzsche who deployed it as on the "slaves" such intellectuals sought to describe.[20] James's use in *Hudson* of the thematic of ressentiment highlights the notion of benevolent morality as a form of revengeful envy, but one that reflects forms of powerlessness or frustrated aesthetic ambitions of the bourgeois patron/philanthropist, not the penniless artist. Interestingly, in *Hudson*, James does not suggest that the artist can free himself from the ressentiment of the powerful sponsor by entering the putatively free market. Instead, in James, the market is always linked to sponsorship. The artist's dependency on his envious and resentful sponsor may, therefore, seem to make his situation hopeless. However, James suggests that the artist can survive the sponsor's ressentiment—in the different forms it takes—if he relies on a professional ethos. The complicated economic and affective relationships James describes, as well as his wishful solution of professionalism, both illuminate and extend Garber's argument, opening up important questions about how to understand and represent the dynamics of literary production in capitalism. James's depiction of the imbrication of the social practices of patronage and philanthropy in modern markets has important implications for both literary historians and James scholars.

Historicizing Patronage and Philanthropy

In an essay that argues for more precision in defining and historicizing modern philanthropy, Susannah Morris argues that scholars need to be clear about the different variables they are focusing on—whether "motivation, action, or outcome."[21] It is notable that James's reading of sponsorship in *Hudson*, as in most of his writings, focuses almost solely on motivation rather than on action or outcome. James is particularly mesmerized by what he sees as a gap between the patron/philanthropist's conscious or stated motives and unconscious or historically determined ones. The careful examination in *Hudson* of the patron/philanthropist's motivation interestingly deflects from a focus on the artist himself, emphasizing the anti-Romanticism that imbues James's allegory of artistic vocation.[22] In his introduction to the New York edition of 1909, James says unequivocally that the story focuses on the patron, Rowland Mallet, not on the eponymous artist, Roderick Hudson. Writes James, "The centre of interest throughout 'Roderick' is in Rowland Mallet's consciousness, and the drama is the very drama of that consciousness." The focus on the "friend's and patron's ... view and experience of him [Hudson]," according to James, was "what really saved" the book from failure. Two issues emerge immediately: the patron is the "centre" of what James significantly calls his "first" novel, emphasizing the economic issue of sponsorship that James criticism has generally ignored, and the patron is also called a "friend," underlining the centrality of psychic or affective issues.[23]

James is somewhat disingenuous here in that he erases a previous novel, *Watch and Ward* (serialized in 1871). *Ward*, however, has much to tell us about *Hudson*. In *Ward*, a wealthy, awkward, unattractive, middle-aged man adopts a working-class, orphaned child, sparing no expense to raise her up as a lady. His explicitly stated hope from the very beginning is that the child's indebtedness to him will be so great that she will marry him. When she comes of age, and after a brief flirtation with a penniless man of her own age, the girl does indeed marry her adoptive guardian out of a sense of gratitude and indebtedness. Here James explores the blurred lines between putatively benevolent or disinterested and self-interested actions across economic divides and power differentials. Equally important, he explores the erotics or affect associated with sponsorship, particularly the question of gratitude—which James figures in economic terms as returns on debt.

In *Hudson*, James builds on *Ward* through a queer, rather than heterosexual, love story, and through the rubric of cultural sponsorship. Thus in *Hudson*, a wealthy, awkward, unattractive, middle-aged man simultaneously falls in love with and decides to sponsor an impoverished, handsome young artist, sparing no expense in his education and training. The sponsor acts apparently disinterestedly and benevolently as a "connoisseur" who hopes to help both a young artist and an American city by donating his collected art to a new museum.[24] As the novel proceeds, however, the sponsor's disinterestedness increasingly is called into question, as the kinds of gratitude, or returns, he requires are increasingly evidenced. In other words, *Hudson* explores the blurred lines between the self-interested and disinterested motivation associated respectively with patronage and philanthropy, the erotics and affect constituting such motivation, and the issue of gratitude as returns.

In exploring the historical—rather than transhistorical—motivations of the patron/philanthropist, the novel begins with a brief but pointed analysis of

Rowland Mallet's family, its connection to charitable giving, and how that family history has shaped Mallet's character and consciousness. The analysis links James's account of philanthropy as disinterested benevolence to Max Weber's analysis of the Protestant ethic in the history of capitalism, and to the stringent ethos of duty and asceticism that enables capitalist accumulation, as well as charitable giving.[25] Of "rigid Puritan stock," Mallet's wealthy father had consistently worked to ensure that his child was not "corrupted by luxury" and that he would be compelled to exercise a "rigorous... abstinence." James dryly writes that Mallet's father kept up his child's abstinence "at great expense," emphasizing the asceticism that inheres in capitalist accumulation, as well as the necessary defeat of that asceticism through capitalist accumulation.[26] At the same time, James highlights here the hypocrisy of Puritan ethics, as Mallet's father wields unnecessary abstinence as an expensive punitive disciplinary tool on his son.[27] James further criticizes these ethics by charting their relation to the motivation behind charity: "Mr. Mallet was consistent, but the perfection of his consistency was known only on his death. He left but a third of his property to his son, and devoted the remainder to various public institutions and local charities."[28] In leaving "but a third" of his property to his son, in making the "perfection" of his Puritan morality "known" on his deathbed through charity, and in also thereby disciplining and punishing his son financially yet again, James suggests that Mr. Mallet's morality really is self-interested and sadistic self-aggrandizement.[29] James's Weberian analysis of Mallet's father combines a notion of the links, on the one hand among Protestant asceticism, duty, and charity and on the other hand, capitalist accumulation, self-interested self-aggrandizement, and personal cruelty.

Mallet's father's story is shown to be important in two ways for understanding his son. On the one hand, Mallet inherits his father's beliefs: "[He] had been brought up to think much more intently of the duties of this life than of its privileges and pleasures." In short, Puritan ethics (which James has so thoroughly criticized) are central to the son. On the other hand, Mallet also inherits "a private plot of sentiment" from his "singularly unhappy" "saint" of a mother, who has "spent her life in trying to look in the face" the "immitigable error" that is her marriage. Such sentiment and identification enables him to rebel against the "exclusively salutary" fate of "rigorous abstinence" that his father had planned for him. *Sentiment*, however, is a complex term for nineteenth-century male artists like James. In this novel, the term appears to be linked to femininity and, through that, in a positive sense to an aesthetic sensitivity that exceeds "abstinence" but in a negative sense to failures of perception and blocked or mistaken erotics.[30]

The end result of such a family history, in James's narrative, is that Mallet's plan for his life combines his father's (complexly motivated) charitable practice with his mother's (complexly described) "sentiment": he plans to travel abroad to "purchase certain valuable specimens of the Dutch and Italian schools as to which he had received private proposals, and then present his treasures out of hand to an American city, not unknown to aesthetic fame, in which at that time there prevailed a good deal of fruitless aspiration toward an art museum." In this regard, Hudson is an early figuration of James's most famous cultural patron and philanthropist, Adam Verver of *The Golden Bowl*. Hudson, and later Verver (also described as a Puritan), both plan to contribute to the civically inclined museum building of the time. Mallet explains this goal to his cousin Cecilia this way: "I am tired of myself, my own thoughts, my own affairs, my own eternal company. True happiness, we are told, consists in getting out of one's self. . . . [One] must have some absorbing errand." James highlights here that Mallet's motivation for his cultural philanthropy can be linked, on the one hand to Puritan duty and ethics (to an "absorbing errand," to "getting out of one's self") and on the other hand to the feminized "sentimental" rebellion against it through "happiness" and aesthetics.[31]

However, James complicates this historical analysis of the residual elements of Puritanism embedded in a newer sentimental and civic cultural philanthropy. For example, when Mallet explains to his cousin Cecilia his dream of social usefulness through cultural philanthropy, she curtly responds, "What an immense number of words . . . to say you want to fall in love."[32] While Cecilia's statement appears a profoundly reductive account of his motives—given the historical analysis the book has just outlined—James nonetheless also validates Cecilia's analysis. Cecilia tells Mallet that while she cannot find him a "pretty girl" to fall in love with, she "can at least show [him] a pretty boy."[33] The "pretty boy" is a statue she has been given of a young boy slaking his thirst, which leads Mallet to another pretty boy: the statue's creator, Roderick Hudson. Mallet's goal of cultural philanthropy (purchasing European art for an American art museum) is instantly redirected into one of individual patronage of an American artist. In this way, the historical account James has provided us of the transformation of Puritan charity into systematic and sentimental cultural philanthropy also works backward as a story of individual patronage, and both stories are connected to complex psychic and libidinal motivations. So if the story has a historical trajectory, it also refuses any simple account of changes in forms of sponsorship. James describes social practices that could be indistinguishably defined as philanthropy or patronage—institutional and civic-minded sponsorship as well as individual and affective; putatively disinterested and complexly self-interested.[34]

At the same time, James boldly layers the Weberian account of the double-edged Protestant ethic involved in sponsorship or "charity" onto a Nietzschean one about ressentiment. What precipitates love in *Hudson* is apparently envy—the envy of the weak (artistically if not economically) for the lordly and masterly. Mallet sees himself as "neither fish nor flesh nor good red herring" and has failed in his one and only aspiration—that of being "a vigorous young man of genius without a penny." James structures the narrative so that Mallet sees Hudson's statue of a "pretty boy" before Hudson has met Mallet. The result is that the wealthy connoisseur's first feeling toward Hudson is not love but "a pang of something akin to envy" for "what he [Mallet] failed of in action and missed in possession": "[The statue] had the stamp of genius. Rowland envied the happy youth who, in a New England village, without aid or encouragement, without models or examples, had found it so easy to produce a lovely work." But Rowland's envy is redirected by Puritan morality; it is "half suppressed . . . for conscience sake." As in Nietzsche's theory of ressentiment, envy turns into morality—into an expression of admiration and friendship *as* benevolent philanthropy. Thus, the scene of Mallet's proposal to Hudson finds him "blush[ing]" when he offers to take Hudson to Europe and become his patron. Mallet describes himself to Hudson not as a patron but as "a friend with a good deal more [money] than he wants." Such blushing seems to highlight how envy has been redirected into a modest, humble, and disinterested friendship—a friendship that shrinks in embarrassment from its financial power. Such blushing could also be read more ambiguously as an expression of embarrassment at the mixed emotions of envy and conscientious philanthropy.[35]

The blushing tells us another story as well: envy that is also love and admiration motivates Mallet's patronage and philanthropy of Hudson, and this envy and love informs the homosocial triangle that James constructs between Mallet, Hudson, and Hudson's fiancée, Mary Garland. Hudson states that he falls in love with Garland and proposes to her at the same time that Mallet has offered Hudson his patronage. He says, "You [Mallet] . . . put me into such ridiculous good-humour that I felt an extraordinary desire to tell some woman that I adored her." Likewise, Mallet apparently falls in love with Mary Garland, as James himself notes in the preface, "at the same hour" that he offers Hudson his patronage.[36] This timing highlights the interconnected tissues of envy and admiration, envy and love that James is suggesting are constitutive of aesthetic sponsorship. Thus, it is no surprise that as the novel progresses, Mallet comes to fantasize consciously about destroying Hudson. Writes James of Mallet's thoughts:

> When of old a man was burnt at the stake it was cruel to have to be present; but if one were present it was a charity to lend a hand to pile up the fuel and make the flames do their work quickly and the smoke muffle up the victim. With all deference to your charity, this was perhaps an obligation you would especially feel if you had a reversionary interest in something the victim was to leave behind him.[37]

In a subtle link to his Puritan father and, behind him, New England's witch burnings, as well as to the disciplinary and punitive use of charity in which his father engaged, Mallet's philanthropic leanings take on a new color. He sees himself as having a charitable "obligation" to help "kill" Hudson, especially since there is a "reversionary interest in something the victim was to leave behind."

Garland is implicitly the "something the victim was to leave behind," but she is clearly only a traditional placeholder in the homosocial triangle for the different ways in which Hudson's destruction can benefit Mallet. For after all, Hudson's death can also end Mallet's continuous envy of and need to monitor Hudson's wide-ranging and apparently heterosexual amorous adventures, indirectly sponsored by Mallet's money, and which include but are not limited to Garland. But, more importantly, James suggests a broader reading of how the artist's destruction can serve the patron. Hudson's destruction can benefit Mallet by ending the latter's envy of the former's artistic abilities, of what the patron "fail[s] of in action and misse[s] in possession."[38] The novel ends with Hudson's suicide or death and Mallet's continuing romantic pursuit of Garland, which demonstrates the seriousness of James's depiction of the philanthropic patron's ressentiment of the sponsored artist. Philanthropic patronage is the love that kills. Like Nietzsche's "slave" who practices "the secret black art of truly *grand* politics of revenge, of a farseeing, subterranean, slowly advancing . . . revenge," Mallet describes himself in the last lines of the book as he continues his pursuit of the bereaved Garland as "the most patient [of mortals]!"[39] Such a reading of patronage and philanthropy dramatizes the life-threatening dangers of sponsorship for the artist.

Accountability, Debt, Speculation

So far I have focused on the motivations—historical and personal—that James associates with patronage and philanthropy. I want to turn now to a more extensive analysis of James's account of how the economics of patronage and philanthropy endanger the author. One challenge of such an exploration is that James carefully obscures any literal depiction of monetary exchange; we never know what exactly constitutes the financial arrangements between Mallet and Hudson. Nonetheless, *Hudson* is noteworthy, as Andrew Lawson also argues, for its emphasis on metaphors of accounting and accountability. Lawson links this emphasis to the particular kind of "*rentier* ethos" James inherited from his father.[40] While of the *rentier* class, the Jameses' financial well-being was somewhat precarious, Lawson argues. So on the one hand, the family emphasized transforming capital into aesthetic experience, but on the other hand, they engaged in anxious hoarding, since "all sums are limited and their expenditure [must be] zealously controlled."[41] Lawson's reading helpfully explains the repeated discussions of accountability in the novel. Mallet sees himself and is seen by others as "accountable" for Hudson's behavior, as well as for his artistic failures or success.[42] While Hudson says to Mallet of the latter's view of his accountability, "That's a view of the situation I can't accept," Hudson is nonetheless even more obsessed with accountability, spending much of the book in his own accounting exercises: adding up credit but more often (and this is a key point) attesting to his debt to Mallet.[43] When, for example, Hudson first falters in his work, he asks Mallet for money to travel in the hopes he will be artistically rejuvenated, a request that Mallet misunderstands as a desire to travel together. Hudson responds carefully: "I needn't say I prefer your society to that of any man living. . . . But I have a perpetual feeling that you are expecting something of me, that you are measuring my doings by a terrifically high standard. You are watching me; I don't want to be watched. . . . It is not that I don't know what I owe you: it is not that we are not friends."[44] There is both monetary and affective accounting here. Mallet is watching Hudson as a patron who feels he is accountable for Hudson's actions, as his friend, and as an aspiring lover of Garland or Hudson (or both).[45] Hudson knows he is being watched; that he is expected to pay back equally in art and in a gratitude that is expressive of friendship and love.[46]

As must be self-evident here, while accounting and accountability are key to the novel—as Lawson shows—that language blurs quickly into that of debt, and also, and more importantly, speculation.[47] Mallet is figured in the novel as a speculator, but oddly enough, Hudson becomes a debtor. Early on in the novel, for example, Garland asks Mallet if he "mean[s] to do a great deal for [Hudson]?" The following conversation ensues:

> "What I can. But my power of helping him is very small beside his power of helping himself."
> For a moment she was silent again. "You are very generous," she said almost solemnly.
> "No, I am simply very shrewd. Roderick will repay me. It's a speculation."[48]

The syntax here is peculiar. To be assured of repayment is not to speculate. A speculation usually means a risk in which one may either win or lose, but Mallet seems to have certainty that he will be repaid. Therefore, when Hudson announces later in the novel that he is "bankrupt" and that he "shall never repay," Mallet's risk-free speculation seems to have gone awry. Mallet will not be repaid in art or love. Mallet seems to be left only "with the stale residuum of his own generosity." The ending of the novel, however, seems to justify Mallet's notion of risk-free speculation. Certainly, Hudson's words in his final confrontation with Mallet ("I can shut up shop now") suggest he plans to commit suicide. But whether he commits suicide or the deus ex machina of an alpine thunderstorm kills him, Hudson's debt—as noted earlier—is potentially repayable with his death as Mallet "patient[ly]" waits for Garland. The patron, the "generous" philanthropist, the speculator in James's depiction of the economic and affective relation of sponsorship, risks nothing with his benevolence; the artist, however, racks up debt that must ("will") be repaid even, or especially, with death. Such repayment comes here in the form of a person (Garland), but implicitly exceeds such a form—whether in terms of emotions of a certain kind or in art objects that are owned by the sponsor and can be sold—if the patron/philanthropist is as "patient" as Hudson is.[49]

Lest the novel's ambiguous deus ex machina seem to muddle James's critical analysis of the paradoxically risk-free speculative economics that inhere in the patron-philanthropist relation, consider James' parallel plot to that of Mallet and Hudson: the story of the American Christina Light.[50] Unlike Hudson, Christina does not have a patron. She does, however, have something comparable mediating her relation to the market—namely, her mother, whom James figures as a kind of pimp. Throughout the novel, James has Mrs. Light identify a community of interest between herself and Mallet, working to ally herself to him, and describing to him at length her ambitions for and anxieties about Christina. Like Mallet's relation to Hudson, Mrs. Light's relation to Christina is one of envy and hatred as well as love and admiration. Mallet has failed at his one dream of being "a vigorous young man of genius without a penny" and envies Hudson his artistic ability but then displaces this envy into benevolent love. Likewise, Mrs. Light has "failed to make her own fortune in matrimony [and] has transferred her hopes to her daughter." If Mallet sponsors Hudson, Mrs. Light sponsors her daughter, stating unequivocally, "Oh, the money alone that I have put into this thing would melt the heart of a Turk!" James therefore links Mallet and Mrs. Light as speculators: Mallet speculates on Hudson's genius, and Mrs. Light speculates on Christina's beauty. The creepiness of a mother's speculation on her daughter's beauty works to defamiliarize normative views of the acceptability of the patron's right to "speculate" on the artist and receive "returns."[51]

In a long monologue, Mrs. Light recounts Christina's story for Mallet. Mallet observes that Mrs. Light has "a real maternal conscience; she considered that she had been performing a pious duty in bringing up Christina to set her cap for a prince." To Mallet, this "real maternal conscience" presents the spectacle of a "conscience upside down." Yet while Mallet views Mrs. Light critically, we cannot help but see that Mrs. Light's conscience is but an exaggerated version of Mallet's. When Christina turns five, Mrs. Light realizes her daughter is a great beauty. From then on, she says, "I lived only for my daughter. I watched her, I fondled her from morning to night, I worshipped her. . . . I was determined she should be perfection." The language of watching and of attaining perfection reminds us of the accusation that Hudson levels at Mallet of "watching" and of measuring "[his] doings by a terrifically high standard." In the case of Christina, the result of such watching and such perfectionism, says Mrs. Light in resonantly economic language, is that "if my daughter is the greatest beauty in the world some of the credit is mine."[52] She explains further:

By the time she was ten years old she was beautiful as an angel, and so noticed, wherever we went, that I had to make her wear a veil like a woman of twenty.... I had a passionate belief that she might marry absolutely whom she chose, and she might be a princess out and out. I have never given it up, and I can assure you that it has sustained me in many embarrassments. Financial, some of them; I don't mind confessing it! I have raised money on that girl's face! I have taken her to the Jews and bidden her put up her veil, and asked if the mother of that young lady was not safe! She, of course, was too young to understand me.[53]

James suggests here how the mother's failed matrimonial ambitions are redirected into a conscientious duty to serve as a pimp for her child, to give Christina the ability to "marry absolutely whom she chose," which, as the story develops, comes to mean the highest bidder that her mother chooses. The mother's conscientiousness entails both speculating on her child's beauty and using her child to raise credit for the speculation. She makes debts ostensibly for the sake of Christina, but the debts somehow become only Christina's. Mrs. Light is "safe" as "the mother of that young lady," while Christina's indebtedness grows, just as Mallet is safe because Hudson "will repay" him. Or, as Madame Grandoni puts it, again in the language of speculation, "Of course it is Christina's beauty that floats her [Mrs. Light]." The mother's desire to help her daughter, her putative benevolence, renders her daughter a debtor. The Orientalist language used for Christina's story (involving as it does Turks, Jews, and a "slave market") suggests that James reads a kind of historic barbarism into the mother's conscientious speculation, which likewise inflects his reading of the conscientious philanthropic speculation on artists. In this dramatic juxtaposed rejection of benevolent conscientiousness, James links the patron/philanthropist to the pimp as equivalent figures whose speculative benevolence involves no speculation, whose investments have few costs and many different possible returns. If later male modernist authors depicted themselves as prostitutes in the market (one thinks here of Ernest Hemingway and F. Scott Fitzgerald's critical—albeit self-pitying—accounts), James's focus here is on the patron/philanthropist who pimps the artist/prostitute in capitalism.[54]

Patronage, Philanthropy, and Professionalism

Although the parallel story of Christina Light and her mother throws yet another lurid light on James's reading of the artist-sponsor relation, James refuses a simplistic account in which the sponsor is the single cause of the artist's tragic failure and death. While the novel exposes the murderous ressentiment of the patron/philanthropist, it also indicts Hudson's model of artistry and offers alternative models that do not fail. The novel's allegory of artistic vocation implies that only through a professional work ethic can the artist retain independence from the barbarous economic power of patronage/philanthropy. For example, early on in the novel, Mallet aggrandizes Roderick Hudson's "genius" and compares it critically to the sculptor Gloriani's "worldly motive, skill unleavened by faith, the mere base maximum of cleverness" and to the painter "Poor little Singleton" who "pass[es] for an embodiment of aspiring candour afflicted with feebleness of wing." In this early section of the novel, and despite Mallet's critical perception of Gloriani's "mere . . . cleverness," Gloriani correctly predicts Hudson's downfall: "My dear fellow, passion burns out, inspiration runs to seed. . . . [The artist] must learn to do without the Muse! When the fickle jade forgets the way to your studio, don't waste any time in tearing your hair and meditating on suicide. Come round and see me and I will show you how to console yourself." Gloriani provides no specifics of how to do without the muse when "inspiration runs to seed"; nonetheless, the novel itself suggests that in removing obstacles from Hudson's path, Mallet has encouraged Hudson's self-indulgent laziness, his "not altogether masculine" and "mollycoddle" tendencies. Obstacles, James suggests through Gloriani, are what test an artist's courage and must be overcome through an unfaltering professionalism. Hudson has genius but does not have the professional courage to succeed, so when genius fails him, instead of "Be[ing] a man," he becomes shamefully "querulous" and follows the route to failure and death that Gloriani had predicted for him.[55]

James puts heavy pressure on this thematic of a courageous and masculine professional work ethic in his 1909 preface, as well. Reflecting on himself as a young artist, who before *Hudson* had written only short stories and was "master as yet of no vessel constructed to carry a sail," he implicitly compares his masterly success to Hudson's failure. Highlighting the issue of sponsorship in his comparison, James repeatedly discusses the "terror" of the artist as he "at last . . . put[s] quite out to sea" and the "discipline" that is required to overcome this terror: "Art would be easy indeed if, by a fond power disposed to 'patronize' it, such conveniences, such simplifications, had been provided." The quotation marks around the word *patronize* emphasize the reference he is making to the plot of his own novel. No one can help the artist. Neither muse (Christina Light) nor patron/philanthropist (Mallet) can provide conveniences and simplifications for the artist. The real test of the artist is the professional courage and endurance he relies on as he faces the terrors of the open sea.[56]

But courage is not all there is to professionalism; diligence is also required. Thus, for example, the aptly named Singleton, who at the beginning of the novel is reduced to pathetic diminutives ("Poor, little Singleton"), triumphs by the end. Singleton, like Hudson, is sponsored financially by Mallet. But both Mallet and Hudson figuratively patronize him as well, the latter regarding his fellow artist with "amusement" and "levity."⁵⁷ But both literal and figurative patronage have no effect on Singleton:

> "Ah, don't envy our friend," Rowland said to Singleton . . . on [the latter's] expressing with a little groan of depreciation of his own paltry performances his sense of the brilliancy of Roderick's talent. "You will sail nearer the shore, but you sail in smoother waters. Be contented with what you are and paint me another picture."
> "Oh I don't envy Hudson anything he possesses," Singleton said, "because to take anything away would spoil his beautiful completeness."⁵⁸

Singleton's industry protects him from either being destroyed by the envy of the patron/philanthropist or experiencing envy himself. Singleton practices "happy frugality" and continues "with patient industry" to hone his "slender and delicate" "talent"; he therefore improves at each stage of the novel, gaining "more facility," and is increasingly filled with a "great happiness" rather than the great despair of Hudson. At the end of the novel, Mallet and Hudson are watching the sun set in the mountains of Switzerland when they see a "colossal figure as it made its way downward along the jagged silhouette of the rocks." It turns out to be none other than "little Sam Singleton," whose "unflagging industry" "pointed a moral" to the failed Hudson. Indeed, it is Singleton who finds Hudson's body after the latter "fall[s] from a great height" to his death. Professional diligence and a work ethic protects the artist from envy, prevents him from dramatic falls from grace, and eventually turns a little man into a "colossal figure."⁵⁹

However—and this is a key point—even as James posits that professionalism will inoculate the artist from the patron/philanthropist's ressentiment and create his success, he does not presume that sponsorship therefore disappears. Thus, even as Singleton's professional courage and diligence ensure his success, James nonetheless makes clear that he too depends on Mallet's sponsorship.⁶⁰ James refuses the opposition of the "standard narrative" of literary history, in which unfree sponsorship stands on one side and the free market and professionalism stand on the other side. Whatever role the market plays in an artist's work, in James's account, sponsorship remains the basic necessity of the artist. The result is that professionalism in *Hudson* is a form of self-protection from the sponsor within a market economy.

James's historical interpretation of the change and continuity within the social practices of patronage and philanthropy and his critical account of both the motivations of the patron/philanthropist and the economics of speculation and debt that govern sponsorship provide useful insights that contextualize Garber's transhistorical claims about sponsorship. Patronage and philanthropy, as James describes them, change over time, and the problems that he charts are not simply those of "art-in-the-world," as Garber puts it, but specifically of "art-within-capitalism."[61] Unlike Garber, James does not imagine that equality between sponsor and artist can occur within capitalism; however, he does fantasize about strategies that will protect the artist in his or her subordination. His interpretation opens up at least two avenues for future research in terms of both the modern literary field and James himself. First, as we rethink the standard narrative of modern literary economics, we need to continue to explore the kinds of social practices and forms of sponsorship, including but not limited to patronage and philanthropy, that are important in literary history. Likewise, we can explore the forms of protection that authors created or imagined for themselves. Authorship studies, an old-fashioned terrain of study, may nonetheless be one specific place to begin broader historical analyses of interventionism in literary markets. Instead of presuming that the market is the central factor in modern writers' literary careers, we can more carefully explore different kinds of sponsorship in authors' lives, how those forms of sponsorship operate within a variety of publishing venues (elite, mass-market, middlebrow), how their significance can change over the course of a career, and how artists responded critically to those practices. From these individual studies, we can expand outward.

In terms of James's own personal story, we need to remember, as Lawson emphasizes, that he was a member of the rentier class. Such biographical details should not limit or reduce our readings of James's work, but they can expand both our understanding of his representation of economics and the economic dynamics of the literary field. Lawson, thus, usefully analyzes the way James's family's precarious rentier status affects *Hudson*, but other issues emerge as well. For example, Anesko explains how, in 1873, James's father offered to pay for the publication of *Hudson*. James, however, demurred, writing to his father that he wanted "to start [him]self on a remunerative and perfectly practical literary basis."[62] Given James's critical analysis of the patron/philanthropist's revengeful envy and the economics of speculation and debt in *Hudson*, it is not a surprise that he refused his father's offer. Nonetheless, throughout his career, James was in fact his own sponsor, in the sense that he did not rely solely on his literary publications for his living. Indeed while Anesko argues that James only once made the mistake of letting his father sponsor his work, Anesko's brilliant research in fact reveals that James was always partially supported by money from the family's Syracuse real estate holdings, especially after 1893, when James's share of the family inheritance grew dramatically.[63] In addition, as Anesko shows, James had not only familial money but also familial connections in the literary world, which helped him along.

Relying on Anesko's research, we might furthermore ask: What did increased private revenue after 1893 mean for James? Can we connect it to the formal experimentations of his later years? How does James's rentier status and self-sponsorship likewise relate to the development of professionalism, an ethos so deeply embraced by James? Furthermore, how can we connect James to the recent work demonstrating the centrality of rentier sponsorship more generally in experimental literary modernism? And if we can connect it, how does rentier sponsorship inflect the themes and politics of such work?[64] Furthermore, what do self-sponsorship and family connections mean to a writer practically? One can imagine a range of implications associated with such connections and sponsorship. But also how might those forms of sponsorship and connections inflect James's analysis of a broader capitalist culture that, in contrast (and disingenuously), aggrandizes "a vigorous young man of genius without a penny"?[65]

And this leads to the second avenue of research: What happens to our analysis of literary texts when we rethink the significance of patronage and philanthropy (among other social practices)? As James's refusal of his father's help and his notion of starting out "on a remunerative and perfectly practical literary basis" suggests, James felt some pressure not only to sell his writings but also to see himself as selling his writings—to see himself as "remunerative."[66] Geoffrey Turnovsky has argued that "commerce" represents a "stylized image" that writers don to claim their intellectual independence, but which literary historians have adopted uncritically.[67] While Turnovsky's point is well taken, one could also argue for the genuine ideological commitment to imagining one's writing as being "remunerative." Such commitment makes *Hudson* legible as a novel about patronage and philanthropy in yet another way. There are certainly salutary and prescient features in James's critical and suspicious account of the economics of accounting, speculation, and debt in patronage and especially philanthropy. One thinks of contemporary analyses of the way philanthropy has hijacked radical social movements, or how philanthropy—in the name of and with the intention of doing good—has helped in the enforcement of brutal neoliberal policies.[68]

Nonetheless, and at the same time, if to James the patron/philanthropist's envy is motivated by his failure to be a "vigorous young man of genius without a penny," and if his revenge is gained by his "conscientious" desire to help a talented young artist, then James implicitly criticizes the bad faith that inheres in the notion of one's duty to help others. His critique of the desire to be socially useful becomes even more scathing, extensive, and outraged in his novels about social movements—about the sponsorship of socialism by the former Christina Light in *The Princess Casamassima* and the sponsorship of the women's movement by Olive Chancellor in *The Bostonians*. More emphatically than Nietzsche's notion of benevolence as revenge, James seems to posit benevolence in capitalism as murderous.[69]

Thus, in *Hudson*, when Mallet tells Cecilia of his decision to sponsor Hudson, Cecilia "exhibited a certain fine displeasure." She tells him that "the boy is doing very well. Let well alone!" She continues by accusing Mallet of "meddling."

As Hudson begins his decline, Mallet writes to Cecilia, "My dear wise cousin, you were right and I was wrong: you were a shrewd observer, and I was a meddlesome donkey!"[70] Indeed, one moral of *Hudson* seems to be that if the patron/philanthropist had not meddled, the artist might have survived and achieved, or if he was not meant to succeed, he would have at least lived. To intervene through financial aid is to "meddle," and to "meddle," in the context of this story, is to obstruct ethical freedom. Indeed, returning to Susannah Morris's notion of the different factors in philanthropy, James's focus on motivation (rather than on actions or outcomes) suggests his indebtedness to liberal economics. To James, without entirely pure motives—a purity that is impossible given what the liberal economics of Adam Smith along with Puritanism theorize as the "natural selfishness and rapacity" of man, or what James later calls the "terrible . . . heart of man"—neither actions nor outcomes matter in any form of helping others.[71] To put it another way, while James's suspicious reading of the patron/philanthropist is useful (given what has been done in the name of philanthropy in James's time as well as ours), suspicious readings themselves have their own histories that bear examination. In James's case, his anxiety about all forms of "interventionism"—whether for the artist or otherwise—itself bears scrutiny within the nineteenth-century discourse of philanthropy.

FRANCESCA SAWAYA is Professor of English and American Studies at the College of William and Mary. Her publications include *The Difficult Art of Giving: Patronage, Philanthropy, and the American Literary Market* and *Modern Women, Modern Work: Domesticity, Professionalism, and American Writing, 1890–1950*.

Notes

1. Garber, *Patronizing the Arts*, 1.
2. Ibid., ix (emphasis in original).
3. Ibid., xi–xiii, xiv, 1, 2.
4. The term *standard narrative* comes from Turnovsky, *The Literary Market*, 5.
5. Some central accounts of the discourse of professionalism in literature and otherwise include Bledstein, *Culture of Professionalism*; Glazener, *Reading for Realism*; Haber, *Quest for Authority*; Haskell, *Professional Social Science*; Robbins, *Secular Vocations*; and Wilson, *Labor of Words*.
6. Garber, *Patronizing the Arts*, xii (emphasis in original). Critics of professional discourse have long disputed the claims of professional autonomy that Garber seems to depend on implicitly in her critique of the status of the artist. For a stringent Marxist analysis of professionalism and its claims, see Larson, *Rise of Professionalism*, and for a measured one, see Robbins, *Secular Vocations*.
7. For other critiques of the "standard narrative," see Bigelow, *Fiction, Famine, and the Rise of Economics*; Jackson, *Business of Letters*; Osteen and Woodmansee, introduction to *The*

New Economic Criticism; and Sawaya, *Difficult Art of Giving*. Scholars of the "new economic criticism" have particularly shown the problems with the standard economic narrative—the continuing difficulty in periodizing the shift from sponsorship to free market but, more importantly, the faulty conceptual apparatus borrowed from the fictions of liberal economics about free and competitive markets that render highly questionable the empirical validity of such a narrative.

    8. Garber, *Patronizing the Arts*, 4–7, 11–12, 13.

    9. On occasion, Garber herself indirectly notes this. In the middle of the book, she suddenly makes a distinction between government "patronage" and what she calls "cultural philanthropy," by which she means corporate-based sponsorship. But she does not explain this switch in terminology and promptly recurs to the term *business patronage*. Garber, *Patronizing the Arts*, 97. Nowhere does she actually explain why she has used *patronage* to describe so many different forms of sponsorship or why corporate sponsorship deserves the much more positively inflected language of *philanthropy* than other forms of sponsorship.

    10. See Holzknecht's classic study, *Literary Patronage*.

    11. Gross, "Giving in America," 44–45, 37, 31. For the implications of the transformation from charity to philanthropy on literary form, see Christianson, *British and American Fiction*.

    12. See particularly the Bourdieu-inspired analyses of philanthropy in Adam, *Philanthropy, Patronage, and Civil Society* and Adam, *Buying Respectability*.

    13. James, *Roderick Hudson*, 10. The Penguin edition I use here is the 1878 edition, with the 1909 preface affixed to it.

    14. Anesko, *"Friction with the Market."*

    15. Polanyi, *Great Transformation*, 33, 138.

    16. I have found only one essay that focuses primarily on the relation between patronage and philanthropy and aesthetics: Andrew Lawson's very useful "Perpetual Capital." I discuss the essay below. Two illuminating essays whose suggestive discussions of patronage are nonetheless subordinated finally to psychosexual and aesthetic issues respectively are Mendelssohn, "Homosociality and the Aesthetic," and Saint-Amour, "Transatlantic Tropology."

    17. The term *collecting mania* and an analysis of the civic and nationalistic effect it had in the late nineteenth century comes from Harris, *Cultural Excursions*, 251. I have also relied on Burt, *Palaces for the People*; Pohl, *Framing America*; Saisselin, *Bourgeois and the Bibelot*; and Tinter, *Museum World of Henry James*.

    18. James makes the point about the relation between American and European sponsorship but also the national specificity of each version in later novels, especially *The Golden Bowl*. See Sawaya, *The Difficult Art of Giving*, chap. 1.

    19. For Nietzsche's account of ressentiment, see Nietzsche, *On the Genealogy of Morals*. While James apparently never read Nietzsche, there are nonetheless important links. For more on the James-Nietzsche connection, see Donadio, *Nietzsche*, 16–22; and McDonald's "Tragic Henry James."

    20. Jameson, *Political Unconscious*, 202.

    21. Morris, "Changing Perceptions," 139.

    22. I borrow the term *allegory of vocation* from Bruce Robbins, who defines such allegories as "critical works which, while doing whatever other interpretive tasks they set themselves, also perform a second, most often implicit function: they invent and arrange their concepts and characters so as to narrativize and argue for the general value and significance of the intellectual vocation they exemplify." Robbins, *Secular Vocations*, 190. While this may seem to simply repeat the notion of a künstlerroman, it usefully highlights the mixed genres of *Hudson* for a present-day reader, with its critical preface as well as its fictional narrative. For

more on the anti-Romanticism of the novel, see Saint-Amour, "Transatlantic Tropology"; and Duquette, "'Reflected Usefulness.'"

23. James, *Roderick Hudson*, 20, 19, 10.

24. Ibid., 36.

25. A Weberian reading of philanthropy is not unprecedented in history and sociology. For a particularly strong and effective use of Weber in terms of philanthropy, see Chernow, *Titan*.

26. James, *Roderick Hudson*, 28, 30.

27. While some critics note that a "mallet" is an artistic tool, its connotations emphasize violence. The *Oxford English Dictionary* defines a mallet thus: "I. Senses relating to the tool. 1. a. A kind of hammer, usually of wood, but sometimes of other materials, smaller than a maul or beetle and usually with a relatively large head ... II. In extended uses. 3. a. A person or agency that hits, beats down, or crushes something or someone." *Oxford English Dictionary*, 3rd ed., s.v. "mallet."

28. James, *Roderick Hudson*, 31. James emphasizes Mr. Mallet's hypocritical disciplinary morality by having one of the charities to whom he has left his money rather comically sue Rowland for more of his father's estate than was originally stipulated by the will. After winning the case against said charity, however, Mallet reveals his own Puritan ethos by promptly donating the given sum to another charity.

29. An autobiographical element is evident in this critique of Puritan morality. William James, who made the family's fortune, left his son Henry James Sr. a "derisory" sum of money on his death as a punishment for his "dissolute college days." Lawson, "Perpetual Capital," 179. Henry James Sr., like Mallet, contested the will successfully.

30. James, *Roderick Hudson*, 28, 31, 32, 30.

31. Ibid., 26, 27.

32. Ibid., 27.

33. Ibid., 33.

34. For another reading of Mallet's actions as purely self-aggrandizing and egoistic, see Duquette, "'Reflected Usefulness.'"

35. James, *Roderick Hudson*, 30, 33, 35, 84, 44.

36. Ibid., 73, 21.

37. Ibid., 216.

38. Ibid., 84.

39. Nietzsche, *On the Genealogy of Morals*, 35 (emphasis in original); James, *Roderick Hudson*, 350.

40. Lawson, "Perpetual Capital," 184.

41. Ibid., 187.

42. James, *Roderick Hudson*, 157.

43. Ibid.

44. Ibid., 101.

45. Mallet's profound disappointment, for example, in the bad returns he receives on Hudson's travel in terms of his artistic productivity appears inextricable from his disgust with Hudson's heterosexual, amorous adventures during it. James, *Roderick Hudson*, 106–107, 109. In fact, his disappointment seems more to do with friendship and love than with aesthetic productivity, since Hudson continues to produce good work at this point in the novel.

46. Mendelssohn interestingly argues that patronage in the novel gives Mallet "the right to sight," what Mendelssohn calls "scopophilia." This right is the return on Mallet's "investment." Mendelssohn, "Homosociality," 514, 519.

47. Mendelssohn usefully focuses on the language of "investment" with Mallet, and Saint-Amour on the language of debt. Neither, however, notes the relation that James establishes between the patron's speculation or investment and the artist's debt.

48. James, *Roderick Hudson*, 70.
49. Ibid., 283, 331, 340, 350.
50. Lawson also notes the story is parallel, emphasizing the commodification of Christina by her mother and Hudson by Mallet in trying to sell his work to the philistine American, Leavenworth. Lawson, "Perpetual Capital," 186–187.
51. James, *Roderick Hudson*, 33, 124, 268.
52. Ibid., 175, 176, 101.
53. Ibid., 177.
54. Ibid., 70, 142, 268, 177, 132.
55. Ibid., 98–99, 61–62, 36, 47, 114.
56. Ibid., 10, 11, 19.
57. Ibid., 99, 140.
58. Ibid., 140.
59. Ibid., 111, 89, 321, 322, 348. Duquette, like me, argues that Singleton is elevated as a model for the artist over Hudson. Unlike my argument, however, her argument focuses not on professionalism but on morality, arguing that James highlights the "pedestrian example" of Singleton over the Emersonian "exemplary genius" of Roderick Hudson. Duquette, "'Reflected Usefulness,'" 158. Nonetheless, Duquette's ideas about morality fit into the discourse of professionalism. Saint-Amour argues that James uses Gloriani as his model for the artist, albeit with critical irony. Saint-Amour, "Transatlantic Tropology." I would agree that Gloriani can be read as embodying a professional ethos, but it is Singleton's professionalism that James unironically embraces in the novel.
60. James, *Roderick Hudson*, 89, 110, 140. Likewise, Lawson argues that the philistine collector Leavenworth, who commissions a sculpture from Hudson, represents the market. Lawson, "Perpetual Capital." While this is a useful point, Leavenworth is explicitly described by James as a "patron" of American artists and a private collector. James, *Roderick Hudson*, 140–141. In other words, James is continually interested in "interventionism" in and *as crucial to* the market in this novel.
61. Garber, *Patronizing the Arts*, ix.
62. Quoted in Anesko, *"Friction with the Market,"* 32.
63. Anesko, *"Friction with the Market,"* 32, 172, 223n1.
64. For both the importance of rentier patronage to modernism and two completely different readings of what it means for the art produced, see Delany, "Who Paid for Modernism?"; and Rainey, "Cultural Economy of Modernism."
65. James, *Roderick Hudson*, 33. For recent work on the disingenuousness of the classic narrative of upward mobility, see Laird, *Pull*; and Robbins, *Upward Mobility*.
66. James, *Roderick Hudson*, 32.
67. Turnovsky, *Literary Market*, 5.
68. Some prominent examples of critique include Allen, *A Guide to Black Power in America*; INCITE! Women of Color against Violence, *Revolution Will Not Be Funded*; and Klein, *Shock Doctrine*.
69. We might ask, for example, why Hudson and Light do not simply default on their debts to their patrons/pimps. Mallet says to Hudson right before Hudson dies that Hudson is "incredibly ungrateful." James, *Roderick Hudson*, 337. So the reader is forced to ask: Why do Hudson and Christina not become "incredibly ungrateful" together? Why must they pay the debts that their sponsors have racked up for them with their lives? The novel seems to presume that they must, and thus the gift becomes murder.
70. James, *Roderick Hudson*, 51, 202.
71. Smith, *Theory of Moral Sentiments*, IV.I.10; James, *Golden Bowl*, 566.

Bibliography

Adam, Thomas, ed. *Buying Respectability: Philanthropy and Urban Society in Transnational Perspective, 1840s to 1930s*. Bloomington: Indiana University Press, 2009.

———. *Philanthropy, Patronage, and Civil Society: Experiences from Germany, Great Britain, and North America*. Bloomington: Indiana University Press, 2004.

Allen, Robert L. *A Guide to Black Power in America*. London: Victor Gollancz, 1970.

Anesko, Michael. *"Friction with the Market": Henry James and the Profession of Authorship*. New York: Oxford University Press, 1986.

Bigelow, Gordon. *Fiction, Famine, and the Rise of Economics in Victorian Britain and Ireland*. New York: Cambridge University Press, 2003.

Bledstein, Burton. *The Culture of Professionalism*. New York: W. W. Norton, 1976.

Burt, Nathaniel. *Palaces for the People: A Social History of the American Art Museum*. Boston: Little, Brown, 1977.

Chernow, Ron. *Titan: The Life of John D. Rockefeller, Senior*. New York: Random House, 1998.

Christianson, Frank. *Philanthropy in British and American Fiction: Dickens, Hawthorne, Eliot, and Howells*. Edinburgh, UK: Edinburgh University Press, 2007.

Delany, Paul. "Who Paid for Modernism?" In *The New Economic Criticism*, edited by Mark Osteen and Martha Woodmansee, 335–348. New York: Routledge, 1999.

Donadio, Stephen. *Nietzsche, Henry James, and the Artistic Will*. New York: Oxford University Press, 1978.

Duquette, Elizabeth. "'Reflected Usefulness': Exemplifying Conduct in *Roderick Hudson*." *Henry James Review* 23, no. 2 (2002): 157–175.

Garber, Marjorie. *Patronizing the Arts*. Princeton, NJ: Princeton University Press, 2008.

Glazener, Nancy. *Reading for Realism*. Durham, NC: Duke University Press, 1997.

Gross, Robert. "Giving in America: From Charity to Philanthropy." In *Charity, Philanthropy, and Civility in American History*, edited by Lawrence Friedman and Mark D. McGarvie, 29–48. Cambridge: Cambridge University Press, 2003.

Haber, Samuel. *The Quest for Authority and Honor in the Professions*. Chicago: University of Chicago Press, 1991.

Harris, Neil. *Cultural Excursions: Marketing Appetites and Cultural Tastes in Modern America*. Chicago: University of Chicago Press, 1990.

Haskell, Thomas. *The Emergence of Professional Social Science*. Urbana: University of Illinois Press, 1977.

Holzknecht, Karl Julius. *Literary Patronage in the Middle Ages*. 1923. Reprint, London: Octagon Books, 1966.

INCITE! Women of Color against Violence. *The Revolution Will Not Be Funded: Beyond the Non-profit Industrial Complex*. Cambridge, MA: South End Press, 2007.

Jackson, Leon. *The Business of Letters: Authorial Economics in Antebellum America*. Palo Alto, CA: Stanford University Press, 2008.

James, Henry. *The Golden Bowl*. 1910. Reprint, London: Penguin, 1985.

———. *Roderick Hudson*. 1878. Reprint, London: Penguin, 1981.

Jameson, Fredric. *The Political Unconscious: Narrative as Socially Symbolic Act*. Ithaca, NY: Cornell University Press, 1981.

Klein, Naomi. *The Shock Doctrine: The Rise of Disaster Capitalism*. New York: Metropolitan Books, 2007.

Laird, Pamela. *Pull: Networking and Success since Benjamin Franklin*. Cambridge, MA: Harvard University Press, 2006.
Larson, Magali Sarfatti. *The Rise of Professionalism*. Berkeley: University of California Press, 1977.
Lawson, Andrew. "Perpetual Capital: *Roderick Hudson*, Aestheticism, and the Problem of Inheritance." *Henry James Review* 32, no. 2 (2011): 178–191.
McDonald, Henry. "Nietzsche, Wittgenstein, and the Tragic Henry James." *Texas Studies in Literature and Language* 34, no. 3 (1992): 403–449.
Mendelssohn, Michele. "Homosociality and the Aesthetic in Henry James's *Roderick Hudson*." *Nineteenth-Century Literature* 54, no. 4 (2003): 512–554.
Morris, Susannah. "Changing Perceptions of Philanthropy in the Voluntary Housing Field in Nineteenth- and Early Twentieth-Century London." In *Philanthropy, Patronage, and Civil Society: Experiences from Germany, Great Britain, and North America*, edited by Thomas Adam, 138–162. Bloomington: Indiana University Press, 2004.
Nietzsche, Friedrich. *On the Genealogy of Morals*. Edited by Walter Kauffman, translated by Walter Kauffman and R. J. Hollingdale. 1887. Reprint, New York: Vintage Books, 1989.
Osteen, Mark, and Martha Woodmansee. Introduction to *The New Economic Criticism*, edited by Mark Osteen and Martha Woodmansee, 1–40. New York: Routledge, 1999.
Pohl, Francis K. *Framing America: A Social History of American Art*. London: Thames and Hudson, 2002.
Polanyi, Karl. *The Great Transformation*. New York: Farrar and Rinehart, 1944.
Rainey, Lawrence. "The Cultural Economy of Modernism." In *The Cambridge Companion to Modernism*, edited by Michael Levenson, 33–69. New York: Cambridge University Press, 2003.
Robbins, Bruce. *Secular Vocations: Intellectuals, Professionalism, Culture*. New York: Verso, 1993.
———. *Upward Mobility and the Common Good: Toward a Literary History of the Welfare State*. Princeton, NJ: Princeton University Press, 2007.
Saint-Amour, Paul K. "Transatlantic Tropology in James's *Roderick Hudson*." *Henry James Review* 18, no. 1 (1997): 22–42.
Saisselin, Remy. *The Bourgeois and the Bibelot*. New Brunswick, NJ: Rutgers University Press, 1984.
Sawaya, Francesca. *The Difficult Art of Giving: Patronage, Philanthropy, and the American Literary Market*. Philadelphia: University of Pennsylvania Press, 2014.
Smith, Adam. *The Theory of Moral Sentiments*. Edited by D. D. Raphael and A. L. Macfie. Indianapolis, IN: Liberty Fund, 1984.
Tinter, Adeline R. *The Museum World of Henry James*. Ann Arbor: University of Michigan Research Press, 1986.
Turnovsky, Geoffrey. *The Literary Market: Authorship and Modernity in the Old Regime*. Philadelphia: University of Pennsylvania Press, 2010.
Wilson, Christopher. *The Labor of Words: Literary Professionalism in the Progressive Era*. Athens: University of Georgia Press, 1985.

7

"Witnessing Them Day after Day"
Ethical Spectatorship and Liberal Reform in Walter Besant's Children of Gibeon

Tanushree Ghosh

"Suppose a girl were to learn . . . some of the worst wrongs that are inflicted on women in the city," proposes a character in the opening chapters of Walter Besant's 1886 reformist romance, *Children of Gibeon*, "wrongs that can only be realized *by actually sharing them or witnessing them* day after day. Do you suppose women could be treated so if we made up our minds that they should not?"[1] Even as this quote forwards a reformist social vision, it predicates reform on the crucial equivalence between "sharing," an embodied and experiential modality, and "witnessing," a form of ethical spectatorship. Following in the wake of the quite successful *All Sorts and Conditions of Men* (1882), which espoused a distinctively late-Victorian liberal discourse of philanthropy, Besant's *Children of Gibeon* not only reiterates the discursive stance of its predecessor but also crucially introduces "witnessing," or ethical spectatorship, as the constitutive element of social reform. The novel, via its aristocratic protagonist, Valentine, makes a case for the social and cultural elite to travel and live in the East End and see for themselves the actual lives of the working classes. The premise is that once the dismal living conditions of the working classes in the East End have been made sufficiently visible, reform will follow. Instead of empty curiosity or voyeurism, the novel posits a model of ethical spectatorship—looking as a socially necessary duty.

In *All Sorts and Conditions of Men*, Besant had described the lack of any cultural and educational institutions in the East End. The wealthy protagonist, Angela Messenger, establishes the "Palace of Delights" to provide the working classes with access to culture, education, and pleasure and thereby alleviate their grim existence. Interestingly, a project funded by the legacy of the philanthropist Barber Beaumont for a center for education and recreation in the East End, much like Besant's fictional Palace of Delight, was in the making as Besant published his novel in 1882. His novel was instrumental in garnering popular support and funding for this institution, appropriately named the People's Palace. Besant was one of the trustees of the People's Palace from 1887 to 1891 and edited its weekly *Palace Journal*. *Children of Gibeon* also forwarded quintessentially liberal solutions of individual responsibility and cultural transformation toward late-Victorian social problems, such as sweated labor and the working-class housing crisis. Indeed, Simon Joyce's perceptive description of late-Victorian charity as proposing "a magical form of resolution for a range of concrete social problems while simultaneously eliding their economic and social basis" holds true for the model of social reconstruction offered in *Children of Gibeon*.[2] More specifically, by imagining reform as the cultural and moral transformation of working-class individuals as well as the inculcation in them of self-governance, self-restraint, and patience through this cultural education, *Children of Gibeon* allies itself with the larger trend within late-Victorian liberal reformist discourse to imagine social change in specifically ameliorative terms.

While epitomized by individuals, like Rev. Samuel A. Barnett, Alfred Toynbee, Charles Booth, Benjamin Seebohm Rowntree, and Octavia Hill, as well as organizations like the Charity Organization Society, liberal reformist discourse was truly polyphonic and diverse in its aims and ideological visions. However, roughly speaking, late-Victorian Liberal reformist discourse revolved around the ideas of progress, character, education, private charity, and individual initiative.[3] However, the 1880s revealed a growing tussle between the midcentury classical liberalism and the emergent social and political philosophy of New Liberalism. Despite New Liberalism's heightened awareness of structural inequalities and growing acknowledgment of the need for state-led initiatives, liberal reformist discourse continued to also employ classical liberalism's moralistic vocabulary of individual responsibility, or fault, and to defend the free market. Putting it briefly, there was a disjunction between late-Victorian liberalism's theory and praxis: in theory, liberals recognized the exploitative nature of capitalism as well as the systemic nature of oppression, but, in practice, they stuck to a more conservative rhetoric of cultural reform and social gradualism.[4]

A text emblematic of New Liberalism, *Children of Gibeon* forwards a constitutive relationship between reform and spectatorship by strategically privileging Valentine's model of personal charity, driven by the specular will and agency of the reformer, over the possibilities of a working-class revolution. These acts of ethical spectatorship become integral to the self-definition of liberal subjects in Besant's novel. The lower-class slum becomes the site for the moral evolution of the liberal protagonist—the one who sees and feels—while the working-class characters are victimized and transformed into objects of diagnosis and remedy. The spectator-reformer and the spectacularized working-class victim together foreground the individualist poetics of liberal reform in the novel, particularly its concern with present, immediate suffering containable in the figure of a visible, particular sufferer. As the novel focuses on the pains of the spectating subjects, like Valentine, who dutifully look at suffering and perform their affective states, it simultaneously displaces working-class suffering onto the realm of aesthetic representation, mostly by codifying lower-class realities into the representational type of the seamstress.

Looking as Reform

Children of Gibeon begins with a prologue wherein a certain Lady Mildred Eldridge adopts her former servant's daughter to lessen the servant's burden of multiple children and meager earnings. As the adopted ward bears a striking resemblance to her own daughter, Lady Eldridge embarks on a social experiment directly in conversation with late-Victorian debates about character and environment: she decides to conceal the actual parentage of both girls and raise them in exactly the same manner. The novel reopens with both girls turning twenty, but with only one of them having claim to a substantial fortune. Before their parentage is revealed, Lady Eldridge presents both girls with the possibility of a dramatic change in fortune: a fall from aristocratic privilege to working-class origins. The impact on the two girls is dramatically different. While Violet—in keeping with her name—shrinks from working-class associations, Valentine is galvanized into action. Valentine decides to move to Hoxton, a working-class neighborhood, to get a room in the same tenement as her possible sister, Melenda. By living close to Melenda and looking at how she lives, Valentine attempts to better understand her and the rest of her potential family. As the plot progresses, Valentine discovers that she is actually Lady Eldridge's daughter. Despite discovering her aristocratic lineage, Valentine refuses to give up her associations in the Hoxton neighborhood and continues with her plans of social transformation. The novel ends with Valentine and her brother-turned-lover, Claude (actually, Melenda's brother, whose law education had also been funded by Lady Eldridge), affirming both their mutual love for each other and their commitment to social reform.

In positing spectatorship as foundational to Valentine's philanthropic efforts, Besant relies on the extant Victorian cultural discourse on sympathy. In his famous "Art of Fiction" lecture, he defined "sympathy" as a "power of vision and of feeling."[5] Besant's conceptualization of "sympathy" as both "vision" and "feeling," as both spectatorial capability and affect, offers a productive rubric to understand the particular alliance between ethical spectatorship and reform in late-Victorian formulations of *ethos*, and particularly in *Children of Gibeon*. Victorian philanthropy, especially in its liberal articulations, was underwritten by Adam Smith's theorization of sympathy as a model for self-regulation and social interaction.[6] Within the Smithian schema, the self itself is split into the actor and the impartial spectator, the agent and the judge. Knowing always the feelings and experiences of others are not their own, Smithian subjects approach others and even themselves as spectacles, making the dialectic of sympathy at once affective and spectatorial. Revolving around questions of what it means to be a sympathetic spectator and how to react or respond appropriately to scenes of suffering, liberal ethics is Smithian in its ultimate focus on *and* concern with the spectator-subject. While my focus on *Children of Gibeon* here foregrounds the particularities of late-Victorian philanthropic discourse, the historical trajectory of spectacular sympathy begins in the eighteenth century and extends well into contemporary expressions of philanthropic thought. Karen Halttunen traces how, from the eighteenth century onward, the "pornography of pain" became integral to the Anglo-American humanitarian sensibility, which increasingly defined sympathy as spectacular and deemed watching the pain of others as both taboo and titillating.[7] In their book *Distant Suffering*, Luc Boltanski and Graham Burchell also point to the fraught nature of ethical action and spectatorship in the age of global media, in which images of people suffering elsewhere are beamed right into the living rooms of unaffected viewers.[8] In my essay "Gifting Pain: The Pleasures of Liberal Guilt in *London, a Pilgrimage* and *Street Life in London*," I also explore the intermingling of voyeuristic and ethical pleasures in nineteenth-century reformist writing by examining how images of the suffering poor were included in Christmas "gift-books."[9]

Advocating for increased social engagement among its upper- and middle-class readers, *Children of Gibeon* offers a particularly interesting configuration of reform: ethical spectatorship as the basis for social change. The novel's premise for reform—Valentine's move to Hoxton to see for herself—is directly inspired by Toynbee Hall and the settlement movement, which advocated that the socially and culturally privileged people live among the working classes to counteract institutional blindness.[10] Writing on the settlement movement, Samuel Barnett opposed the complete relegation of philanthropic efforts to the governmental "machinery":

> The best-devised mechanism can have neither eyes nor feeling. It must act blindly. . . . Settlements stand as an acknowledgement of the claims of all the citizens to a share in these good things, and as a protest against meeting those claims by the substitution of philanthropic machinery for human hands and personal knowledge. They express the desire on the part of those "who have" to see, to know, and to serve those "who have not."[11]

Barnett proposed the settlement movement as a much more personal and embodied approach toward social work against the unseeing, impervious apparatus of institutionalized aid. In resonance with Besant's definition of sympathy,

Barnett's understanding of philanthropy also establishes a constitutive relationship between vision and ethical affect, between *eyes* and *feeling*, and the significant role of ethical looking in reformist interventions.

Throughout the novel, looking at suffering and being justifiably moved by the extant misery is posited not only as an exercise of sympathy but also as viable reformist practice. Valentine's move to Hoxton, for instance, is inspired by her very first visit to Melenda's room. The narrative describes the impact of that encounter on Valentine in strikingly visual terms: she is haunted by a "grisly spectre always before her eyes."[12] In other words, Valentine is unable to escape the scene that she witnesses; her initial act of spectatorship yields a series of inescapable hauntings where images of poverty and want flash before her, causing her concern and pain. The "spectre of the work-girl, half-starved, overworked" becomes a potent visual symbol, which evokes the initial reformist angst in Valentine, causing her to dramatically uproot her life of privilege and comfort.[13] From the beginning, then, Valentine's reformist interventions are presented as acts that inextricably combine looking with feeling.

Appropriately, Valentine's primary mode of engagement with Hoxton is also specular. As she begins to explore the neighborhood, the narrative abounds with descriptions of exteriors of working-class homes, shop fronts, and the vibrant energy of the streets. The narrator comments that Valentine had begun to "see Hoxton."[14] The way in which the novel employs seeing or looking in this instance is again multivalent: on the one hand, Valentine is able to look beyond the sensationalized descriptions of the East End, which abounded in late-Victorian urban journalism, and discover a much less morally decrepit, hardworking populace in Hoxton; on the other hand, the emphasis on vision *sans* the other senses emphasizes the crucial role of distance necessary to these spectatorial acts. As Valentine visually engages with the bustling East End streets, the prose rarely mentions any olfactory or haptic experiences. The privileging of vision in comparison to other sensorium in the novel suggests—in Jonathan Crary's terms—"the rebuilding of an observer fitted for the tasks of spectacular consumption" in the nineteenth century.[15] Vision separated from smell or touch serves to preserve distance between Valentine as the spectator and the spectacle of the East End.

Significantly, distance functions as an integral element within the Smithian sympathetic transaction: if the suffering is too excessive or close enough to threaten the person of the spectator, the sympathetic circuit is ruptured.[16] Dependent on a safe distance between her as the spectator and East End views, it is safe to venture that Valentine's visual engagement with Hoxton resonates with structures of sympathy routinely imagined in Victorian liberal literature and culture as acts of identification between the subject-spectator, at once distanced and proximate, and the sufferer.

As the novel posits ethical spectatorship as the solution to social ills, it simultaneously configures a lack of awareness among the privileged about the condition of the working classes as the key obstacle to reform. Under attack from Melenda, who vigorously protests against the low wages and long work hours of the seamstresses, Valentine can only exclaim, "But the ladies do not know."[17] Throughout the novel, reform-minded characters, particularly Valentine, attempt to evoke the concern or pity of other upper-class characters by asking them to engage in the cognitive act of sympathetic spectatorship. "If you could see the girls in their pain" becomes the constant refrain in the novel, as the privileged are exhorted to look at the oppressed.[18] In fact, Lady Eldridge—the mastermind behind the social experiment involving Valentine and Violet—emphasizes the need for women to "see evil," to step out of their protected worlds and look at "dark places and injustice."[19] She prophetically observes that Valentine will "suffer" in "seeing for herself" the misery present in Hoxton.[20] Witnessing, or looking at suffering even at the cost of personal pain or displeasure, is thus understood in the novel as the labor of ethical spectatorship.

Adopting a similar stance toward exploitation, Claude argues that businessmen would not dare to ill-use working-class women if they feared exposure in the press. Claude compares the power of the press to "setting up electric lamps in dark places." "Opinion," he observes, "is the will of the people. Let us get opinion on the side of the girls. And then light, more light."[21] His vision of social reform thus depends on a vocabulary of illumination: of making visible that which is hidden. To look becomes evidence not only of an ethical self but also of sufficient action. Indeed, even at the level of the plot, the novel does not attempt to forward material solutions to the problem of the exploited seamstresses. Instead, it models for its readers an appropriate mode of spectatorship, which would indicate sympathetic engagement with the lower classes.

The bildungsroman-like evolution of Valentine's character, in fact, hinges on her ethical spectatorship as a form of social engagement and develops in opposition to the selfish ignorance of bourgeois women, who deliberately refuse to perform the unpleasant looking at the exploited seamstresses. While Valentine's increased agency after her move to Hoxton may suggest the novel's essentially feminist framework, such a reading is belied by the several misogynistic invectives in the novel against unsympathetic ladies.[22] The doctor in Hoxton, who treats Melenda's invalid seamstress friend, explains the problem of exploitation in terms of spectatorial disengagement: "Ladies deliberately shut their eyes; they won't take trouble, they won't think; they like things about them to look smooth and comfortable; they will get things cheap if they can. What do they care if the cheapness is got by starving women?"[23] Unlike Valentine, who looks and "suffers," these women, according to the narrator, prefer to "shut their eyes" or look at "smooth and comfortable" things. In identifying selfish upper-class women as the cause of working-class misery—specifically, the exploitation of working-class women—*Children of Gibeon* circumscribes social critique at the level of individual faults and domestic economy. The sheltered existence and the social myopia of wealthy women becomes an easy target in this novel as selfish, well-to-do women are blamed for the misery of working-class women. The novel blithely displaces blame from systematic capitalist exploitation and the lack of any institutional support for working-class women to domestic economy—namely, women, who like things cheap.

The doctor's caustic critique of selfish "ladies," who like things "cheap" even at the cost of the misery of other women, is followed by a narratorial diatribe against the "young lady who sits at home in ease" surrounded by all the signifiers of wealth and comfort, like food, fire, trinkets, books, and music. The narrator advises the lady to stand in front of the mirror and discover common humanity, or "the unseen self," which is universally present in her and in the working-class girl alike.[24] Significantly, the act of mirroring, wherein the privileged young woman sees herself in the place of the obscured seamstress, connects again the act of looking with the process of sympathetic cognition of the pains of another.

Viewing the Needlewoman

Interestingly, as the narrator exhorts readers, especially female readers, to look at the hidden suffering of working-class women, the novel seems to be engaging metatextually with the myriad literary and cultural representations that present models of ethical looking, especially the visual tradition representing suffering working-class women. An illustration in G. W. M. Reynolds's novel *The Seamstress; or, The White Slave of England* (1851), for instance, represents the binary between self-absorbed, rich women and the exploited seamstresses (figure 7.1).

The two juxtaposed panels of the illustration present readers with an opposition between an overworked seamstress sewing ball dresses and fashionable women with their backs turned toward this exploited figure. The two panels are joined together with a giant pair of scissors and spool of thread, representing the chain of exploitation that linked the world of feminine fashion and privilege to the sweated labor of the seamstresses. The narrator's exhortation to privileged young ladies to look at the mirror and find the "unseen self" similarly resonates with John Tenniel's cartoon, "'The Ghost' in the Looking-Glass," published in *Punch* (July 1863), which depicts a fashionable woman looking in the mirror to see the pale and gaunt ghost of an exhausted seamstress beside her own reflection (figure 7.2).

Middle-class viewers of this cartoon are encouraged to identify with the well-dressed, prosperous-looking woman in the image, only to be startled into

Figure 7.1 Illustration by Henry Anelay in G. W. M. Reynolds's novel *The Seamstress; or, The White Slave of England*, 1851.

a sudden awareness of the exploited seamstress. Even as Tenniel's cartoon, much like Besant's novel, indicts the self-absorbed, upper-class woman for neglecting her working-class counterpart, her shock and possible guilt (much in contrast to the smug satisfaction of the sweatshop owner also in the image) presents viewers with the possibilities of a more aware and engaged spectatorship.

In fact, as it suggests possible modes of ethical looking, *Children of Gibeon* also spectacularizes the working classes by strategically employing the seamstress figure—a key visual and literary type—as an object of sympathy. Since the mid-nineteenth century, the seamstress had been one of the pathetic female figures represented regularly in Victorian culture. Seamstresses had become a matter of great public interest and concern following the Children's Employment Commission's 1843 report, which detailed how these women were coping with starvation wages and oppressive work conditions. Exhibited six months after the publication of Thomas Hood's poem "Song of the Shirt" (1843), Richard Redgrave's *The Poor Sempstress* (1844) depicts an isolated seamstress in a dark room as dawn breaks outside, gazing upwards, her face etched with tiredness and despair (figure 7.3). Paintings, such as Anna Blunden's *For Only One Short Hour* (1854; figure 7.4) and Frank Holl's *The Song of the Shirt* (1875), also followed

Figure 7.2 John Tenniel, "The Haunted Lady; or, 'The Ghost' in the Looking-Glass," *Punch; or, The London Charivari*, July 4, 1863, L. Tom Perry Special Collections Library, Harold B. Lee Library, Brigham Young University, Provo, UT.

suit by representing the seamstress as a figure of pathos in the manner of Redgrave's painting.

The seamstress occupied a significant place in the literature of the 1840s and 1850s, figuring in pamphlets, like *Confessions of a Needlewoman* (1840) and Charlotte Elizabeth Tonna's *The Wrongs of Woman* (1843); journalistic works, such as Henry Mayhew's *London Labour and the London Poor*; and novels, like Elizabeth Stone's *The Young Milliner* (1843), Frances Trollope's *Jessie Phillips* (1844), G. W. M. Reynolds's *The Seamstress; or, The White Slave of England* (1851), and Elizabeth Gaskell's *Mary Barton* (1848) and *Ruth* (1853).

Julian Treuherz observes, "Together Hood and Redgrave created a visual type which was to be frequently painted by others; they made the seamstress into the most commonly depicted social realist subject in Victorian painting."[25] Often represented as a middle-class woman fallen on bad days, the seamstress figure combined Victorian middle-class notions of respectability with a lower-class setting. Represented as shut away in a garret, surrounded with broken, faded, and dying things that connoted genteel decay, the seamstress figure allowed the

Figure 7.3 *The Poor Sempstress*, by Richard Redgrave, 1844, watercolor. © Victoria and Albert Museum, London.

middle classes to view her labor as domestic, or, at least, not completely commercial. The domestic connotations of the seamstress's labor also allowed authors and visual artists to imbue her with an idealized bourgeois femininity, as opposed to the more rough and masculine appearance of "real" working-class women.

Critics such as T. J. Edelstein, Beth Harris, and Patricia Zakreski have noted the various ideological functions of—to use Beth Harris's phrase—"the seamstress narrative" in Victorian culture.[26] Referring to visual representations of the seamstress from the 1850s, Edelstein argues that these isolated and passive female figures evoke the sympathy of the uninvolved middle-class viewer. However, the seamstress figure in *Children of Gibeon* indicates not only the influence of eighteenth-century sentiment, as Edelstein argues, but also, more specifically, the presence of Victorian formulations of sympathy within reformist discourse.[27] The need for an appropriate victim, or the proper subject within the sympathetic circuit conflates ethical priorities with aesthetic preferences; it also foregrounds the rather fraught nature of the sympathetic transaction, wherein the burden

Figure 7.4 *For Only One Short Hour*, by Anna Blunden, 1854, oil on canvas. Yale Center for British Art, Paul Mellon Fund.

of eliciting sympathy from the viewer is placed firmly on the sufferer.[28] Besant's choice of the seamstress—the helpless woman engaged in a suitably quasi-middle-class labor of sewing shirts—thus seems calculated to evoke the sympathy of a bourgeois-liberal audience for a familiar, identifiable victim.[29]

The mix of class and gender politics mobilizing Besant's choice of the seamstress figure is apparent in one of his nonfiction pieces, "The Endowment of the Daughter" (1888). His paternalist attitude toward female labor is unmistakable as he makes a case for rescuing women from direct participation in the marketplace: "My brothers, let our girls work if they wish; perhaps they will be happier if they work; let them work at whatever kind of work they desire; but not—oh not—because they must."[30] In *Children of Gibeon*, the narrator describes the seamstresses as "hands . . . nothing but hands" to critique their dehumanization in the marketplace; however, by virtue of her femininity and the semidomestic nature of her work, she remains respectable enough for the middle-class reader to sympathize with her.[31]

Besant follows convention in presenting the seamstress as having little or no education and being completely disconnected from the outside world, with no other skills and very little understanding of her own industry. Like "steam-engines," which are kept working until the wheels stop, these girls keep sewing as long as possible, almost around the clock and until their bodies break down and they die.[32] The novel imagines the working-class women as having been abandoned by their fathers and brothers who are involved in "their clubs, their drinks, and their amusements."[33] Neglected by society and without any protection, which itself is imagined in patriarchal terms, these women are subject to the vagaries of supply and demand. Unlike working-class men, women have no idea how to better their conditions by organizing or striking and are thus suitable victims because of their vulnerability and passivity. "They are," the narrator notes, "weak of body and have no power of speech; they are as dumb sheep because they do not even bleat in complaint."[34] Significantly, Valentine imagines Hoxton as a community of women waiting for aid: "the world where the women suffer."[35] The neighborhood seems populated by children and working-class women of all ages with invalid or unemployed husbands.[36] The question of reform is located firmly within the domestic space; it is concerned with saving women neglected both by the upper classes as well as by working-class men. Other than Valentine's supposed brother, Joe, there is not a single working-class male character in this novel but instead a host of oppressed working-class girls, like Lottie, Lizzie, and Melenda.

In the novel, Besant employs the two most common seamstress narratives; Lizzie's character represents the seamstress lured into prostitution through want, while Lottie's character represents the seamstress losing her health and dying from overwork and fatigue. Both Lizzie and Lottie, like the typical seamstress figure in fiction, have middle-class origins. The novel's emphasis on Lizzie's refined features and potential beauty also indicates the influence of the usual narrative of the seamstress as a gentlewoman fallen on bad days. With her fiery energy and defiant refusal of charity, Melenda's character seems to be Besant's most original interpretation of the seamstress figure. Her short and stocky stature, large hands, broad shoulders, and strong chin would indicate to Victorian readers a working-class physique. She is intensely aware of her exploitation and perpetually angry about the unfair system, which demanded so much labor and paid so little.

While Melenda's character makes room for the articulation of working-class frustrations in the novel, she is rendered increasingly passive, vulnerable, and dependent on Valentine's help over the course of the novel. Besant informs readers about a rather cruel punishment named "drilling" doled out by the shops to women who turned in rough or imperfect work. By making them wait for several hours, sometimes numerous days, for payment and the next batch of work, the store owners disciplined "errant" seamstresses through physical pain and public humiliation. Since seamstresses were used to sitting and sewing all day and had only a light meal before coming to the shop, they bore pangs of hunger and extreme bodily pain as they were forced to stand for long periods of time. The narrator notes that the effect of extended drilling turned the punished woman into "nothing at all from head to foot but a collection of aches and pains."[37]

Yet effective protest against this horrible practice comes not from Melenda or any other working-class woman but from Valentine. When Melenda is "drilled" by the shop owner, this characteristically fiery girl "stood perfectly quiet and waited."[38] Valentine's indignant remonstrance directed at the senior partner of the store is the only voice, a privileged voice, raised against the cruel practice of drilling. Her ability to protest and the weight it carries depends on her being "the daughter of Lady Mildred Eldridge."[39] Suffering matters, it seems in this novel, when someone with ample social clout, like Valentine, witnesses it. Although, ultimately, Valentine's outburst costs Melenda her employment, it has enough impact on the senior partner to make him brood about the damage the young lady and her "friends" might cause to the reputation of his business. Besant's novel, of course, does not depict any such redemption for the working-class women or any punishment to those who exploit and torture them. The novel is not invested in systemic solutions (in fact, it suggests there aren't any) but rather proposes a culmination of the reformist impulse in Valentine's spectatorship of Melenda's oppression, and in the latter's expression of outrage and indignation at the unfairness of drilling helpless women.

As the working-class figures in the novel are rendered passive, Valentine gains agency and voice. Just as Valentine performs and validates her ethical self through sympathetic spectatorship, readers of this novel are assured of their moral well-being through their acts of reading about the suffering of others and simultaneously learn to emulate the model of ethical spectatorship proposed in the text.[40] The despair and rage of those living in subhuman conditions and the violence wreaked on those left at the mercies of market-determined employment and wages have no purchase in this novel unless they are mediated by ethical spectatorship and appropriately contained in the figure of a working-class victim.

Aestheticization as Reform

In a manner akin to the aestheticization of working-class misery in the seamstress figure, the reformist project forwarded in *Children of Gibeon* is predicated on the emptying out of the East End of any distinct cultural character and a visible aestheticization of the place and its people. Emphasizing the aesthetic remaking of working-class individuals, their preferences, and their homes, the novel envisions reform as the reshaping of working-class subjectivity in the manner of an idealized middle-class subject.[41] Through its model of cultural transformation, this novel advances a bourgeois-liberal argument about citizenship and participation in the public sphere.

On her first night in Hoxton, Valentine sits in her room taking stock of her new residence and the neighborhood; the narrator observes, "Valentine looked across the space between the two 'backs,' and as she had eyes stronger than most she could see through the open windows opposite, and could catch a glimpse of interiors which filled her soul with pity."[42] From the safety of her room—a significant reiteration of the necessity of distance in the configuration of ethical spectatorship in this novel—Valentine looks inside the houses of her working-class neighbors to note firsthand their insalubrious living conditions. The unwholesome and unkempt appearance of the homes is connected constitutively with the moral despondence and the social stagnation of its inhabitants. The emphasis on her powerful vision, which is "stronger than most," moreover, suggests the possibility of the novel using Valentine's range of vision more than just literally to imply her sympathetic capacity, especially since the prose immediately connects her strong eyesight to her "soul" filled with "pity." Even as this moment functions as another significant instance of ethical spectatorship, it also demonstrates the primary mode of reformist change in the novel.

The novel presents the East End, or, more specifically, Hoxton, as peopled by decent folk but as a visually unappealing and culturally barren space.[43] East End streets become an undesirable form of public commons where men talk politics and women socialize "noisily."[44] Ivy Lane—the street where Melenda and her companions live—is drab and dirty, with "mean" and "squalid" houses.[45] Melenda's room is in a similar state of disrepair and neglect; the narrator describes her room as consisting of a broad wooden bed with a hard mattress that sags in the middle, a yellowed blind that does not keep out the sun, a rusty grate, plaster peeling off the ceiling and the walls, no carpet, and old utensils that seem to have not been used in quite some time.[46] In describing this "abode of grinding, wretched, hopeless poverty," the narrative suggests that the ugliness of the room suits Melenda, Lizzie, and Lottie's lack of prospects.[47] The text suggests a correlation between the nature of surroundings and the internal character of an individual: the novel asks readers to draw parallels between the dreariness of Melenda's room and her social and personal stasis.

In direct contrast to Melenda's room, Valentine's quarters are cramped but tastefully decorated: "The room was certainly very small, yet Claude had made it pretty." The description of her room details not only freshly painted walls and ceilings but also lingers on the smallest furnishings, like a French green and gold iron bed, candlesticks, lamps, an embroidered tablecloth, a vase filled with flowers, a rug, and a fireplace. The narrative repeatedly highlights the visual charms of various pieces of furniture: the "pleasing design" of the counterpane, the "pretty curtains," the "pretty lamp," "pretty" tiled fireplace, and "aesthetic tablecover."[48] The emphatic use of "pretty" in the description of Valentine's room, especially juxtaposed with the portrayal of working-class homes as drab and dirty, manages to convey to readers both the necessity of improving working-class living conditions and, more importantly, that the essential nature of that reform is the aestheticization of their living spaces.

Having configured the problem in aesthetic terms—that is, the dreariness of the working-class home and person—the novel thus proceeds to provide an aesthetic solution: Valentine's task becomes, essentially, a makeover. Although my usage of this term from popular culture is anachronistic, its connotations of surface-level, ornamental alterations make it rather appropriate in this case. When Valentine wants to help, she gives Melenda one of her pretty dresses and changes her hairstyle. She refurnishes Melenda's room with new blinds, chairs, and bedstead and finishes by putting flowers on the table.

Even as *Children of Gibeon* adapted the model of neighborly charity suggested by the settlement movement, it subtly changed the power dynamic between the classes in its proposed model of social transformation. While Barnett had made a case for reformers understanding East End neighborhoods by living there and learning from working-class residents, who possessed valuable local knowledge and experience, Besant proposed a rather more top-down model of culture, where upper-class emissaries brought cultural enrichment to the monotonous lower-class lives and modeled for the latter the way to live, the way to use their leisure time, and, really, the way to be. Besant envisioned cultural education or training—the latter word perhaps being more appropriate given the apprentice-like position imposed on the working-class individual within his reform program—as part of an endeavor that targeted working-class identity formation. In an essay on Ratcliffe parish, one of East End's most impoverished neighborhoods, Besant writes:

> The people being such as they are—so poor, so hopeless, so ignorant—what is done for them? How are they helped upward? How are they driven, pushed, shoved, pulled, to prevent them from sinking still lower? For they are not at the lowest depths; they are not criminals; up to their lights they are honest; that poor fellow who stands with his hands ready—all he has got in the wide world—only his hands—no trade, no craft, no skill—will give you a good day's work if you engage him.[49]

Here, as in the novel, Besant uses the image of hands to indicate how workers without education or skills become the most exploited, as their labor is exchangeable and undervalued. The portrait he paints of the working-class man in this quote also corresponds with the picture he presents of Hoxton inhabitants: not criminal but lacking "self-restraint."[50] The tension between "help" and verbs like *driven, pushed, shoved,* and *pulled* indicate that despite Besant's claims of change emerging from within the working classes, he accords a dominant prescriptive position to the middle classes and imagines the lower classes as passive entities waiting to be molded into shape.

The disciplinary aspects of Besant's cultural education become clear in the oppositions he posits between existing working-class pastimes and the proposed uplifting and character-building activities at institutions like the People's Palace. Thus, instead of decadent "amusements," aimless loitering on the streets, and incendiary political clubs, Besant recommends "recreation," activities that demand "skill, patience, discipline, drill, and obedience to law."[51] Brad Beaven, in *Leisure, Citizenship, and Working-Class Men in Britain, 1850–1945*, observes that the prescriptive tone and the attempts to direct working-class leisure activities were part of attempts to "create the model citizen" and, thereby, to control the subversive potential of male leisure as it took the shape of radical politics located in public houses and social events.[52] The working classes are targeted at both physical and intellectual levels as Besant imagines a new working class that would mirror bourgeois-liberal social values and tastes. Within such a context, cultural and moral education—core elements of Besant's reform agenda—becomes the means not only of cultivating an honest working class but also of preserving extant social hierarchies. Instead of talking in the streets or in clubs, Besant offers libraries as spaces, which would better channel the curiosity of the working classes. The noisy happiness of working girls in the street, which Besant incredibly characterizes as "mirthless laughter," would be stopped with a "hot supper of chops fresh from the grill," which would incline them toward "rest, reflection, instruction, and a little music."[53] The hegemonic implications of culture are more than apparent in these homilies that set up bourgeois-liberal subjecthood as an aspirational goal for the working classes.

Working-class spectatorship functions very differently in this novel than the empowering effects of ethical looking on Valentine's character. The novel imagines working-class characters as acting on the basis of a monkey-see, monkey-do rationale. The moment when the three seamstresses first see Valentine's room becomes an exemplary instance:

> Valentine had now pulled down the blind, drawn her curtains, and lit the pretty reading lamp with its coloured shade. "Oh—h!" the girls gasped. They had never before seen a pretty room, and the prettiness of this room took their breath away. Even Melenda, who had been prepared to admire nothing, was taken by surprise. They went round, looking at and examining everything, the easy-chair, the fireplace, the bookshelves, the table, and the pictures.[54]

The "prettiness" of Valentine's room—the aesthetic charm of this well-decorated room—draws the girls' admiration and is posited as an aspirational ideal. The very act of looking places Melenda and her friends in a state of inadequacy and apprenticeship: they must learn how to keep house from this space. However, as the text offers this moment as a paradigm-altering experience for the working-class girls who have never seen such a tastefully furnished room, it offers a very classed material culture as a model for improvement. In fact, a vocabulary steeped in aesthetic priorities allows the novel to posit a bourgeois domesticity as the desirable "artistic" home.[55]

Jordanna Bailkin comments perceptively on the relationship between liberalism and Victorian material culture: "The belief that people were molded through their environments prompted an unprecedented moralization of possessions, a worldview in which material objects were seen to have moral sway over those who owned and saw them."[56] Beginning with the adoption of Violet by Lady Eldridge, *Children of Gibeon* participates in late-Victorian discussions about the effect of environment on character—a conversation that finds its most significant articulation in the way in which reform is imagined in the novel.

Through reformist interventions that emphasize aesthetic values, such as initiation into "good" art, music, and books and the "right" food, attire, and homes, and by configuring working-class spectatorship as a prolonged tutelage, Besant sets forth an argument about sociopolitical legitimacy. An abstracted, idealized domesticity becomes a means of simultaneously defining bourgeois-liberal identity as normative mode of citizenship and depoliticizing the conversation. Valentine and Claude form the Earthly Tract Society, which publishes tracts called the "Domestic Series," describing appropriate domestic behavior, proper amusements, apparel, hairstyles, and hygiene for the lower classes, or, as Valentine describes it, "the improvement of the world in comfort, culture, and manners."[57] In her reading of the ideological use of the "domestic ideal," Mary Poovey points out how classed versions of domesticity and, more generally, bourgeois identity were sublimated as "representative" English identity even as the domestic space was removed from the forces of the marketplace.[58] Removed, by virtue of her gender and aristocratic lineage, from the actual economic transactions of the market, Valentine's reformist interventions, too, are situated within the domestic space.[59] She remakes Melenda, her room, and then the "homes" of the entire street. Her reconfiguration of working-class homes to meet normative bourgeois domesticity signals the novel's social program of reshaping working-class identity after the hegemonic middle-class model; as Valentine remarks to Claude, "It would be easier to move men in the right direction if we first endeavoured to make them more careful about their homes."[60] The novel expresses an investment in the domestic space, coded in terms of discipline and productivity, as a prescriptive path toward citizenship.

However, despite its desires to remold working-class identity through the working-class home, the novel's focus on domestic space, in fact, serves to postpone the possibilities of working-class political legitimacy and autonomy. The effect of Claude and Valentine's "Domestic Series" tracts is such that Ivy Lane, the reader is informed, becomes a visually inviting and aesthetically pleasing "show street" with flowers and white blinds adorning clean windows, clean doors, and scrubbed floors. Its inhabitants, moreover, are men who are sober and women who do not scream or quarrel; they have "grown critical" over their food, attire, spending, and speech. The tracts on the "duties and privileges of the English subject," the narrator reveals, would be published much later.[61] To gain equal participation in the public sphere, to claim citizenship, Besant's novel suggests, the lower-class individual needs first to become more like a bourgeois-liberal subject—a trajectory that remains incomplete in the novel. Keeping in mind the rise of radical working-class politics in the late nineteenth century, *Children of Gibeon* ultimately seems invested in regulating working-class participation in the public space; who gets to speak and how are latent questions in the more obvious and overt discussions regarding the cultivation of the proletarian subject and the working-class home in the novel.

Visible Victims

The novel imagines Valentine and Claude as mediators working to alleviate the hostility and misunderstanding between the classes. As the biblical title of the novel itself indicates, Valentine and Claude are the "Children of Gibeon," or ambassadors bringing a peace treaty to a more powerful nation.[62] The necessity of fostering better relations between the two classes finds clearest articulation through the character of Lady Eldridge as she observes:

> We cannot afford to laugh at the ignorance of the people anymore, because we have given them all the power, though they don't know yet that they have got it; but they will find out very soon, and then—. . . . [T]he more we of our set learn what working people want and think, and how they judge things, and the more they, for their part, learn what we think about things, the better it will be for all of us, and the safer.[63]

As the possibility of a working-class revolution loomed on the horizon, *Children of Gibeon* offered reform as a means of ensuring interclass understanding and, quite literally, "safety" for the privileged.[64]

After the Chartist turbulence of the 1830s and 1840s, the 1880s were the beginning of another period of economic depression and increasing attacks on liberalism's support of a laissez-faire economy. The attack on liberalism and on capitalism came from several quarters: the rise of Fabian Socialism, New Liberalism, and working-class organizations led to a reassessment of capitalism and produced foreboding about potential class warfare. *Children of Gibeon* responds to this fraught social context by putting pressure on its own liberal worldview with the introduction of Sam's working-class socialism and its stringent critique of liberal reform. However, despite pitting these two radically different approaches to social reform against one another, Besant's novel eventually validates an individualized poetics of suffering—that is, liberal spectator-reformers forwarding aid to visible victims.

Sam's character and his more radical social theories *almost* seem to provide an effective counterpoint to Valentine's aestheticized approach to reform. He proposes a socialist utopia, wherein all titles and privileged classes would be abolished; land would belong to the people, and there would be equal wages for equal hours of work, free education, universal male suffrage, and no taxes.[65] "Think of it!" he asserts, "No more poverty, no more disease from luxury or from privation, no more ignorance, no more indolence, no more vice!"[66] Sam's critique foregrounds the emphasis on visible, aestheticized, and essentially cosmetic transformations in Valentine's plans for reform when he identifies her as "one of those who go tinkering up a rotten place here and painting over a bad place there, and pretending that everything is sound and healthy"—as people who give concerts, hang a few pictures in the schoolroom, sing a few hymns, and distribute pennies and oranges and call it variously "softening the masses," "introducing art among the lower orders," "bringing religion home to the people," and "bringing the classes together."[67] Sam observes that culture and personal charity become means of furthering—what Deborah Weiner calls "feudal hierarchy"—the unequal relationship between the bourgeois-liberal and working classes.[68]

The novel's dualistic representation of the options for reform ensures that Valentine's specular model of charity appears as the more viable option when compared to socialism's "rivers of blood."[69] While Sam, Melenda's schoolmaster brother, contends that a piecemeal individual-based reform will not do any good unless the "competitive system is destroyed," Valentine insists that she cares for the people she sees.[70] As the novel unfolds, Sam's vision of a more equal, more just society is reduced to a quixotic and abstract solution, which ignores the immediate, embodied reality of present, visible suffering while Valentine's concern with the immediate care of the three individuals—the three girls whose conditions she has personally witnessed—is made heroic. Reinforcing again a model of reform based on ethical spectatorship, she entreats Sam to see them every day as motivation for a "readier," even "temporary," plan for reform.[71] The political implications of the spectatorial basis of Valentine's brand of reform becomes clearer as she insists on helping those she sees while Sam repeatedly negates the value of such individualized poetics of suffering.

In response to Sam's desire for systemic changes, Valentine angrily responds, "I ask you for advice, and you offer me the chance of a new system. Go away and rail at competition while we look after its victims."[72] The concern with present, immediate suffering, containable even in the emphasis on the visible, individual sufferer, moreover, is predicated on the impossibility and inevitable failure of any working-class attempts at revolution. When Melenda demands "justice," Valentine answers with "I can help you three." The pressure-valve function of liberal reform is apparent as Valentine describes herself as a "messenger" of rich ladies and promises "lighter work and better pay" instead of justice.[73] Valentine's response to Melenda also indicates how liberal reform may be complicit with capitalism even as it articulates powerful protest against its ills. Sympathy within a liberal-capitalist society can serve as a substitute for political action; its vocabulary of individual affect ensures that it does not translate into the formation of collective activism.

The narrator sides with Valentine's disbelief in Sam's utopia by noting the inherent selfishness of "human nature"; the "natural man," the narrator observes, "derides equality" and will "go on grabbing all he can."[74] The socialist, then, "may rage furiously, but he will rage in vain."[75] Reform in *Children of Gibeon* is deemed as a successful remedy to social problems as opposed to a working-class revolution because it is in line with classical liberalism's conception of human beings as essentially individualistic and acquisitive. Liberalism's emphasis on what C. B. Macpherson has called "possessive individualism,"[76] or the belief in the autonomy and self-governing character of individuals, is clear in Claude's refutation of Sam's socialist proposition:

> But I am certain that there is no system, or institution, or code of laws, whatever, which can be imposed upon a people, unless they are ready for it and desire it for themselves. You will never live to see your dream realized, Sam, because it will be always impossible to make the men of ability, who are the only men to be considered, desire a system in which they themselves shall not be able to do good to themselves first.[77]

Claude voices here the liberal belief in the freedom of the individual and his proprietorship over "his person and its capacities."[78] In an almost evolutionary twist, the socialist desire to remake society is seen as a restriction of individual choice and thus regressive, as opposed to liberalism's ability to allow expansive freedom to "men of ability." The doctor who tends to Lottie similarly critiques socialism as an attempt to "impose" a scheme on people and curb their "free will."[79] The Enlightenment ideal of the public sphere as composed of self-governing, self-owning individuals, one of the central tenets of classical liberalism, is apparent when he says, "The best chance is when every man feels that he is part of the government."[80] The aesthetic cultivation of the working classes, however, which is the goal of Besant's cultural-reform projects, is a means of postponing the working classes' political participation long after they have been formed along the lines of liberal selfhood.[81] Described in immanent terms as the "feeling" of government in the novel, the possibility of working-class participation in governance is at best postponed, at worst erased. Instead of Sam's working-class revolution, both Valentine and Claude voice their desire to "take the world as it is" and imagine another kind of "revolution," in which working-class "missionaries," having received a liberal education, return "to the soil and to the gutter" to disseminate this knowledge and teach this mode of liberal becoming to others.[82]

The actual example of such "reform" in the novel, however, reveals the dubious emancipatory potential of such transformation. From the start, Melenda's "independence" and her defiant refusal to accept Valentine's help or charity of any kind are ridiculed as irrational obstinacy.[83] It is significant that a novel, which makes much of individual freedom with characters like Claude and Valentine, takes a different view of independence when it comes to working-class characters. Melenda, as the unformed, unfinished working-class subject, is not accorded the rationality or the autonomy—which is given naturally to self-governing subjects—to claim independence.

As the novel progresses, Melenda loses her work at the shop as a result of Valentine's protest against drilling. By the end of the novel, she is completely dependent on Valentine's charity and has no future prospect of work, and thus becomes a "young lady."[84] After Valentine "dresses" her and refurnishes her room, Melenda goes for her usual walk in her neighborhood, where she had previously found pleasure and kinship, and finds that "these things amused her no longer."[85] The reformed Melenda does not "like the crowd" or "the street" but wants to sit quietly in her room.[86] As Melenda is gentrified, the loss of her voice and mobility signals a loss of agency. Melenda's demand for justice is met with Valentine's dream of a cooperative workshop, owned by working-class women, dependent still on the benevolence of rich women who would be made aware of the exploitation of seamstresses: "There must be some sympathy, somewhere in the world."[87] Significantly, the possibility of such a workshop materializing remains doubtful; the deferral of this fictional utopia becomes a powerful symptom of the *Children of Gibeon*'s doubt regarding the efficacy of liberal reform, even as the novel seemingly contents itself with the development of its philanthropist-protagonist through ethical spectatorship.

Conclusion

Elaine Hadley, in her essay "On a Darkling Plain: Victorian Liberalism and the Fantasy of Agency," sees the link between liberal thought and beauty as forming a "liberal cognitive aesthetic." In the face of external pressures, liberal discourse offered an autonomous, self-reflexive, coherent self that created through "purposeful thought a feat of human beauty." Building on Harold Perkins's argument, Hadley rightly recognizes the constitutive relationship between aesthetic and "social aesthetic" within liberal discourse.[88] Besant contrives a relationship between his aesthetic choices within *Children of Gibeon* and the social aesthetic as a way of imagining particular social relationships. His novel presents a certain kind of "realism," which appealed to late-Victorian bourgeois-liberal readers because it allowed them the pleasures of identification and sympathy. A reviewer for *Blackwood's Edinburgh Magazine*, for instance, praised Besant's ability to "open to the reader [irrespective of his social location] . . . a picture of human life in general . . . which may charm him out of his cares, or soothe his pain for an hour or two, with a gain of wholesome images and human sympathy." For this reviewer, Besant's aesthetics were far removed from the "nauseous and abominable inventions" found in naturalist fiction of the day.[89] Other reviewers joined in the applause: a reviewer for the *Athenaeum* noted that "he is never angry,"[90] while another reviewer described his style—in comparison with George Gissing—hiding "truth" in a "pink-silk veil."[91] Besant himself noted in his autobiography that *Children of Gibeon* was the "most truthful" of anything he had ever written and that "it offered the daily life and the manners—so far, as they can be offered without offensive and useless realism—of the girls who do the rougher and coarser work of sowing [sic] in their lodgings."[92]

Within this cluster of scattered remarks and observations, a pattern regarding Besant's liberal aesthetics may be located. Defined against the alienating hyperrealism of naturalist fiction, which emphasized the dirt, grime, and despair of poverty, Besant's fiction not only proposed an aesthetic solution to poverty but also enacted a form of aesthetic closure on the realities of lower-class suffering and deprivation. As working-class characters are rendered into spectacularized victims by Besant's "pink-silk veil," lower-class reality is made not just palatable but pleasurable for his readers.

TANUSHREE GHOSH is Assistant Professor of English at the University of Nebraska, Omaha.

Notes

1. Besant, *Children of Gibeon*, 107 (emphasis added).
2. Joyce, "Castles in the Air," 521.
3. Haggard, *Persistence of Victorian Liberalism*, 1–8.
4. Hurren, *Protesting about Pauperism*, 34; Sykes, *Rise and Fall*, 11.
5. Besant, *Art of Fiction*, 11–12.
6. A significant Victorian philosophical term, *sympathy* was heavily influenced by Adam Smith's theory and the eighteenth-century sentimental novel. James Chandler, Rae Greiner, David Marshall, Audrey Jaffe, and Lara Kees, among others, note the centrality of Smithian formulations of sympathy in Victorian culture. See Chandler, "On the Face of the Case"; Greiner, *Sympathetic Realism*; Marshall, *Figure of Theater*; Jaffe, *Scenes of Sympathy*; and Kees, "Sympathy in *Jane Eyre*."
7. Halttunen, "Humanitarianism," 304.
8. Boltanski and Burchell, *Distant Suffering*, 16.

9. Ghosh, "Gifting Pain."
10. Robert Haggard and Seth Koven provide very informative discussions of the settlement movement. See Haggard, *Persistence of Victorian Liberalism*; and Koven, *Slumming*.
11. Barnett, "University Settlements."
12. Besant, *Children of Gibeon*, 80.
13. Ibid., 81.
14. Ibid., 130.
15. Crary, *Techniques of the Observer*, 19.
16. Smith and Haakonssen, *Theory of Moral Sentiments*, 61.
17. Besant, *Children of Gibeon*, 67.
18. Ibid., 217.
19. Ibid., 106.
20. Ibid., 107.
21. Ibid., 396.
22. At first glance, implied comparison within the novel between the masculine overtones of Valentine's name and the typically feminine connotations of Violet's name, also corroborated by their different personalities, seems to suggest that Valentine possesses capabilities that force an interrogation of the stereotypical Victorian association of femininity with a sheltered, domestic existence. In fact, Lady Eldridge's argument in favor of Valentine moving to Hoxton sounds distinctly feminist, as she emphasizes the need for women to see "evil," to step out of their protected worlds and see "dark places and injustice." Besant, *Children of Gibeon*, 106. However, in light of many well-known female reformers, like Josephine Butler, Octavia Hill, and Annie Besant, this move was not as novel as it seems within the novel. In the context of late-Victorian gender dynamics, it is quite likely that Besant used the figure of the female reformer to both frame the reform question and provide solutions in domestic terms. See Judith Walkowitz's work on new "actors" on the social scene: Walkowitz, *City of Dreadful Delight*, 41–80. Also, see Anna Davin's essay about reform and the imposition of the bourgeois home as a model for the working classes: Davin, "Imperialism and Motherhood."
23. Besant, *Children of Gibeon*, 195.
24. Ibid., 71.
25. Treuherz, *Hard Times*, 26.
26. Edelstein, "They Sang 'The Song of the Shirt'"; Harris, *Famine and Fashion*, 3; Zakreski, *Representing Female Artistic Labor*, 8. Zakreski argues that the "refining" work of sewing endowed the seamstress with femininity and evoked unanimous pity, while Beth Harris notes that the middle-upper-class origins of the seamstress made her appear more feminine than her working-class counterparts and thus evoked the concern of the Victorians.
27. Edelstein, "They Sang 'The Song of the Shirt'," 195–197.
28. See, for instance, Elizabeth Barnes's very perceptive discussion of Smithian sympathy. Barnes, *States of Sympathy*.
29. By the term *bourgeois-liberal*, I wish to indicate the classed nature of the seemingly classless liberal political discourse. Liberalism allowed the British bourgeoisie to simultaneously aid their social ascension and keep the working classes from making a similar claim toward an egalitarian society.
30. Besant, "The Endowment of the Daughter," 23.
31. Besant, *Children of Gibeon*, 101–102.
32. Ibid., 153–154.
33. Ibid., 69.
34. Ibid., 349.

35. Ibid., 380.
36. Ibid., 386.
37. Ibid., 340.
38. Ibid., 343.
39. Ibid., 343–344.
40. Writing about the commodification of compassion or pity in sentimental novels, Simon During notes, "These commodified intensities helped the domain of fiction imagine a society democratized not through actual political participation but through collectivized good will, benevolent action, acute sensitivity to suffering, and tears." During, *Exit Capitalism*, 46. Carolyn Betensky forwarded a similar claim in her book *Feeling for the Poor: Bourgeois Compassion, Social Action, and the Victorian Novel* by drawing our attention to how social-problem novels portray reading as a socially significant act that "*mattered* in and of itself." Betensky, *Feeling for the Poor*, 5. Besant's novel may be understood within a similar rubric since it allows readers the possibility of imagining an increased ethical responsibility through sympathetic spectatorship.
41. Besant's emphasis on an aesthetic education of the working classes bears comparison with John Ruskin's protest against the degradation of the working classes involved in mechanized, industrial labor in *Unto This Last* and *Fors Clavigera*, a series of essays published in the 1860s and 1870s. While Ruskin also stressed the aesthetic education of the working classes and protested against the soul-crushing nature of labor, especially in mechanized settings, he held pronounced antidemocratic views. There are telling overlaps between Ruskin's and Besant's models of reform, which reveal a shared paternalistic attitude toward the working classes and their fear of a revolution despite different political philosophies. For an extended discussion of Ruskin's views regarding reform, see Cockram, *Ruskin and Social Reform*.
42. Besant, *Children of Gibeon*, 92.
43. P. J. Keating contrasts Besant's description of the lack of any genuine cultural expression in the East End with Charles Booth's acknowledgment of proletarian culture, such as music halls, theaters, Sunday debates in Victoria Park, and political clubs. Keating, *Working Classes in Victorian Fiction*, 118–119.
44. Besant, *Children of Gibeon*, 280.
45. Ibid., 61.
46. Ibid., 155–156.
47. Ibid., 280.
48. Ibid., 90–91.
49. Besant, *As We Are and As We May Be*, 125–126.
50. Ibid., 126.
51. Ibid., 57–58.
52. Beaven, *Leisure*, 16. For an analysis of the Victorian bourgeoisie's concerns regarding leisure activities, also see Bailey, "'A Mingled Mass of Perfectly Legitimate Pleasures.'"
53. Besant, *As We Are and As We May Be*, 281.
54. Besant, *Children of Gibeon*, 93.
55. Deborah Cohen comments on the late-Victorian trend of the aestheticized domestic space, "'Artistic' became a term of praise for a well-furnished dwelling, and 'inartistic' a much dreaded censure. From the ubiquitous 'art furniture' displayed in store windows to the 'artistic' effects achieved by those who decorated according to the popular 'Art at Home' series of household manuals, the home had become *the* haven for art." Cohen, *Household Gods*, 65.
56. Bailkin, *Culture of Property*, 84.
57. Besant, *Children of Gibeon*, 268.

58. Poovey, *Uneven Developments*, 10–12.

59. Both Keating and Wim Neetens note the "declassed"—to use Neetens's term—nature of Besant's protagonists. While Neetens chooses to see this particular characterization as part of Besant's contradictory "humanist" project, I agree more with Keating's critique of Besant as a writer of "slum pastorals"—a fictional mode in which class struggle is suppressed in favor of a utopia of social harmony—where middle-class characters are conveniently distanced from capitalism. Keating, *Working Classes*, 167–198; Neetens, "Problems of a 'Democratic Text.'"

60. Besant, *Children of Gibeon*, 266.

61. Ibid., 269.

62. Gibeon was a Canaanite city conquered by Joshua, the leader of Israelites after the death of Moses. The Gibeonites trick the Israelites into a peace treaty (see Nehemiah 7:25 KJV). While Besant clearly acknowledges the greater power of the working classes by comparing them with Israelites, there is a note of guilt in comparing the middle classes with Gibeonites who have to resort to deceptive tactics to ensure their survival. Yet this note of guilt, which I have identified in Besant's use of the biblical reference, is not really visible elsewhere within the novel.

63. Besant, *Children of Gibeon*, 415–416.

64. Ibid., 416. For a discussion of the emergence of New Liberalism, see Freeden, *New Liberalism*, 175–184.

65. Besant, *Children of Gibeon*, 93–94, 203–205.

66. Ibid., 205.

67. Ibid., 199–200.

68. Weiner, *Architecture*, 164. Weiner uses the phrase to describe Samuel Barnett's invitation to educated young men to "come and be the squires of East London." Weiner, *Architecture*, 164. Besant was much inspired by the settlement movement, especially Barnett, and quite often spoke of reformers as secular "missionaries" who lived among the people and educated them.

69. Besant, *Children of Gibeon*, 100.

70. Ibid., 206, 203.

71. Ibid., 203, 208.

72. Ibid., 209.

73. Ibid., 163.

74. Ibid., 397. Regenia Gagnier notes that around 1871, political theory began to emphasize the insatiability of the "economic man" imagined increasingly as a consumer. Gagnier, *Insatiability of Human Wants*, 4–5. The acceptance of essential human nature as "selfish" in Besant's novel may thus be understood in light of Gagnier's explanation of a shift in post-1870s political theory. However, the validation of "self-interest" had been quite intrinsic to classical liberal political theory ever since Adam Smith's *Wealth of Nations*.

75. Besant, *Children of Gibeon*, 397.

76. Macpherson, *Possessive Individualism*, 3.

77. Besant, *Children of Gibeon*, 395.

78. Macpherson, *Possessive Individualism*, 3.

79. Besant, *Children of Gibeon*, 196.

80. Ibid., 196.

81. Jonathan Parry remarks, "They [liberals] encouraged individual self-improvement within all classes not least because of their ingrained assumption that the class structure was preordained and that men of property were society's natural leaders." Parry, *Rise and Fall*, 5.

82. Besant, *Children of Gibeon*, 394, 395.

83. Ibid., 131, 167.
84. Ibid., 353, 355.
85. Ibid., 354.
86. Ibid., 355. H. L. Malchow observes that reformers engaged in urban development viewed the streets as dark, ungovernable public spaces in opposition to the park promenades, which were easily kept under surveillance. Malchow, "Public Gardens."
87. Besant, *Children of Gibeon*, 356.
88. Hadley, "On a Darkling Plain," 95–96.
89. "Novels," 778.
90. "Children of Gibeon," 668.
91. Sichel, "Two Philanthropic Novelists," 518.
92. Besant, *Autobiography of Sir Walter Besant*, 247–248.

Bibliography

Bailey, Peter. "'A Mingled Mass of Perfectly Legitimate Pleasures': The Victorian Middle Class and the Problem of Leisure." *Victorian Studies* 21, no. 1 (1977): 7–28.
Bailkin, Jordanna. *The Culture of Property: The Crisis of Liberalism in Modern Britain*. Chicago: University of Chicago Press, 2004.
Barnes, Elizabeth. *States of Sympathy: Seduction and Democracy in the American Novel*. New York: Columbia University Press, 1997.
Barnett, Samuel. "University Settlements." In *University and Social Settlements*, edited by Will Reason, 11–26. London: Methuen, 1898. http://infed.org/archives/e-texts/barnet2.htm.
Beaven, Brad. *Leisure, Citizenship, and Working-Class Men in Britain, 1850–1945*. Oxford: Manchester University Press and Palgrave, 2005.
Besant, Walter. *All Sorts and Conditions of Men*. 1882. Reprint, London: H. M. Caldwell, 1896.
———. *The Art of Fiction*. London: Chatto and Windus, 1884.
———. *As We Are and As We May Be*. London: Chatto and Windus, 1903.
———. *Autobiography of Sir Walter Besant*. London: Hutchinson, 1902.
———. *Children of Gibeon*. 1886. Reprint, New York: Elibron Classics, 2005.
———. "The Endowment of the Daughter." In *As We Are and As We May Be*, 1–23. London: Chatto and Windus, 1903.
Betensky, Carolyn. *Feeling for the Poor: Bourgeois Compassion, Social Action, and the Victorian Novel*. Charlottesville: University of Virginia Press, 2010.
Boltanski, Luc, and Graham Burchell. *Distant Suffering: Morality, Media, and Politics*. Cambridge: Cambridge University Press, 2011.
Chandler, James. "On the Face of the Case: Conrad, *Lord Jim*, and the Sentimental Novel." *Critical Inquiry* 33, no. 4 (2007): 837–864.
"Children of Gibeon." *The Athenaeum*, no. 3082 (1886): 668–669.
Cockram, Gill G. *Ruskin and Social Reform: Ethics and Economics in the Victorian Age*. London: Tauris, 2007.
Cohen, Deborah. *Household Gods: The British and Their Possessions*. New Haven, CT: Yale University Press, 2006.
Crary, Jonathan. *Techniques of the Observer: On Vision and Modernity in the Nineteenth Century*. Cambridge, MA: MIT Press, 1990.

Davin, Anna. "Imperialism and Motherhood." *History Workshop* 5 (1978): 9–65.
During, Simon. *Exit Capitalism: Literary Culture, Theory, and Post-secular Modernity*. New York: Routledge, 2010.
Edelstein, T. J. "They Sang 'The Song of the Shirt': The Visual Iconology of the Seamstress." *Victorian Studies* 23, no. 2 (1980): 183–210.
Freeden, Michael. *The New Liberalism: An Ideology of Social Reform*. Oxford: Clarendon Press, 1978.
Gagnier, Regenia. *The Insatiability of Human Wants: Economics and Aesthetics in Market Society*. Chicago: University of Chicago Press, 2000.
Ghosh, Tanushree. "Gifting Pain: The Pleasures of Liberal Guilt in *London, a Pilgrimage* and *Street Life in London*." *Victorian Literature and Culture* 41, no. 1 (2013): 91–123.
Greiner, Rae. *Sympathetic Realism in Nineteenth-Century British Fiction*. Baltimore, MD: Johns Hopkins University Press, 2012.
Hadley, Elaine. "On a Darkling Plain: Victorian Liberalism and the Fantasy of Agency." *Victorian Studies* 48, no. 1 (2006): 92–102.
Haggard, Robert F. *The Persistence of Victorian Liberalism: The Politics of Social Reform, 1870–1900*. Westport, CT: Greenwood Press, 2001.
Halttunen, Karen. "Humanitarianism and the Pornography of Pain in Anglo-American Culture." *American Historical Review* 100, no. 2 (1995): 303–334.
Harris, Beth. *Famine and Fashion: Needlewomen in the Nineteenth Century*. Aldershot, UK: Ashgate, 2005.
Hurren, Elizabeth T. *Protesting about Pauperism: Poverty, Politics and Poor Relief in Late-Victorian England, 1870–1900*. Woodbridge, UK: Boydell Press, 2007.
Jaffe, Audrey. *Scenes of Sympathy: Identity and Representation in Victorian Fiction*. Ithaca, NY: Cornell University Press, 2000.
Joyce, Simon. "Castles in the Air: The People's Palace, Cultural Reformism, and the East End Working Class." *Victorian Studies* 39, no. 4 (1996): 513–538.
Keating, P. J. *The Working Classes in Victorian Fiction*. New York: Barnes and Noble, 1971.
Kees, Lara. "Sympathy in *Jane Eyre*." *SEL Studies in English Literature 1500–1900* 45, no. 4 (2005): 873–897.
Koven, Seth. *Slumming: Sexual and Social Politics in Victorian London*. Princeton, NJ: Princeton University Press, 2004.
Macpherson, C. B. *The Political Theory of Possessive Individualism: Hobbes to Locke*. 1962. Reprint, Oxford: Clarendon Press, 2010.
Malchow, H. L. "Public Gardens and Social Action in Late-Victorian London." *Victorian Studies* 29, no. 1 (1985): 97–124.
Marshall, David. *The Figure of Theater: Shaftesbury, Defoe, Adam Smith, and George Eliot*. New York: Columbia University Press, 1986.
Neetens, Wim. "Problems of a 'Democratic Text': Walter Besant's Impossible Story." *Novel* 23, no. 3 (1990): 247–264.
"Novels: 'The Children of Gibeon'; 'Princess Casamassima'; 'Sir Percival'; 'A Bachelor's Blunder.'" *Blackwood's Edinburgh Magazine* 140, no. 854 (1886): 776–798.
Parry, Jonathan. *The Rise and Fall of Liberal Government in Victorian Britain*. New Haven, CT: Yale University Press, 1993.
Poovey, Mary. *Uneven Developments: The Ideological Work of Gender in Mid-Victorian England*. Chicago: University of Chicago Press, 1988.

Sichel, Edith. "Two Philanthropic Novelists." *Murray's Magazine: A Home and Colonial Periodical for the General Reader* 3, no. 16 (1888): 506–518.

Smith, Adam, and Knud Haakonssen. *The Theory of Moral Sentiments*. Cambridge: Cambridge University Press, 2002.

Sykes, Alan. *The Rise and Fall of British Liberalism*. London: Longman Press, 1997.

Treuherz, Julian. *Hard Times: Social Realism in Victorian Art*. London: Lund Humphries and Manchester City Art Galleries, 1987.

Walkowitz, Judith. *City of Dreadful Delight: Narratives of Sexual Danger in Late-Victorian Britain*. Chicago: University of Chicago Press, 1992.

Weiner, Deborah E. B. *Architecture and Social Reform in Late-Victorian London*. Manchester, UK: Manchester University Press, 1994.

Zakreski, Patricia. *Representing Female Artistic Labour, 1848–1890 : Refining Work for the Middle-Class Woman*. Aldershot, UK: Ashgate, 2006.

8

"The Orthodox Creed of the Business World"?

Philanthropy and Liberal Individualism in Edith Wharton's The Fruit of the Tree

Emily Coit

In the wake of the success of *The House of Mirth* (1905), Edith Wharton turned away from the plush drawing rooms of New York, seeking fresh subject matter in the factories of rural New England, which she visited like a good naturalist in order to get her details right.[1] The novel that emerged from this experiment, *The Fruit of the Tree* (1907), represents relations between business owners and factory operatives and is one of her most explicitly political works. Wharton positions her reforming protagonists against those who advocate "the orthodox creed of the business world." According to this creed, "Business was one thing, philanthropy another; and the enthusiasts who tried combining them were usually reduced to paying fifty cents on the dollar, and handing over their stock to a promoter presumably unhampered by humanitarian ideals"; those who espouse this creed impose unsafe conditions on workers because their single aim is "to make it pay better."[2] Wharton's protagonists, by contrast, embrace "humanitarian ideals," integrate philanthropy into business, and accept that as business owners they have a social responsibility to care for their workers.

The "orthodox creed" that Wharton represents so unflatteringly anticipates the economist Milton Friedman's influential axiom, pronounced some fifty years later, that "the social responsibility of business is to increase its profits."[3] In subjecting this creed to stern critique and valorizing the efforts of those who oppose it, Wharton's novel might seem to participate in the long and robust tradition of collectivist dissent that questions the assumptions of Friedman's discipline and objects in particular to the liberal individualism at its center. But any student of Wharton will know that her opposition to various forms of collectivism was explicit and consistent. Her novel about business and philanthropy, in fact, has a far more complex and far less antagonistic relation to the assumptions of the emergent academic discipline of economics. This relation becomes more evident when we recognize the novel's participation in the larger discourse of philanthropy; its political and ethical commitments emerge when we situate it within a transatlantic conversation about the social responsibilities attendant on industrial wealth. This chapter reads *The Fruit of the Tree* with an eye toward contemporary writing on business and philanthropy, taking up the industrialist Andrew Carnegie's widely disseminated exhortations as well as the eminent economist Alfred Marshall's lecture on "economic chivalry." Situating the novel thus allows us to see that its opposition to "the orthodox creed of the business world" is in fact a steady endorsement of the liberal individualist principles that economists like Friedman would promote.

Liberal is a problematic word in that it has frequently carried multiple unstable meanings, even within the same historical moment. Here I use the term to refer to the set of ideas within classical liberalism that emphasize the value of an individual liberal subject's autonomy in relation to the state; this set of ideas within classical liberalism is not synonymous with later twentieth-century economic liberalism, though this essay investigates how the former may figure in the history of the latter. Wharton's novel, I want to suggest, participates in the cultural work that makes Friedman's statement possible, and its argument about the proper relation between philanthropy and business is also an argument about the proper relation between the citizen and the state. Wharton shares with Carnegie and Marshall a pattern of reference to organic metaphor and thus to organic models for understanding social organization; read together, the three texts treated here thus prompt us to consider the relation between organicism and liberal individualism in early twentieth-century thinking about wealth. For Wharton especially, organicism is the foundation for an argument that the wealthy individual ought to be autonomous: to the extent that *The Fruit of the Tree* advocates a laissez-faire economics, it does so on the premise that free-market decisions are made in an organic society. In the context of such a society, philanthropy is for Wharton not merely an autonomous practice, but a form of luxury consumption. By representing philanthropy thus, she actually goes farther than either Carnegie or Marshall in suggesting that the individual is sovereign: the sovereignty of her liberal individual is specifically the sovereignty of the consumer, and she represents citizenship and consumption as overlapping practices.

As consumers, Wharton's individuals are creatures of capricious desire, and the genre in which she represents them allows her to emphasize that capriciousness. While Marshall's and Carnegie's individuals are abstract devices for argumentation, Wharton's are fully rendered characters, and she advocates their sovereign autonomy in spite of their peculiar caprices and flaws. The novel's formal possibilities crucially enable her argument, in that the genre's capacity for representing ambiguities and local particulars allows her to express an organicism that rejects abstract, uniform, and externally mandated solutions to complex, specific problems. The solutions to such problems, she suggests, must always be themselves local and specific—and must therefore begin with the free actions of individuals rather than with systems or policies imposed on individuals.

Wharton sets her story in an industrial town in the hardscrabble rural New England that would later be the ground of the much more celebrated *Ethan Frome*. Her male protagonist, the factory manager John Amherst, wishes to make reforms at the Westmore Mill; when he marries Bessy Westmore, the wealthy widow of the mill's late owner, he mistakenly understands their love to be grounded in a mutual desire to do good. Bessy's actual frivolity hampers his projects, however, and the couple grow estranged. Justine Brent, the intelligent and capable nurse who has shared Amherst's reformist vision from the start, attempts to help them salvage their marriage. While Amherst remains away, Bessy has an equestrian accident and is left in a semiconscious state of paralyzed agony. Before he can get home, Justine secretly gives Bessy a fatal, merciful dose of morphine. When Justine and Amherst subsequently marry, this act haunts and ultimately destroys their relationship. They work as partners to spend the Westmore fortune in a way that benefits the millworkers, but their marriage is an empty shell.

A number of readings of the novel have attempted to find coherence in its rather overloaded plot; others have sought to show how the novel anachronistically exhibits a late-twentieth-century feminism.[4] More recently, Jennie A. Kassanoff has given fresh attention to the novel's expression of Wharton's conservative politics; her important book observes that a "don't ask don't tell approach to Wharton's conservatism" has been part of "a widespread tendency in American criticism to oversimplify and patronize conservative politics," a tendency in which "conservatism has been the straw man of choice, a flimsy opponent easily dismantled by the sophisticated instruments of liberal democratic thought." Her productive efforts "to take Wharton at her word" in *The Fruit of the Tree* focus on the plot about euthanasia, arguing that the "prostrate woman incarnates Wharton's fear of oligarchic collapse" and that the novel proposes "a strategy of elite control" while expressing "Wharton's deep-seated fears of political and cultural democratization." She also points to the 1907 financial collapse that immediately followed the novel's publication. Noting that the collapse prompted a public debate about the ethical and political issues around high finance and massive industrial fortunes, she argues that the novel "anticipates this national discussion."[5]

In this reading, I extend Kassanoff's efforts to take Wharton's conservatism seriously, but I see *The Fruit of the Tree* intervening in a discussion that was already well underway when Wharton was writing the novel, during the years from 1905 to 1907, rather than merely anticipating the discussion that would follow the collapse.[6] The conversation in which the novel intervenes includes muckraking novels, self-help success manuals, and, not least, Theodore Roosevelt's ongoing commentary about corruption and honesty in the realm of business and finance and the policy initiatives that accompanied that commentary. In the 1906 speech that also treats the function of "the Man with the Muck-rake," Roosevelt declares that Americans must "grapple with the problems connected with the amassing of enormous fortunes, and the use of those fortunes, both corporate and individual, in business." He goes on to express support for some sort of "progressive tax on all fortunes, beyond a certain amount either given in life or devised or bequeathed upon death to any individual—a tax so framed as to put it out of the power of the owner of one of these enormous fortunes to hand on more than a certain amount to any one individual. . . . Such taxation should, of course, be aimed merely at the inheritance or transmission in their entirety of those fortunes swollen beyond all healthy limits."[7] Wharton was a great admirer of Roosevelt and notably supported his imperial tendencies, but her novel interrogates these ideas about how to address "the problems connected with the amassing of enormous fortunes."[8] We need to recall, moreover, that Roosevelt's words participate in the larger early twentieth-century discourse of philanthropy that also includes thinkers like Carnegie and Marshall. This discourse is the site of conversations about, among other things, the ethics of possessing a large fortune, the wealthy citizen's right to private property, and the question of whether social responsibility for the needy lies with the wealthy citizen or with the state.

"The Fruit of the Tree": Organicism and the Distribution of Wealth

Wharton's title has been read as a reference to the Bible and to Milton's lost paradise, and it surely has those resonances.[9] But as the title of a book about an industrial-era factory town, "the fruit of the tree" also describes production and products in surprisingly agricultural terms, locating Wharton's treatment of modern questions about money and factory management in a premodern register of growth and harvest. It thus points to the organic society that the novel proposes, one in which change is gradual and paternalism benevolent. In both art and politics, Wharton objects to inorganic rupture, to the forceful, spontaneous, or unnatural application of ideas.[10] She writes in 1923 to Bernard Berenson of her dislike for literary modernism: "The trouble with all this new stuff is that it's à thèse: the theory comes first, & dominates it."[11] *Theory* here should be distinguished clearly from preexisting rules and established order; Wharton does not oppose regulation grounded in tradition—au contraire. What she opposes is the a priori application of a conjectural, untried theory regardless of local circumstances and particularities. James Tuttleton persuasively reads *The Fruit of the Tree* as a critique of "abstract idealism"; this idealism is analogous to the "à thèse" approach that Wharton disparages in her letter to Berenson, and the novel's critique of it expresses an organic logic that figures in her thinking about both literature and politics.

For Carnegie and Marshall as well, the idea of an organic society provides a framework within which to explain the role of the wealthy individual in addressing social ills. In their prose, too, the commonplace trope of trees and fruit figures organic change that is slow and pragmatic and exposes the danger of change that is rapid and violent. This pattern of imagery functions in the work of all three authors to argue for conservative, gradualist politics, supporting a status quo in which property is held by the rich and disparaging collectivist programs for redistribution, including some forms of taxation. Their claims about the social obligations of the rich imply that certain key solutions to the social problems attendant on industrialization lie with individuals rather than with the state. Philanthropy provides a model for redistribution of wealth that is consistent with liberal individualism; collectivist approaches to redistribution, as understood here, depend instead on some form of government taxation and potentially disrupt a steady, safe, organic progress. In the former model, improvements arise from within, while in the latter, they are imposed artificially by external systems that operate, as Wharton might put it, "à thèse."

The contexts for Carnegie's and Marshall's deployments of organic imagery differ. Marshall's "Social Possibilities of Economic Chivalry" is an address delivered at the Royal Economic Society in January 1907 and published in expanded and polished form in *The Economic Journal* in March of the same year.[12] Its audience is thus substantially composed of economists, and one of his aims in the piece is to define ethical and social duties for the discipline. Carnegie's program on the ethics of wealth speaks to a broader audience. He published his philosophy of philanthropy, "Wealth," in the *North American Review* in 1889; the piece received a great deal of attention on both sides of the Atlantic, earning a positive, engaged critique from William Gladstone himself. It was a reprint for the British market that gave the essay its now-famous title, "The Gospel of Wealth," which Carnegie adopted as his own. Carnegie answered his critics and fans in subsequent essays in the *North American* and in the *Nineteenth Century*. In 1906, prompted partly by Roosevelt's expressed support for a graduated estate tax, Carnegie requested that the *North American* reprint the "Gospel" and followed it with a new piece, "The Gospel of Wealth II," which he subsequently expanded for inclusion in his book *Problems of To-day: Wealth, Labor, Socialism*. In addition to these publications, Carnegie also promoted his ideas in numerous speaking engagements.

For Carnegie, the image of a tree and its fruit contrasts the wrongness of "endeavoring to uproot" or provoking "revolution" with the rightness of evolutionary progress within an existing system: "All we can possibly or profitably accomplish . . . is to bend the universal tree of humanity a little in the direction most favorable to the production of good fruit under existing circumstances."[13] Those circumstances involve immutable laws and principles that may be the cause of inequality and injustice but are "the soil in which society has so far produced the best fruit."[14] Marshall, too, deploys the imagery of the fruitful tree to express his pragmatic gradualism: "In recent years we have suffered much from schemes that claim to be practical, and yet are based on no thorough study of economic realities . . . that even propose to tear up by the roots family life, the tree whose fruits and flowers contribute much more than half to the sum total of all that is known of beauty and happiness by the people in general."[15] Marshall acknowledges the problem of unequal distribution of wealth but criticizes radical or "utopian" efforts to address it: "The reasonable dissatisfaction, with which every thoughtful person must regard the existing distribution of wealth, is in danger of being perverted towards ill-considered measures of reform by Utopian schemers . . . who imply, if they do not explicitly state, that, if wealth were equally divided, everyone would have access to means of comfort, refinement, and even luxury which are far out of the reach of the working classes at present." This view, Marshall states, is quite mistaken: acquaintance with economic particulars convinces him that "many prosperous artisan's families" would actually suffer under such an arrangement.[16]

Carnegie, too, opposes forms of socialism or communism. Heavily influenced by Herbert Spencer, he understands those models of governance as regressive. "To those who propose to substitute Communism for this intense Individualism," he writes in 1889, "the answer, therefore, is: the race has tried that. All progress from the barbarous to the present has resulted from its displacement. Not evil, but good, has come to the race from the accumulation of wealth by those who have the ability and energy to produce it." In 1906, he repeats this refrain, affirming that "in Individualism lies the secret of the steady progress of civilization." Carnegie's thrust is that the rich man must give his money away during his lifetime, and he must have freedom to do so as he sees fit; upon his death, however, the state is justified in imposing an essentially punitive estate tax. Carnegie writes with characteristic subtlety: "By taxing estates heavily at death the state marks its condemnation of the selfish millionaire's unworthy life." The rich man has a moral imperative to give, he explains, because "enormous fortunes are dependent upon the community; without great and increasing population, there could be no great wealth. Where wealth accrues honorably, the people are always silent partners." In addition to endorsing a graduated estate tax, Carnegie also allows that a dividend tax on corporations might be acceptable. However, he sternly opposes a personal income tax: "Of all taxes," he writes, "this is the most pernicious. It demoralizes a nation." Through redistribution, "the people" must be rewarded for their role in generating vast wealth—but that redistribution should occur in the same individualistic fashion as the accumulation of wealth that makes it possible. For the nation and the race to benefit, the rich man must have autonomy to distribute his wealth as he likes.[17]

Marshall, too, argues for the autonomy of the individual in relation to the state. He asserts that "governmental intrusion into businesses which require ceaseless invention and fertility of resource is a danger to social progress"; noting that although civil servants are numerous, they produce few inventions, he declares, "Government creates scarcely anything." But creation, he suggests, is after all not government's proper purpose; implementation, regulation, and infrastructure, it would seem, are the right functions and duties of the state. Innovation, however, is the work of the individual. Marshall puts it pithily: "A government could print a good edition of Shakespeare's works, but it could not get them written." The same is true in the sciences: "The carcase of municipal electric works belongs to the officials; the genius belongs to free enterprise."[18] Marshall's biographer, the historian of economic thought Peter Groenewegen, sums up the project of "Social Possibilities of Economic Chivalry" as an attempt to "argue strongly for the severe curtailment of state social activities by confining them basically to municipal works; and to present competition and private initiative as vastly superior vehicles for achieving social aims."[19] Marshall argues that the government should "do work which is vital, and which none but the government can do efficiently": within the "work which none but the government can do" he includes "inquiry where agents betray their trust, or where fraudulent producers or dealers can outwit the consumer" and notes "its imperative duty to inspect and arbitrate, for that cannot be discharged by anyone else, except it be the ever-ready writers in newspapers."[20] Like Carnegie, Marshall does express some support for redistributive taxation, and in particular for an estate tax on the death of the wealthy man. He observes that "a vast increase of happiness and elevation of life might be attained if those forms of expenditure which serve no high purpose could be curtailed, and the resources thus set free would be applied for the welfare of the less prosperous members of the working classes," but he opposes "retrenching the lavish expenditure of the rich, and dividing income equally."[21] The distinction between this desirable "curtailing" and this undesirable "retrenching" may seem elusive; for Marshall, it is a distinction that depends on the autonomy of the wealthy in relation to the state, as well as their right to private property. He advocates a state that works actively for the welfare of its people by exercising some redistribution, as well as monitoring and regulating businesses, but he feels that the policies advocated by collectivists—the collective rather than private ownership of property, the forced redistribution of wealth and state—will actually compromise the welfare of the vast majority, lowering a standard of living only recently raised.

Marshall's and Carnegie's arguments both work against socialist and communist ideas by swallowing them whole. For Carnegie, the supreme autonomy of the rich man (and his right to private property) is justified partly because the rich man's property is actually the property of the broader public: "The surplus wealth for the few will become, in the best sense, the property of the many, because administered for the common good, and this wealth, passing through the hands of the few, can be made a much more potent force for the elevation of our race than if it had been distributed in small sums to the people themselves."[22] Carnegie's "property of the many" attributes communism's putative benefits to the policies of individualism; similarly, Marshall defines socialism in a way that allows him to claim its attractions for the system he endorses. He boldly identifies himself—and, indeed, "nearly every economist of the present generation" as a "socialist."[23] "Economists," he writes, "generally desire increased intensity of State activities for social amelioration that are not fully within the range of private effort, but they are opposed to that vast extension of state activities which is desired by collectivists." What Marshall opposes, then, is the "collectivism" of "utopian schemers"; "collectivists" he defines as "those who would transfer to the State the ownership and management of land, machinery, and all other agents of production." "Socialists," however, he defines commodiously as "everyone who strenuously endeavors to promote the social amelioration of the people." Both the economist and the industrialist, then, use language strategically to suggest that solutions to the problem of poverty lie with individuals.[24]

Wharton's novel, like Carnegie's and Marshall's more overtly polemical prose, also magisterially takes control of language in order to make a political argument. The book does not discuss communism and socialism; the words *socialism* and *communism* and their variants are absent from the text, with the exception of two passing mentions by Bessy's man-of-business father Mr. Langhope: a reference to "low mongrelly socialist mill-hands" and an exclamation that Amherst is "no better than a socialist, then!" But Amherst is most certainly not a socialist. The fact that his enemy, the business-minded Langhope, would apply that term to him points us to one of the novel's central tactics for political argumentation: Wharton erases ideas and strategies that might be called socialist, collectivist, or communist by silently foreshortening the political spectrum. In a move that recalls Carnegie's redefinition of publicly held property and Marshall's redefinition of socialism, Wharton appropriates the language of socialism or radicalism for her conservative argumentation. The effect is to make actual socialist or radical meanings less visible and less thinkable. Views labeled "radical" in the novel are in fact rather conservative, and actual radicalism is absent.

Because Wharton does not discuss, for instance, labor unionization or political solutions to social problems, she is able to position Amherst—whose views are quite moderate—as the extremist in her book. Amherst's strategy for improving the lives of millworkers initially centers on ensuring that "the hands should work and live under healthier conditions." The novel does not consider legislative or collectivist means by which this aim might be accomplished. Rather, Amherst argues ardently for certain choices to be made independently by the owners of the mill: "Floorspace of the mills must be enlarged, and the company must cease to rent out tenements, and give the operators the opportunity to buy land for themselves." Later in the novel, Amherst (along with Justine) develops his efforts further by advocating for the provision of leisure facilities for millworkers.[25]

Amherst's reforms are positioned against "the orthodox creed of the business world," placing above the profit motive "humanitarian ideals" such as interpersonal sympathy between workers and managers. He argues that employers must develop a "sounder understanding" of the needs of workers, and the two groups must learn "to regard each other not as antagonists but as collaborators," thus accomplishing a "readjustment of the whole industrial relation." He urges Bessy to disregard "business" and concern herself with her "personal relation to the people" who work in the mill. Understanding would develop between workers and employers, he believes, if "the employers proved their good faith by the deliberate and permanent sacrifice of excessive gain to the well-being of each employed." In direct opposition to the "orthodox creed of the business world," Amherst's reform platform demands, in fact, that "revenues should be materially and permanently reduced." Bessy points out that her father and his associates have told her that Amherst's spending is "imprudent" and his plan "unbusinesslike."[26]

But Amherst's aims are not really so distant from the creed they presume to oppose. The profit motive, or at least due deference to it, is folded within his reforms. In his efforts to persuade the selfish Bessy, he says, "In the end I believe such sympathy produces better work, and so benefits the employer materially"; later, he promises, "You would certainly have less money for a number of years; after that, I believe you would have more rather than less." His schemes for reform, moreover, are meant to provide opportunities for workers to exercise the sort of individualism that leads to fortunes: his reforms will strike "at the roots of the baneful paternalism which was choking out every germ of initiative in the workman." Part of the problem with slum tenements, it would seem, is that such living conditions prevent workers from exercising the "initiative" that might make them successful, independent strivers who buy and own.[27]

Wharton solidifies Amherst's otherwise unlikely status as an extremist reformer by situating him within a distorting juxtaposition: she places him next to Bessy, a dim and pliant wife backed by a pack of wolfish businessmen led by her father, Mr. Langhope. Her reformist projects are "superficial"; his, in contrast, are "radical." Her often aesthetically oriented and female-implemented schemes serve as the foil to his more substantive reforms.[28] Amherst dismisses in frustration as "purely superficial" Bessy's "minor projects": her organization of Christmas celebrations for the workers, her plans for establishing a "Mother's Club," recreation grounds, a hospital, night schools, a library, and a gymnasium. Wharton has Amherst argue—in organic terms that echo the gradualism implicit in the novel's title—that working on Bessy's projects is "like picking flowers and sticking them in the ground to make a garden—unless you transplant the flower with its roots, and prepare the soil to receive it, your garden will be faded tomorrow. No radical changes have yet been made at Westmore; and it is of radical changes that I want to speak." But a genuine radical of Wharton's time might say the same to Amherst about his own schemes for change.[29]

The Rich Man: Talent and Chivalry

In locating the cure for the social ills of advanced industrial capitalism in the activity of the autonomous private individual rather than the collectivist or socialist state, Wharton, Carnegie, and Marshall all imagine the wealthy individual as a man possessed of faculties that justify this autonomy. Amherst is a fine specimen: handsome, gifted, and nobly concerned with the "humanitarian ideals" that Langhope and the others among Bessy's backers would dismiss. As Kassanoff has noted, Wharton's protagonists, Amherst and Justine, are marked as superior to those around them in a way that depends at least partly on race: "John Amherst is in reality the descendant of a long line of genteel Americans" and "Justine . . . is in fact the descendant of an old-stock family that has fallen on hard times." Wharton, she concludes, "is careful to certify that all of the characters who are in the position to control industrial production are sufficiently 'aristocratic.'" So, although ownership and control of wealth is a complicated issue in Wharton's plot, the organic society within which she imagines philanthropic spending would seem to have leaders whose gifts are to a significant extent natural. Amherst's princely superiority acquires added significance when we consider Carnegie's and Marshall's accounts of the rich man: the "natural elite" that Kassanoff observes in *The Fruit of the Tree* has analogues in the wealthy as imagined by both of these thinkers.[30]

Carnegie observes that generally, in the cases of rich men, "there can be traced in their careers some special form of ability upon which their success depended, thus distinguishing them from the mass of competitors," and he further suggests that "the great administrator, whether as railroad builder, steamship owner, manufacturer, merchant, banker, is an exceptional man. . . . [M]illions honestly made in any useful occupation give evidence of ability, foresight, and assiduity above the common and prove the man who has made them a valuable member of society."³¹ "The Gospel of Wealth" suggests not just that success is evidence of these exceptional abilities but that the employer who grows rich can hardly do otherwise: "Talent for organization and management . . . secures for its possessor enormous rewards, no matter where or under what laws or conditions. . . . [I]t is inevitable that their income must exceed their expenditures, and that they must accumulate wealth." He concludes, "It is a law, as certain as any of the others named, that men possessed of this peculiar talent for affairs, under the free play of economic forces, must, of necessity, soon be in receipt of more revenue than can be judiciously expended upon themselves; and this law is as beneficial for the race as the others."³²

Within Carnegie's logic, the man who rises to wealth is necessarily superior and necessarily capable of doing better than the poor because wealth accrues inevitably and exclusively to those who are innately talented and capable. The power that wealth confers is thus necessarily justified by the inevitable merits of its possessor. To deny the wealthy man that power would be to cede it to the less intelligent, less hardworking, and the less deserving, which would in turn diminish the progress of the race. Carnegie argues that the man of business must increase his profits as much as possible because those profits will be spent philanthropically. In fact, given the proper practice of philanthropy, Carnegie asserts, "It becomes the duty of the millionaire to increase his revenues. The struggle for more is completely changed from selfish or ambitious taint into a noble pursuit. Then he labors not for himself, but for others; not to hoard, but to spend. The more he makes, the more the public gets."³³

Although his perspective is less explicitly racialized and less deterministic, Marshall similarly posits a rich man of business whose status marks him as exceptionally able. Rather than a racialized rhetoric of evolutionary fitness, he deploys a medievalizing rhetoric of paternalistic hierarchy to articulate his ideas about superiority. The autonomy of private wealth and of business in relation to the state is justified by the potential for what Marshall calls "economic chivalry," and the economists who are his audience have a role to play in fostering such chivalry. "I want to suggest," he says, "that there is much latent chivalry in business life, and that there would be a great deal more of it if we sought it out and honoured it as men honoured the medieval chivalry of war." Doing so, he continues, will nurture a "chivalry of wealth," provoking an "elevation of life which has been achieved by training the finer elements of human nature to full account in the production of wealth and its use."³⁴ It is the duty of economists to assist in this process by distinguishing "that which is chivalrous and noble from that which is not." The chivalry of wealth that economists must assist the public in perceiving is akin to the glories achieved in war and in the arts. Marshall calls on medieval tropes to evoke both the independent courage of the warrior and the nobility of careful craft:

Chivalry in business includes public spirit, as chivalry in war includes unselfish loyalty to the cause of prince or of country or of crusade. But it also includes a delight in doing noble and difficult things because they are noble and difficult: as knightly chivalry called on a man to begin by making his own armour, and to use his armour for choice in those contests in which his skill and resource, his courage and endurance, would be put to the severest tests. It includes a scorn for cheap victories, and a delight in succouring those who need a helping hand. It does not disdain the gains to be won on the way, but it has the fine pride of the warrior who esteems the spoils of a well fought battle, or the prizes of a tournament, mainly for the sake of the achievements to which they testify, and only in the second degree for the value at which they are appraised in the money of the market.[35]

Marshall proposes the idea that business calls on creative and ethical faculties and is only secondarily driven by profit; he develops this idea throughout his essay, reiterating that innovation in business is analogous to innovation in art and science. "Epoch-making discoveries," he writes, "come from men who love their work with a chivalrous love. . . . Creative science can be evoked only by the force which evokes creative art and creative literature—the force of chivalrous emulation." This force has room to exert itself in the realm of entrepreneurship, in the atmosphere of "the bracing fresh air which a strong man with a chivalrous yearning for leadership draws into his lungs when he sets out on a business experiment at his own risk."[36]

Carnegie's overtly Spencerian and racial account of the rich man's superiority differs considerably from Marshall's rather Ruskinian, medievalizing account of voluntary paternalistic chivalry—the former makes the rich man's correct benevolence inevitable, while the latter suggests that economists have a duty to coax it out. Carnegie and Wharton both draw from Spencerian thinking to imagine a biologically superior rich man—but, unsurprisingly, their visions of superiority differ: the innate merit of Wharton's hero is manifest not in a "talent for organization and management" but in attributes such as a sensitivity to the pleasures of Shakespeare.

The Philanthropist as Consumer

Wharton, like Carnegie and Marshall, argues against collectivist solutions to social ills; like them, she imagines the wealthy man of business as a man possessed of an exceptional skill that justifies his autonomy. Her argument takes a further turn, however, one that is distinctly literary: *The Fruit of the Tree* disrupts genre conventions and exploits the capacity of the novel for meaningful self-contradiction. The book presents itself as a text that might fall into the category of the muckraking industrial novel, the social problem novel, the progressive problem novel, or some interesting mix of those genres—and, indeed, Wharton's investigative visits to factories during the book's composition suggest the same.[37] But the novel that begins with set pieces in the mills shifts its focus to the luxurious milieu of those who own them: it moves from the scene of production to the scene of consumption. Some readers have suggested that what we see here is a faddish industrial interest that succumbs to a resurgent, inveterate tendency to describe the world Wharton knew: she cannot represent factories and poor people, they suggest, because she knows nothing about them, and so the novel wanders helplessly back into the drawing rooms with which its author was so familiar.[38] But this reading of *The Fruit of the Tree* as a failed industrial novel that veered ineluctably off course neglects to note the argumentative implications of this shift.

In fact, the novel's political force derives from its preoccupation with private spending by the owners of industry. An industrial novel that focuses on private consumption is not necessarily a failed industrial novel; it is an industrial novel that makes a specific argument about how to address industrial problems. In turning from the scene of production to the scene of consumption, *The Fruit of the Tree* locates the solution to the social ills of advanced industrial capitalism in the autonomous individual of talent and merit—in his role as sovereign consumer, spending his freely accumulated wealth wisely. Social solutions are thus dependent on a market that permits such accumulation and a government that does not restrict the individual's right to do with his wealth as he sees fit.

The novel represents consumption extensively, even laboriously, and it locates philanthropic spending within that consumption. It dwells on debates about how those profiting from the mill should spend their money: on lavish weeklong house parties, new horses, private swimming pools, and rare sets of Chinese vases? Or on enlarging the workspace in their mills in order to prevent further injury to workers? These are the questions that drive the plot. The marital conflict between Amherst and Bessy pits her will to spend on luxuries at their home, Lynbrook, against his will to spend on making improvements at the mills that bear her name. Their disagreement is a zero-sum game, so that, as Mr. Langhope says, "the golden age at Westmore" is "likely to be the age of copper at Lynbrook." Langhope and his lawyer feel obliged to point out to Bessy that "every philanthropic outlay at Westmore must entail a corresponding reduction in her income." Because they dislike Amherst and his reforms, they consistently try "to encourage her in some new extravagance to which the work at the mills must be sacrificed." Bessy is infuriated when she discovers that she is "ruined" and that there is no money to build her private recreation facilities: "She had expected to find herself cramped, restricted—to be warned that she must 'manage,' hateful word! . . . But this! This was incredible! Unendurable! There was no money to build the gymnasium—none at all! And all because it had been swallowed up at Westmore."[39]

Bessy is, among other things, a portrait of the modern consumer: she is notable for her hedonism, sensuousness, excessive desire, and sensitivity to the social implications of her purchases. She is childish, even animal-like, and her favorite pleasure is intense athletic activity. Wharton writes, "Bessy combined great zeal in the pursuit of sport—a tireless passion for the saddle, the golf-course, the tennis court—with an almost oriental inertia within doors"; in that interior realm, her behavior is marked by an "indolence of body and brain." In using the words *oriental* and *indolence*, Wharton evokes a vast body of antiluxury literature, and in speaking of "zeal" and "passion," she emphasizes the irrational character of Bessy's amusements. Later, Bessy appears "filled with a feverish desire" to build her new leisure facilities—a squash court, a bowling alley, a swimming tank, and a gymnasium—as fast and as grandly as possible. In keeping with her status as a modern hedonistic consumer, she seeks her pleasures not casually, but desperately: she wants not enjoyment, but relief. The luxuries of equestrian sport and lavish entertaining are for her exactly what a drug is to its addict. "She had grown," Wharton writes, "to depend more and more on the distractions of a crowded house"; later, we read that "of late nothing but a hard gallop had availed to quiet her nerves."[40]

Bessy marks herself as a creature of the social world described by Thorstein Veblen in that she consumes in part to consolidate her elevated social status in the existing order.[41] Her friend Blanche Carbury, the novel's sole one-dimensional villain—a tasteless, ill-mannered, and indiscreet adulteress—takes her to New Jersey (a destination, one feels, not arbitrarily chosen) to see similarly conceived private leisure facilities "on which a friend of Mrs. Carbury's had lavished a fortune." Blanche herself is a grotesque version of the modern consumer: her rudeness takes the form of wastefully consuming household luxuries with an almost parodic intensity. As a houseguest, she lingers endlessly, "somewhat aggressively in possession, criticizing and rearranging furniture, ringing for servants, making sudden demands on the stable, telegraphing, telephoning, ordering fires lighted or windows opened, and leaving everywhere in her wake a trail of cigarette ashes and cocktail glasses." Bessy comes back from her New Jersey jaunt with this vulgar creature "brimming with the wonders she had seen" and is freshly inspired to build big and build soon. More significantly, she is filled with a "dread of appearing, under Blanche Carbury's eyes, subject to any restraining influence of economy." Wharton thus in one stroke represents Veblen's "pecuniary emulation" and his "conspicuous consumption."[42]

The zero-sum game of spending in the novel means that Bessy's conspicuous consumption is parallel to Justine and Amherst's "philanthropic" spending on improving the lives of millworkers. Just as Bessy's "superficial" schemes to help workers serve in the novel as a foil to Amherst's ostensibly more substantive "improvements," Bessy's greedy frivolity serves to set her rival Justine's sober virtues in relief. And yet the novel suggests that these forms of altruism bleed problematically into one another. Wharton presents Justine's philanthropic work as strikingly similar to Bessy's; like Bessy's philanthropic efforts, Justine's are at least in part costly forms of self-gratification. "In her eager adoption" of her husband's ideas, Wharton writes, Bessy "had made a pet of the mills." This sounds rather suspect, but later, Justine says cheerfully to Amherst of her interest in the poor, "It's the same kind of interest I used to feel in my dolls and guinea pigs—a managing, interfering old maid's interest. I don't believe I should care a straw for them if I couldn't dose them and order them about." For both women, then—not just for the shallow, materialistic Bessy—working with the poor delivers the same sort of amusement provided by a docile domesticated rodent or a child's plaything. Justine has the wise self-awareness to admit that "philanthropy is one of the subtlest forms of self-indulgence." Wharton again positions philanthropy as a form of luxury consumption when Mr. Langhope, acknowledging the unseemly truth that his daughter has begun to play bridge for money, says, "Well, she may make something, and offset her husband's prodigalities," making reference to Amherst's lavish spending on improvements at the mills. His ironic rhetoric makes gambling for cash over a decadent bridge table an act of pecuniary responsibility and dismisses the dispensing of funds to help poor workers as the feckless move of an improvident prodigal. Langhope's remark is snide, but it reinforces a pattern in the novel that recognizes philanthropy as one form of luxury consumption among others.[43]

In making philanthropic spending a self-gratifying activity that is precisely parallel to similarly gratifying conspicuous consumption, Wharton represents philanthropy as a form of luxury spending. Having located the solution to social problems in the independent philanthropic decisions of the autonomous liberal subject—rather than the collectivist efforts of a government—she takes one step farther, marking such philanthropy as a practice driven by a variety of personal desire akin to the desire that drives purchases of thoroughbreds and chocolates. In this respect, her examination of the social responsibilities of business is more incisive and bold than Carnegie's or Marshall's. Like them, she advocates the autonomy of the liberal subject, but her novel acknowledges more fully than either thinker the potential implications of that autonomy. Her rich man, like Carnegie's and Marshall's, is a superior being deserving of the power his wealth confers—but unlike the one-dimensional paragons imagined by those thinkers, Wharton's philanthropists are fully developed characters, and their shining altruism is mixed with selfishness and error. Wharton's rich also differ from Carnegie's and Marshall's in that they are sometimes women. Her novel, in fact, offers an essentially misogynist critique of the idea that a rich man's merits will always justify his control over his wealth by suggesting that, in practice, this wealth may be spent by the idiot female to whom he is married. Wharton, then, is willing to advocate the supremacy of the autonomous liberal subject even while acknowledging that his autonomy is never total and that his autonomous decisions will sometimes amount to foolish whim. Marshall does not dwell on this as fully, and Carnegie denies it entirely. Their cleaner, more polemical texts must rely to some extent on generalizations; they veer, in this sense, into the realm of abstraction and theory. But as a writer of novels, Wharton expresses a more thoroughgoing commitment both to liberal individualism and to an organicist rejection of arguments in which "the theory comes first, & dominates it."

Wharton's novelistic attention to local particulars and resistance to universal certainty sounds the keynote of her political thinking. As Tuttleton shows, *The Fruit of the Tree* as a whole functions as a rebuke to all forms of "absolute idealism"—and in this respect, the novel carries the same central message as Wharton's other explicitly political novel, *The Valley of Decision* (1902), not to mention her politically inflected objections to the literary modernism that seemed all too "à thèse" to her taste.[44] In her great, chastened revelation at the conclusion of *The Fruit of the Tree*, Justine realizes that "life is not a matter of abstract principles, but a succession of pitiful compromises with fate, of concessions to old tradition, old beliefs, old charities and frailties." This humbled heroine comes to see that "human relations" are "a tangled and deep-rooted growth, a dark forest through which the idealist cannot cut his straight path without hearing at each stroke the cry of the severed branch: '*Why woundest thou me?*'"[45] Wharton's dark forest here offers yet another organic metaphor; Justine's mistake is to ignore the complexity and specificity of this organic form. She wanders into ambiguous sin because of her unswerving devotion to an ideal: it is not, in fact, clear how the abstract principle of support for euthanasia should apply in this particular case, and Justine's lie about the merciful dose of morphine she administers suggests that she realizes this. Wharton's novel similarly refuses to deliver easy truisms on questions about business and philanthropy: Wharton endorses the ideology of liberal individualism with the caveat that all theories and ideologies are flawed, emphasizing that their abstract principles cannot ever apply universally. She advocates a free-market logic within the context of an organic society, but her organic society is not perfect: its natural elite occasionally falters, and its fruitful trees stand alongside dark forests. The novel positions itself overtly against the "orthodox creed of the business world" that disparages "humanitarian ideals," but it also regards those ideals with some suspicion, simply because they are ideals.

As we have seen, Carnegie and Marshall, too, reject the logic of the "orthodox creed" that Wharton portrays: if this is orthodoxy, the celebrated industrialist and the prominent economist are themselves surprisingly heretical. The orthodoxy within the novel declares that "business was one thing, philanthropy another," but these thinkers see a complex interrelation for business and philanthropy. We should therefore be careful not to identify Wharton's fictional orthodoxy too quickly with analogues in history, tempting though that may be when Carnegie asserts that it is "the duty of the millionaire to increase his revenues" or when Friedman announces that "the social responsibility of business is to increase its profits." Carnegie and Friedman are, in fact, saying very different things, and neither of them is simplistic in the manner of Wharton's orthodoxy.

The "orthodox creed of the business world" that Wharton represents features in a novel that emphasizes the inadequacy of *all* inflexible orthodox creeds and valorizes instead an adaptive, pragmatic approach that gives the autonomous individual the supreme right to choose spending, splurging, saving, or giving. That supreme right to choose is, of course, the signature prerogative of the consumer. In that the sovereignty of her individual is the sovereignty of the consumer, Wharton goes beyond the arguments of her contemporaries Carnegie and Marshall to contemplate the possibility of an indistinction between the consumer and the citizen. She notably does not dwell on the question of what such an indistinction might mean for those without great wealth to spend. But as she locates the solution to social ills in the private spending of private wealth, she also imagines the fallibilities of the particular private spender—for whom spending on golf and horses might appeal more than spending to help the poor. This insistence on complexity and local particularity, along with this rejection of abstract universality, is the foundation of her conservatism both in politics and in matters of literary form. For Wharton, the realist novel, in its rich accommodation of such complexity and particularity, offers a literary form that can serve such conservatism well.

EMILY COIT is Lecturer in the Department of English at the University of Bristol.

Notes

1. See Lewis, *Edith Wharton*, 181; Lee, *Edith Wharton*, 207.
2. Wharton, *The Fruit of the Tree*, 195–196, 102.
3. Friedman expressed this idea with particular sharpness in an article in the *New York Times Magazine*; see Friedman, "A Friedman Doctrine." He argues that those who insist that "business has a 'social conscience'" are in fact "preaching pure and unadulterated socialism." It is important to note that Friedman distinguishes between the private individual and the corporate executive: the former may take on whatever social responsibilities he wishes, but the latter may not. The corporate executive, he explains, "is an employee of the owners of the business," and his "responsibility is to conduct the business in accordance with their desires, which generally will be to make as much money as possible." Ibid., 33. For Friedman, corporate executives who transgress the bounds of this responsibility by seeking greater social good rather than greater profit in effect arrogate powers of taxation and expenditure that properly belong

to democratically elected officials; they spend the money of business owners and customers in ways that those individuals might not wish. Friedman develops these ideas at greater length in his influential book *Capitalism and Freedom*.

4. Elizabeth Ammons, Deborah Carlin, and Margaret B. MacDowell read the novel as a critique of patriarchy and the patriarchal institution of marriage; these interpretations depend on reading Bessy Westmore and her divorcée friend Blanche Carbury as positive figures entrenched in a fight against patriarchy. The novel, however, clearly condemns both women as morally corrupt and intellectually vapid. As James W. Tuttleton points out in his vociferous critique of these feminist readings, such interpretations also depend on reading Justine's actions as obviously right, when in fact the text represents them as morally somewhat muddy, and achieves its greatest artistic merit precisely by asking us to contemplate this kind of moral uncertainty. See Ammons, *Edith Wharton's Argument with America*; Carlin, "To Form a More Imperfect Union"; MacDowell, "Viewing the Custom of Her Country"; Tuttleton, *"Fruit of the Tree."*

5. Kassanoff, *Edith Wharton and the Politics of Race*, 1, 2, 63.

6. Wharton began writing the novel at the end of the summer of 1905; it was serialized in *Scribner's* starting in early 1907 and published in book form by Macmillan in October of that year. See Lee, *Edith Wharton*, 205–207.

7. Roosevelt, "Muck-Rakers," 374, 375. An article in the *New York Times* highlighted this paragraph of the long speech and asserted, "It was not the muck rake feature of the address that attracted attention; it was his new scheme for the progressive taxation of fortunes." "Roosevelt for Tax on Wealth," 1.

8. See Wegener, "'Rabid Imperialist'"; Kassanoff, *Edith Wharton and the Politics of Race*, 68–69; Lee, *Edith Wharton*, 156–157.

9. For more on the book's title, see Kassanoff, *Edith Wharton and the Politics of Race*, 61; and Carlin, "To Form a More Imperfect Union," 57–58.

10. Wegener observes a "pervasive organicism clearly shaping Wharton's temperament as a critic" and suggests that the logic of her criticism extends into her politics. Wegener, "Enthusiasm Guided by Acumen," 20; see also Wegener, "Form, 'Selection,' and Ideology." Kassanoff develops this argument by showing that Wharton's political aesthetic is very much a "racial aesthetic—a theory of language and literature encoded a deeply conservative . . . model of American citizenship," expressing "neo-nativist laws of 'pure English'" and "a colonial determination to suppress 'pure anarchy in fiction.'" Kassanoff, *Edith Wharton and the Politics of Race*, 5.

11. Lewis and Lewis, *Letters of Edith Wharton*, 461.

12. Marshall would incorporate some of the material from this piece into later editions of his *Principles of Economics*, where he proposes a scheme for redistributive taxation of the rich. See Marshall, "Social Possibilities of Economic Chivalry"; and Marshall, *Principles of Economics*.

13. Carnegie, *"Gospel of Wealth,"* 5–6.

14. Ibid., 5.

15. Marshall, "Social Possibilities," 13. Marshall's expression of gradualism is not confined to this one address; his influential *Principles of Economics* (1890) takes the "principle of continuity" as its central axiom, and he takes as his epigraph "Natura non facit saltum" (Nature never moves in leaps).

16. Marshall, "Social Possibilities," 12.

17. Carnegie, *"Gospel of Wealth,"* 4, 57, 7, 64.

18. Marshall, "Social Possibilities," 21, 22.

19. Groenewegen, *Alfred Marshall*, 119. Groenewegen usefully draws distinctions between the "welfare state" as generally understood today and as envisioned by Marshall, observing

caution mixed with optimism in the economist's injunction to "Let the State be up and doing!" which Groenewegen describes as a "reinterpretation of a more restrictive laissez-faire policy." Groenewegen, "Marshall on Welfare Economics and the Welfare State," 26.

20. Marshall, "Social Possibilities," 20.
21. Ibid., 12–13.
22. Carnegie, *"Gospel of Wealth,"* 8.
23. Marshall, "Social Possibilities," 11, 17. Marshall had himself been a socialist in the stricter sense of the term, earlier in life. Groenewegen writes that "the evils of class war, combined with socialist misunderstandings of the positive role of capital, were the attitudes of socialists which eventually led Marshall to abandon his youthful tendency to socialism, to enter into the self-help avenues of cooperation and the politics of neo-liberalism." Groenewegen, *Alfred Marshall*, 118–119. David Reisman suggests, however, that scholarship has generally understated the extent of Marshall's socialist sympathies; see Reisman, *Alfred Marshall's Mission*.
24. Marshall, "Social Possibilities," 17.
25. Wharton, *Fruit of the Tree*, 216, 469, 194.
26. Ibid., 195, 192, 194.
27. Ibid., 100, 204.
28. As critics have pointed out, the novel's own objections to industrial poverty are often aesthetic. Tuttleton, *"Fruit of the Tree,"* 160.
29. Wharton, *Fruit of the Tree*, 123, 181, 190–191.
30. Kassanoff, *Edith Wharton and the Politics of Race*, 69, 70.
31. Carnegie, *"Gospel of Wealth,"* 63, 64.
32. Ibid., 3–4.
33. Thus, as Carnegie's biographer David Nasaw notes in his introduction to *The "Gospel of Wealth" Essays and Other Writings*, Carnegie's "commitment to giving away his fortune did not make him a more philanthropic employer . . . he became if anything more ruthless in pursuit of profits once he had determined that those profits would be distributed during his lifetime" Nasaw, "Introduction," xii. Carnegie's "Gospel" makes this ruthlessness a force for good—and it was a gospel broadly heard: business historians note that "Carnegie's tract, substantiated by his own example and that of Rockefeller, was embraced by the ruling elite and, with media approval, helped persuade the masses in the United States and beyond to tolerate on-going inequalities." Identifying Carnegie as "the progenitor of modern-day entrepreneurial philanthropy," they observe that "by voluntarily 'giving back' to communities, entrepreneurs might demonstrate that inequality was a temporary phenomenon which, through wise spending, could deliver public benefit. In exchange for their munificence, entrepreneurs turned philanthropists would gain the right to engage in world making on a grand scale." See Harvey et al., "Andrew Carnegie," 445.
34. Marshall, "Social Possibilities," 14.
35. Ibid.
36. Ibid., 16, 17.
37. Criticism has helpfully examined the question of the novel's genre. Ammons considers the ways it conforms to the conventions of the "economic novel," the muckraker novel, and fictions of New Woman; see Ammons, *Edith Wharton's Argument with America*, 23–26. Ellen Dupree finds in *Fruit* an immanent feminist critique of the genre of the progressive problem novel; see Dupree, "New Woman." Mary V. Marchand argues that formal integrity becomes evident when we cease to view it as a failed attempt at muckraking and instead attend to its investigation of women's roles in industrial reform; see Marchand, "Death to Lady Bountiful."

38. Ammons, too, objects to readings that focus on Wharton's failure to represent industry accurately: "What keeps the novel from realising its muckraking potential is not really a simple matter," she argues; "Wharton gives a comparatively sloppy, vague picture of factory life in *The Fruit of the Tree* because, finally, she is only vaguely interested in industrial reform." Ammons, *Edith Wharton's Argument with America*, 44–45. For Ammons, Wharton's central interest in the novel is the relationship between Justine and Amherst.

39. Wharton, *Fruit of the Tree*, 216, 181, 176, 366.

40. Ibid., 219, 356, 261.

41. Veblen and Wharton together have been a fruitful subject for critics. Ruth Bernard Yeazell reads *The House of Mirth* alongside Veblen's *Theory of the Leisure Class* (1899) and notes that "Wharton never specifically mentions having read *Theory of the Leisure Class*, but . . . the evidence of *The House of Mirth* suggests that she was familiar with its argument and vocabulary." See Yeazell, "Conspicuous Wasting of Lily Bart," 732n3.

42. Wharton, *Fruit of the Tree*, 364, 354.

43. Ibid., 181, 457, 156, 217.

44. Lewis and Lewis, *Letters of Edith Wharton*, 461.

45. Wharton, *Fruit of the Tree*, 624 (emphasis in original). See also Tuttleton, "*Fruit of the Tree*," 165.

Bibliography

Ammons, Elizabeth. *Edith Wharton's Argument with America*. Athens: University of Georgia Press, 1980.

Carlin, Deborah. "To Form a More Imperfect Union: Gender, Tradition, and the Text in Wharton's *The Fruit of the Tree*." In *Edith Wharton: New Critical Essays*, edited by Alfred Bendixen and Annette Zilversmit, 57–96. New York: Garland, 1992.

Carnegie, Andrew. *The "Gospel of Wealth" Essays and Other Writings*. Edited by David Nasaw. New York: Penguin, 2006.

———. *Problems of To-day: Wealth, Labor, Socialism*. New York: Doubleday, 1908.

Dupree, Ellen. "The New Woman, Progressivism, and the Woman Writer in Edith Wharton's *The Fruit of the Tree*." *American Literary Realism* 32, no. 2 (1999): 44–62.

Friedman, Milton. *Capitalism and Freedom*. Chicago: University of Chicago Press, 1962.

———. "A Friedman Doctrine: The Social Responsibility of Business is to Increase Its Profits." *New York Times Magazine*, September 13, 1970 pp. 32–33, 122–124.

Groenewegen, Peter. *Alfred Marshall: Economist, 1842–1924*. New York: Palgrave Macmillan, 2007.

———. "Marshall on Welfare Economics and the Welfare State." In *No Wealth but Life: Welfare Economics and the Welfare State in Britain, 1880–1945*, edited by Roger E. Backhouse and Tamotsu Nishizawa, 25–41. New York: Cambridge University Press, 2010.

Harvey, Charles, Mairi Maclean, Jillian Gordon, and Eleanor Shaw. "Andrew Carnegie and the Foundations of Contemporary Entrepreneurial Philanthropy." *Business History* 53, no. 3 (2011): 425–450.

Kassanoff, Jennie A. *Edith Wharton and the Politics of Race*. New York: Cambridge University Press, 2004.

Lee, Hermione. *Edith Wharton*. London: Chatto and Windus, 2007.

Lewis, R. W. B. *Edith Wharton: A Biography*. New York: Harper and Row, 1975.

Lewis, R. W. B., and Nancy Lewis, eds. *Letters of Edith Wharton*. New York: Scribner's, 1988.
MacDowell, Margaret B. "Viewing the Custom of Her Country: Edith Wharton's Feminism." *Contemporary Literature* 15, no. 4 (1974): 521–538.
Marchand, Mary V. "Death to Lady Bountiful: Women and Reform in Wharton's *The Fruit of the Tree*." *Legacy* 18, no. 1 (2001): 65–78.
Marshall, Alfred. *Principles of Economics*. New York: Macmillan, 1890.
———. "The Social Possibilities of Economic Chivalry." *Economic Journal* 17, no. 65 (1907): 7–29.
Nasaw, David. "Introduction." In *The "Gospel of Wealth" Essays and Other Writings*, edited by David Nasaw, vii–xiii. New York: Penguin, 2006.
Reisman, David. *Alfred Marshall's Mission*. London: Routledge, 2011.
"Roosevelt for Tax on Wealth," *New York Times*, April 15, 1906, p. 1.
Roosevelt, Theodore. "Muck-Rakers." In *The Roosevelt Policy: Speeches, Letters and State Papers, Relating to Corporate Wealth and Closely Allied Topics*, vol. 2, edited by William Griffith, 367–378. New York: Current Literature, 1908.
Tuttleton, James W. "*The Fruit of the Tree*: Justine and the Perils of Abstract Idealism." In *The Cambridge Companion to Edith Wharton*, edited by Millicent Bell, 157–168. New York: Cambridge University Press, 1995.
Wegener, Frederick. "'Enthusiasm Guided by Acumen': Edith Wharton as a Critical Writer." In *Edith Wharton: The Uncollected Critical Writings*, edited by Frederick Wegener, 3–52. Princeton, NJ: Princeton University Press, 1996.
———. "Form, 'Selection,' and Ideology in Edith Wharton's Antimodernist Aesthetic." In *A Forward Glance: New Essays on Edith Wharton*, edited by Clare Colquitt, Susan Goodman, and Candace Waid, 116–138. Newark: University of Delaware Press, 1999.
———. "'Rabid Imperialist': Edith Wharton and the Obligations of Empire in Modern American Fiction." *American Literature* 72, no. 4 (2000): 785–786.
Wharton, Edith. *The Fruit of the Tree*. Amherst, MA: Prometheus Books, 2004.
Yeazell, Ruth Bernard. "The Conspicuous Wasting of Lily Bart." *ELH* 59, no. 3 (1992): 713–734.

9

SUSTAINING GENDERED PHILANTHROPY THROUGH TRANSATLANTIC FRIENDSHIP
Jane Addams, Henrietta Barnett, and Writing for Reciprocal Mentoring

Sarah Ruffing Robbins

IN 1893, THE Thomas Y. Crowell publishing company issued *Philanthropy and Social Progress*, seven essays that had originally been delivered as lectures for the summer 1892 session at the School of Applied Ethics in Plymouth, Massachusetts.[1] The opening and closing pieces in this collection marked the ongoing work of the school and the volume itself as transatlantic enterprises, with the first two chapters reprinting talks by Jane Addams of the Hull-House settlement in Chicago and the last recording an address by Bernard Bosanquet of London.[2]

Analyzing the 1893 collection's discourse patterns today, we can see how Bosanquet's piece highlights an increasing emphasis in Anglo-American philanthropy on collaborative social organizations (which he, at the time of his writing, contrasted with older versions of benevolent charity work).[3] Addams's two essays—"The Subjective Necessity for Social Settlements" and "The Objective Value of a Social Settlement"—strike similar themes for us now. She defines the settlement in the latter lecture-essay as "social, educational, and humanitarian," as well as "civic." Addams also takes pains to distance it from more traditional forms of philanthropy by emphasizing in "Subjective Necessity" that Hull-House was providing at least as many benefits to its well-educated middle-class "residents" as to its "neighbors," and by noting in the "Objective Necessity" chapter that immigrants from the Halsted Street community were coming to the settlement for "social intercourse" rather than charity.[4]

The emphasis Addams's and Bosanquet's essays place on a cooperative brand of social activism resonates with philanthropic discourse within other chapters in *Philanthropy and Social Progress*, partly, Henry C. Adams's introduction suggests, because the contributors all initially combined "extended investigation" of "the problem of social progress" with being "practical philanthropists." Thus, as Adams's framing text for the collection suggests, the consistent discourse of philanthropy evident across the book's content logically emerges from leaders who "have devoted their lives to the realization of principles which they advocate." In characterizing the book's authors as part of a network of leaders sharing philosophical principles as well as pragmatic strategies, Adams's overview also stresses how those interpersonal connections helped sustain both the movement's overarching goals and the members of that transnational community themselves.[5] Similarly, within her two chapters, Jane Addams underscores the efficacy of that network by referencing ways in which Hull-House drew on English models. In particular, she singles out the example of Toynbee Hall, led by "Mr. and Mrs. Barnett, of St. Jude's, Whitechapel" and the "hearty sympathy" they brought to long-standing ties between the two settlements.[6]

The rich archive of Addams's personal correspondence held in the Richard J. Daley Library Special Collections at the University of Illinois, Chicago (UIC), provides clear evidence that the "hearty sympathy" linking Hull-House and Toynbee did have strong personal—as well as programmatic—dimensions. For instance, when Jane Addams wrote to Henrietta Barnett in March of 1903, the American Hull-House leader declared, "I want to thank you for your dear letter; coming as it did just after I had read your fine and vivid article in the XIX Century. It gives me the impression of having really talked with you—and that you must know is a rare and abiding pleasure."[7] In a parallel personal missive to Addams dated March 1, 1920, Barnett included this request in reference to the recently published biography of her husband: "I shall be most grateful if I could be sent a few American reviews of my Book. They teach me about America."[8] One month earlier, when writing to her longtime London friend about laying groundwork for Barnett's forthcoming US lecture tour, Addams had predicted that American readership for the book would likely be expanding, partly because of the impact of more reviews having appeared. Those reviews, actually, would include her own strategically placed contributions: "I have been asked to review it for various magazines and have accepted The Atlantic and the Yale Review. It has had very favorable notices thruout the country and should of course be featured in relation to your coming."[9]

In documenting a decades-long friendship, examples like these from the long-standing Barnett-Addams correspondence underscore, for us today, how transnational social networking—which we sometimes represent as dependent on the tools of "new" media—consistently facilitated construction of collaborative discourse created by women philanthropists in a much earlier era. Thus, revisiting their textual exchanges is interesting, on one level, simply as an example of sustained transatlantic communication. But the discursive strategies they developed through textual exchange are equally significant as one window into the Anglo-American culture of philanthropy at the turn into the twentieth century. Both women played a central role in shaping their respective settlement-house enterprises—Addams at Hull-House and Barnett at Toynbee Hall—as well as other large-scale fields of social activism, such as Addams's connection to the international peace movement and Barnett's to model neighborhood design. Therefore, we can mine the archive of their transatlantic networking to track both the socially affirming nature of philanthropy and its dependence on interpersonal connections. Further, consistent with a pattern identified by Gertrude Himmelfarb within a British context, "almost everyone involved in this philanthropic world [where Addams and Barnett operated] was personally associated with not one but several causes and institutions: the result was something like a network of interlocking directorates."[10] Accordingly, the diverse philanthropic publications produced by these two women, over time, now show both remnants of the overlap in their work and distinctive individual commitments. In the relational support they originally built up through their writing *to* each other, on the one hand, and the crucial contributions that writing *about* each other made to their efforts to claim social influence, on the other, we can see how producing interactive, strategically gendered discourse on philanthropy helped these two women become visible leaders.[11] Recapturing the intellectual milieu in which both developed as Progressive-era role models, therefore, involves tracking ways that their philanthropic discourse responded to each other's writings within a context of transatlantic rhetoric simultaneously providing for each woman's personal growth and contributions to settlement praxis.

In the retrievable record of this Addams-Barnett connection, we find telling evidence of how their efforts to advance altruistic projects necessarily involved attentive, purposeful self-promotion, which each repeatedly reinforced for the other. We can also see how that publication-linked affirmation of women's philanthropic leadership could be bolstered through collaborative discursive interventions that countered gender-related constraints by providing access to reciprocal mentoring from within a privileged social class. Private and published discourse came together to enable both Addams and Barnett to succeed as significant public figures in a crowded assembly of would-be leaders shaping (and shaped by) the culture of nineteenth- and early twentieth-century philanthropy. By revisiting how their writing *about* and *to* each other functioned in this context during their lifetimes, we gain insight into the broader transatlantic network guiding philanthropic theory and practices in their day.[12] That is, through this specific case, we can track evidence of the "common set of cultural imperatives" that Frank Christianson identifies in the "increasingly prominent philanthropic discourse in mid to late nineteenth-century Britain and the United States," including its alignment with the emergence "of a transnational middle class" and its increasingly "professional ethos."[13] Accordingly, my recovery of the Addams-Barnett writing-enhanced relationship affiliates with and affirms Christianson's call to highlight the "rhetorical components of philanthropy."[14] At the same time, my examination here of the long-standing Addams-Barnett relationship foregrounds how their shared identity-construction process linked to philanthropic leadership was based as much in gender as in social class.

Tracking a Gendered Bond

Studying transatlantic culture typically requires considering cross-space relationships over time.[15] So revisiting the Addams-Barnett friendship, which spanned close to fifty years and reached repeatedly across transatlantic space, requires a temporal mapping. Their connection emerged in the late 1880s, launched by the tradition of the Grand Tour for well-to-do Americans, when Addams first visited Toynbee Hall. Their relationship shifted over the years, even as their shared interests and mutual respect kept the two women intellectually and emotionally close up to Addams's death in 1935. In the early years, Addams positioned herself as a learner, studying the methods of both Barnett and her husband, Samuel. Eventually, though, the American author-activist became an international celebrity herself. After the death of Canon Barnett in 1913—a personal loss as well as a change in social status for his widow—Henrietta several times turned to Addams for support. Addams, meanwhile, drew solace from this friendship in the period when her peace activism caused her to become as vilified in some quarters of US society as she had previously been revered.

As scholars revisiting these exchanges, we can identify features characterizing the shifts and continuities in their relationship. During the final stage of their long friendship, for example, though noting signs of reversal from the original hierarchy of role model and mentee, we can still see Barnett asserting her position as a longtime leader with an associated right to dole out directions to Addams in a tone others would not have adopted when interacting with such a famous woman. The candor evident in their private correspondence, on both sides, provides a telling counterpoint to their persistent public praise for each other, an equally crucial element in their ongoing discourse of gendered support.

One factor enabling their mutual mentoring was, clearly, their shared commitment to social reform and their experience as settlement founders in their respective home nations. Despite the two women's having grown up in different countries with nearly ten years between them in age (Barnett born in 1851 and Addams in 1860), parallels in their personal backgrounds from presettlement years surely came into play. Both had lost their mothers at a very early age—Henrietta Rowland shortly after her birth, as the last of eight children, and Jane Addams when she was only two years old. Both then built intense, identity-shaping bonds with their charismatic, highly successful fathers, both of whom nurtured their daughters intellectually and emotionally while also providing life opportunities available only to the very well-to-do. Both Barnett and Addams benefited from stimulating and affirming all-female boarding school experiences at a time when most young women had very limited educational opportunities. As an adolescent, Barnett studied at the Dover Academy run by Carrie and Margaret Haddon, whose practice of involving all their students in one of the local "ragged" charity schools sowed seeds for Barnett's future leadership of antipoverty programs. Addams attended Rockford College; there, she forged gendered relationships and honed womanly leadership skills that later carried over into her Hull-House career.[16] Through their settlement work, both women acquired impressive professional networks. Thus, Addams's ties to the likes of John Dewey and Alice Hamilton had a parallel in Barnett's links to British counterparts such as William Beveridge and Beatrice Webb. Overall, each sought a public brand of philanthropic leadership at a time when gender roles were both extending and still confining upper-middle-class women's reach into social arenas.

Just as significant as such parallels, however, were some telling differences in Barnett's and Addams's life histories—factors that probably helped keep their relationship from being competitive rather than supportive. As the younger of the two, Addams became one of the first generation of college women, with Rockford Seminary literally becoming a college while she was enrolled, so that she had greater access to formal education than Henrietta Rowland did. Perhaps even more significantly, Addams successfully repelled attempts by her family to marry her off to her stepbrother, whereas Rowland first resisted for months, but eventually agreed to wed the then-unknown and professionally insecure prelate Samuel Barnett in 1873, and afterward devoted much of her energy, for many years, to his career. In the meantime, Addams, drawing both financial and emotional support from her women's network at Hull-House, was able to make herself the primary public figure of the Chicago settlement, with the role of her longtime companion Mary Rozet Smith often paralleling Henrietta's place in the marriage with Samuel.

Consistent with other recent studies of nineteenth-century women writers' transatlantic friendships (such as Harriet Beecher Stowe's ties to Lady Byron and the Duchess of Southerland),[17] interpreting this relationship in our own present moment requires attention to spatial as well as temporal factors. For most years of the friendship, each lived in a well-appointed domestic setting that could easily accommodate a lengthy visit from the other. Travel by both parties supported their connection, with their relative wealth enabling multiple transatlantic crossings. Besides personal trips (by ship and on at least one occasion by air), ready access to new technologies also enabled them to shrink the space between London and Chicago. For instance, though regular, speedy air mail had not yet come into play, the two women augmented their letters with telegrams, especially when faced with time constraints in planning for transnational visiting. Both women had secretarial support to help manage correspondence—but both also had time-consuming social responsibilities that sometimes impeded their communications. Furthermore, countering the geographic distance between them and the pull of other responsibilities was a network of associates whose publications both women studied and whose travel back and forth between Britain and the United States supplemented Addams's and Barnett's own individual journeys. This community, in turn, reinforced such bonds as their compatible commitments to social issues and their shared awareness of gender constraints and possibilities.

The start of their connection—Addams's visit to Toynbee Hall in the late 1880s—provides a fascinating portrait of how the links between these two women emerged when they were at very different points in long public careers, with Jane Addams very much the starry-eyed admirer and Henrietta Barnett the well-established social leader as cofounder with Samuel of the already-famous London settlement.[18] Differing accounts of this initial contact also point to ways in which representing their personal connections for public audiences would become useful to both women, helping them move their own individual and shared agendas forward through savvy rhetoric.

Dame Henrietta Barnett offers a succinct 1919 depiction of Jane Addams's first coming to Toynbee, set within the memorializing biography of Canon Samuel Barnett, whose death in 1913 Henrietta was still working to process: "In 1887 Miss Jane Addams came to see us. We greeted her with the same patient or impatient civility with which we greeted the large number of unknown visitors, and soon forgot all about her." Besides giving a different date from the one Addams would report in her own published versions of the occasion, Barnett implicitly reminds readers of the status of Toynbee Hall as a foundational location for settlement work. In this sentence, she and her husband are cast as the famous figures constantly dealing with "unknown visitors," and Addams (whose own celebrity would eventually eclipse her friend's) is "soon forgot."[19]

I return to this passage later, setting it in the context of the Canon Barnett biography, but first I turn to Addams's regular depictions of Toynbee and its leaders' influence as a technique she used for validating women's leadership at her settlement.

Addams on Barnett: Affirming Women's Philanthropic Work

In the "Arts at Hull-House" chapter of her *Twenty Years* memoir, Addams simultaneously points to the Barnetts as role models and to their founding of the

Toynbee gallery as a vital inspiration in line with an Arnoldian view of philanthropic settlement outreach.[20] She opens this chapter by recounting,

> The first building erected for Hull-House contained an art gallery well lighted for day and evening use and our first exhibit of loaned pictures was opened in June, 1891, by Mr. and Mrs. Barnett of London. It is always pleasant to associate their hearty sympathy with that first exhibit, and thus to connect it with their pioneer efforts at Toynbee Hall to secure for working people the opportunity to know the best art, and with their establishment of the first permanent art gallery in an industrial quarter.[21]

Hull-House, specifically, and settlements, in general, have understandably been critiqued at times for cultivating a patronizing, elitist stance toward local working-class and immigrant communities being "served" through community programming.[22] Projects like the art gallery and book clubs that studied canonical authors—as well as Addams's writing about these endeavors—have come under particular fire. However, Addams herself counters such critique in "Arts at Hull-House" by invoking the Barnetts' prior work to promote the arts at Toynbee and by offering a parallel set of anecdotes a few paragraphs later to describe the responses of Halsted Street neighbors to the gallery. Notes Addams, "An Italian expressed great surprise when he found that we, although Americans, still liked pictures, and said quite naïvely that he didn't know that Americans cared for anything but dollars—that looking at pictures was something people only did in Italy." Similarly, she observes how one of the neighborhood Greek immigrants "was much surprised to see a photograph of the Acropolis," since he "had never before met any Americans who knew about this foremost glory of the world." This lover of classical images recounted how he had, up to then, tried unsuccessfully to sell his own colored drawings of Athens at a stall near the railroad station. Relieved to find his negative assessment of Americans as uninterested in "'ancient times'" and related art works undermined by the opening of the gallery at Hull-House, he thereby affirmed the importance of such projects for the settlement. Closing out this episode of her memoir by characterizing these art shows as precursors for the Art Institute of Chicago, Addams, as so often in her writing, exhibits a fine sense of narrative structure. In this case, she employs the figures of the Barnetts as a starting point for an anecdotally framed argument about the place of art within the urban neighborhood, and then closes this brief story by characterizing her two exemplary neighbors ("an Italian" art aficionado and the Greek "graduate of a school of technology") to combine an invocation of canonical cultural capital with an assertion about immigrant, working-class neighbors' compatible aesthetic values.[23]

Henrietta Barnett's 1919 description of this event mirrors and somewhat extends Addams's. Barnett explains, in her biography of Samuel: "When we were in

Chicago in 1891 we stayed with her in Hull House, and for me she had reserved the pleasure of opening their first Art Exhibition, Mr. Barnett giving one of his suggestive, elusive, indefinite addresses so specially attractive to the American mind." Reading this single sentence today, we see signs of the complex rhetorical dance Henrietta was attempting with the biography of her husband—to combine an assertion of his rightful place in social history while simultaneously documenting her own equally important role as a leader of settlements and social reform.[24]

Over the long years of their friendship, Addams supported this ongoing agenda, thereby both assisting Henrietta's efforts to claim authority for herself and using the example of Mrs. Barnett to help establish the right of Hull-House's many women affiliates to meaningful leadership. For example, in an essay for *The Ladies Home Journal* in 1906, Addams invokes not just Toynbee Hall but the specific influence of Henrietta. "It was at the End of the Second Year," Addams recalls,

> that we received a visit from the Warden of Toynbee Hall and his wife as they were returning to London from a journey around the world. They had lived in East London for many years, and Mrs. Barnett had been identified from the beginning with Octavia Hill's improved housing plans. They were much shocked and surprised that, in a new country with conditions so plastic and the possibility of change so hopeful, we had paid so little attention to experiments and methods of amelioration which had already been tried; and they looked in vain through our library for Blue Books and governmental reports which recorded painstaking study into the conditions of English cities.[25]

"Blue Books" here refers to the already-established Toynbee approach of applying the new social sciences to gather data about urban issues and, in turn, to use such reports to promote reform. What Addams chose to omit in referencing this critique from the British side is that Toynbee's residents were men who had Oxbridge educations and, hence, unquestionable rights to carry out formal research. Instead, she used the Barnetts' (purportedly) surprised disappointment at finding no formal, published research done by US settlement residents as a rationale for having Hull-House women undertake such studies themselves.

Meanwhile, Addams's reference here to Mrs. Barnett's collaboration with well-known British reformer Octavia Hill might seem to us now, on first reading, to be a throwaway line. However, in the next few paragraphs of this article, published in a venue that was then straddling a line between conservative gender politics and progressive possibilities,[26] Addams provides a telling example of how references to her alignment with Toynbee supported the gradual yet determined assertion of *women's* leadership of urban reform, including using such traditionally masculine approaches as data-based studies from the new social sciences. By positioning Mrs. Barnett as linked "from the beginning with Octavia Hill's improved housing plans," Addams asserts a model of womanly leadership that was, in 1906, still seeking full acceptance in the pre-women's-suffrage United States.[27] Over several successive paragraphs, Addams builds justification for a project now often referenced as a turning point in the evolution of Hull-House's position as a rigorous producer of applicable academic-style knowledge—the formalized study of urban conditions led by female residents such as Florence Kelley. Playing this Barnett validation card adeptly, Addams describes how, in response to the Barnetts' critique of there being no research products then in place similar to those being generated at Toynbee, Hull-House women residents carried out a "careful investigation of the sweat-shops of the neighborhood." This project, in turn, led to Kelley's being "appointed the first factory inspector with a deputy and a force of twelve inspectors to enforce the first law" enacted by the state of Illinois to protect child welfare.[28]

By invoking the Toynbee "Blue Books" and Henrietta Barnett's encouragement of such studies, Addams clearly sought to capitalize on what Robert L. Payton and Michael P. Moody identify as "the principles of scientific philanthropy that were altering the charitable landscape at the time" and that were being put into practice at the London settlement by university-trained residents there. At the same time, though, Addams apparently recognized the potential danger of turning Halsted Street neighbors into objects of analytical study: such a stance could undermine the very democratic principles she was also seeking to foster at the settlement. So, here and elsewhere in her writing, she simultaneously casts the work of Hull-House's women leaders as reaffirming reciprocal approaches to gendered benevolence, such as depicting residents' forays into the tenements as shared municipal housekeeping rather than efforts to reform immigrants' and working-class members' social practices.[29]

Barnett on Addams as an Icon of Gendered Leadership

If Addams made good use of Barnett's cachet to justify forays by Hull-House's women residents into formerly male bastions of social action, Barnett made equally astute use of her affiliation with Addams to cast her own (and her husband's) feminized approaches as effective philanthropic tools. Unlike Hull-House, with its mixed-gender blend of residents, Toynbee was conceived as a site for university men to come together in shared study and social action, learning leadership through service in London's East End.[30] Henrietta Barnett was the sole female resident and, as such, she occupied a liminal space that would have made carving out a visible leadership position quite difficult. This constraining context might help explain why Barnett, known from childhood onward for feistiness (even, at times, brusque assertiveness) continued to cultivate that aspect of her personality as Toynbee Hall cofounder with her more shy, patient, and, we might say, "feminized" husband. Indeed, in "Henrietta Barnett: The (Auto)Biography of a Late-Victorian Marriage," Seth Koven notes her repeated attribution of feminine qualities to her husband and, by extension, masculine traits to herself in the biography of Samuel.[31] One result of this pattern over the course of the narrative was to begin claiming the wife's social authority in the wake of her husband's death. But finding the proper blend of assertiveness and sensitivity was as tricky in that era as it is today.[32] Barnett and Addams used discourse linked to their philanthropy work to navigate those very gender stereotypes.

With this framework in mind, we should note how, within the biography of Canon Barnett, Henrietta crafted a striking portrait of Addams in action to help readers understand the complex challenges both women and men philanthropists faced when trying to position themselves in response to masculine and feminine models of leadership in the late nineteenth century. Referencing her first visit to Hull-House in 1891, Henrietta recalls:

> The organisation she controlled was then large, but she daily spent some hours in housework, and tended babies meanwhile. . . . The front door was in the centre of the building. . . . One morning during our visit naughty boys came again and again and rang the front bell, and again and again Miss Addams, with a sickly and sickening baby in her arms, answered the bell, only to find no one there. Thinking to aid her, I waited in the side wing, and next time that the troop of little demons appeared I administered an argument which they quite understood. But on telling Miss Addams, her beautiful eyes filled with tears, and she said in her gentle, undulating American voice: "You have put my work back, perhaps years. I was teaching them what is meant by 'resist not evil.'" I did not understand her then, and I don't now, but my husband did, for . . . his nature would make him prefer to continue to answer a mischievously rung bell than to use force to protect his own comfort.[33]

Here, Barnett exhibits a striking willingness to engage in self-critique mounted in gendered terms. Aligning Jane Addams's feminized approach to philanthropic leadership with Canon Barnett's, Henrietta explains that her Chicago counterpart was by 1891 blending masculine administrative management over a "large" "organisation" with a continued commitment to feminine duties, including "housework" and "tend[ing] babies." Henrietta Barnett seems at first to resist that model by inserting herself aggressively into Addams's interactions with the neighborhood. She chastises, in no uncertain terms, the group of "naughty boys" who had repeatedly disrupted Addams's efforts to tend to a "sickly . . . baby." Although Barnett asserts that the boys "quite understood" the rough verbal medicine she administered, she describes how her hostess's "tears" punctuated the "gentle" rebuke given in an "undulating American voice." Insisting that "I did not understand her then, and I don't now," Barnett seems initially to reject outright Addams's wish to "teach" the boys a Christian lesson, but the British author then corrects her own view of the situation by linking Addams's approach with Samuel's more feminine "nature," which "would make him prefer to continue to answer a mischievously rung bell than to use force to protect his own comfort." By associating Addams's strategy with her husband's embodiment of Christian principles, Barnett heightens the authority of both settlement leaders. And, given the overarching aim of the biography of Canon Barnett, in which this anecdote appears, she simultaneously reinscribes an appropriately gendered role she had been enacting since their 1873 marriage, putting his image ahead of her own.

To appreciate fully how Addams might have felt upon reading such high praise for herself in Mrs. Barnett's 1919 book, we need to remember that, at the time this text was published, Addams's own position as the international celebrity "Saint Jane" had come under furious assault as a result of her active involvement in the peace movement during World War I. She had gone from being revered to being characterized by Theodore Roosevelt as "the most dangerous woman in America."[34]

In this light, Henrietta Barnett's multiple moves in the biography of her husband to paint Jane Addams as a remarkable woman appear now all the more generous, especially when we consider that one of the nations that had been most impatient for the United States to enter the World War I conflict had been the widow's home country. In that context, effusive descriptions of Addams in *Canon Barnett* merit rereading. For example, in a section referenced earlier, where Barnett writes that she and her spouse paid no special attention to Addams the first time the American visited Toynbee Hall, Barnett follows up that admission with a sequel, noting how, through subsequent networking over time,

> we realised that she was a great soul, and took pains to show her much and tell her more. How she went back to America, and started that most wonderful of all Settlements, Hull House, where men and women live and work together, is known to all the world, but the value of the gift of her friendship to us both is known only to us. Whenever she could she has visited us during the years that have intervened, and on each occasion fresh depths of her character have been revealed, new spiritual forces realized.[35]

While on one level this passage reads as a sentimental personal reminiscence, situated in the context of the attacks being mounted against Addams's very "character" at this point in the American's career, we can appreciate Barnett's determined defense of her friend.

Equally affirming—perhaps even more so—is Barnett's invocation of high praise for Addams from a range of British political leaders, all men, in a passage that strategically couples their assessments with Barnett's pointed endorsement of Addams's involvement in the peace movement:

> Since I have been alone [i.e., since Canon Barnett's death], I have seen much of Miss Addams on her visits to England in relation to her hopes for international peace, and concur with the opinion of four men, all so different that it makes their estimate of weight. Sir John Gorst, Mr. John Burns, Mr. Sidney Webb, and my husband, after seeing her at home and abroad, said of her: "She is the greatest man in America." So like men to appraise her as a man![36]

Barnett's final touch of wry humor is, of course, striking, but so is her cagey approach of portraying Addams as possessing a rightful (that is, male-acknowledged) access to authority by virtue of the very activities that had drawn condemnation from others.[37]

Beyond the biography of Samuel, Barnett's recurring praise of Addams also appears around the same time in the British periodical *The Woman's Leader*, underscoring their shared commitment to women's active involvement in politics. In an article straightforwardly titled "Jane Addams" and authored by "Mrs. S. A. Barnett, C.B.E.," we find a vivid characterization of Addams's leadership pitched even more clearly to the gendered audience invoked by the periodical's title than in *Canon Barnett*. This text begins with a series of vignettes that establish Barnett's long-standing knowledge of Addams as her subject and the necessity of acknowledging the American's greatness:

> I have often tried to analyse what makes people of all sorts and conditions agree to call Miss Jane Addams a "great woman." I have known her for forty-six years, and have seen her in Chicago carving forcibly and rapidly at the head of the table around which sat the forty residents of Hull House. I have heard her as she faced a great audience electrically charged with war fever and pleaded for peace. I have tended her as she lay in bed when, as our guest at Clifton, she was exhausted with rapid travelling to obtain her coveted interview with Tolstoi. I have watched her as she played the courteous sightseer and tried to understand and be interested in vast machinery as explained to her by the factory owner. I have listened as in conference she acted as Chairman to earnest men and women from all parts of the United States who had met to discuss knotty practical questions affecting the lowest stratum of imported foreigners, their sufferings and their sins. I have tried to teach her to bicycle and heard her merrily laugh, as we all did, when the iron pony threw her off. I have heard her speak many times to audiences of all sizes and standards of education, sometimes splendidly, and sometimes inadequately, because neglectful of preparation; and I have to confess that none of these things does she do better than any other woman whose powers and inclinations have led her to enter the public service.
>
> Why, then, do all who know her agree that she is a "great woman"? An opinion I echo with emphasis.[38]

Here, as in the biography of her husband, Henrietta Barnett's account makes the British writer herself a pivotal character in a publication purportedly focused on another's success. Accordingly, woven in with details that characterize Addams as the admirer of Leo Tolstoi, a "courteous sightseer," and skilled facilitator are details that, at the least, demonstrate Barnett's close association with and, implicitly, her ongoing contributions to, Addams's career. Thus, Barnett references gently "tend[ing] her as she lay in bed . . . as our guest at Clifton," on the one hand, and persuading her to try a bicycle, on the other—nurse during illness, companion in fun. Later in this sketch, she reports that "Addams telephoned to me from Tilbury that she had arrived in England, and . . . we sat tete-a-tete in my workroom," where Addams recounted her efforts to persuade "the belligerents . . . to stay the cruel war." More recently, Barnett's story declares, Addams had come to visit on Boxing Day (December 26) in 1922. "After many telegrams," Barnett writes, "she reached me at the Hampstead Garden Suburb, coming direct from the International Women's Peace Conference," which the movement's best-known American figure then described in detail to her friend. Afterward, says Barnett's report, at multiple stops while on a "journey around the world," Addams wrote "from Egypt, India, and Burmah," with each letter continuing to "display her passion for peace" and her wish to assist the oppressed. At the same time, Barnett's account notes, these letters bore clear marks of "her unchanging capacity for friendship," a bond here reasserted by quoting directly from one of her counterpart's letters, with Addams's own assessment of Barnett and their bond: "For you, dear friend, hold my heart in the hollow of your hand now as evermore."[39]

If, when writing *Canon Barnett*, Henrietta deemphasized her role in the work she shared with her husband, in this periodical piece she veered in a different direction, positioning herself as Jane Addams's equal by virtue of their special friendship. When we read this biographical feature in the larger context of their textual exchanges, however, we can see how it also resonates with motifs recurring throughout their writing. These themes include their consistent emphasis on women leaders learning from one another, on celebrating each other's successes while openly admitting to shortcomings, and, more broadly, on the epistemic and moral efficacy of personal relationships in efforts to claim leadership of philanthropic enterprises.

Writing off the Record

The depictions of each other that Jane Addams and Henrietta Barnett originally crafted for publication offer compelling evidence of how these two women used writing *about* each other to advance a gendered model of leadership. Another significant indication of the strength of their friendship—and its contributions to their shared social commitments—emerges when we turn to their personal correspondence. This private archive reveals a richer, more complex picture of their reciprocal mentoring than we would glean through published texts alone. Accordingly, in putting their private writing in conversation with their public texts about each other and their shared social commitments, we can recover a sense of how their strong personal ties shaped their participation in a gendered discourse of philanthropy, and vice versa.

We can also retrieve a more nuanced personal portrait of each woman than is available in the public record. On Barnett's side, reading their exchanges heightens our appreciation of her role in multiple, interrelated reform movements, countering, at least in part, her own tendency, in published texts, to safeguard her husband's legacy over her own. Further, to see Henrietta Barnett through Jane Addams's eyes within their private exchanges is to recognize a softer, more vulnerable side to a woman who tends to be cast as the crankier, more pretentious half of a Victorian-era marriage that was also a partnership for social reform.[40] On Addams's side, recovering private texts from this decades-long friendship provides a valuable counterweight to the idealized mythology that grew up around her in the 1930s, the final "Nobel laureate" stage of her life, a view frequently echoed in the burgeoning body of recent work reclaiming her as a pivotal feminist.[41]

In private correspondence, Addams and Barnett felt as free to make pointed requests of each other—and even to voice complaints—as they did to offer encouragement. Back-and-forth communication in their decades-long friendship reflected this pattern, underscoring a key element within their gendered professional networking: mutual, candid critique.

One striking example of this frank stance surfaces when we trace a series of exchanges related to Barnett's organizing a US book tour in connection with the publication of her biography of Samuel. These letters—supplemented by telegrams—address a diverse yet connected set of topics, ranging from identifying the best possible dates for Dame Henrietta to come to the United States to selecting a speakers' bureau to manage her bookings and even to deciding on the most suitable subjects for her lectures.

In these letters, Addams assertively redirects her friend to a different timeline than the one originally proposed. She is equally candid when responding to questions about the content of proposed lectures, pointing to topics likely to interest the women's clubs that she anticipated would be Barnett's major US audience. When the Pond lecture agency rejected the chance to manage Barnett's appearances, Addams offered alternatives and tried to soothe her colleague's clearly hurt feelings. Along the way, Barnett occasionally voices frustration at Addams for being slow to respond to queries and for a mix-up involving failure to send materials essential to the Englishwoman's travel. Barnett sets these relatively minor critiques in the larger context of complaining that Addams, in general, had grown inattentive at precisely the time—during the years after Samuel's death—when Dame Henrietta was most in need of a solicitous friend. Addams, in the meantime, avoids offering any direct apology, focusing instead on providing thoughtful, well-informed advice for making the most of this trip to America, personally and professionally. It is tempting to say, given the content and tone of some letters in this sequence, that they mark a reversal in their original positions, since Addams gives the majority of the advice here. A careful reading, however, demonstrates that Barnett continued to assert the egalitarian nature of the friendship, freely commenting on Addams's shortcomings while, at the same time, acknowledging that she herself had much to learn from her Chicago-based connection.

One sign of Barnett's trust in Addams is signaled in the British reformer's reliance on her American colleague's guidance for safeguarding Samuel's legacy as a visionary philanthropist. For instance, soon after Canon Barnett's death, an array of appreciative salutes to his work emerged in America—a development his widow welcomed but about which, in writing to her close friend Addams, she expressed concerns. Accordingly, in a letter dated July 20, 1913, Addams forecasts plans to hold "a little memorial service for Canon Barnett" at an upcoming "meeting of the American Federation of Settlements in Pittsburg[h] on September 24." Responding to misgivings already voiced by her friend, however, Addams observes: "Of course, you are quite right in what you say about not using Canon Barnett's name to exploit any undertakings, even the very best." She explains, "His name is incorporated . . . in many settlements and we are indebted to you and to him, not only for the first formulating of the settlement idea but also for holding it to its best possible achievement."[42] She also reassuringly notes that "many letters from settlement people hoping that some such service would be held" had prompted these plans, both to provide "recognition to Canon Barnett" and to ensure that those "of the younger people" who might not be fully versed in his contributions could learn more.

In succeeding years, both women were eager to shape the records of their own and other women's leadership of philanthropic projects. For instance, the death of longtime Hull-House colleague Julia Lathrop prompted Addams to write a forceful account of Lathrop's leadership for the journal *Social Service Review* in 1932 and then to expand that account into an appreciative book-length biography, *My Friend, Julia Lathrop*, published soon after Addams's death in 1935. Lathrop, whose ties to Addams dated back even further than Barnett's, had risen from influential local leadership of various charitable causes in Illinois, to national management of the Children's Bureau under both William Taft and Woodrow Wilson, to international prominence through the Child Welfare Committee of the League of Nations. If in some ways we might read this biography as a parallel to Barnett's account of Samuel's career, it is certainly also a sign that, by this time, Addams was considering how to locate her own legacy within a tradition of women-led philanthropy.[43]

Though older by almost a decade, Dame Henrietta outlived her treasured friend long enough to help generate highly personal public texts for major tributes held in England and in Scotland to celebrate Addams's own career, thereby providing a counterpoint to the transatlantic recognitions for Canon Barnett, which Addams had facilitated twenty years earlier. On June 5, 1935, Dorothy Williams (charged with assisting preparations for a memorial service for Addams at "St. George's West . . . in Edinburgh") wrote "Dear Dame Henrietta" to request "a message touching the *Settlement* side of Miss Addams' work." Noting "how all her [Addams's] work at Hull House was built on the inspiration of Toynbee Hall," Williams predicted that "a living word from you [Barnett] would delight & cheer the settlement workers as no other word would."[44] On June 9, just before the June 11 memorial, Williams penned a glowing handwritten thank-you to Barnett for the tribute she had sent to be read at the service. In a wistful yet hopeful tone, Williams observed, "I should like the young to realize all that splendid passion for the oppressed that centered round Toynbee Hall and Hull House," and, she predicted, Barnett's "beautiful message" would help achieve that goal.[45] A few days later, Williams's report on the service itself again credited the power of Barnett's account of Addams's life and their friendship as carrying a special weight for those seeking to learn from their example. "Your beautiful message meant a great deal," Williams declared, but "it specially helped those who knew nothing" of Addams's private side, who had not had the gift of Barnett's own decades-long ties.[46] In Barnett's opening lines, in fact, she had invoked both Addams's remarkable leadership traits and her own deep personal knowledge of them: "I can truthfully say that she is the noblest character I have ever met[,] & I knew her intimately in many circumstances."[47]

Yet even in this memorializing moment, Henrietta continued the two women's shared habit of blending praise of the individual with broader affirmations of women's leadership. Thus, in the tribute Barnett prepared for the Edinburgh memorial, she celebrated Addams's loyalty and spunk for taking an "aeroplane [flight] from Paris to London" to see her old friend one last time and linked the achievements of Hull-House to Addams's charitable vision, bringing "together people of all Nations," united with "sympathy & aspiration." Barnett also depicted the connections between Toynbee and Hull-House as reciprocally productive, referencing trips she had made to the Chicago settlement and saluting, in particular, its openness to new ideas, quoting Addams's own assertion that the "greatest pride at Hull House" was having "adaptability." In typical Barnett style, though, she also noted of Addams's visits to England: "She came to

Toynbee Hall and to some of the other East London settlements, and wherever she went she offered friendly criticism and suggestive improvements & always in such a humble attitude of mind that no one was hurt."[48]

Henrietta Barnett herself, despite her own occasionally brusque manner, had, within the praxis of this friendship at least, strived for a similarly rigorous yet generously supportive stance and had even worried on occasion that she might not have achieved it. In a March 1, 1920, letter to Addams, for instance, she begins by confessing to being relieved that her American friend had been able to accept Barnett's contrasting position on a social issue they had been debating in their correspondence. "I had allowed all sorts of fears to arise in case my views had separated you from me," Barnett confesses. "But however much one will otherwise, one has to think and judge and decide with the best heart and brain that one possesses, even if one knows some one nobler thinks differently." Closing this note with "Yours ever in a big strong humble way,"[49] Barnett here, as so often in their exchanges, locates their writing to each other within a relationship that could contain both feminine and masculine models of personal interaction.

Big, strong, humble. With such verbal gifts of their writing to and about each other, Addams and Barnett together supplement the many other texts they bequeathed to us with a revealing interpersonal record of gendered philanthropic discourse in action. In this archive, combining both public and private texts, the two women offer up a window into a potent transatlantic network. This record today remains compelling, certainly, for its durability but also for its astute mapping and promotion of gendered philanthropic leadership. Through this strategic writing, Jane Addams and Henrietta Barnett reaffirm a shared vision of settlement-based cultural intervention as characterized by historian Gertrude Himmelfarb in her study of Toynbee Hall and Hull-House. As Himmelfarb notes, these leaders certainly "sought to elevate [others] morally, spiritually, culturally, and intellectually, as well as materially." For Himmelfarb, this agenda may be vulnerable to charges of authoritarianism on some counts, but it was, nonetheless, "eminently democratic" as well, promoting the capabilities and commitment of all those affiliated with the movement. In that context, Himmelfarb asserts, we should remember that the "moral needs" being addressed by both Toynbee Hall and Hull-House included those of the leaders themselves.[50] And perhaps nowhere is that pattern of reciprocal benefit for both sides of philanthropic relationships clearer than in the writings that Henrietta Barnett and Jane Addams generated to limn their own transatlantic bond. There, within a model of institutionalized activism simultaneously asserting a very personal claim, we see philanthropic leadership as astutely framed around proactive gender-identity construction and, at the same time, around the ongoing social enterprises that both of these bold, visionary women writers promoted.

SARAH RUFFING ROBBINS is Lorraine Sherley Professor of Literature, Texas Christian University, and Professor Emerita, Kennesaw State University. Her publications include *Learning Legacies: Archive to Action through Women's Cross-Cultural Teaching*, *Bridging Cultures: International Women Faculty Transforming the US Academy*, and *The Cambridge Introduction to Harriet Beecher Stowe*.

Notes

Acknowledgment: Especially given that this chapter is about two women's reciprocal approaches to developing leadership, I should certainly salute the very crucial contributions to the chapter made by Carrie Tippen, Lorraine Sherley Research Fellow for 2013–2014, who helped move this work forward from lectures for different audiences to its current written form. Thanks go as well to Tyler Branson and Adam Nemmers, 2014–2015 and 2015–2016 Fellows, whose editorial assistance aided subsequent steps in preparing the manuscript for publication.

1. Adams, *Philanthropy and Social Progress*.

2. Addams would later adapt her essays for inclusion in *Twenty Years at Hull-House*, her best-selling memoir; this practice was one she followed throughout her career—first giving a lecture and then revising it for print publication, often in general-interest magazines to start and, later, as book chapters. See Addams, "The Subjective Necessity for Social Settlements"; and Addams, "The Objective Value of a Social Settlement." While Addams generally used the hyphen when referencing her settlement (Hull-House), and the Jane Addams Hull-House Museum in Chicago does for their print materials and website, other writers (including Henrietta Barnett and some scholars today) have often omitted the hyphen. In this chapter, I adopt Addams's typical use.

3. Bosanquet, "The Principles and Chief Dangers of the Administration of Charity." Bosanquet contrasts charity, which he classifies as ultimately ineffectual "alms-giving," with the type of strategic philanthropy he advocates: "concerted action in neighborly service." Ibid., 249, 250. Similarly, in describing the work of effective philanthropic organizations in England, he suggests that "as the committee becomes fused with the neighborhood, the relief work of the committee passes, as it ought, into the relief work of *the neighborhood in consultation.*" Ibid., 258 (emphasis in original). Philosophically, therefore, though Bosanquet does not directly invoke the specific example of Hull-House, his characterizations of effective social interaction are consistent with Addams's views as expressed in her descriptions earlier in the volume and throughout her oeuvre.

4. Addams, "Objective Value," 33. Intriguingly, in the context of the overarching themes explored in this book, as well as the philanthropy focus of the collection in which her essay originally appeared, Addams declares in "Objective Value," "I am always sorry to have Hull House regarded as philanthropy, although it doubtless has strong philanthropic tendencies, and has several distinct charitable departments which are conscientiously carried on." Ibid., 55. Emphasizing the cooperative dimensions of the settlement's activities over its more charitable ones, Addams echoes points from "Subjective Necessity," where she stresses that both residents and neighbors tied to the settlement affirm "the solidarity of the human race" and thereby achieve reciprocal benefits, so that settlement work "is not philanthropy nor benevolence. It is a thing fuller and wider than either of these." Addams, "Subjective Necessity," 23, 16.

5. Adams, introduction to *Philanthropy and Social Progress*, viii. See, along similar lines, Butler, *Critical Americans*. Focusing on male social arbiters like Charles Eliot Norton and

Thomas Wentworth Higginson in the United States, Butler argues that the "transatlantic liberal community" of the nineteenth century was knit together not only by a cohesive social class identity but also by "shared ambition" and a shared "sense of duty" to the larger society. Butler suggests these ties were reinforced through institutional connections (such as university education) as well as access to transnational communications networks such as periodicals. Butler, *Critical Americans*, 5–6.

6. Addams, "Objective Value," 42. See also Addams, "Subjective Necessity," 16.

7. Letter from Jane Addams to Henrietta Barnett, March 1903, Dame Henrietta Barnett Papers, Jane Addams Memorial Collection, Special Collections and University Archives, University of Illinois at Chicago (DHBP).

8. Letter from Henrietta Barnett to Jane Addams, March 1, 1920, DHBP.

9. Letter from Jane Addams to Henrietta Barnett, February 3, 1920, DHBP. One review of Dame Henrietta's biography of her husband was penned by Mary McDowell, which praised the book as "the story of a modern mystic, whose spirituality expressed itself in simple common services for the neediest, through a philanthropy that believed in eliminating itself gradually by securing social legislation and making public service a religious and a patriotic duty." McDowell, Review of *Canon Barnett*, 644.

10. Himmelfarb, "Victorian Philanthropy," 382.

11. Butler makes a similar claim about the role of writing in the development of strong transatlantic ties among male social leaders of this era and, in that context, calls for a "connected" more than a "comparative" approach to studying such relationships. Butler, *Critical Americans*, 6.

12. The Addams-Barnett relationship and its ongoing expression in writing serves as a parallel to the cross-fertilization of ideas that Cherry Schrecker and others have traced in the development of sociology as evolving from a transatlantic reciprocal exchange fed by both personal travel (that is, trips by leading thinkers back and forth across the ocean) and the migration of ideas through writing. See Schrecker, *Transatlantic Voyages and Sociology*.

13. See Christianson, *Philanthropy in British and American Fiction*, 1.

14. Ibid., 6.

15. Robbins and Hughes, introduction to *Teaching Transatlanticism*. See also Weisbuch, *Atlantic Double-Cross*; Giles, *Transatlantic Insurrections*; Claybaugh, *The Novel of Purpose*; Bannet and Manning, *Introduction to Transatlantic Literary Studies*.

16. For a discussion of Addams's multifaceted learning while at Rockford Seminary/College, see Robbins, "Rereading the History of Nineteenth-Century Women's Higher Education."

17. For examples, see Lueck, Bailey, and Damon-Bach, *Transatlantic Women*.

18. Henrietta and Samuel actually met through Octavia Hill, and Hill is said to have encouraged her protégée's marriage to Barnett. By the time of Addams's first visit to Toynbee Hall, Mrs. Barnett was already publishing the kind of arguments for social reform that Addams herself would later generate. See, for instance, Barnett, "'At Home' to the Poor." More than for settlement-house philanthropic work, Henrietta is recognized today for her leadership after Samuel's death in a planned community outside London that brought together housing for differing social classes in one locale. See Creedon, *"Only a Woman."* However, she also remained actively engaged, throughout her career, in issues such as child welfare, as seen in her essays "The Home or the Barrack for the Children of the State," "Town Children in the Country," and "The Children's Country Holiday Fun." The influential *Practicable Socialism*, coauthored with her husband, was published in the United States after Samuel's death. See Barnett and Barnett, *Practicable Socialism*. Recently, a biography by Micky Watkins has highlighted Dame Henrietta's role as a writer and public speaker who played a central role in

Toynbee Hall's development, including the Art Gallery that inspired Addams to similar efforts in Chicago. See Watkins, *Henrietta Barnett in Whitechapel*.

19. Barnett, *Canon Barnett*, 30.

20. Himmelfarb, in "Victorian Philanthropy," discusses "why Toynbee Hall resembled a civic and educational institution more than a charitable institution," noting that "it did not dispense relief or charity; it dispensed education, culture, and civic amenities." Himmelfarb, "Victorian Philanthropy," 378.

21. Addams, "Arts at Hull-House," 371. Here, as elsewhere in this chapter, quoting whole passages from writing by Addams or Barnett is essential, since both women carefully assembled their retrospective anecdotes to gradually draw together numerous interrelated threads, guiding the reader through narrative depiction of a specific episode toward a more expository point. Addams and Barnett used such strategies to counter the constraints on women's discourse that Nan Johnson describes in *Gender and Rhetorical Space in American Life, 1866–1910*, where she notes that "a highly conservative cultural agenda regarding public rhetorical space and gender roles was still the dominant cultural viewpoint as the nineteenth century ended." Johnson, *Gender and Rhetorical Space*, 6. As Johnson documents, even though emerging pedagogical materials purported to guide women to effective public rhetoric, the lingering vision for women's social position as necessarily domestic called for back-door discursive approaches that avoided seeming to undermine traditional roles. Thus, narrative modes, more than expository ones, played a key role for writers like Addams and Barnett.

22. In literature from the early twentieth century, perhaps the most biting critique came from Anzia Yezierska, whose *Salome of the Tenements* (1923) and *Arrogant Beggar* (1927) both treat the social class hierarchies and prejudices that could undermine the very cross-class solidarity that many settlement leaders—Addams included—claimed to be seeking. For more recent scholarship criticizing Addams's writings and work as exhibiting a pernicious and constraining class bias, ironically based in maternalist sameness-promoting rhetoric, see Fiesta, "Unsettling Working-Class Commonplaces." For a counter of such critiques, see Seigfried, "Cultural Contradictions."

23. Addams, "Arts at Hull-House," 372.

24. Barnett, *Canon Barnett*, 30–31.

25. Addams, "Jane Addams's Own Story," 11.

26. For a discussion of Edward Bok's careful editing of *Ladies' Home Journal* over the years to manage conflicting pressures between his own progressive gender ideas and conservative visions linked to the need for advertising revenue, see Steinberg, *Reformer in the Marketplace*.

27. As Daphne Spain points out, "Most American settlement house histories begin, and sometimes end, with Jane Addams and Hull House," but that view underacknowledges the pivotal role of Toynbee Hall, including Henrietta Barnett (who, she notes, Canon Barnett credited with attracting "the most progressive thinkers into their sphere" through the magnetism of her "tea table"), as well as the Barnetts' earlier association with and learning from Octavia Hill. Spain, "Octavia Hill's Philosophy," 107, 113. Spain reports, "According to Henrietta, Samuel was profoundly influenced by Hill and admired her to the point of veneration." Ibid., 113.

28. Addams, "Jane Addams's Own Story," 11. In her biography of Samuel, Mrs. Barnett comments very favorably about this move by Hull-House into research by reasserting its ties to British influence while simultaneously reaffirming the mutual benefits to the movement, in both nations, of sharing such success stories. Summarizing an 1895 meeting of leaders at Toynbee Hall, she notes that Sir John Gorst, who had recently returned from a visit to the United States, praised Kelley's and Addams's work there, including the influence it was garnering for women as social agents. Thus, he "told also the story of her [Addams's] workers investigating

the condition of child labour in Chicago and the reforms obtained by them from the Illinois State legislation, and, moved with a tenderness which so often surprised his listeners, he described how they got a woman appointed State Inspector with 'power to watch and obtain the due execution of the law for the protection of little helpless children.'" From Gorst's and Mrs. Barnett's perspective, this shift in practice had been influenced by her husband as predecessor and supporter. Barnett, *Canon Barnett*, 50.

29. Payton and Moody, *Understanding Philanthropy*, 149. In this regard, Addams was distancing the settlement's philosophy and practice from a growing trend in privileged women's benevolence at the turn into the twentieth century. As Lori D. Ginzberg notes in *Women and the Work of Benevolence: Morality, Politics, and Class in the Nineteenth-Century United States*, often the "heirs of antebellum benevolence had strikingly different perspectives and agendas than their predecessors," with the later group taking on less of a "mission of moral regeneration" and assuming in its place "a responsibility to control the poor and 'vagrant.'" Ginzberg, *Women and the Work of Benevolence*, 5. At the root of this evolving stance, Ginzberg argues, was an "increasingly class-stratified and class-conscious society," a view which Hull-House leaders self-consciously resisted. Ibid. While pushing back against class distinctions, Addams and her colleagues were nonetheless embracing, through their moves into social science–like research, the kind of enhanced philanthropic professionalism Ruth Crocker associates with changing roles and increased educational access among women of this era. See Crocker, "From Gift to Foundation."

30. The complex interplay of gender and class identities associated with Toynbee and the related complexities in its links to Hull-House are evident in Daniel T. Rodgers's treatment of the two sites. In one chapter of *Atlantic Crossings: Social Politics in a Progressive Age*, Rodgers seems dismissive of Toynbee Hall's class and gender identity, describing the London enterprise as exhibiting "Oxford pretenses set prissily in the slums." In another discussion of the settlement-house movement earlier in the same book, however, he situates it in the context of "transatlantic social Protestantism's" shared vision and analyzes points of agreement and contrast between practices on each side of the Atlantic. He points out that an array of US-based settlement leaders "all visited Toynbee Hall before setting out institutionally on their own" and even reports that "at Hull House, an irresistible way stay station for reformers from abroad, Jane Addams read Henrietta Barnett's letters aloud at dinner time." At the same time, however, Rodgers asserts gender- and class-based differences between the American and British sites. On the one hand, he reports, "the American movement was much more quickly and deeply feminized than its English model," which he critiques for its "Oxford cultural pretensions . . . (with its fine arts exhibits and reading rooms wreathed in pipe smoke)" and "its residents' easy, Oxbridge-greased access to government policy making." Yet, he admits, the American settlements' moves into formal "social investigations" were inspired by "the London original." Rodgers, *Atlantic* Crossings, 270, 64.

31. Koven, "Henrietta Barnett."

32. Sheryl Sandberg points out in her bestseller, *Lean In*, that women leaders have seemingly always faced the problem of being judged as "too aggressive" and "not a team player" when exhibiting the same traits that, for men, generate what Sandberg classifies as "positive reinforcement." See Sandberg, *Lean In*, 39–51.

33. Barnett, *Canon Barnett*, 31.

34. For an example of sources attributing this designation to Teddy Roosevelt, see Westheimer, "Teaching Students," 135. Others have attributed the "dangerous woman" designation to J. Edgar Hoover rather than Theodore Roosevelt. See, for instance, Reardon, "Why You Should Care about Jane Addams." In each case, the negative assessment is associated with her

commitment to foiled peace efforts by an international group of women—cast in these reports as naïve, at least, or worse, "dangerous."

35. Barnett, *Canon Barnett*, 30.
36. Ibid., 31.
37. In that vein, several additional descriptions of Addams in *Canon Barnett* merit rereading. For example, Dame Henrietta recalls how, in the 1895 meeting of many settlement leaders at Toynbee Hall, Sir John Gorst gave a stirring report of Addams's work in America, based on having made a recent visit. Barnett notes how Gorst "spoke with enthusiasm of Miss Jane Addams, who 'exercised a strong and beneficial influence in public affairs.'" Barnett, *Canon Barnett*, 50.
38. Barnett, "Jane Addams." The *Woman's Leader*, published in Britain between 1920 and 1932, was a periodical advocating social reform on issues such as women's having full access to political participation, equality in pay, and birth control. David Doughan positions the *Woman's Leader* as one of a cluster of that decade's women-centered British periodicals aiming for a sober look and tone while promoting feminist causes. Doughan, "Periodicals," 268. A few sample issues are available on the website *Women's Print Media in Interwar Britain*; see "The Woman's Leader."
39. Ibid.
40. In this context, see Addams's notes to Mrs. Barnett just after the death of Samuel. Printed in *Canon Barnett* along with a cluster of others that focus only on Canon Barnett himself, Addams's condolences include praise of his spouse: "He is mourned all over the world by the hundreds of people he has helped and made one, and they are all filled with gratitude and admiration for you who made possible so much of his beneficent activity." Barnett, *Canon Barnett*, 383.
41. One example is the appreciative biography by Jean Bethke Elshtain, *Jane Addams and the Dream of American Democracy*, and Elshtain's edition of writings by Addams, *The Jane Addams Reader*. For a response revisiting critiques of Addams and her approach to philanthropy, see Joel Schwartz, "Flawed Reformer."
42. "The Settlement and Democracy," an unsigned 1913 report in *The Outlook*, suggests that Addams successfully navigated this presentational challenge of honoring but not exploiting Canon Barnett. This article praises "a most inspiring service in memory of Samuel A. Barnett, Canon of Westminster, and founder of Toynbee Hall, the first settlement in London, thirty years ago." Anticipating the linkage between Addams and Barnett that his widow would later invoke in her biography, this article asserts, "No better person could have been chosen to take charge of this memorial meeting in honor of the man who labored in the interests of giving the workingman opportunity for culture than Jane Addams, who is giving herself heart and soul to the welfare of the people." "Settlement and Democracy," 292.
43. For a fuller reading of Addams's *My Friend, Julia Lathrop*, her appreciative biography of Lathrop, see Robbins, *Learning Legacies*, where I suggest that the Hull-House founder's final book was, in notable ways, modeled on Henrietta Barnett's biography of Samuel.
44. Letter from Dorothy Williams to Henrietta Barnett, June 5, 1935, DHBP (emphasis in original).
45. Letter from Dorothy Williams to Henrietta Barnett, June 9, 1935, DHBP.
46. Letter from Dorothy Williams to Henrietta Barnett, June 13, 1935, DHBP.
47. Letter from Henrietta Barnett to Dorothy Williams, June 7, 1935, DHBP.
48. Ibid. This exchange between Williams and Barnett, with Williams seeking direction from the British settlement leader for an occasion honoring Addams, was not unique. Barnett had received a parallel request from Catherine E. Marshall, writing "on behalf of the Executive

Committee" of the London-based Women's International League, for which Addams had served as "International President." Marshall asked permission to visit with Barnett in person "to tell you all we are planning" and garner Barnett's input for that group's "Memorial Service to dear Jane Addams," to be held at St. Martin-in-the-Fields, since Barnett's poor health would likely prevent her attending in person. Letter from Catherine E. Marshall to Henrietta Barnett, May 29, 1935, DHBP.

49. Letter from Henrietta Barnett to Jane Addams, March 1, 1920, DHBP.

50. Himmelfarb, "Victorian Philanthropy," 384.

Bibliography

Adams, Henry C., ed. *Philanthropy and Social Progress: Seven Essays by Miss Jane Addams, Robert A. Woods, Father J. O. S. Huntington, Professor Franklin H. Giddings, and Bernard Bosanquet*. New York: Thomas Y. Crowell, 1893.

Addams, Jane. "Arts at Hull-House." In *Twenty Years at Hull-House with Autobiographical Notes*, 371–399. New York: Macmillan, 1912.

———. "Jane Addams's Own Story of Her Work: The First Five Years at Hull-House." *Ladies Home Journal* 23, no. 5 (1906): 11–12.

———. *My Friend, Julia Lathrop*. New York: Macmillan, 1935.

———. "The Objective Value of a Social Settlement." In *Philanthropy and Social Progress*, edited by Henry C. Adams, 27–56. New York: Thomas Y. Crowell, 1893.

———. "The Subjective Necessity for Social Settlements." In *Philanthropy and Social Progress*, edited by Henry C. Adams, 1–26. New York: Thomas Y. Crowell, 1893.

Bannet, Eve Tavor, and Susan Manning, eds. *Introduction to Transatlantic Literary Studies, 1660–1830*. New York: Cambridge University Press, 2012.

Barnett, Henrietta O. "'At Home' to the Poor." *Cornhill Magazine* 43, no. 257 (1881): 579–589.

———. *Canon Barnett: His Life, Work, and Friends by His Wife*. Vol. 2. London: John Murray, 1918.

———. "The Children's Country Holiday Fun." *Living Age*, June 1, 1912, pp. 524–529.

———. "The Home or the Barrack for the Children of the State." *Contemporary Review*, no. 66 (1894): 243–258.

———. "Jane Addams." *Woman's Leader*, June 1, 1923.

———. "Town Children in the Country." *Nineteenth Century* 48, no. 281 (1900): 100–107.

Barnett, S. A., and Mrs. S. A. Barnett. *Practicable Socialism*. New York: Longmans, Green, 1915.

Bosanquet, Bernard. "The Principles and Chief Dangers of the Administration of Charity." In *Philanthropy and Social Progress: Seven Essays by Miss Jane Addams, Robert A. Woods, Father J. O. S. Huntington, Professor Franklin H. Giddings, and Bernard Bosanquet*, edited by Henry C. Adams, 249–268. New York: Thomas Y. Crowell, 1893.

Butler, Leslie. *Critical Americans: Victorian Intellectuals and Transatlantic Liberal Reform*. Chapel Hill: University of North Carolina Press, 2007.

Christianson, Frank. *Philanthropy in British and American Fiction: Dickens, Hawthorne, Eliot, and Howells*. Edinburgh, UK: Edinburgh University Press, 2007.

Claybaugh, Amanda. *The Novel of Purpose: Literature and Social Reform in the Anglo-American World*. Ithaca, NY: Cornell University Press, 2006.

Creedon, Alison. *"Only a Woman": Henrietta Barnett, Social Reformer and Founder of Hampstead Garden Suburb*. Chichester, UK: Phillimore, 2006.

Crocker, Ruth. "From Gift to Foundation: The Philanthropic Lives of Mrs. Russell Sage." In *Charity, Philanthropy, and Civility in America*, edited by Lawrence J. Friedman and Mark D. McGarvie, 199–216. New York: Cambridge University Press, 2004.

Doughan, David T. J. "Periodicals by, for, and about Women in Britain." *Women's Studies International Forum* 10, no. 3 (1987): 261–273.

Elshtain, Jean Bethke. *Jane Addams and the Dream of American Democracy*. New York: Basic Books, 2002.

———. *The Jane Addams Reader*. New York: Basic Books, 2008.

Fiesta, Melissa J. "Unsettling Working-Class Commonplaces in Jane Addams's Settlement House Rhetoric." In *Who Says? Working Class Rhetoric, Class Consciousness, and Community*, edited by William DeGenaro, 69–87. Pittsburgh, PA: University of Pittsburgh Press, 2007.

Giles, Paul. *Transatlantic Insurrections: British Culture and the Formation of American Literature, 1730–1860*. Philadelphia: University of Pennsylvania Press, 2001.

Ginzberg, Lori D. *Women and the Work of Benevolence: Morality, Politics, and Class in the Nineteenth-Century United States*. New Haven, CT: Yale University Press, 1990.

Himmelfarb, Gertrude. "Victorian Philanthropy: The Case of Toynbee Hall." *American Scholar* 59, no. 3 (1990): 373–384.

Johnson, Nan. *Gender and Rhetorical Space in American Life, 1866–1910*. Carbondale: Southern Illinois University Press, 2002.

Koven, Seth. "Henrietta Barnett: The (Auto)Biography of a Late-Victorian Marriage." In *After the Victorians: Private Conscience and Public Duty in Modern Britain*, edited by Susan Pedersen and Peter Mandler, 31–56. New York: Routledge, 1993.

Lueck, Beth L., Brigitte Bailey, and Lucinda L. Damon-Bach, eds. *Transatlantic Women: Nineteenth-Century American Women Writers and Great Britain*. Lebanon, NH: University Press of New England, 2012.

McDowell, Mary. Review of *Canon Barnett, His Life and Friends*, by Henrietta O. R. Barnett. *American Journal of Sociology* 25, no. 5 (1920): 643–644.

Payton, Robert L., and Michael P. Moody. *Understanding Philanthropy: Its Meaning and Mission*. Bloomington: Indiana University Press, 2008.

Reardon, Patrick T. "Why You Should Care about Jane Addams." *Chicago Tribune*, June 11, 2006. http://articles.chicagotribune.com/2006-06-11/news/0606110193_1_jane-austen-abigail-adams-peace-and-freedom.

Robbins, Sarah R. *Learning Legacies: Archive to Action in Women's Cross-Cultural Teaching Narratives*. Ann Arbor: University of Michigan Press, 2017.

———. "Rereading the History of Nineteenth-Century Women's Higher Education: A Reexamination of Jane Addams' Rockford Education as Preparation for her *Twenty Years at Hull-House* Teaching." *Journal of the Midwest History of Education Society*, no. 21 (1994): 27–46.

Robbins, Sarah R. and Linda Hughes. Introduction to *Teaching Transatlanticism: Resources for Teaching Nineteenth-Century Anglo-American Print Culture*, edited by Linda K. Hughes and Sarah R. Robbins, 1–17. Edinburgh, UK: Edinburgh University Press, 2015.

Rodgers, Daniel T. *Atlantic Crossings: Social Politics in a Progressive Age*. Cambridge, MA: Harvard University Press, 1998.

Sandberg, Sheryl. *Lean In: Women, Work, and the Will to Lead*. New York: Knopf, 2013.

Schrecker, Cherry, ed. *Transatlantic Voyages and Sociology: The Migration and Development of Ideas*. Burlington, VT: Ashgate, 2010.

Schwartz, Joel. "Flawed Reformer." *Philanthropy*, May–June 2002. http://www.philanthropyroundtable.org/topic/excellence_in_philanthropy/flawed_reformer.

Seigfreid, Charlene. "Cultural Contradictions: Jane Addams' Struggles with the Life of Art and the Art of Life." In *Feminist Interpretations of Jane Addams*, edited by Maurice Hamington, 55–80. University Park: Penn State University Press, 2010.

"The Settlement and Democracy." *The Outlook*, October 11, 1913, pp. 291–292.

Spain, Daphne. "Octavia Hill's Philosophy of Housing Reform: From British Roots to American Soil." *Journal of Planning History* 5, no. 2 (2006): 106–125.

Steinberg, Salme Harju. *Reformer in the Marketplace: Edward W. Bok and The Ladies' Home Journal*. Baton Rouge: Louisiana State University Press, 1979.

Watkins, Micky. *Henrietta Barnett in Whitechapel: Her First Fifty Years*. London: Micky Watkins and the Hampstead Garden Archive Trust, 2005.

Weisbuch, Robert. *Atlantic Double-Cross: American Literature and British Influence in the Age of Emerson*. Chicago: University of Chicago Press, 1989.

Westheimer, Joel. "Teaching Students to Think about Patriotism." In *The Social Studies Curriculum: Purposes, Problems, and Possibilities*, 4th ed., edited by E. Wayne Ross, 127–138. Albany: State University of New York Press, 2014.

"The Woman's Leader." *Women's Print Media in Interwar Britain*. http://interwarfeminism.omeka.net/collections/show/4 (accessed May 23, 2017).

Yezierska, Anzia. *Arrogant Beggar*. 1927. Reprint, Durham, NC: Duke University Press, 1996.

———. *Salome of the Tenements*. 1923. Reprint, Urbana: University of Illinois Press, 2005.

Conclusion

Frank Q. Christianson and Leslee Thorne-Murphy

As Angela Burdett-Coutts asserted in her volume on Anglo-American women's philanthropy, British and American philanthropists were "co-inheritors and fellow-workers" in their efforts.[1] This collaborative work is recognized and reflected in the chapters included in this book. As a whole, these chapters draw out the common narrative strands that constitute the philanthropic record of the period, including issues of gender, economic disparity, race and ethnicity, urbanization, sympathy, and patronage. It would be easy to conclude that these strands confirm many of the common platitudes regarding charity work of the time, leading to an overall sense that philanthropic rhetoric from 1850 to 1920 retained a sense of social superiority and condescension. As the chapters demonstrate, however, the truth is much more complex.

In particular, the collection reinforces the role that gender played in philanthropic discourse. Seven of the chapters in the book focus specifically on actual or fictional philanthropic work by women, often demonstrating the fraught nature of women's involvement. Sarah Ruffing Robbins's study of the letters of Jane Addams and Henrietta Barnett forefronts the means each woman took to negotiate generational, national, and temperamental difference. Their interactions allow Robbins to investigate the issues involved in women stepping into leadership roles. A similar dynamic enters into Suzanne Daly's study of Mary Carpenter's *Six Months in India* and Rosamond Webb's review of Carpenter's treatise. Daly not only elaborates the sectarian, political, and philosophical divisions between the two writers but also manages to incorporate glimpses into the perspectives of native women who taught in the schools that Webb's organization helped sponsor. These ideas are further elaborated in Dorice Williams Elliott's study of upper-class women's philanthropy in England and India, which demonstrates both the possibilities and limitations of women's roles in leading civil society. These scholars' studies join a significant and growing body of scholarship about the professionalization of women's philanthropic roles, an avenue of scholarly inquiry that promises to remain fruitful.

Francesca Sawaya's chapter, concerning patronage in the work of Henry James, takes an alternate approach to the study of gender, investigating male homosocial relationships as negotiated through patronage. Sawaya's approach adds to the work of such scholars as Seth Koven and James Eli Adams on concepts of masculinity within social reform work, yet another topic that remains an area of study inviting further elucidation.

All of the chapters in the book engage in some manner with the notion of sympathy, which has economic, moral, and aesthetic dimensions. For Daniel Bivona, a developing concept of sympathy in the work of Adam Smith and Edmund Burke becomes a means of understanding the potential of philanthropic endeavor in Charles Dickens's *Bleak House*, as well as the demise of this ideal a generation later in George Gissing's work. Similarly, Tanushree Ghosh uses Smith's notion of sympathy to understand ethical spectatorship and aesthetic reform in Walter Besant's *Children of Gibeon*. The work of both these scholars reveals the economic underpinnings of the discourse of philanthropy. Terms such as *charity* and *benevolence* may be grounded in a religious tradition of almsgiving, but the institutional manifestation of philanthropy relies equally on the philosophy of political economy that, ironically, was so often used to contest the logic of philanthropy. Emily Coit continues to develop this topic in her study of Edith Wharton's *The Fruit of the Tree*. Placing Wharton's discussion of philanthropic work within the context of Andrew Carnegie's gospel of wealth and Alfred Marshall's notion of economic chivalry, Coit explores the fine line that Wharton treads between the logic of business and the practice of philanthropy. Explaining how economic thought informed philanthropic effort is essential to understanding how philanthropy did (and still does) act within local, national, and global markets.

In an increasingly urban setting, Anglo-American writers of the late nineteenth century grappled with issues of poverty and need that traditional systems of relief could not satisfy. As Lori Merish discusses, the image of the poor unwed mother became a symbol of anxieties about poor relief on the urban frontier. Writers such as Margaret Fuller and Louisa May Alcott would expand on earlier depictions of urban poverty, as Monika Elbert relates in her chapter on the journalism and correspondence of these women. Indeed, the urban landscape became a background for depicting and exploring many issues germane to philanthropic work, as seen in Ghosh's chapter on depictions of the needlewomen of London, Robbins's work on women's correspondence in the transatlantic settlement movement, and Bivona's study of the urban settings favored by Dickens and Gissing.

The book as a whole illustrates how the strands of philanthropic discourse overlap and commingle in each of the individual chapters and in the texts on which they are based. Though certain chapters forefront specific strands, they also interweave several others seamlessly. In Daly's chapter, "Education as Violation and Benefit: Doctrinal Debate and the Contest for India's Girls," the rhetoric of gender is interwoven with observations on ethnic and political divisions within Indian native cultures, Christian sectarianism, and each writer's class and social backgrounds. In Lori Merish's "The Poverty of Sympathy," the gendered image of the young and poor unwed mother becomes a way of understanding Smithian concepts of sympathy within the new urban landscape. Conversations regarding poverty, patronage, sympathy, urbanization, economic disparity, as well as class, race, gender and ethnicity, all weave themselves through the work included in this book. They mutually inform one another within the language of philanthropy.

Collectively, these chapters describe a transformative moment in the history of philanthropy and its modes of representation. Philanthropic discourse, as drawn from the novels, newspapers, poetry, economic treatises, and broadsides—in short, from the print culture of the late nineteenth and early twentieth centuries—was transatlantic in nature. It crossed national and colonial borders within the Anglo-American span of influence. It demonstrates the common discursive elements behind a seemingly inconsequential American pamphlet novel of 1840, *Mary Bean: The Factory Girl*, and Swarnakumari Debi's Indian novel of 1892, *The Uprooted Vine*, and joins these works, in turn, with the political economy of Adam Smith, the psychological realism of Henry James's *Roderick Hudson*, and the correspondence of Jane Addams.

In her afterword, historian Kathleen McCarthy encourages philanthropic studies to "follow the money" to better understand the nature of philanthropy's nineteenth-century transformation. In particular, she identifies the funding patterns of charitable associations large and small as a source for some of the defining themes of the era. While philanthropy as an *economy* left a transactional record of money and materials, philanthropy as a *discourse* yielded a rich corpus of writing that represented, rationalized, and shaped that economy. Each line of prospective "analytic possibility" that McCarthy identifies charts a course for both material and rhetorical investigations to follow. McCarthy's work prompts new directions of inquiry that have particular resonance for the period bounding the chapters in this book. Taken together, these chapters showcase a remarkably diverse written tradition registering the broader transformation of Anglo-American culture during a formative moment in the development of philanthropy.

FRANK Q. CHRISTIANSON is Associate Professor of English at Brigham Young University. He is author of *Philanthropy in British and American Fiction: Dickens, Hawthorne, Eliot and Howells.*

LESLEE THORNE-MURPHY is Associate Professor of English at Brigham Young University.

Note

1. Burdett-Coutts, *Woman's Mission*, xxi.

Bibliography

Burdett-Coutts, Angela, ed. *Woman's Mission: A Series of Congress Papers on the Philanthropic Work of Women by Eminent Writers.* New York: Charles Scribner's Sons, 1893.

Afterword
Follow the Money

Kathleen D. McCarthy

Sometime during the late nineteenth century, the meaning of philanthropy dramatically changed. Americans initially interpreted it as both giving and voluntarism. Before the Civil War, social reformers as well as charity advocates were often categorized as philanthropists. Most giving tended to be small and mass based, with even colleges started by subscriptions. However, there were some large gifts, such as the bequest that established the Lowell Institute in Massachusetts. The largest came from immigrants and foreign donors such as Stephen Girard and James Smithson. After the war, the rise of great fortunes and the modern corporation lifted giving to previously unimagined heights. Johns Hopkins created the country's first modern university, John D. Rockefeller transformed a stagnating Baptist college into the University of Chicago, and Andrew Carnegie planted libraries in cities and towns across the country. Suddenly, philanthropy was reinterpreted as big gifts, eclipsing the historically embedded significance of collective giving and voluntarism.

The period also marked a reversal in the flow of philanthropic models. Until the arrival of the big foundations, America stood at the margins of international philanthropic innovation. Almost all of the institutions that cropped up in the United States during the nineteenth century, from the antislavery movement to the modern university, were imported from Europe. But with the heyday of big donors, money and philanthropy suddenly went hand in hand, and philanthropy itself was recast as an American invention. Historians have managed to restore the notion that gifts of time are as valuable as gifts of money in tracing the history of philanthropy over the arc of the nineteenth century. But most have ignored the impact of hard cash in the belief that monetary philanthropy equals millionaires' philanthropy, a resoundingly unappealing notion for a profession committed to rewriting history from the bottom up. Nonetheless, institutional budgets can reveal a great deal about working-class preferences, as well as those of corporate moguls like John D. Rockefeller.[1]

Indeed, budgets are often informational gold mines that can yield data on everything from working-class attitudes about worthy and unworthy behavior to middle-class women's hidden economic and political roles. For example, in *American Creed* I examine the investments listed in the budgets published in charitable annual reports to trace the economic roles of middle-class white women, elite white males, and African Americans in what Stephen Innes terms "communal capitalism." The United States had a cash-scarce economy during the early decades of the nineteenth century and was heavily dependent on foreign investment. Because they received donations, charitable organizations were magnets for capital, and even modest charities often built an investment plan into their charters. Mutual aid societies, which technically fell outside the realm of philanthropy (unless they provided aid beyond their members) also often had very strict rules about who was worthy—and unworthy—of support. Drinking and disorderly behavior could disqualify members for aid, providing a fascinating window onto the differences and similarities between middle- and working-class assistance. Clearly, there were variations in working-class culture, from the literate journeymen who headed associations in Sean Wilentz's work to the far rowdier Irish canal diggers described by Peter Way. Associational records provide a unique perspective on the values of one subset of this heterogeneous universe, particularly when money was concerned.[2]

They also provide clues about the role of philanthropy in fueling America's economic takeoff during the antebellum era. Northern philanthropic dollars helped bankroll the Massachusetts textile industry and the Erie Canal. To a far greater degree than in the South, philanthropic dollars helped fuel a broad universe of Northern economic investments, from small loans and stock purchases by women's and African American charities to industrial development and the transportation revolution.[3]

This has theoretical implications as well. Robert Putnam's *Making Democracy Work* linked voluntarism and social capital to economic development, with the notion that collective endeavors build trust, leading people to invest together. This is an appealing notion, but it is highly abstract. Budgets provide a different slant, affording concrete evidence of the ways in which philanthropy did or did not fuel economic development.[4]

Similarly, in *Women's Culture* I trace the subterranean economy that middle-class white women developed for the production and sale of goods produced by and for women through their associations. At a time when middle-class and elite women were thought to be isolated in the home and steeped in the idiom of separate spheres, and therefore resoundingly outside the entrepreneurial economy, charitable and associational budgets provide a different slant on their legacies and lives. They also reveal the incentives for cloaking these economic roles from public view. At least in terms of cultural institutions, whenever the endowments or profits of female- run philanthropic ventures grew too hefty, they ran the risk of a male takeover under the pretense of ensuring that the funds were "properly" used. By downplaying their financial skills, the women who ran these organizations protected their administrative roles but did a disservice to their sisters and themselves by perpetuating the idea that women were incapable of managing significant sums.[5]

The twentieth century yields a different set of analytical possibilities. My current research on women, power, and money looks at the role of high-net-worth female donors over the course of the twentieth century, particularly those who made major donations for feminist ends. But there are a number of other questions that merit research. For example, far less is known about the development of highly capitalized philanthropic institutions in Europe, especially around the time of the World War I. Did the war's devastation play a role in cementing American dominance in this field? Why, when so many of Rockefeller's major gifts, from the University of Chicago to the Rockefeller Institute, were grafted directly on European models, did the notion that philanthropy was an American export become paradigmatic? How did giving in the United States compare to that in the United Kingdom and Germany, and how did its political and economic roles vary?

Oliver Zunz's book *Philanthropy in America* does a superb job of mapping out the political roles of big philanthropy, particularly in shaping foreign policy. Philanthropic organizations can establish a beachhead in countries where their governments do not have formal diplomatic relations or are not welcome. Nineteenth-century missionary societies are an example of the first scenario; foundations of the second. For example, the Ford Foundation made grants in Burma (Myanmar) and Guinea during the Cold War after the US government's overtures were rejected, forging an American presence outside governmental diplomatic channels. Foundations can also quietly provide a neutral ground for meetings where government funding would have a very different meaning. Is this a uniquely American phenomenon, or has philanthropy played a similar role in other countries?[6]

Large-scale philanthropy also has a great deal of definitional authority, from the funding that helped build the field of area studies to the effects of initiatives like the Flexner Report on medical education. Foundation funding played a key role in winnowing "good" from "bad" professional practices in a variety of fields. It also helped define which universities would be most influential via a concerted effort to "make the peaks higher" in the United States and a variety of developing countries by burnishing individual and institutional reputations and resources. Philanthropy also brought new issues to public policy agendas, testing possible solutions and expanding the role of the state through public-private partnerships to bring their projects to scale. In the American South, for example, Rockefeller-funded philanthropies grafted the foundation's hookworm eradication campaigns onto state departments of public health. Philanthropy has always played a definitional role; large donors amplified these activities by working to reshape the state.[7]

Some associations even became significant businesses in their own right. In Europe, for example, medieval *montes di pietà* grew into some of Italy's largest banks. In the United States, New York's Irish Emigrant Society spun off the Emigrant Savings Bank to channel remittances to Ireland, creating a major financial institution that also underwrote mortgages and loans for Irish immigrants and a constellation of local charities in New York. Indeed, we know very little about the role of foundations and nonprofit organizations as investors. Some, like the Salvation Army and New York's Trinity Church, own large swaths of valuable urban real estate, playing invisible but important roles in urban development. The finance committee is often the most important committee in heavily capitalized institutions. Highlighting who served in these positions, as well as how they invested the funds, could reveal a great deal about the role of philanthropy in shaping local and national economies, as well as in institutional development.

Much of the literature on philanthropy to date has focused on service provision and the relationships between institutional entrepreneurs and the poor, with social control as an enduring leitmotiv. More recently, the agency of those who used these services has emerged as a compelling theme. During the 1990s, interest in civil society and political culture shifted attention to the role of giving and voluntarism in expanding practitioners' political roles, while more recent cultural studies such as Seth Koven's *Slumming* cast a spotlight on the cultural chasms that separated reformers and the poor. Still untapped is the role of philanthropic funding in the development of capitalistic societies and how this differed among various groups and from one country to the next. Following the money can illuminate a new slant not only on philanthropy but on the history of capitalism writ large.

KATHLEEN D. MCCARTHY is Professor and Director of the Center on Philanthropy and Civil Society at the Graduate Center, the City University of New York. Her publications include *American Creed: Philanthropy and the Rise of Civil Society, 1700–1865* and *Women's Culture: American Philanthropy and Art, 1830–1930*.

Notes

1. My comments about the United States and philanthropic innovation are based on a project that I am currently researching on philanthropy in the United States and France during Alexis de Tocqueville's lifetime. See also Adam, *Buying Respectability*.
2. McCarthy, *American Creed*; Innes, *Creating the Commonwealth*; Wilentz, *Chants Democratic*; Way, *Common Labour*.
3. McCarthy, *American Creed*, chap. 4.
4. Putnam, *Making Democracy Work*.
5. McCarthy, *Women's Culture*, chap. 3. See also Sander, *Business of Charity*; Boylan, *Origins of Women's Activism*; and Sklar, "Who Funded Hull House?," 94–115.
6. Zunz, *Philanthropy in America*.
7. See, for example, Ettling, *Germ of Laziness*; O'Connor, *Social Science for What?*; Lagemann, *Private Power for the Public Good*; Lagemann, *Politics of Knowledge*; Johnson and Harr, *Rockefeller Century*; Johnson and Harr, *Rockefeller Conscience*; and Sealander, *Private Wealth and Public Life*.

Bibliography

Adam, Thomas, ed. *Buying Respectability: Philanthropy and Urban Society in Transnational Perspective, 1840s to 1930s*. Bloomington: Indiana University Press, 2009.

Boylan, Anne. *The Origins of Women's Activism: New York and Boston, 1797–1840*. Chapel Hill: University of North Carolina Press, 2002.

Ettling, John. *The Germ of Laziness: Rockefeller Philanthropy and Public Health in the New South*. Cambridge, MA: Harvard University Press, 1981.

Innes, Stephen. *Creating the Commonwealth: The Economic Culture of Puritan New England*. New York: W. W. Norton, 1995.

Johnson, Peter, and John Ensor Harr. *The Rockefeller Century*. New York: Scribner, 1988.

———. *The Rockefeller Conscience: An American Family in Private and Public*. New York: Scribner, 1991.

Koven, Seth. *Slumming: Sexual and Social Politics in Victorian London*. Princeton, NJ: Princeton University Press, 2006.

Lagemann, Ellen Condliffe. *The Politics of Knowledge: The Carnegie Corporation, Philanthropy and Public Policy*. Middletown, CT: Wesleyan University Press, 1989.

———. *Private Power for the Public Good: A History of the Carnegie Foundation for the Advancement of Teaching*. Middletown, CT: Wesleyan University Press, 1983.

McCarthy, Kathleen D. *American Creed: Philanthropy and the Rise of Civil Society, 1700 to 1865*. Chicago: University of Chicago Press, 2003.

———. *Women's Culture: American Philanthropy and Art, 1830–1930*. Chicago: University of Chicago Press, 1991.

O'Connor, Alice. *Social Science for What? Philanthropy and the Social Question in a World Turned Rightside Up*. New York: Russell Sage Foundation, 2007.

Putnam, Robert. *Making Democracy Work: Traditions in Modern Italy*. Princeton, NJ: Princeton University Press, 1993.

Sander, Kathleen Waters. *The Business of Charity: The Woman's Exchange Movement, 1832–1900*. Urbana: University of Illinois Press, 1998.

Sealander, Judith. *Private Wealth and Public Life: Foundation Philanthropy and the Reshaping of American Foreign Policy from the Progressive Era to the New Deal.* Baltimore, MD: Johns Hopkins University, 1997.

Sklar, Kathryn Kish. "Who Funded Hull House?" In *Lady Bountiful Revisited: Women, Philanthropy, and Power*, edited by Kathleen D. McCarthy, 94–115. New Brunswick, NJ: Rutgers University Press, 1990.

Way, Peter J. *Common Labour: Workers and the Digging of North American Canals, 1780–1860.* Cambridge: Cambridge University Press, 1993.

Wilentz, Sean. *Chants Democratic: New York and the Rise of the American Working Class, 1788–1850.* New York: Oxford University Press, 1984.

Zunz, Olivier. *Philanthropy in America: A History.* Princeton, NJ: Princeton University Press, 2012.

Index

Addams, Jane, 7, 211, 213–215, 225, 236; "Arts at Hull-House," 217; as feminist, 224; on Grand Tour, 214; and Henrietta Barnett, 213, 214, 215–216, 218, 221, 222, 223, 225–227; and international peace movement, 213, 214, 221, 222, 223, 231–232n34; leadership of, 215, 219, 220–221, 222, 225, 226, 227; legacy of, 226; as mentored by Henrietta Barnett, 223, 224; *My Friend, Julia Lanthrop*, 225–226; as Nobel laureate, 224; as "Saint Jane," 221; self-promotion by, 213; *Twenty Years at Hull-House*, 216, 228n2; writings about Henrietta Barnett by, 213, 214, 217, 218; and writings to Henrietta Barnett, 213, 224–225, 232n40. *See also* Barnett, Henrietta; Hull-House settlement

aesthetics, 7, 46, 183; versus action, 86; aesthetic patronage, 142, 147; aesthetic values, 6, 7, 178, 217; in *Children of Gibeon*, 44; Edmund Burke on, 34; of poverty, 105; relation between economics and, 141; relationship between aesthetic and social aesthetic, 182; of suffering, 95; and sympathy, 237. *See also* domestic space, aestheticization of; working class: aesthetic cultivation of

Alcott, Abigail "Abba," 85–86, 98–99, 100

Alcott, Bronson, 86, 89, 98–99, 100–101

Alcott, Louisa May, 87–88, 98–107; on Christian path of helping others, 99; *Eight Cousins*, 105–106; and family income, 98–99; on genteel poverty, 98; *Little Women*, 100–101, 105; prison visits by, 103; as reformer, 88; and view of poor in New York, 87–88, 92, 106

almsgiving, 85, 129; as cause of poverty, 16; as emotional, 16; ineffectiveness of, 228n3; religious tradition of, 237

almshouses, 15, 89, 90, 103

American Federation of Settlements, 225

Anderson, Amanda, 41–43

Anesko, Michael, 141, 154

aristocratic women, 115–119, 126–127; self-restraint of, 121; submissiveness of, 120. *See also* social class

Aristotle: and civility, 116; and suffering onstage, 34

Arnold, Matthew, 44, 46, 217

Arnoldian-aestheticist mission, 44, 46

artists and professionalism, 153

arts: disinterest and self-interest in, 144, 146; as supported by philanthropy rather than patronage, 140; as supported by rich sponsors, 139; in working-class neighborhood, 217. *See also* Hull-House settlement: art gallery of

authors and market, 154

autonomy, 75, 182; loss of, 182; in relation to the state, 191, 196; and religious instruction, 73; of the rich, 196, 197, 199, 201; sovereignty of, 181, 192; and Victorian philanthropy, 40; of the working class, 178

awareness, 90, 167, 168, 169, 182

Bailkin, Jordanna, 178

Barnett, Canon Samuel, 214, 215, 218, 225; feminine traits of, 220–221; legacy of, 225; on philanthropy, 165–166; on the settlement movement, 165, 176

Barnett, Henrietta, 7, 212, 213–215, 236; *Canon Barnett*, 216, 217–218, 220–221, 222, 223, 224–226, 232n37; and Jane Addams, 213, 214, 215–216, 218, 219, 221, 222, 223, 225–227; leadership of, 215, 216, 219–220, 225, 227, 229–230n18; self-promotion by, 213, 216, 220, 227; and social reform movements, 224; writings about Jane Addams by, 213, 214, 216, 217–218, 220–222, 226, 232n37; and writings to Jane Addams, 213, 214, 224, 227. *See also* Addams, Jane; Toynbee Hall

Barnett, Samuel A., 163

Bartels, Peggy, vii–viii

Beaumont, Barber, 162

Beaven, Brad, 177

benevolence literature, 5

Berenson, Bernard, 193–194

Bergman, Jill, 5

Bermeo, Nancy, 116, 134n5

Besant, Annie, 184n22

Besant, Walter, 7, 44, 163; *All Sorts and Conditions of Men*, 31, 162; *Children of Gibeon*, 7, 44, 162, 164–165, 166–168, 169, 171, 172–174,

247

248 | Index

Besant, Walter (*continued*)
   175–176, 177–182, 183; "The Endowment of the Daughter," 172; on exploitation of the working class, 176; social reform projects of, 181; on sociopolitical legitimacy, 178–179; as trustee of People's Palace, 163
Beveridge, William, 215
Bivona, Daniel, 5
Blanchard, Paula, 93
"Blue Books," 218, 219
Blumberg, Ilana, 6
Blunden, Anna, 169, 172
Boltanski, Luc, 165
Booth, Charles, 163
Bosanquet, Bernard, 211, 228n3
bourgeois-liberal class, 172, 174, 177, 178, 180, 182, 184n29. *See also* social class
Brace, Charles Loring, 20
Brahmo Samaj, 66, 72, 75
Buffett, Peter, 76
Burchell, Graham, 165
Burdett-Coutts, Angela, 2–3, 7, 236
Burke, Edmund, 8, 36, 43, 237; on aesthetics, 34; on desire, 43–44; on dissymmetry of power, 41; *Philosophical Enquiry into Our Ideas of the Sublime and Beautiful*, 34; on social duty to the sufferer, 47; on sympathy, 48, 54. *See also* Schadenfreude
Burroughs, Charles, 16–17
Burton, Antoinette, 79–80n43, 130
business: art as supplementary to, 139; of charity, 105; chivalry in, 201; of educating poor children, 60; and fortunes, 193; governmental intrusion into, 196; mutual self-interest and social inequality in, 141; and philanthropy, 190–191, 205; and profit, 200–201; social responsibilities of, 193, 204, 206
Butler, Josephine, 65, 184n22

Canning, Charlotte, 123
capitalism, 24, 110n82, 139, 141, 151, 163; artists and sponsors within, 140, 154; capitalist accumulation, 145; communal, 241; criticism of, 179; exploitative nature of, 163, 168; global philanthropic, 61; industrial, 199, 202; liberal reform as complicit with, 181; philanthropy within, 142
Carnegie, Andrew, 191, 193, 204–206, 237, 240; on abilities of rich men, 199; on dividend versus income tax, 196; and moral imperative to give, 195; opposition to socialism or commu-
nism, 195; and philosophy of philanthropy in "Wealth," 194; as progenitor of modern-day entrepreneurial philanthropy, 208n33; and publications on wealth, 194
Carpenter, Mary, 61, 64–66, 71, 75, 76, 77, 236; and colonial pedagogy, 65; critique of, 71–74; on educational reform, 69, 71–74; as English philanthropist, 118, 125, 133; and recommendation for a Female Normal Training School, 70; religiosity of, 66; on religious instruction, 71, 73, 74; *Six Months in India*, 67, 69–74; and Unitarianism, 71. *See also* enabling violation
Carter, Stephen L., 116
caste system, 66
Catholic generosity on holidays, 90–91
Channing, William Ellery, 13
character, 163; nature of surroundings and, 164, 175, 178; of the poor, 16; reform of, 16
charitable guerilla(s), 114, 119, 120, 122, 124, 126, 131, 134
charity: as cause of inequality between classes, 180; charity bazaar, 135n34; Christian, 92, 100; in London, ix; organized, 102; as prevalent on holidays, 86, 88–90, 101; private, 163. *See also* philanthropy
Charity Organization Societies (COS), 4, 31, 163
Chartist turbulence, 179
chastity, 13–14
Child, Lydia Maria, 20, 87–88
Children's Bureau, 225
Children's Employment Commission, 169
child welfare, 219, 229–230n18, 230–231n28
Child Welfare Committee of the League of Nations, 225
Christian duty, 92, 108–109n26, 143; charity as, 91; to preach the gospel, 74; public service as, 229n9
Christian missionary efforts in India, 60, 63; Victorian, 67. *See also* mission schools
Christian principles, 221. *See also* Christian duty
Christianson, Frank, 6, 30, 33, 56n23, 157n11, 213–214
Church Missionary Society (CMS), 67
civility: crisis of, in Anglo-Indian romances, 124; and English masculinity, 124; qualities of, 116; superiority in, 123. *See also* civil society
Civil Service and colonial government, 124
civil society, 3, 9, 115, 116; of Anglo India, 117, 123, 124; banishment from, 117; definition of, 134n5; and education of Indian women, 125;

limited participation of Indian women in, 118, 132; masculinized structure of, in India, 129; organizations formed to give women access to, 133; women defined as essence of, 117
Claybaugh, Amanda, 6
Cobbe, Frances Power, 65, 66
Cody, Lisa, 17
collecting mania, 142
Collins, Jennie, 14, 23-26
Collins, Wilkie, 72
communism, 195, 197
condescension, 37
Congress on Charities, 2
conservatism, 192, 206
consumers, 202, 203
Crary, Jonathan, 166
cultural education, 176, 177, 185n41
cultural institutions, 162, 242
cultural reform, 163, 227

Dauble, M. S., 72, 80n53
Davidson, Cathy, 18
Debi, Swarnakumari: as social reformer, 130, 133; *The Uprooted Vine*, 115, 118, 119, 126-133
degeneration, 49, 51, 52, 54
dehumanization, 172
demoralization, 53
depoliticization, 55n4
"deserving" poor, 31-32, 44
detachment. *See* disinterestedness
Dewey, John, 215
Dickens, Charles, viii, 30, 36-41, 114, 122; *Bleak House*, viii-ix, 36-40, 49, 53-55, 114; on philanthropic motives, 45; on transference, 41, 42
disinterestedness: Adam Smith and, 47; Charles Dickens and, 39, 41, 43; disinterested philanthropy, 40-41; Edmund Burke and, 47; George Gissing on, 45, 46; morality of, 38; surrendering self-interest, 41. *See also* self-interest
Disraeli, Benjamin, 44, 46, 47
District Visitor, 114, 121
domestic space, aestheticization of, 173, 178, 179, 185n55
Dorsey, Bruce, 15
Duff, Alexander, 75

East End. *See* London's East End
East India Company and missionary work, 123
economics: academic discipline of, 191; and aesthetics, 141; art as supplementary to, 139; of patron-artist relation, 142, 148; speculative, 149-151
Edelstein, T. J., 171
education, ix, 9, 92, 163, 172; and civil society, 125, 133; colonial, 60, 65, 71; cultural, 176, 177, 185n41 (*see also* working class: aesthetic cultivation of); and doctrinal-secular divide, 69-71; educational reform, 65, 69, 74; institutions of, 162; lack of, and exploitation, 176; moral, 177; and social class, 69, 163; of women, 63, 66, 69, 125, 132, 215, 231n29; for working class, 163
educational philanthropy, 59, 63; and enabling violation, 69, 76; imperial, 63, 64, 77; religious, 60-61, 64
Elbert, Sarah, 105
Elliott, Dorice Williams, 5, 10
Ely, Ezra Stiles, 15
egalitarian society, 184n29
elite benevolence, 142
envy as an element of patronage and philanthropy, 147, 153
Emerson, Ralph Waldo, 88, 89, 90, 93; "Self-Reliance," 85, 91-92, 106
enablement: and education 70, 71, 76; religion in the name of, 76; and violation, 76
enabling violation, 61, 62, 64, 76
Enlightenment, 30, 40, 54, 181
Ethan Frome (Wharton), 192
ethical affect, 165, 166, 181
ethical spectatorship, 162, 163, 167, 169, 171, 174, 182; in the age of global media, 165; call for, 174; compared to working-class spectatorship, 177; distance as necessary for, 166, 175; as foundational for social reform, 164, 165, 166, 167, 180; and giving aid, 180; models of, 168, 174; modes of, 169; reading as, 185n40; as social duty, 162, 164; spectatorial disengagement, 167; sympathetic spectator, 165, 172. *See also* suffering; sympathy
ethics, 49, 165
ethos, 117, 143, 164
eugenics, 47, 50, 54
exploitation, 167, 168, 176; and capitalism, 163, 168

Fabian Socialism, 179
feminism, 66; British, 65, 74, 232n38, 242; *Children of Gibeon* and, 167; *Ethan Frome* and, 192; politics and sympathy of, 25; and publications, 71, 232n38; Victorian, 65
feminists: British, 65, 75, 130; Indian, 75

Fern, Fanny, 103, 111n88
Fitzhugh, George, 15
Forbes, Geraldine H., 125
forced sterilization, 50
For Only One Short Hour (Blunden), 169–170, 172
Foster, George, 20–23
free market, 163. See also capitalism
Friedman, Milton, 190, 206–207n3
The Fruit of the Tree (Wharton): consumption portrayed in, 202–203; as critique of abstract idealism, 194; and financial collapse of 1907, 192–193; and laissez-faire economics, 191; as muckraking industrial novel, 201; natural elite in, 199; as organicism, 193
Fuller, Margaret, 86–97, 100, 106–107; "The Great Lawsuit," 88–89; on plight of oppressed classes, 92; as reformer, 88; and view of poor in New York, 87–88; visits to penitentiaries by, 89, 94; *Woman in the Nineteenth Century*, 88–89

Garber, Marjorie, 139–140
Gaskell, Elizabeth: *Mary Barton*, 170; *Ruth*, 170
gender, 68; and authority, 69; and benevolence, 219; constraints related to, 213, 215, 216, 230n21, 231n32; and identity, 227, 231n30; and leadership, 220, 231n32; and politics, 172, 218; and relationships, 214, 215; and religion, 74; and roles in philanthropy, 213, 221, 227; and stereotypes, 184n22, 220. See also women
Gerard, Jessica, 119
Ghose, Indira, 129, 135n17
"'The Ghost' in the Looking-Glass" (Tenniel), 168, 169, 170
Gibbons, Abby, 104
Gissing, George, 30; on disinterestedness, 45, 46; on failure of philanthropy, 47; *The Netherworld*, 44, 47, 48–55; and sympathy, 44; *Thyrza*, 44–46, 48, 51; and Walter Besant, 44, 183
The Golden Bowl (James), 146
Goodlad, Lauren, 6, 116
Gorst, John, 230–231n28
Gott, Gill, 75
Grand Tour, 214
gratitude: expectation to repay, 149; and indebtedness, 144
Greeley, Horace, 88, 89, 107
Greiner, Rae, 33
Groenewegen, Peter, 196, 207–208n19
Gross, Robert, 140

Hadley, Elaine, 182
Halttunen, Karen, 165
Hamilton, Alice, 215
Harris, Beth, 171
Harrison, Brian, ix
Hill, Octavia, 31–32, 163, 184n22, 229–230n18, 230n27; compared to fictional characters, 53; housing plans of, 218, 219
Himmelfarb, Gertrude, 227, 230n20
holiday charitable acts, 86, 88–91, 101
Holl, Frank, 169–170
Hood, Thomas, 169, 170; "Song of the Shirt," 169
Hoover, J. Edgar, 231–232n34
The House of Mirth (Wharton), 190
housing for working class, 31, 163. See also domestic space, aestheticization of
Howe, Julia Ward, 101, 102, 104
Hull-House settlement, 211, 213, 215, 220, 222, 225; achievements of, 226; art gallery of, 217–218, 231n30; as educational institution, 219; as influenced by British models, 212, 226; research done by, 230–231n28; viewed as philanthropy, 228n4; women leaders of, 219. See also Addams, Jane; Himmelfarb, Gertrude; settlements; Toynbee Hall
human nature, 181. See also selfishness

identity, 182; and gender, 227, 231n30; and social class, 231n30
idolatry, 70, 73, 74
Idolatry (Perrin), 115, 118, 119, 125–129, 131, 133
imperialism, 65
impoverishment, 13
India: class divide in, 123; education in British-controlled, 60–65, 69, 124; missionary work in, 123; social reform in, 66, 75
individualism: versus collectivism, 197; extreme, 86; ideology of liberal, 190, 191, 194, 205; laissez-faire, 25; as leading to fortunes, 198; possessive, 181; transcendentalist self-reliance and, 92
inequality, structural, 163
inherited criminality, 51
inhumanity, 19; of neo-Malthusianism, 53; of working-class life, 48
initiative, 163
Innes, Stephen, 241
innovation: in business, 201; philanthropic, 240; in work of the individual, 196
institutional philanthropy, 36, 48, 49, 165
International Congress of Charities, Correc-

tion, and Philanthropy, 1
international peace movement, 213, 214, 221, 222, 223, 231–232n34
International Women's Peace Conference, 223
intervention, 31, 55n4, 142, 178

Jacobs, Harriet, 20
Jaffe, Audrey, 35–36, 183n6
James, Henry, 141–156, 157nn18–19, 158nn28–29, 158n47, 159nn59–60
Jameson, Frederic, 143
Jane Eyre, rejection of missionary work in India in, 122
Johnston, Anna, 70
Jones, Gavin, 5
Joyce, Simon, 163
justice, 85, 94, 181, 182

Kassanoff, Jennie A., 192, 199, 207n10
Kelley, Florence, 219
Klaver, Claudia, 6
Koven, Seth, 5, 56n35, 184n10, 220, 237, 243
künstlerroman, Roderick Hudson as, 141

Ladies Committee of the British and Foreign School Society, 122
Lady Bountiful, responsibilities of, 118–119, 134
laissez-faire economy: and *The Fruit of the Tree*, 191; and liberalism, 179
Lamarckism, 49, 51, 53
labor, ix, 18, 176; soul-crushing nature of, 185n41. *See also* sweated labor
labor unionization, 198
Larsen, Timothy, 66
Lathrop, Julia, 225
Lawson, Andrew, 148–149, 154, 157n16, 159n50, 159n60
Le Sueur, Meridel, 25
liberal ethics, 165
liberalism: classical, 163, 181, 186n74, 191; criticism of, 179; discourse of, 182, 184n29; economic, 13, 23, 191; late-Victorian, 163; New Liberalism, 163, 179; and support of laissez-faire economy, 179; and sympathy, 181; and Victorian material culture, 178. *See also* liberal reform
liberal reform, 181; as complicit with capitalism, 181; critique of, 179, 182; discourse of, 163; poetics of, 164. *See also* liberalism; social reform
London's East End, 44, 50, 162, 219; in *Children of Gibeon*, 162, 166, 175; cultural expression in,
185n43; Ratcliffe parish, 176; reformist project proposed for, 174
looking. *See* ethical spectatorship
love, 19; as cover for sexual desire, 45; and disinterestedness, 47; as element of patronage and philanthropy, 147, 149; as a form of suffering, 46; of opulence, 94; romantic, 45–46, 47; as threat to philanthropy, 46

Macaulay, Thomas Babington, 64
Macpherson, C. B., 181
Mandler, Peter, 23
Malthus, Thomas, 13–15, 47. *See also* Malthusianism; neo-Malthusianism
Malthusianism, 50
Marshall, Alfred, 191, 193, 204–206; and autonomy of the individual, 196; on definition of socialism, 197; "Social Possibilities of Economic Chivalry," 194; on unequal distribution of wealth, 195
Marshall, David, 32–33, 183n6
Martineau, Harriet, 65
Mary Bean: The Factory Girl (J. A. B.), 18–20
Mayhew, Henry, and *London's Labor and the London Poor*, 170
McCarthy, Kathleen, ix
Mearns, Andrew, 50
Melville, Herman, 21
mentoring, 213, 214, 223, 224
metaphorical suffering. *See* suffering
middle class. *See* social class
Midgley, Clare, 66, 122
Miller, Julie, 21
Miller, William, 75, 80n66
mirroring, 40, 49, 53, 54, 168
missionaries as teachers, 63, 72, 75, 123
mission schools, 63, 69, 71, 74, 75. *See also* Christian missionary efforts in India; religious instruction
Mitchell, Sally, 66, 78–79n23
Moody, Michael, 219
moral needs, 227
Morris, Susannah, 143, 156
motive, 39, 54; curiosity as, 56n34; disinterestedness as, 45; suffering as, 40, 41; sympathy as, 48; unconscious, 49. *See also* disinterestedness; self-interest; sympathy
muckraking, 193, 201

Nair, Janaki, 125
neighborhood design, 213

neo-Malthusianism, 47, 52. See also Malthusianism
networks, 215, 216; transnational networking, 212, 227; women's networks, 215, 224, 227. See also civil society
New Life Children's Refuge, 59–60, 65
New Poor Law, 17
New York by Gaslight (Foster), 20–22
Nietzsche, Friedrich, 143, 146–147, 148, 155, 157n19
Nightingale, Florence, 123, 132; aggressiveness of, 120; as aristocratic philanthropist, 119; as model for girls, 119
nonprofit institutions, ix
Nord, Philip, 116
the novel, 30, 35; loss of moral authority of philanthropy traced in, 31; as most influential literary form, 30; muckraking novels, 193, 201; new aristocratic woman conceived in, 120; philanthropic duties dramatized in, 35, 51, 166; and power to influence opinion and actions, 115; sentimental novels, 185n40; "slum pastorals," 186n59; social-problem novels, 185n40

Old Poor Law, 16–17
organicism, 191, 193
overpopulation, 50. See also neo-Malthusianism

patronage, 139–156, 236; as changing over time, 153; focus on, in *Roderick Hudson*, 143–148; as mutual self-interest, 141; and philanthropy, 140, 141; as a transatlantic phenomenon, 142–143
Patronizing the Arts (Garber), 139–140
Payton, Robert, 219
Peabody, Elizabeth Palmer, 89, 100–101
Peck, Dennis L., 116–118
People's Palace, 44, 162–163, 177
Perrin, Alice, 115, 118, 119, 125, 127–129
philanthropic organizations: collaborative social organizations, 211; homes as the domain of, 115; institutions as the domain of, 115; in the nineteenth century, ix; women's, 2
philanthropy: causes of, 213; and civil society, 134; as a contest, 48; criticism of conventional, 50; critique of capitalist organization of charity, 14; culturalist, 44; culture of, 213; definition of, x; and dependence on interpersonal connection, 213, 223; and Dickens, 36; discourse of, 114–115, 162, 165, 213, 214, 227; disinterested, 40–41; as duty of the millionaire, 200; educational, 63, 69; efficacy of, 47; futility of, 54; in India and Britain, 124, 125, 129; as an institution, 36, 48, 49, 165; leadership in, 214, 215, 225, 227; as luxury consumption, 191, 204; misplaced, 36, 38; in modern markets, 140, 141, 143; as a movement, 4; practical, 211; practices of, 213; properly supervised, 121; and publications, 213, 216, 232n38; and redistribution of wealth, 194, 195; and Schadenfreude, 40, 41, 53; scientific, 219; and settlements, 217, 227; as shaped by Puritanism in America, 142, 146; and social responsibility, 190; and spending, 202, 204; strategic, 228n3; study of, 9; suffering as motivation for, 41; as threat to social class, 46, 47; telescopic, viii–ix, 36–37; theory of, 213; as transatlantic phenomenon, 6, 142; women philanthropists, 212
pity. See sympathy
Polanyi, Karl, 141
politics, women's involvement in, 222, 232n38
Poole, Andrea Geddes, 5
poor: "deserving," 31–32, 44; poor women, 17–23; sentimental versus real picture of, 87; "undeserving," 31–32, 44; and women writers, 85, 88–90, 96, 102
The Poor Sempstress (Redgrave), 169–170, 171
Poovey, Mary, 25, 178
postbellum period, art patronage during, 142
poverty: aestheticization of, 105; antipoverty programs, 215; as cultural condition, 5; descriptions of, 166; despair of, 183; and the individual, 196; as inheritance, 13; as moral failure, 15; sexual behavior as cause of, 13–15, 47, 50, 51, 52; solutions to, 50, 51, 55, 167; urban, 4
power, philanthropy as, 48
prison reform, 65, 69
prisons, 69–70, 72, 88–89; Fuller's and Alcott's visits to, 90, 102–103; as places for philanthropic work, 115
Prochaska, Frank, ix, 65, 78n16, 78–79n23
Progressive era, 213
prostitution, 22–23, 173
Protestant self-reliance, self-interest, and greed, 90
protests, 173, 174
Puritan ethics, hypocrisy of, 145
Putnam, Robert, 241

ragged schools, 66, 215
Ramusack, Barbara, 66

Raza, Rosemary, 124–125
Redgrave, Richard, 169, 170, 171
Red Lodge reformatory, 66. See also ragged schools
religious instruction, 66, 69, 71; autonomy and, 73. See also mission schools
ressentiment, 143, 146–147, 153; Nietzsche's definition of, 143
Reynolds, G. W. M., and *The Seamstress*, 168, 170
Riis, Jacob, 87, 95
Robbins, Bruce, 13, 36, 56n14, 157–158n22
Robinson, Harriet, 19
Roderick Hudson (James): art patronage as a transatlantic phenomenon in, 142–143; criticism of Puritan ethics in, 142, 145–146; debt and accountability in, 148–151; eroticism in, 144, 146; focus on patron in, 143–148; as *künstlerroman*, 141; on professionalism of artist, 151–154; on relation between patronage and philanthropy, 141–143, 155–156; and *ressentiment*, 143, 146–148, 153
Roosevelt, Theodore, 193, 221, 231–232n34
Rowntree, Benjamin Seebohm, 163
Roy, Anindyo, and *Civility and Empire*, 124
Roy, Raja Ram Mohan, 66
Ruskin, John, 185n41

Sakhi Samiti, 130, 133
Sangari, Kumkum, 129
Sarkar, Tanika, 129
sati, 71, 118, 122, 132
Schadenfruede, 46, 48, 54; as creating communal relationship, 41; description of, 34; as grounds for earnest philanthropy, 40, 41, 53; *Schadenfreudliche* delight, 34–35, 37, 40, 41, 44, 48; social justification of, 35. See also Burke, Edmund
seamstresses, 169, 174; in *Children of Gibeon*, 171, 172–173; critique of "seamstress narrative," 171; exploitation of, 167, 168, 182; images of, 168–174; labor of, seen as domestic, 170–171; in literature, 168–169, 170, 173; as objects of sympathy, 169; and overwork, 173; and prostitution, 173; as a type, 170–171. See also sweated labor
self-interest, 38; as motive for philanthropy, 45, 54; in relationships, 41; validation of, 186n74
selfishness, 167, 181, 186n74; as argument against utopia, 181. See also self-interest
self-recognition, 54

self-transformation, 45, 46. See also social transformation
Sengupta, Parna, 75
sentiment in *Roderick Hudson*, 145
Seton, Rosemary, 67
settlements, 165, 225, 230n27, 231n30; criticism of, 217; and cross-class solidarity, 230n22; cultural intervention based on, 227; definition of, 165, 211; founders of, 214, 215, 216, 218, 225; and neighborly charity, 176; philanthropic settlement outreach, 217, 227; research done by, 218; settlement praxis, 213; Walter Besant as inspired by, 186n68. See also Hull-House settlement; Toynbee Hall
sexuality: as cause of poverty, 47, 52, 117; and civility, 117; illicit, 21; in narratives of poor women, 14, 17–23; objectification of women, 19; sexual "fall" of poor women, 18–20; Victorian mores of, 20; zenanas as sites of unruly, 125
Sharpe, Jenny, 125
Siegel, Daniel, 5, 37
Silsby, Laura, 59
Silverman, Gillian, 14–16
single mothers, 17–20
slumming, 45, 56n34
Smith, Adam, 8, 13, 20, 32–33, 156, 238; and metaphorical knowledge, 40, 41, 43; on sympathy, 54, 164–165, 166, 183n6; *Theory of Moral Sentiments*, 41; *Wealth of Nations*, 186n74
Smith, Mary Rozet, 215
social activism: cooperation in, 211; by Fuller and Alcott, 88; institutionalized, 227; large-scale, 213; and philanthropic discourse, 211; sympathy and, 181; women and, 213, 214
social class: boundaries of, 47, 231n29; change in, 45, 47, 164, 170; class benevolence, 24; and education, 69, 163; hostility between, 179, 186n59; and identity, 231n30; interclass understanding, 179; labor suitable for, 172; and leadership, 214; philanthropy as a threat to, 46, 47; and politics, 172; transnational middle class, 214, 215. See also aristocratic women; working class
social conscience, 45, 206–207n3
social domain. See civil society
social duty, 46, 47; ethical spectatorship as, 162, 164
social gradualism, 163, 199
social inequality: contentedness with, 46; contexts of, 140; as discussed in Women's Congress in Syracuse, 102; reform due to, 88

socialism, 155, 179, 195, 197; critique of, 180, 181
social order, 54; liberal-capitalist, 26
social progress, 54, 163; problem of, 211
social realism, 6, 86
social reform, 65, 164; commitment to, 164, 214; discourse of, 171; ethical spectatorship as foundational for, 164, 165, 166, 167, 180; lack of awareness as obstacle to, 167; leaders in, 218; promotion of, 218, 232n38; as remedy to social problems, 181; vision of, 162. *See also* liberal reform
social responsibility of needy, 193, 204
social sciences, 218, 231n29
social sphere. *See* civil society
social transformation, 163, 174, 175. *See also* self-transformation
Societies for the Prevention of Pauperism, 15–16
Society for Promoting Female Education in the East (FES), 61; female teachers for, 63, 64; Rosamond Webb as secretary of, 67
sociopolitical legitimacy, 178–179
The Song of the Shirt (Holl), 169–170
spectatorship. *See* ethical spectatorship
Spencer, Herbert, 195
Spivak, Gayatri Chokravorti, 59, 61–65, 76
sponsorship: as motivation of art, 143, 144, 151; as obstructing ethical freedom, 156
status. *See* social class
Steedman, Carolyn, 23
Stone, Elizabeth, and *The Young Milliner*, 170
Stoneley, Peter, 102, 110n78
strikes, 173, 174
suffering, 33–36, 41, 87, 94, 167, 174; aestheticization of, 95; in lieu of money, 99, 101; love as a form of, 46; poetics of, 180; response to scenes of, 165, 166; vicarious, 40–41, 54; of working class, 164, 167, 168, 181. *See also* ethical spectatorship; Schadenfreude
suffrage, women's, 219, 232n38
sweated labor, 163, 168, 219; and "drilling," 173–174, 182. *See also* exploitation
sweatshops. *See* sweated labor
sympathy, 8, 13–26, 165, 171, 183n6; in *Bleak House*, 41, 44; conditions for, 41; definition of, 164; discourse on, 164; disgust rather than, 49; institutional, 31–32; within a liberal-capitalist society, 181; mirroring as an act of, 168; moral imperative of, 49, 51; in *The Netherworld*, 49; pleasures of, 183; reading as sympathetic spectatorship, 185n40; and social class, 44; spectatorship as a form of, 166; as substitute for political action, 181. *See also* ethical spectatorship

Taft, William, 225
talent, 200
taxes: dividend, 196; estate, 195–196; income, 196; for redistribution of wealth, 193–194, 196; Roosevelt and, 207n7
teaching as philanthropy, 63, 64
tenements, 198
Tenniel, John, 168, 169, 170
theatricality, 32–35, 41
Thoreau, Henry David, 89, 92, 93, 97, 106
Tinling, J. B., 75
Tonna, Charlotte Elizabeth, and *The Wrongs of Woman*, 170
Toynbee, Alfred, 163
Toynbee Hall, 213, 214, 216, 219; art gallery of, 229–230n18, 231n30; as civil and educational institution, 230n20; as inspiration for *Children of Gibeon*, 165; as model for Hull-House settlement, 212, 217, 226, 229–230n18; research done by, 218, 219; residents of, 218, 219. *See also* Himmelfarb, Gertrude; Hull-House settlement; settlements
transatlantic communication, 212–213, 215. *See also* Addams, Jane; Barnett, Henrietta; networks
transatlantic culture, 214
transcendentalism: and self-reliance, 91, 96; and women turned reformers, 86–88, 98
transference, 41, 42
transnational middle class, 214, 215
Treuherz, Julian, 170
Trollope, Frances, and *Jessie Phillips*, 170
Turnovsky, Geoffrey, 155
Tuttleton, James, 194, 205, 207n4

"undeserving" poor, 31–32, 44
Unitarianism, 66, 71
urban issues, 218; study of, 219
urbanization, 7, 14
urban reform, 218
utopia in *Children of Gibeon*, 180, 181, 186n59

Vaid, Sudesh, 129
The Valley of Decision (Wharton), 205
Veblen, Thorstein, 203
vicarious suffering, 40–41, 54. *See also* ethical spectatorship
Victoria, Queen, 44

Victorian era, 35; feminism in, 65; liberal literature of, 166
Virgin Mary as Madonna of the Slums, 91
Viswanathan, Gauri, 76

Watch and Ward (James), 144
Waterston, R. C., 16
wealth: chivalry of, 200; complacent, 92; ethics of, 193; in New York, 97; right of individual to spend, 202; talent and, 200; twentieth-century thinking about, 191. *See also* Carnegie, Andrew
Webb, Beatrice, 215
Webb, Rosamond, 61, 64–77
Webster, Daniel, 88
Weiner, Deborah E. B., 180, 186n68
Wharton, Edith, 190–194, 197–199, 201–206, 207n10, 209n38, 209n41
Whately, Edward, 68
Whately, Richard, 68
White, Arnold, 50
Wilberforce, William, 64
Wilford, Florence, 114, 115, 119, 120, 124, 134
Williams, Dorothy, 226
Wilson, Harriet, 24
Wilson, Woodrow, 225
women: birth control for, 232n38; and civilizing missions, 117; derogation of, 18–22, 24; English and Indian, 122, 124; equality in pay for, 232n38; and expectations for chastity, 13–14, 18–22; as integral to representation of philanthropy, 4; as leaders, 213, 214, 216, 218, 219, 225, 226, 230–231n28, 231n32 (*see also* Addams, Jane; Barnett, Henrietta); missionary work of, 122; and participation in the marketplace, 172; as philanthropic volunteers, 116; political participation of, 219, 232n38; as rich in *The Fruit of the Tree*, 204; as role models, 213; women writers, 115, 124. *See also* gender
Wood's Despatch, 62–63
working class: aesthetic cultivation of, 174, 175–176, 179, 180, 181, 185n41; apparent roughness of, 171, 173; condition of, 167; education for, 163; frustrations of, 173; homes of, 175–176; and housing crisis, 163; identity formation of, 175, 178; and liberal reform, 181; men of, 173; middle class as a model for, 177; misery of, 168, 174, 177; organizations of, 179; as passive, 176; political participation of, 181; recreation of, 177; revolution of, 179, 181; and socialism, 179; and spectatorship of middle class, 177–178; suffering of, 164, 167, 168, 181; upper-class neglect of, 173; women of, 173. *See also* social class
workingwomen, 19, 24–26. *See also* working class
World's Columbian Exposition, 1–2, 4
World War I, 221, 242

Zakreski, Patricia, 171, 184n26
zenanas, 68, 117, 123, 125, 129, 135n14. *See also* education

www.ingramcontent.com/pod-product-compliance
Lightning Source LLC
Chambersburg PA
CBHW050435240426
43661CB00055B/2394